The Battle over Peleliu

WAR, MEMORY, AND CULTURE

The Battle over Peleliu

Islander, Japanese, and American Memories of War

Stephen C. Murray

The University of Alabama Press
Tuscaloosa

The University of Alabama Press
Tuscaloosa, Alabama 35487-0380
uapress.ua.edu

Hardcover edition published 2016.
Paperback edition published 2019.
eBook edition published 2016.

Typeface: Garamond

Cover image: The Bai ra Ngermelulau in Ngerdelolk, Peleliu, 1936; Kondo, Micronesian Expedition, Bishop Museum, Honolulu; CN 18835
Cover design: Kyle Anthony Clark

Paperback ISBN: 978-0-8173-5978-2

A previous edition of this book has been catalogued by the Library of Congress as follows:
Library of Congress Cataloging-in-Publication Data
Murray, Stephen C., 1945–
The battle over Peleliu : islander, Japanese, and American memories of war / Stephen C. Murray.
pages cm. — (War, memory, and culture)
Includes bibliographical references and index.
ISBN 978-0-8173-1884-0 (cloth : alk. paper) — ISBN 978-0-8173-8889-8 (e book)
1. Peleliu, Battle of, Palau, 1944. 2. World War, 1939–1945—Campaigns—Palau—Peleliu Island. 3. Collective memory—Palau—Peleliu Island. 4. Historic sites—Palau—Peleliu Island—Conservation and restoration. 5. Peleliu Island—Social life and customs. 6. Peleliu Island—History. 7. Japan—Relations—Palau. 8. Palau—Relations—Japan. 9. United States—Relations—Palau. 10. Palau—Relations—United States. I. Title.
D767.99.P4M87 2016
940.54'2666—dc23
2015022948

This book is dedicated to the three women who considered me a son:

Barbara Curran Murray Henderson,
1919–1992,
Seattle and Bainbridge Island, Washington,
my mother;

Olga Davis Murray,
Sausalito, California, and Kathmandu, Nepal,
my stepmother; and

Aliil Betok Nakamura,
1909–1988,
Ngerchol, Beliliou, Belau,
my Palauan mother.

Contents

Illustrations

Maps

Figures

Acknowledgments

Throughout this project I received encouragement and sturdy assistance from numerous friends, relatives, and colleagues. I hereby offer them my deepest thanks.

In Palau I received unstinting support from members of my wife's family and from the various Nakamura families who welcomed back their prodigal brother. I thank Ambassador Daiziro Nakamura, the late speaker Tosiwo Nakamura and his wife, Sabeth, their children, Steven and Imelda, and former president Kuniwo Nakamura for information, suggestions, and hospitality.

I thank the staffs of the library at Palau Community College, the Belau National Museum, the Historic Preservation Office, and the Palau Visitors Authority. Officials at the Bureau of Lands and Surveys helped untangle the difficult subject of land matters. Kyonori Tellames of the Office of Planning and Statistics was generous with census data.

Masaharu Tmodrang, Techetbos William Tabelual, Jonathan Emul, Kathy Kesolei, and Kempis Mad explained Palauan ways of history. On Guam I received hospitality and advice from Professor Dirk Ballendorf and his wife, Francesca. Professor Don Shuster also shared ideas. Nancy Farrell provided helpful information on archaeology and the search for remains.

I am particularly indebted to two Japanese researchers I met in Palau, Iitaka Shingo and Mita Takashi. They shared their knowledge of Japanese history, politics, and wartime memories. Shingo generously translated inscriptions of Japanese monuments and explained their choice of language and subtleties in points of view. Kurata Yoji told me his life story as a scientist and soldier in Palau.

Clearly my deepest gratitude goes to the people of Peleliu and Ngaraard, who shared their private stories so that I could bring them into the public record. On Peleliu I particularly thank Governor Timarong Sisior, Chief Obak Isao Singeo, Chief Uchelsias Etibek Shmull, Chief Obaklechol Ichiro Blesam, and Chief Renguul Donald Haruo for their interviews. Special thanks go to other elder collaborators who shared their pasts at unusual length: Tokie Morei, Lorenza Pedro of Angaur, Reiko Kubary, Spesungel Ichiro Dingilius, Matichau Ilemelong, Dilchuuch Ermang Ngiruous, Olikong ra Tikei Kokichi Ingas, Diltpak Merkii Napoleon, Susong Smau, Dirribukel Ngirametuker, Chief Obak's father, Singeo, and Peleliu historian Smau Amalei Ngirngesang. Kent Giramur contributed many acute observations concerning tourism on Peleliu today. I received warm family support from Margarete Ichiro, Des Matsutaro and his guide firm, Peleliu Adventures, and from Emaredong. In Ngaraard I am especially indebted to Imelda Blailes, Julius and JeRome Temengil, and the historian Andrew Shiro, who offered invaluable information and advice.

On Peleliu my research assistants and translators, Fuanny Blunt and Bouwel Iekar, helped me in the long and demanding interviews and made important suggestions regarding whom to talk with, what to inquire about, and what to see on the island and elsewhere in the archipelago.

I thank Professor John W. Dower for encouragement and advice, and for introducing me to Professor Franziska Seraphim, who in turn introduced me to the politically charged landscape of Japanese war memory. Her insights framed my understanding of how this disputed memory manifests itself on Peleliu. I am also indebted to Professor Peter Black, a friend from Peace Corps days, who, like Professor Seraphim, read the manuscript with care and made many valuable recommendations. I thank Professors Geoff White and David Hanlon in Hawaii for their support, and the staff of the National Park Service in Honolulu. Nico Tripcevich produced the maps of Palau and Peleliu. I am also grateful to friends and colleagues in Santa Barbara who discussed the project and read drafts: Mike Jochim, David Cleveland, Don Brown, and A. F. "Sandy" Robertson. The staff at University of Alabama Press, including Dan Waterman, Joanna Jacobs, J. D. Wilson, and Susan Harris, were helpful and professional at every step.

I was buoyed by the continuous interest in the project shown by a lifelong friend of my parents who became family, E. M. Mac Gardiner. My two sons, Sean Henderson Murray and Colin Umerang Murray, showed patience for and understanding of my reasons for pursuing the research. I thank my wife's elder sister, Meikam Chin Weers, of Peleliu and Melekeok, for decades of conversations about Palau's past, present, and future.

I could not have managed this project without the love, assistance, and encouragement I received from my wife, Hirmina (Fermina) Brel Murray, of Melekeok, Palau. Hirm acted as my chief source of information on all things Palauan, coached me in cultural matters, ran the household during my lengthy absences, read and critiqued my drafts, challenged my preconceptions, nursed me in illness, and nudged me tactfully when I bogged down.

The Battle over Peleliu

Introduction

My connection with Peleliu began in 1966 when I joined the first Peace Corps program to deploy to the Palau Islands in the western Pacific. I was adopted by a woman from Peleliu Island, Aliil Betok Nakamura. Since Palau follows matrilineal descent, I became a person of Peleliu as well. We lived 25 miles north of the island, in Palau's urban capital of Koror. I knew that a fierce battle had occurred on Peleliu in 1944 between American invaders and Japanese defenders, but nothing could have prepared me for what I found on my first visit to the island. Everywhere beneath its regrown forests and small gardens, even 23 years after the battle, lay rusted guns, smashed planes, caves filled with weapons and human skeletons, countless tons of unexploded ordnance, and shattered buildings. This was no Civil War battleground of well-groomed fields and orchards with winding paths, stone markers, rows of crosses, guides, museums, and bookstores. It was a raw and grisly battlefield, and it was hard to imagine what forces brought Japan and the United States to expend the lives of 12,600 men and vast wealth in a struggle over an island that they both had now abandoned and, it seemed, forgotten entirely.

At that time Peleliu had only a few memorials raised by American soldiers in the aftermath of the battle. Starting in the late 1960s, however, Japanese citizens began coming to Peleliu in a steady stream to comb its shorelines and mountains for remains of their fighting men, and to erect monuments around the island. Over the years both Japanese and American veterans and historians published many historical works telling their particular versions of the battle. However, with few exceptions, the visitors to Peleliu and their historiographies share the same trait: they focus obsessively on their own war stories and concerns and completely ignore the residents of Peleliu, the third people caught up in the maelstrom of the battle, as if their history has no importance.

The Palauans most definitely have their own memories and tales to tell, versions of the past that are fascinating and affecting. They are maintained as oral histories by the elders who lived through the turbulent decades of the midcentury. But few of these stories had been written down by the early 2000s, and the numbers of elders were being thinned rapidly by time. With the opportunity to record their experiences slipping away, I undertook writing this book in order to capture as many of their oral recollections as possible. Most people I spoke with voiced their concerns that the old stories were not being passed down to the younger generations and that they needed to be preserved in writing.

The Pacific War, however, was only the violent climax to an imperial rivalry between Japan and the United States that dated to the early 20th century. Japan ruled and colonized the Micronesian islands of the Pacific (including Palau) from 1914 until losing them to the United States in 1945. America's conquests from 1898 had left it in possession of a Pacific empire that included Hawaii, Guam, American Samoa, the Philippines, and other small but valuable islands. The victory over Japan won the United States undisputed dominance throughout the Pacific Rim. America viewed the strategically placed islands of Micronesia as vital to its postwar position and administered them as a de facto colony for 50 years. The United States retained vital powers over the various island governments that evolved in Micronesia during the 1980s and 1990s. The imperial aims of these two great powers have now shaped Palauans' lives for a full century.

Thus, as the first goal of the book, I asked Peleliu's elders to help me document their own distinctive experiences, memories, and judgments across these decades of colonial rule, war, and foreign intrusions into their way of life. The results occupy parts I and II. Besides preserving remembrance, these parts of the book argue that the history of the violent clash on Peleliu remains incomplete until careful consideration is given to its impacts on the native inhabitants of the island. I present the prewar way of life of the people of Peleliu in detail in order to give the reader a sense of what they lost from foreign rule and the cataclysm of 1944. The book describes the islanders' kin-based social and political system, the subsistence economy built on fishing and farming, social relations, and the steady encroachment of Japanese power in the 1930s. The story continues with the people's wartime hardships: first their exile from Peleliu, then their shock at its devastated condition after the fighting and their frustrated efforts to rebuild their lives while adjusting to American rule. The battle obliterated the way of life that had sustained Peleliu's inhabitants for 3,000 years.

Palauans' views of Japanese and American colonial rule, the war, and of history itself are radically different from those of the two combatants. On Peleliu scarce land is the key subsistence asset, but it also plays multiple cultural roles. Personal identity flows from a family lineage that is defined by the lands it controls. History is conceived geographically, as movements of people among islands and across landscapes, and how they obtained land. Lands and landmarks serve as prompts

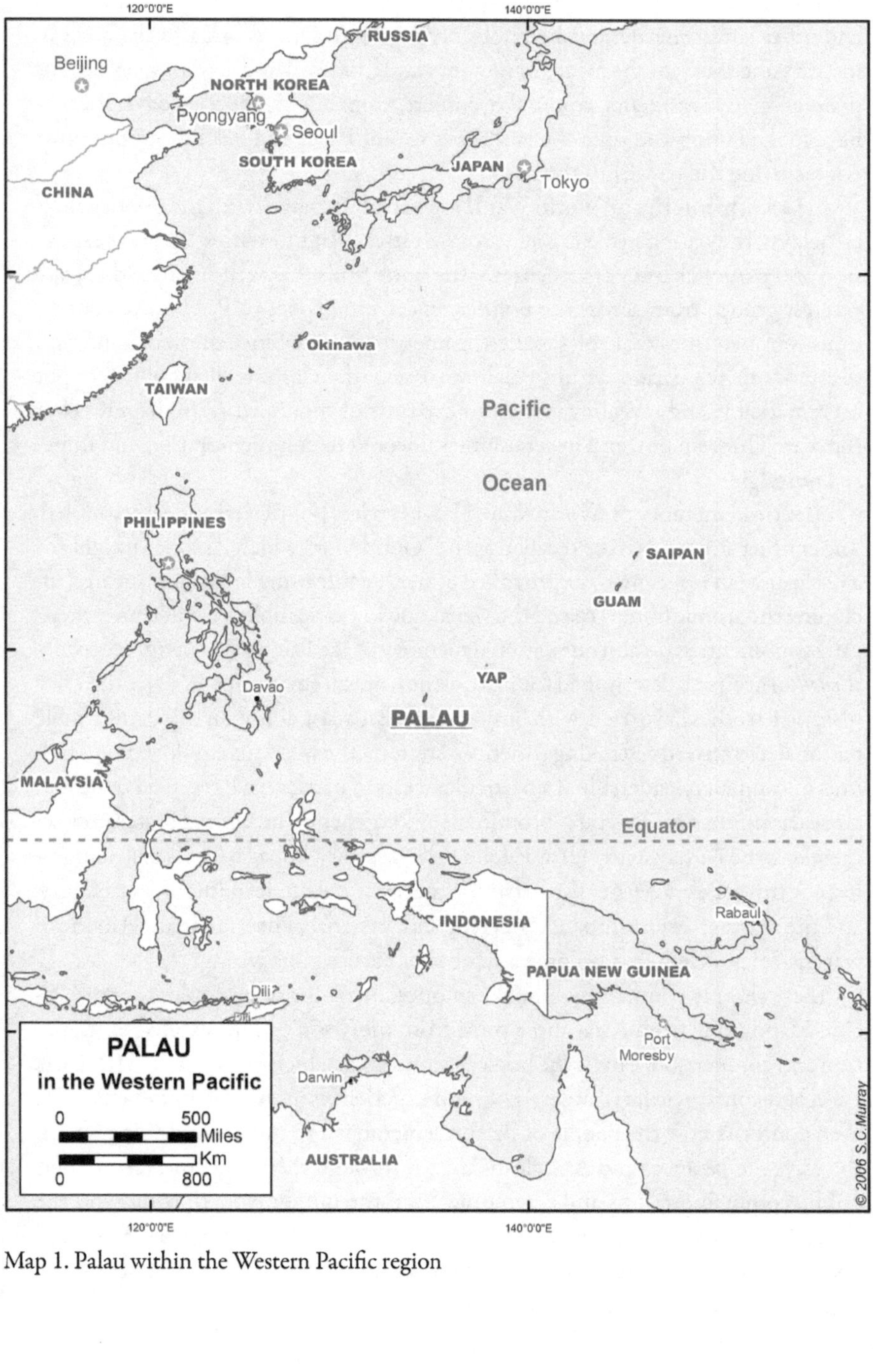

Map 1. Palau within the Western Pacific region

of memory for the oral stories that make up local history. For the islanders, then, the invasion's destruction of the villages, farms, cemeteries holding the ancestors, and other landforms demolished not only productive assets but also the roots of identity and much of the means of memory and history. The different ways various people—native residents, colonial occupiers, combatants, tourists, developers—have looked upon and used the lands and seas of Palau and Peleliu through time is a recurring theme within the book.

In Japan, memories of World War II are fiercely debated, with the political Left criticizing the nation's role as aggressor, while the Right excuses Japanese expansion and denies charges of atrocities.[1] The book finds that well-organized private interest groups from across the political spectrum export to Peleliu the contentious war memories that roil Japanese domestic politics. Since they encounter no resistance or regulation within Peleliu or Palau, the clashing viewpoints are put on remarkable and revealing display in the texts of monuments, in disputes over the search for remains, and in ceremonies devoted to commemoration and imperial nostalgia.

American memory of World War II has been less politicized and less troubled. The conflict still tends to be recalled as the "Good War," which America fought for a just cause (in response to unprovoked attack), while using legitimate means (including the atomic bomb) to end the war as quickly as possible. Peleliu's few American monuments proclaim our national memory of the Pacific War: a righteous victory won against a determined foe in a hostile tropical environment. Over the years historical studies have tried, with limited success, to cast doubt on this comfortable national narrative, questioning American strategy, the weapons employed, and failures of campaign leadership. In particular, certain battles have received close and critical examination. Peleliu is prominent among them. The United States now remembers the 74-day struggle for Peleliu for its ferocity, but also for its many lingering controversies: whether the battle was necessary, American intelligence faulty, and the marines' leadership incompetent and wasteful of lives. In many American war histories, Peleliu has become a symbol of battles gone wrong.

These sharply conflicting public memories, involving one people from the Pacific Islands, one from Asia, and a third from the West, call for explicit examination and comparison. This is the book's second goal, which occupies part III. Parts I and II reconstruct the islanders' lives and experiences in the wartime era. Part III then contrasts how the people of Peleliu remember and understand this era with the ways the Japanese and Americans treat it through their tours of Peleliu, their public commemorations and ceremonies, and the monuments they raise on the island. The analysis continues further by examining the two foreigners' published histories, memoirs, fiction, and documentaries of the battle, which, by sheer weight and volume overwhelm the voices of the islanders.

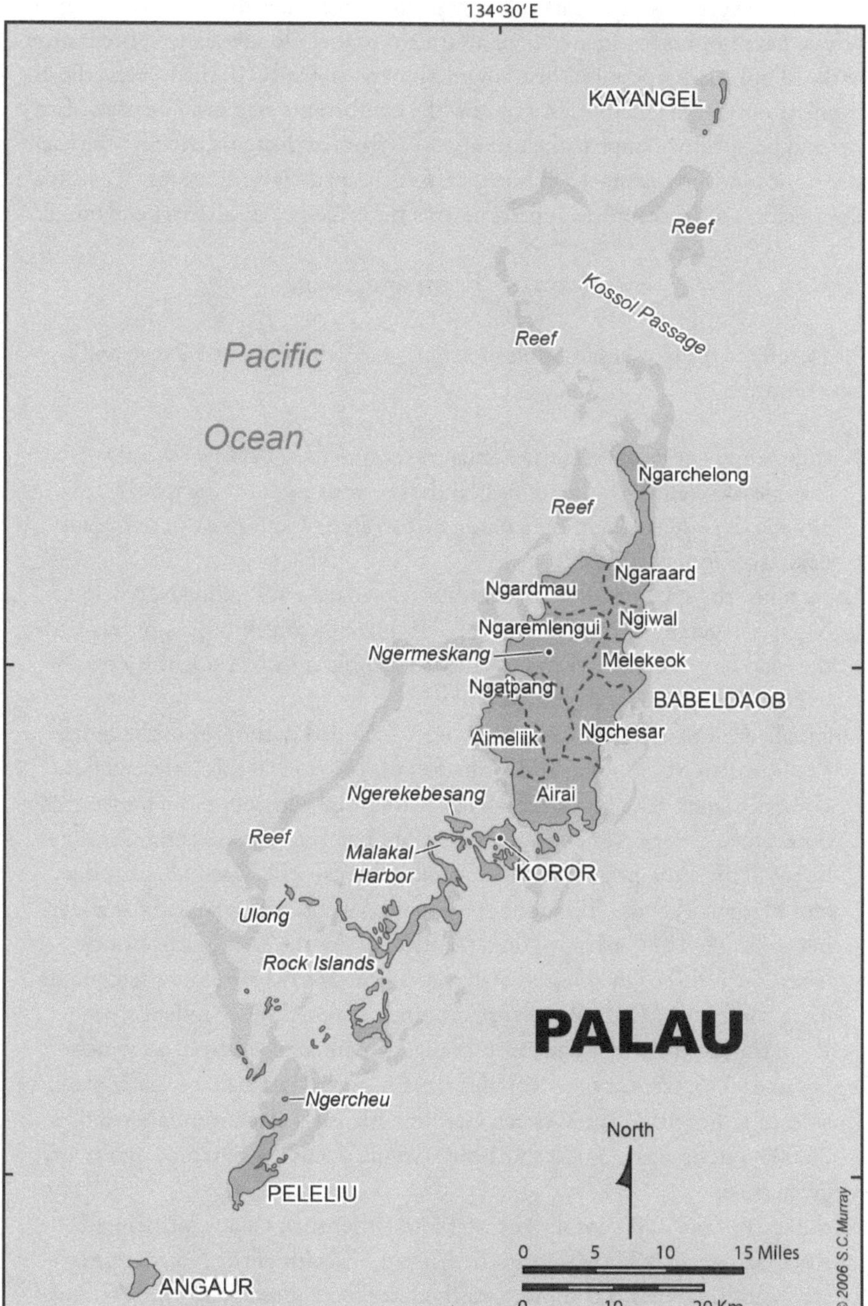

Map 2. The archipelago of Palau

Even 70 years after the battle, Japanese and Americans drawn to the story of Peleliu have not yet broadened their awareness to include adequate consideration of the island's native people. The triangulations within part III, then, reveal the incompatibility of the memories, and how the combatants' narrowly focused histories and perspectives impede the three peoples from exchanging and revising their war stories and judgments—a failure that has delayed their finding mutual consolation within a more complete appreciation of the tragedy they all share and mourn.

Notes on Terms and Usage

Please refer to the glossary for pronunciations and definitions of Palauan and Japanese terms.

For inhabitants of Peleliu I use the Palauan term *chad ra Beliliou* (literally "people of Peleliu") or the terms islanders or natives, believing that by employing the last as a legitimate synonym for "indigenous" we can remove its pejorative connotations.

I have taken the spelling of the five traditional villages on Peleliu (Ngerdelolk, Ngesias, Ngerchol, Ngerkeyukl, and Teliu) from a tourist brochure created by the islanders. It breaks with the standard orthography by using the letter "y" in Ngerkeyukl, rather than Ngerkiukl.

Originally four major groups of islands were included in the area of the central Pacific called Micronesia. Today's nation of Kiribati was formerly called the Gilbert Islands. As a British colony they followed a history different from the other three groups. When Spain lost its hold on the Marianas and Carolines in 1898, the remaining three Micronesian chains—the Marshall, Caroline, and Mariana Islands—became a single colonial entity that passed from Germany (1898–1914) to Japan (as a mandate under the League of Nations from 1919–45) to the United States (as a Trust Territory under the United Nations, from 1947 until various groupings achieved independence, with Palau the last in 1994). The exception was Guam, in the Marianas, which became a U.S. territory in 1898 and remains so today. Palau is usually considered to lie within the Western Caroline Islands. Palauans number about 25,000, but between 5,000 and 10,000 reside outside the archipelago at any given time.

At the start of the 21st century, the Marianas other than Guam (principally Rota, Saipan, and Tinian) form the Commonwealth of the Northern Mariana Islands, CNMI, a commonwealth under the United States. Yap, Chuuk (formerly Truk), Pohnpei (formerly Ponape), and Kosrae (formerly Kusaie) constitute a sovereign state, the Federated States of Micronesia (FSM). The

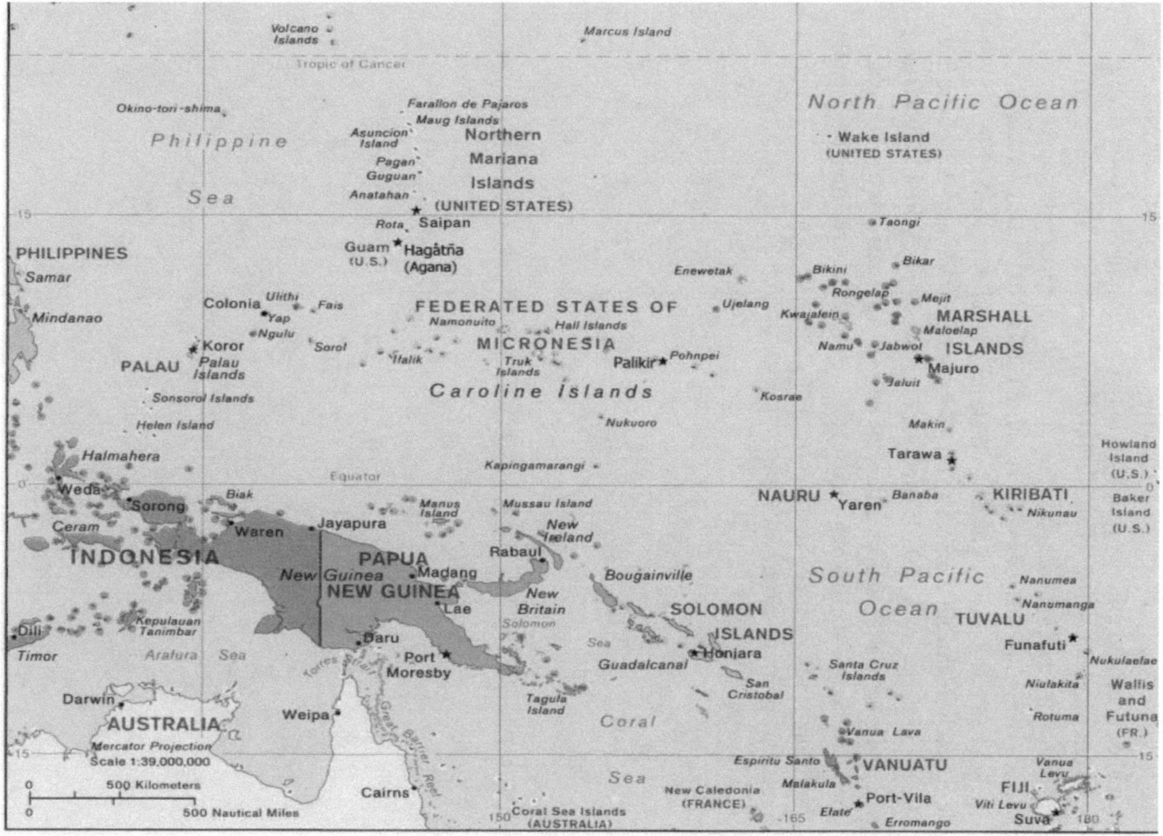

Map 3. Micronesia and the central Pacific region (Courtesy University of Texas Libraries, University of Texas at Austin)

Republic of Palau (ROP) and the Republic of the Marshall Islands (RMI) are also sovereign states, and like the FSM are members of the United Nations. All three nations have special political relationships with the United States. Under compacts of free association, the United States enjoys certain actual or potential military privileges in return for providing defense and generous financial assistance. Additional details on Palau's current government and its arrangements with the United States appear in chapter 6.

Both male and female Palauan elders can hold chiefly titles. Ichiro Blesam, my Palauan uncle, carried the title Obaklechol, and so I refer to him as "Obaklechol Ichiro Blesam." The first-ranked titleholders in each of the five villages I refer to as "Chief." With Japanese names I place the family name first and given name second, unless the person expressed a different preference. The many Palauans of Japanese ancestry who have retained the Japanese family name follow the Western pattern of placing it second.

Distances are given in statute miles.

I

Palauan and Colonial Landscapes

1
History, Memory, and Island Landscapes

The ideal (although seldom-achieved) Western model of history—as truth seeking, public and accessible, unlimited in scope, nourished by open debate, and largely chronological—fits uncomfortably with the ways most Pacific Islanders approach the subject. Islander history operates primarily at the local level, relating family, clan, or village histories. Such kin-oriented stories are exclusive, not inclusive, and in societies like Palau are considered to be confidential, not public. Islander history is frequently political and tendentious. Among the most important family stories or genealogies, for example, are those that explain membership in a particular lineage or clan, or that justify a family's possession of valuable lands or chiefly titles. Because the histories are political, they remain partial, in both senses of the word. No more of a story is released than is necessary, and stories are told with bias, to support a position. Western history telling can also be highly politicized, of course, but islanders seem to take for granted that a primary function of history is to justify power and ownership.[1]

Although growing amounts of island knowledge have been reduced to writing, either by native or outside scholars, island societies maintain their knowledge by a variety of traditional means as well. Most prominent are oral stories, but songs, dances, chants, carvings and artwork, legends and myths are all still widely used.

Palauans have created written histories, notably in a series of pamphlets from their Historic Preservation Office, based on interviews with elders on topics like traditional medicine and leadership. Palauan authors have also produced history texts for schools and compiled volumes of legends. The deepest and most important family stories, however, are still maintained and transmitted orally. As traditional *bai*, structures where the council of village chiefs meets, are gradually rebuilt, their gables and interior tie beams are carved and painted with important legends specific to the village, as was done in the past. Elders can then decode and explain the meaning of the artwork to the young (see figures 1 and 2). Some of the oldest knowledge is retained in the *chesols*, chants performed by men and women of advanced age and rank. In 2003 a segment of Peleliu's wartime history was presented at Palau's annual fair in a dance with singing performed by the island's women.

In Palau, a tightly knit, kin-based society, history is more about human relationships and individual events than about pageants of sweeping change. There are few real "national" stories. Palau was always divided into villages (*beluu*) and these continue to be, along with one's lineage and clan, primary loci of identity and loyalty. Most oral histories therefore focus at the local and family level. The stories I gathered on Peleliu were a mix of public ones that told versions of the prewar and wartime period known to all, and more private and personal versions of events as experienced by the speaker and his family. I did not seek, and was seldom given, deeper more sensitive stories, the *kelulau* (whispers) that are closely guarded. I interviewed 90 people altogether, 49 from Peleliu, of whom I considered 28 to be elders—that is, born before 1935, which placed the youngest of them in their mid-60s at the time of my primary fieldwork in 2002–3.

Stories carried in memory and related orally can readily be altered to suit changed circumstances. Palauans live comfortably with multiple versions of stories, of history. It is accepted that a tale will likely contain "spin." There may be no definitive version of any one of them, but within a locality you will be urged to identify and query the high-ranking elders who hold the key knowledge.

People do not try to distill a final consensus from these rival stories. Beches Iluches Reksid, a titled *rubak* from the village of Ngaraard, told me he appreciated my gathering the war stories from many different persons. This way, he said, I would have enough versions to create a *composite* view of the subject that would be as accurate as could be hoped for. The expectation, then, is not for agreement among competing variants; it is rather for completeness, with the understanding that ultimate harmony of opinion will remain elusive.

Palauans treat the knowledge and histories of others with circumspection. They shun direct conflict and confrontation in all aspects of their lives, and normally this discourages challenging others' stories. A group's history is their business. Consequently, the chad ra Beliliou grant Japanese and American visitors the freedom to tell their versions of the war in books, stone, and ceremony and avoid publicly judging or criticizing such versions.

The connections between history and geography are crucial. As Kathy Kesolei explained to me in an interview, Palauan history is peoples' history as structured by land, with group (not individual) identities at the center. Land and place, she went on, organize history and confer meaning on it. Karen Nero is correct in saying that "the most important dimension to a Palauan sense of history is spatial, geographical." Palauan histories or legends "recount movement through space, through particular geographical places."

It is the same for people, conceived in their group identities. "Histories of clans recount their migrations throughout Palau and ties they established while traveling." Once a group settles, then place and landscape become fixed dimensions, culturally marked space that is used as a mnemonic device for decoding the stories attached to it.[2] The places will be given names, and a lineage or clan will take its basic identity from these named lands and features within a particular village. These may be gardens, *mesei* (taro patches), beachfront, burial grounds, or home plots. These lands and how the group stakes its claim to them represent the most vital portions of its history. Said Kesolei, "A *mesei* is treasured as an heirloom to be passed down. Stories always come with it—how it reached your hands."

Glenn Petersen says of Micronesian society in general, "Embedded in each plot of land, then, is not simply a material source of survival, but a specific history of personal relationships." Loss of such a plot is more than a threat to the group's livelihood. "It is simultaneously a threat to the group's social existence and to its status as part of the community, society, and culture."[3]

The islanders of Palau and Micronesia are hardly unique in the way their landscape continues to be an important repository of the human past. Any settled people who derive subsistence from lands that they have occupied for centuries and who rely on oral traditions rather than written history to transmit their pasts can be expected to intimately know and name land, value it above other possessions, encode stories in it, and use landmarks as mnemonic aids.[4]

In Palau, natural or man-made objects—stones, trees, bead money, titles, burial sites, a tridacna clam shell—frequently serve as aids to prompt recollection of important stories. These aids are called *olangch*. Examples of American olangch would include Plymouth Rock, the Liberty Bell, Bowdoin College's dormitory named for one of its graduates, the Civil War hero Joshua Chamberlain, and almost any statue in a public space.[5]

Kathy Kesolei explained that there were traditionally three elements to a Palauan historical account: the story itself; a chant of it (the chesols) or perhaps a common saying; and the place where it happened, or its associated physical evidence, its olangch. Usually the meaning and importance of an olangch has to be learned from a knowledgeable elder who is qualified to explain it (a further discussion of olangch is found in Parmentier).[6]

The rubak Masaharu Tmodrang described to me the vital connections between migrations, land, olangch, and the burial of ancestors: "Most migration stories [for villages in Koror and Babeldaob] tell how people came from Angaur or Peleliu. Our family has names of places that our ancestors went to and named; these were olangch." Among the most important of olangch are the stone burial platforms called *odesongel*, where kin groups buried important members (see figure 3). "With no writing system, our ancestors used olangch to describe where they first arrived. It's a much stronger story if you can name the *chutem* [land parcel] you landed on; and stronger still if you have an odesongel with ancestors buried there."

The subjects of land, olangch, and burials will appear frequently in this work because they structure so many of the observations and memories that the Palauans shared. For the chad ra Beliliou, land provided their subsistence, the ordering of their society, and much of their identity. The war's devastation of lands was therefore a multifaceted and incalculable loss. For the islanders prior to World War II, their lands, olangch, and memories served the functions largely performed by books, archives, and museums in societies that rely on written language. So damage to the landscape on Peleliu resulted in damage to the means of memory and, hence, to the people's grip on their past.

For foreigners, land on the island was very different. It had economic or military value, and today is sought for either recreation or for preserving wartime history. Nonetheless, for some returned war veterans or committed history buffs, particular portions of the landscape can acquire the kind of personal, historical value that they do for Palauan natives in other contexts—finding a bunker the vet had destroyed or the hill where a memorable assault occurred. Most people in Palau view memorials raised by the foreigners as a form of outsiders' olangch. Islanders spoke frequently of the bonds formed when one kin group has to bury a member in lands of another. Burials and the recovery of remains of their own dead servicemen have also motivated both Japanese and American travelers who have come to Palau and Peleliu; and they remain a source of friction to this day.

As Western historians have turned their attention to the study of public memory, examining which persons and events receive public commemoration and celebration, and how and why these emerge while others are overlooked or suppressed, they found some of their most fertile ground in the study of the great wars of the 20th century.[7] The scale of these cataclysms, their costs in lives and treasure, and the intensity of national mobilizations gave their participants, from the nation-state down to the foot soldier, pressing reasons to want to proclaim and justify their various roles.[8]

By the late 20th century, historians also began to shed long-standing biases against eyewitness accounts of events, recognizing instead the value of the immediacy and details that oral histories and life stories can uniquely provide. The memories of veterans of World War II and the survivors of the Holocaust came to be seen as historical repositories that would soon be gone. James E. Young argues for the joining of historical analysis with personal memory. "What seems to be missing is history-telling that includes both the voice of the historian and the memory of survivors, commentary and overt interpretation of events that deepen the historical record." He also believes that memorial forms like monuments and ceremonies can add a unique element to historic understandings. We achieve better results, he says, if we "add the study of commemorative forms to the study of history, making historical inquiry the combined study of both *what happened* and *how it is passed down* to us."[9]

Paul Connerton reminds us that oral history offers "the possibility of rescuing from silence the history and culture of subordinate groups. Oral histories seek to give voice to what would otherwise remain voiceless even if not traceless, by reconstituting the life histories of individuals."[10] Oral accounts from the chad ra Beliliou therefore become the best means of inserting their experiences, previously missing, into the history of the Pacific War.

There is a confluence here of academic theorizing and indigenous practice. The people of Palau have always used oral discussions to transmit personal or family histories. Oral conversation was, out of sheer necessity, the primary means I used in my field research. Each of the elders who shared stories with me could say, with the poet Virgil, "Cynthius aurem vellit": "Apollo plucked my ear." For them, as for the Romans and the blind poet Milton, the ear was the seat of memory. (Apollo, the god of poetic inspiration, would tug a mortal's ear to remind him to be attentive and remember.) The elders recalled and discussed things that they had learned in one of two ways: through personal experience or from hearing a story and committing it to memory. They were trained from childhood to observe meticulously, to listen carefully, and to remember in detail what they heard and saw. They are the last generation in Palau to learn almost everything they know using only occasional recourse to the written word or artificial images. Their memories were prodigious, and the stories they told fluent and gripping.[11]

Recording the memories of the people of Peleliu, then comparing them against the background of American and Japanese historiography and memory, is the kind of history telling that Young advocates. This work also includes close study of the objects of commemoration—such "material leavings" as war monuments, shrines, and relics on Peleliu—to reveal memories of the Japanese and American soldiers and their countrymen and understand the politics of their representations. It considers such physical remains of Palauan life as village sites, farmlands, odesongel, and other olangch to build the background for the oral histories.

The methods employed, then, combine Palauan and Western notions of history. Source material comes from the Palauan tradition of family oral history and from personal observation. I have supplemented it with written records about Palau and with Japanese and American accounts of their colonial periods and the war. To all these I have provided additional commentary and interpretation. My hope is that reducing the islanders' stories to writing will preserve them but not ossify them, while making the history of the people of Peleliu and Palau available to a wider audience.

The Landscape of Islands

Peleliu is a small island. It has a land area of only 4.78 square miles (12.4 square kilometers). Adding the the shoreline mangrove swamps brings it to 5.73 square miles (14.8 square kilometers).[12] Islands are distinctive for their natural environments. Their smallness and isolation have made many oceanic islands (i.e., those that were never connected to continents, which includes Palau and all of Micronesia) ideal laboratories for understanding the origin, diversification, and extinction of their biota.[13] Those islands furthest from the sources of colonizing species will receive the fewest number of species. Vertebrates in particular disperse poorly.

The result is that the biota of oceanic islands tend to be radically different from those of continents. Oceanic islands are likely to have high rates of endemism—that is, species found nowhere else in the world. In the Hawaiian Islands 94 percent of all flowering plant species are endemic. Guam has (or had) 25 species of birds, 18 of them endemic to the island. By contrast, 852 species of birds have been recorded in Nepal, but only one of them is endemic.[14]

In an influential essay, Raymond Fosberg points out that "isolation and limited size" are the essential traits of insularity, as opposed to continental landmasses. Islands' limited size "makes even relatively small changes capable of rather profound general effects" since the buffering effects of greater size and biological diversity are lacking.[15] Elsewhere Fosberg writes, "Perhaps the thing that most distinguishes at least oceanic islands . . . is their extreme vulnerability, or susceptibility, to disturbance.[16] Guam's birds evolved on an island that had no tree-climbing predators to threaten their nests. But in the 70 years since the accidental introduction of the brown tree snake, this excellent tree climber has wiped out or seriously reduced most of Guam's 25 resident bird species.

This fragility of island ecosystems matters to our story for two reasons. First, we must appreciate the remarkable length of time—between 2,000 and 3,500 years—that Palauan and other natives of western Micronesia, those in Yap and the Marianas, were able to sustain their societies in these delicate environments. Second, the island's fragility is vital in helping us to comprehend the depth of the environmental disaster the people of Peleliu encountered when they returned to their island after the amphibious invasion of 1944.

It would be wrong, though, to assume that this catastrophe marks the first serious disruption of the natural ecosystem of the island. Assumptions that indigenous populations had little measurable impact on native flora and fauna have been dramatically challenged by archaeological discoveries throughout much of Polynesia. Patrick Kirch concludes that there exists "an impressive array of evidence that the indigenous islanders wrought significant and lasting changes to their environments." In the smaller, more remote oceanic islands, where human population densities were high, human effects on the natural biota were frequently "disastrous," including "wholesale decimation and extinction of many species of sea and land birds from these islands, the removal of vast tracts of indigenous forest and . . . erosion and alluviation in the valleys and along coastal plains."[17]

Recent archaeological data suggest that the first humans probably came to Palau from islands in southeast Asia. The first settlers arrived at least 3,000 years ago and possibly a millennium earlier. The archipelagoes of western Micronesia were discovered relatively early, approximately 3,500 years ago for the Marianas and 2,000 for Yap. Hawaii and New Zealand, among the last places on earth reached by humans, were settled around 1,500 and 1,000 years ago respectively. In Palau sediment cores reveal a sudden increase in savanna grasslands and charcoal particles, suggesting removal of forests by fire for agricultural purposes; vast tracts of Babeldaob Island today contain these anthropogenic (human-created) grasslands.[18]

It may be that the disturbances Palauan settlers caused to their landforms and forests had severe effects on native species. We lack the kinds of faunal studies done elsewhere in the Pacific, and for reasons explained in the conclusion, the data for Palau will be difficult to obtain because of the disturbances to the caves of Palau, where humans first took shelter. Whatever the early disruptions, the islanders of Palau developed the means to maintain the productivity of their soils, forests, reefs, and seas for millennia. Their traditions of marine conservation and their extraordinary knowledge of the habits of marine species as of the mid-20th century are documented in one of the signal studies of indigenous knowledge, *Words of the Lagoon* by Robert Johannes.[19]

From the 18th century, and probably long before, Palau's inhabitants had no regular contact with the islands of Southeast Asia, limited contacts with Woleai, in the western Carolines, but more regular visits from Yap, whose people sailed 280 miles to mine their famous stone money disks from aragonite deposits in the Koror area. They were hosted by a succession of ibeduls, the high chiefs of Koror.[20] Recorded and regular contact between Palau and the West did not occur until a British East India packet, the *Antelope*, commanded by Captain Henry Wilson, foundered on Palau's western reef in 1783. The ibedul befriended and protected the foreigners as they built a vessel to return to their world, and he entrusted his son Lebuu to Wilson when the British sailed off to Macau. This intelligent and vivacious young man caused a sensation in English society while he lived in London in 1784. England reacted with genuine grief when he succumbed to smallpox five months after his arrival. In 1788 George Keate published an account of the adventures experienced by those aboard the ship the *Antelope* in which the exemplary dignity, generosity, and naturalness displayed by the Palauan natives toward the shipwrecked British was a central theme. Keate's book proved immensely popular and went through five printings.

Intervillage warfare had been endemic to Palau, and Captain Wilson and his men let themselves be drawn into the battles of their benefactor, the ibedul. The first published description of Peleliu occurs in Keate's book, where he recounts an expedition that the ibedul mounted against Peleliu in October 1783 with over 300 canoes with 10 of Wilson's crewmen along to lend support. The attack was aimed at the village of Ngerdelolk, as the German ethnographer Augustin Krämer discerns. Badly outnumbered, the residents of Peleliu negotiated a settlement. They offered the ibedul Palauan money, two shipwrecked Malays who had been living on Peleliu, and 10 women to take back to Koror. The British briefly went ashore at Peleliu, where they found a stone wall 10–12 feet high defending the entry causeway of the village they visited. They reported that the island appeared populous, mostly flat, and fertile, with houses rather better built than those they had seen in other parts of Palau. Coconut palms were abundant, and the people "courteous, friendly, and well-disposed."[21]

The population of Palau at this time of contact cannot be known with accuracy. Estimates range from 20 thousand to 50 thousand. After European contact the picture is depressingly familiar. Palau, like most island societies in the Pacific, suffered a disastrous decline in indigenous population during the 19th century, reaching a low of 3,000 to 3,750 during the German administration in the early 20th century. The primary cause was "the usual host of diseases—smallpox, influenza, measles, and syphilis" brought by foreigners. Just as isolation made island biota vulnerable to disturbance, it made islanders vulnerable to alien pathogens.[22]

Beaches occur at the dramatic geological margin where land meets the sea. This zone of contact between two utterly dissimilar natural domains has an importance for humans that is rivaled only by the boundary between the life-sustaining envelope of Earth's atmosphere and the void of outer space. Beaches are where islanders and their watercraft most readily entered the sea or left it to come ashore. If islands suggest remoteness, physical separation, and isolation, then beaches summon images of voyaging, exploration, and contact. As Greg Dening writes, beaches are suggestive metaphors for describing cultural contact and conflict between islanders and outsiders. Every islander explorer had to cross a beach in order to construct a new society, as did every species of plant or animal. Beaches were where islanders first encountered the Europeans, who would forever change their lives. For Peleliu, Dening's observation applies to the waves of Palauan settlers, Japanese colonists and combat troops, American invaders, and today's tourists: "From land to sea and from sea to land is a long journey," but once ashore "each new intruder finds a freedom it never had in its old environment."[23]

No geographic feature of the tropical Pacific Islands is more striking than the gloriously beautiful coral reefs, effulgent gardens of multicolored living creatures arrayed on limestone pillars and platforms of every conceivable shape. Reefs consist of limestone (calcium carbonate), which is made from the skeletons of tens of thousands of generations of corals. Only the outermost layer of the reef holds living coral polyps, but they may lie on top of limestone foundations that are thousands of feet thick.

Three different types of reefs are common in Palau. Fringing reefs are attached directly to the shores of islands, from which they extend into the ocean, forming shelves that lie only a short depth below the surface. These are the reefs found along the shores of Peleliu. Barrier reefs, like the long one so visible off the west coast of Babeldaob and running down toward Peleliu, once grew along ancient shorelines when the volcanic landmass was much larger. Today the barrier reefs in Palau are separated from the remaining landmasses by lagoons that are up to 12 miles wide and 130 feet deep. Patch reefs are small coral communities that have grown on top of various underwater rises or other objects.

The limestone mass of Peleliu sits on top of a barrier reef of which it was once part. The island is nearly surrounded by a fringing reef flat, which along the western coast runs for 200 to 400 meters in width. At low tide it dries, while at high tide the depths are over a man's head. To the north of Peleliu the reef flat merges with the vast western barrier reef (which, by creating protected lagoons, allows small boats to travel safely from Peleliu to the northern tip of Babeldaob, a distance of 55 miles).[24]

Coral platforms of limestone like Peleliu are classified as makatea islands, in contrast to high islands like Koror and Babeldaob, or atolls like Kayangel.[25] Peleliu's low-lying southern end is broad and flat. However, the topography of the main peninsula running northeast of the southern lowland contains an irregular system of sharply uplifted and eroded coral ridges known as karst formations. They contain steep-sided cliffs and deep ravines, pocked throughout by caves formed by erosion from rainwater. These ridges stand 200 to 300 feet high; a smaller system dominates the northern end of the island. Peleliu's surface has a hard, marmoreal feel to it. The limestone absorbs and reflects the tropical sun, making Peleliu and Angaur warmer than the high islands. Although rainfall is abundant at 125 inches per year, it is absorbed by the limestone, so there are no running streams. Springs, wells, and catchments provide water for human use.

Basaltic high islands of volcanic origin tend to have the most fertile soils. Koror and Babeldaob's soils are in fact highly eroded, but they are fertile in comparison to Peleliu's. Limestone doesn't erode into good quality soils, which puts gardeners on Angaur, Peleliu, or the Rock Islands at a disadvantage. The luxuriant plant life on Peleliu includes mangrove forests along swampy shorelines and trees, palms, shrubs, and creeper vines that grow on limestone surfaces or in pockets where humus composed of leaf litter and other organic matter provides nutrients to the next generations of plants. Wetland taro swamps are difficult to build, and the deepest variety, mesei, in which the choicest taro is grown, cannot employ the carefully regulated water systems found on Koror or Babeldaob since Peleliu lacks streams.[26]

Prior to World War II the three western villages of Peleliu (Ngerchol, Ngerkeyukl, and Teliu) enjoyed access to the reef and sea from sandy beaches that fronted the communities. Ngesias and Ngerdelolk lie by the protected waters of the mangrove swamps of the eastern shore. Their fishermen poled or paddled canoes and bamboo rafts through channels in the mangroves that opened onto the extensive reef flats lying off the northeastern coasts, with open sea beyond and the protected Rock Island waters to the north. It was these shores, reefs, lagoons, and seas that were the domain of the men, who fished their waters almost every day. The right to fish in the lagoons or to glean on the reefs was controlled by each village, a system that limited access to a given area to those who subsisted on its resources. As Robert Johannes observes in his account of fishing lore in Palau this simple system, widespread in the Pacific, proved an excellent one for conservation of marine resources.[27]

For the native inhabitants, Peleliu's seas, reefs, beaches, lands, and mountains underlay their patterns of subsistence, their social structure, and their sense of history. The powerful foreigners who began forcing themselves into Palauan life in the 19th century viewed these same features very differently, in ways that served their own purposes in establishing a presence in the islands. Between 1885 and 1945 four distant nations would claim the right to rule over Palau. These colonizers caused permanent disruption in the lives of Palau's inhabitants, yet the ancient and complex forms of Palauan society proved remarkably resilient in the face of the forces arrayed against them.

2
Colonial Masters and Island Society

Spanish and German Rule, 1885–1914

Spanish occupation of Guam and the Marianas dates back to Magellan's voyage in the early 16th century, but in the next four centuries Madrid had failed to consolidate its holdings in Micronesia. By the 1880s Germany had become the major trading nation in the Marshall and Caroline Islands. When it staked formal claim to the Marshall Islands and Nauru in the central Pacific, it also agreed to recognize Spain's claims in the Caroline Islands.

Spain's brief attempt to assert authority in the Caroline chain after 1885 began Palauans' kaleidoscopic history as colonial wards. Over the next 109 years they would find themselves subject to rule by Spain (1885–99), Germany (1899–1914), Japan (1914–45), and the United States (under American Naval administration in the immediate postwar, 1945–47, then as a U.N. trust territory administered by the United States from 1947 to 1994). Spanish rule was characterized by energetic missionary activity by Capuchin priests. The Catholic Church became firmly established in the islands and founded the first-ever schools.

But new empires were displacing the old. With its victory in the Spanish-American War of 1898, the United States in a stroke extended its Manifest Destiny across the breadth of the Pacific Ocean, acquiring Hawaii, Midway, Wake, Guam, and the Philippines. Spain was expelled from the Pacific. Germany purchased the remaining islands of the Marianas and all the Caroline Islands from Spain in 1899.[1] Palau's natives found themselves "owned" by yet another European power—this one prepared to alter Palauan economic life to an unprecedented extent in order to make the colony profitable. Germany rapidly exploited the large deposits of phosphate, highly valuable as fertilizer, which it discovered on Angaur. The Germans also found smaller phosphate deposits on Peleliu but never began operations there.[2]

In an effort to boost copra exports, German administrators required Palauan farmers to plant and maintain coconut palms (copra is the dried meat of the mature coconut; oil pressed from copra is used in foods, cosmetics, and industry). Many Palauan men had to ask permission to plant trees on land belonging to other clans. In Palauan custom this would give the planter his copra but leave land title with the owning clan. However, the Germans, hostile to communal tenure, often awarded ownership of such lands to the planters. Such foreign disruptions of Palauan land tenure continued during each of the successor imperial regimes under Japan and the United States, creating a legacy of land disputes that bedevils Palau to this day.[3]

Japan, the Pacific, and the Nan'yō

Peoples of the West are not the only ones subject to the allure of islands. Following the restoration of the Meiji emperor in 1868, both the public and government of Japan developed an interest in the insular regions to their south. Historian Mark Peattie describes how in the 1880s and 1890s hugely popular works of romantic fiction set in Pacific island utopias stirred a "fevered excitement" about this ocean among the youth of Meiji Japan.[4]

But more pragmatic motives also directed Japan's attention to what was nebulously called the Nan'yō, or South Seas. Intent on making Japan a respected and geopolitically competitive power, its leadership concluded that it would have to both industrialize and engage in the race for colonies. The Meiji government soon successfully claimed several nearby island territories, including Okinawa in the Ryuku Islands. The vast landmass of Asia beckoned Japan both for its economic resources and as a buffer against Russian expansion eastward. But influential voices, especially in the navy, argued that the nation's future lay to the south, in the Pacific islands and the lands from French Indochina to the Dutch East Indies, with their vast riches. Two competing visions coalesced around the two armed services. The army favored a northward advance into Asia, while the navy advocated a maritime strategy of a southward advance into the Pacific and Southeast Asia.[5]

In the decades after 1895, Japan acquired the important colonies of Formosa (Taiwan) and Korea. Japan's colonial policy was first and foremost a search for security. As Mark Peattie writes, "No colonial empire of modern times was as clearly shaped by strategic considerations," and, except for Formosa, other holdings were obtained "after a deliberate decision at the highest levels that the territory would meet the strategic interests of Japan." When World War I erupted in 1914, Japan declared war against Germany and quickly dispatched a naval squadron to capture German-held Micronesia. Encountering no opposition, the Japanese Navy accomplished its mission by mid-October. Australia and New Zealand divided up the rest of Germany's Pacific colonies with equal alacrity.[6]

Ever since the stunning defeat the Japanese Navy inflicted on the Russians in 1905 at Tsushima, the U.S. Navy had warily eyed this rising power across the Pacific. The quick and furtive seizure of Micronesia surprised and angered U.S. military planners, for these far-flung islands surrounded the American base at Guam and lay athwart the shipping routes to the Philippine colony and China. The islands were inherently useful to Japan, but both its navy and its exuberant press also saw them as stepping-stones to the economic prizes within Southeast Asia. Quite suddenly, in strategic terms "these tiny remote flecks of land assumed global significance," and the veil of secrecy that the Japanese Navy promptly dropped over the new acquisition only served to stoke American suspicions.[7] The imperial reaches of the United States and Japan had extended to a point where they intersected, setting them on a collision course that would have dire consequences for the inhabitants of Micronesia.

At the Versailles peace conference the former German possessions in the Pacific were doled out as Class C Mandates. These were issued by the League of Nations and supposedly administered, but not owned as colonies, by Japan (Micronesia), Australia (the eastern half of New Guinea), and New Zealand (Samoa). Yet this smoke and mirrors from the Hall of Mirrors could not obscure the harsh truth: these Pacific lands had essentially been annexed by their administrators.[8] Palau's natives found themselves declared unfit to manage their own lives for the third time in 35 years. For the most part they adopted the same accommodating tactics that they had employed with the previous colonizers. But Japan brought attitudes and policies to its new Micronesian colony, generally called the Nan'yō, which would result in transformations of their society beyond anything the Palauan people could have anticipated.

"Japanese colonial policy," writes Mark Peattie, "displayed two overriding continuities: first, the primacy of Japanese interests—largely strategic but to a lesser extent economic—over those of the dependent people, and, second, the absence of any arrangements to prepare those peoples for self-rule, even in the distant future."[9]

Japan's strategic interests in the Nan'yō always guided any other policies it pursued, exactly as it would be in later years when the United States controlled Micronesia. The terms of the mandate forbade Japan from fortifying its island colony. But the vast public works and infrastructure development that the government quickly embarked on—construction of harbors, roads, power plants, water and sewer systems, seaplane ramps, then airfields in the later 1930s—all served both immediate economic goals and later military ones when war loomed in the Pacific. Throughout Japan's 30-year reign in the Nan'yō, projects like these, and the intense levels of administration and economic development that accompanied them, were intended to benefit not the native peoples but the economy back home and the Japanese population in the islands. Saipan and Tinian were turned into vast and profitable sugar plantations. In Palau, heavy investment in fisheries, agriculture, copra, food processing, and services produced a booming economy during the 1930s, where the benefits—first to Japan itself, and second to the Japanese immigrants—accrued as intended.[10]

The second trait of Japanese colonial rule—unwillingness to prepare the colonial wards for self-rule—stemmed from Japan's complex and rapidly changing ideas about race relations within the empire. From the time it emerged as a colonial power after seizing Formosa and Korea between 1895 and 1910, Japan began treating the people it subjugated or considered weaker, especially nonwhites, with arrogance and contempt. An ideology of Japanese racial superiority developed, built on assertions of the nation's unique purity, notions that were codified during the 1930s and 1940s, and carried into the conquests of China and Southeast Asia. Japanese racial attitudes contributed to what John Dower terms "extremely callous and brutal behavior toward non-Japanese" within the wartime empire.[11] In Micronesia, what Japanese administrators perceived as the sheer primitiveness of the natives implied that a vast developmental gulf lay between the two "races." This separateness underpinned the important decision to severely limit the schooling offered to natives. All children received three years, while a select few received five. This relegated Micronesians to only menial positions within the government and economy. In addition, a strict ethnic hierarchy placed the Japanese immigrants at the top, Okinawan and Korean immigrants second, and the islanders at the bottom, officially designated as *santō kokumin*: third-class citizens within their own islands. Japan made concerted efforts to indoctrinate the Micronesian people into Japanese ways through schools, promotion of the Shinto religion, organizing youth clubs, and offering tours of the Japanese home islands to native leaders. But almost no islanders succeeded in obtaining Japanese citizenship; and the highest position any Palauan native attained was as a kind of native police chief.[12]

The Nan'yō was distinguished from other Japanese colonies by the *relatively* large numbers of emigrants who, urged on by the government, sought to make new lives in the islands. The steady flow of the 1920s reached a flood during the 1930s, until the approximately 100 thousand Okinawan and Japanese settlers outnumbered Micronesian natives two to one overall, with a ten to one advantage in Saipan and about five to one in Palau (26,000 to 5,600) when immigration peaked in 1942. The immigrants were very much concentrated in the Mariana Islands and Palau. Okinawans, among the poorest of Japan's citizens and discriminated against for their rustic speech and manners, seized the chance to emigrate. They eventually constituted about 60 percent of all migrants to the mandate and 42 percent of the immigrants to Palau.[13]

Recognizing Palau's advantages in its superior harbor at Malakal next to Koror Island, its large landmass on Babeldaob Island, and the rich marine resources of its great lagoon and offshore fisheries, Japan made Koror the capital of the Nan'yō. Palau's proximity to Asia—1,000 miles from Manila for example—influenced thinking in Tokyo as well. In Koror the Nan'yō-chō (South Seas government) created what most people in Palau remember as an attractive and bustling urban settlement. Koror and two nearby islands to which the Nan'yō-chō built causeways, Malakal and Ngerekebesang, boasted government offices, a hospital, research facilities, seaplane ramps, fish-processing plants, a major Shinto shrine, schools, shops, restaurants, and numerous geisha houses. The Nan'yō's capital boomed with economic activity during the 1930s. Islanders were permitted to seek a modest niche in this commercial hubbub. On Babeldaob the Japanese government established five farming communities, pineapple plantations and canning plants, and experimental farms. On Angaur the German phosphate-mining operation was expanded, with its output shipped directly to Japan. (Tokyo viewed fertilizers as a strategic commodity that was vital for increasing Japan's domestic food production.) The Nan'yō-chō opened mining of the phosphate deposits on Peleliu in 1933.[14]

As Japan tightened its administrative grip and expanded its economic activities, Palauans found their lives increasingly altered. Most were cooperative, with chiefs accepting invitations to visit Japan and parents sending their children to the schools that provided the first steps to possible advancement in the new world that Japan had created. The inhabitants of Peleliu experienced their own unique trajectory in the Nan'yō era, one that elders recall today with a mixture of pride and nostalgia, anger and bitterness. The remainder of this chapter and the following one provide a description of native life on Peleliu, as elders recalled it, in the decade from 1925 to 1935, prior to the first significant intrusions by Japanese settlers and the Nan'yō-chō. Elders considered this era's village-centered way of life to be the last time the chad ra Beliliou lived in their traditional manner, before outside interference forced radical changes upon them. Memories of this period constitute a standard of reference for how they lived when free of overt colonial control with their culture largely intact. These memories retain pointed significance in people's lives to this day. They influence their thoughts about rebuilding the villages destroyed in war, their attitudes toward Japan, their understandings of the war, their assessment of the American administration as Japan's successor, and their reactions to the Japanese and American visitors who return to Peleliu three generations later.

Palauan Society on Peleliu

Palauans divide their archipelago into two distinct moieties, referred to as *bitang ma bitang*, or "side and side." Each is a loose confederation of its constituent main beluu. The Palauan word *beluu* can be glossed many (sometimes confusing) ways:

place, land, nation, state, or village. At its highest and most abstract level beluu means "land" and is considered a paired opposite with *daob*, meaning "sea." In the global community, a person from Palau would consider the entire Palauan archipelago, or the modern nation of the Republic of Palau (ROP), as his beluu, his nation. Within Palau a native would be identified by which of the next lower political units he belonged to; these units are still called beluu, but are also states within the ROP. Peleliu Island as a whole is one of these states, as are Koror, Melekeok, or Ngaraard, for example. Finally, residents of Peleliu are further identified according to which one of the island's five constituent villages, also termed beluu, is their ancestral home. There are 14 beluu or states in the main archipelago (see map 2). The other two states, Sonsorol and Hatohobei, are islands that lie to the southwest of the archipelago. Even though their languages and cultures are different from those of the main islands, their inhabitants are citizens of the ROP and send representatives to the national legislature. The northern moiety is named the same as the largest island, Babeldaob, meaning "upper seas." Its leader is the reklai, the first chief of its first beluu, Melekeok. The southern moiety, to which Peleliu belongs, is Eouldaob, "lower seas," led by the ibedul, the first chief of its first beluu, Koror.[15]

The dominant political units of Palauan society are the beluu, today's states, which are central to a Palauan's sense of identity and loyalty. If you ask who a person is, you will be told not his profession or rank but the beluu from which he comes. These states are assertively autonomous in their dealings with each other and with the national government. The strength of identity within the states and their jealously guarded autonomy is important to keep in mind when considering Peleliu and its dealings with the ROP and the many foreigners who come to the island to press claims.

Peleliu's native name in common usage is Beliliou, combining the word beluu (or possibly *blai*, house) with that for lower, *eou*. In keeping with intervillage rivalries, some Palauans try to demean the beluu by implying that its name reflects its low rank in the hierarchy of villages (see for example, Palau Community Action Agency *History of Palau*, vol. 3:369). But no community names itself with an insult or accepts such a name imposed by outsiders. Rather, *Beliliou* refers to ancient Palauan perceptions of geography and prevailing winds as they relate to sailing, which was Palauans' primary means of transport for thousands of years. As Krämer notes, during the six months of fair weather that accompanies the northeast trade winds (called *ongos*, or east, lasting from early November to mid-May), Babeldaob ("upper seas") is the windward, upwind, direction and Eouldaob ("lower seas") the leeward, downwind, one.[16] Sailing a vessel downwind, with the wind abaft the beam, is quick, quiet, and dry. Sailors often refer to it as sailing "downhill," and leaving an object to leeward is to leave it "below" the vessel. Palauan canoes lacked keels that would reduce leeway, the slipping sideways that occurs when sailing upwind.

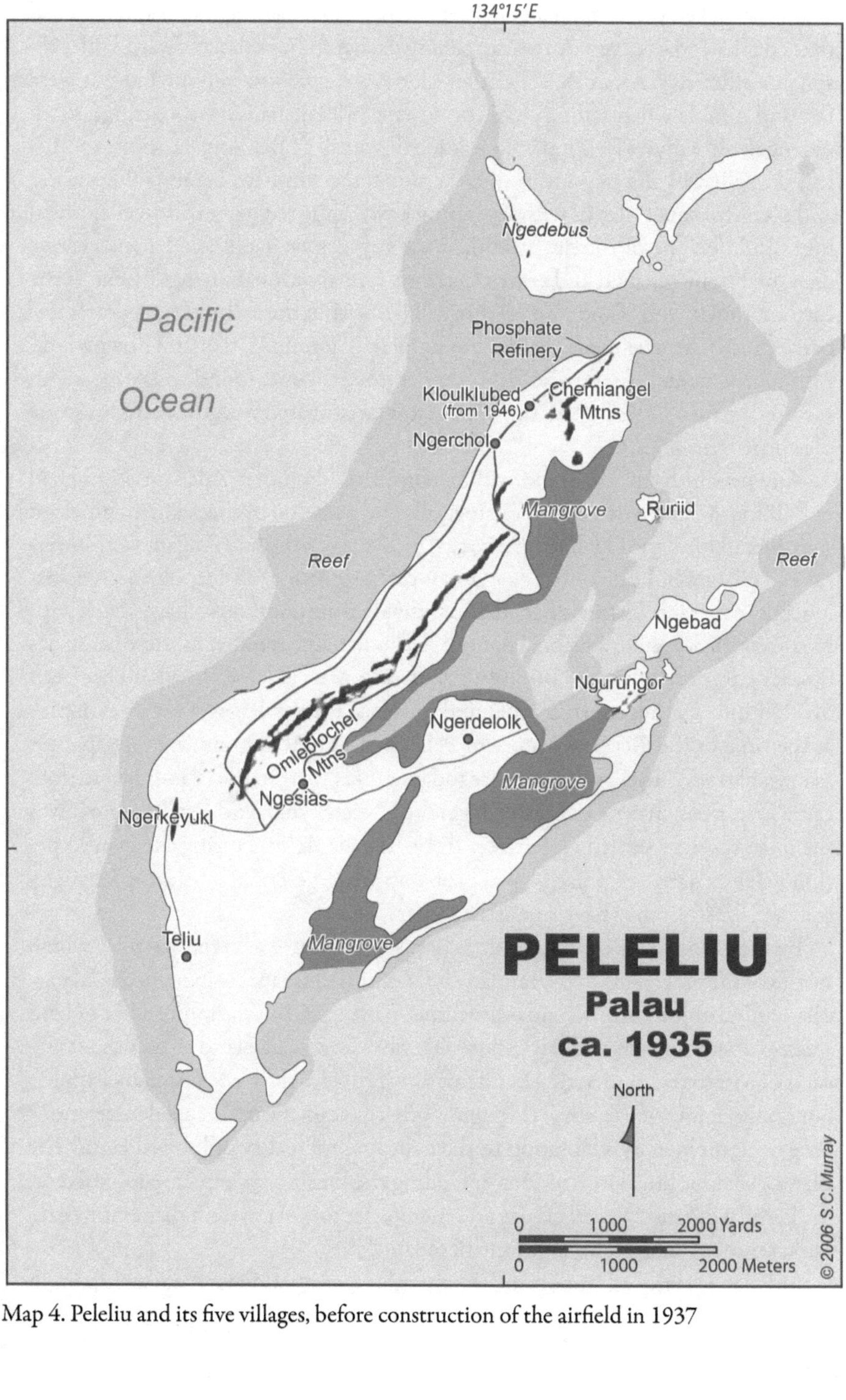

Map 4. Peleliu and its five villages, before construction of the airfield in 1937

They also lacked the aerodynamically effective fore-and-aft rig of jib and mainsail that enables today's Euro-American sailing yachts to beat to windward with reasonable efficiency. As a result, Palauan canoes struggled to sail upwind but were fast and nimble when sailing across or downwind. Palauans have a saying, "kerdi oldengelengl el mora Beliliou": "like going downhill to Beliliou." A trip from Koror, propelled by the ongos through the protected southern lagoon's deep water and plentiful small islands with sheltering bays, while enjoying the excellent fishing, would be one of the most exhilarating voyages available to a Palauan canoe man, one to be relished and remembered in this traditional saying. Peleliu is the furthest downwind island or port that still lies within the archipelago's protective barrier reef. The true meaning of *Beliliou* then, is certainly "the land downwind." Like all the beluu, Peleliu also has an older poetic name, found today mostly in song or legends: Odesangel. (This should not be confused with the word for stone platforms, *odesongel.*)

Any person from the island will be considered by other Palauans as an chad ra Beliliou, a person of Peleliu. Historically the 14 beluu of the main archipelago were hierarchically ranked within the two moieties. Peleliu and Angaur were lower-ranked villages in Eouldaob. The island is often spoken of as if it were a single beluu, but in fact it is further divided into individual autonomous villages, each with its own territory and traditional political structure. The number of these beluu has fluctuated through history. But for the past 125 years at least, the island has been divided into five recognized inhabited villages. These villages were in existence at the time of the German studies of Palau in 1909–10 and during the Japanese Nan'yō period.[17] These were (and are today) ranked within the island: Ngerdelolk came first; then, in order: Ngesias, Ngerchol, Ngerkeyukl, and last, because it was the most recently settled by refugees from Angaur, Teliu. During the Nan'yō period Peleliu's native population was probably the largest of any beluu in Palau; by the early 1940s it may have reached 825 persons.

In discussing islanders' conceptions of history we have seen the extent to which stories of the past reside in the human and natural landscapes—in named land parcels, natural objects, stones, and other forms of olangch. But the importance of land reaches much further. William Alkire describes how scarce land shapes the structures of Micronesian societies. Land not only provides the basic sustenance for life but is also "a way of life, since throughout Micronesia the basic social institutions have been molded by adaptation to the concept and reality of limited land." The islands' sociopolitical institutions, including the kinship system, "are founded on the control of land." Social classes are "manifestations of a system that emphasizes rank, seniority of descent, and control of land."[18]

In Palau it is the all-important chiefly titles, *dui*, that denote leadership, high rank, and the power to direct the disposition of lands. These titles "adhere to the land" with "a specific land parcel associated with a title and [usually] an accompanying taro swamp." As we have seen, the migration histories of one's kin unit—how it reached Palau and how it moved within the islands—and how it obtained land, titles, and alliances are the central facts distinguishing one group from another.[19] There is a saying in Palau that individual members of a lineage or clan live and die, but the land and the dui abide forever. A lineage, its titles, and its lands are then associated with a particular beluu.[20]

An example given by a male elder (rubak) of Ngerchol village demonstrates the attachment of kin groups and dui to particular lands. Ngerchol, like most villages in Palau, has ten ranked clans (*kebliil*). Its third-ranked clan is named Kerkur. It has four lineages (*telungalek*), one of which is named Kebang. There is a parcel of land named Kebang, and the rubak who lives on this parcel assumes the title Ngirakebang. Ngira roughly translates as mister or sir; its female counterpart is Dira, and the rubak's wife would receive the title Dirakebang. Thus the very titles elders hold, their identity as a person of responsibility, reflect their connection to a plot of land.

The most important lands, and those used most productively for farming or home sites, were owned corporately by lineages or clans. (Private parcels became more common as the 20th century progressed, with Germany, Japan, and the United States favoring individual ownership.) The titled heads of lineages or clans were considered *mengkar* (trustees) for most land claimed collectively by their kin group, and they granted use rights in consultation with senior men and women of the group. As the *mechas* (elder female) Dilchuuch Ermang Ngiruous from Ngerchol explained to me, "The chief of a kebliil takes care of land that is owned by the clan. But each telungalek has its own land, and the rubak and mechas of the lineage see that these lands are used well. They are the ones who must know the stories of the lands and mesei." Kent Giramur, who has ties to both Ngerdelolk and Ngerchol, told me this about the role land plays in islanders' lives: "Land in Peleliu is not a commodity; it's part of you, it's your blood, your life."

To appreciate the nature of Peleliu society it is necessary to sketch the basics of the Palauan social structure that is so deeply rooted in the soil of the islands. This requires the introduction of a heavy dose of Palauan terms; see the glossary for pronunciations and explanations. The political and kinship structure of Peleliu is similar to that of all other Palauan beluu. Each of the five beluu of Peleliu typically did, and does today, contain ten strictly ranked clans (kebliil), each made up of three or four lineages (telungalek). Nuclear families related through matrilines constitute the segments of a telungalek. In Palau, as elsewhere in Micronesia, clans tend to be very widespread geographically, and almost no actions are undertaken by the clan as a whole. Marriage exogamy holds, however. Lineages are different in that they are "much more likely to be directly associated with specific places and plots of land," are commonly the basic units owning land, and usually hold or control titles. They are much smaller than clans and often reside together.[21]

Descent in Palau is reckoned primarily through women. A child belongs to the clans and lineages of both his mother and father but has the stronger claim to the mother's line. The mother's clan is centered on one particular beluu, and so the child is typically considered to be "from" that beluu. This model can be complicated considerably given the prevalence of adoption from outside the clan, the possibility of a child being reared in his father's village, which may be different from the mother's, or the case of a child earning merit, and eventually a title, within his father's clan rather than his mother's.

Most telungalek and every kebliil are led by a male elder who is known by his dui; he has a female counterpart, an elder who holds her own title. Lower ranking male dui also have female counterparts. The eldest women choose which men will receive a vacant title, and they may depose chiefs who are judged inadequate in performance. A person becomes eligible for a title by being born to a woman whose lineage holds the rank to claim that title. But the system is wonderfully flexible. Ambitious and able individuals can win support of influential clan members through long service to the group. Clearly unqualified persons may be denied a title regardless of their claims from descent. In the capitalist economy of Palau today, wealth derived from business confers influence and power, and increasingly supports claims to the highly prized traditional titles.

The ten male kebliil chiefs constitute the council of chiefs (*klobak*) for the village, the beluu. The highest-ranking chief of the klobak, and of the village, is the chief of the top-ranked kebliil. The bulk of the power within the klobak resides with the chiefs of the four highest-ranking kebliil; they are called the four corner posts of the village (the *ewaul saus*) since they are viewed as the pillars who hold up the community. In the past they provided the main support for the village in leadership and expenditures of wealth on public projects. (Today large village public works are funded by the central government.) Some elders I spoke with on Peleliu insisted that their beluu have only four kebliil and that the other six chiefs are truly just heads of lineages subordinate to those kebliil.

The klobak met in the building that was the civic heart and symbolic center of every Palauan village, the bai, a beautiful large, narrow, high-gabled wooden structure erected on a stone platform. Said to be the largest wooden indigenous structures between Indonesia and the North American continent, bai were built without nails or fastenings. The most important and most elaborately decorated bai was the one reserved for the sitting klobak and was often referred to as the rubak bai. Bai were also used for important feasts and to host visiting parties from other villages. Men's and women's clubs, ranked by age, exist on Peleliu today; in the past each would have had its own bai. Almost all bai were destroyed in the war or allowed to deteriorate. Five traditional-style bai, however, have been rebuilt in Palau in recent decades. The bai remains Palau's most famous and ubiquitous symbol, found today in art, government seals, and tourist souvenirs and brochures.[22]

Historically the klobak was the ruling authority in the village, combining legislative, executive, and judicial functions. Any matter of village-wide import came before the klobak, and given the Palauan preference for making decisions by consensus, even the lowest clans wielded some power in village councils. Each clan ran its own business without interference from the others. In the early 20th century, the klobaks' powers were increasingly circumscribed by the German and Japanese colonial authorities. Nonetheless, on Peleliu as elsewhere, the system of lineages, clans, chiefs, and ruling councils continued, exercising power in the local, family, and traditional spheres that lay outside the vision of foreign officials.[23] Despite the extensive social change Palau has undergone in the past 100 years, the system remains very much in place today, its components easily recognizable in ethnographic accounts from a century ago. Its rivals for power and influence today are the democratically elected state and national governments, whose powers derive from written constitutions and their control over the public purse.

The Five Villages of Peleliu

Ngerdelolk

Ngerdelolk, which in 1940 had a population of about two hundred, holds the position of first-ranked village on Peleliu. This is due, I was told, to its being the seat of the powerful *chelid* (spirit, god) Ngirabeliliou, who safeguards the island. The leading chief of the village, and hence the highest-ranking chief of Peleliu, is called obak, or sometimes obakdelolk. It is believed that he has a special relationship with the chelid. He is the only chief not chosen by the high-ranking women of his clan; instead he is selected by Ngirabeliliou. It is obak who still maintains the shrine, named Omuchel el Tekoi ("the beginning of the word"), that is dedicated to the god. The rubak bai of Ngerdelolk was named Ngermelulau. Like all the bai on Peleliu, it was destroyed in World War II. Its name comes from the word *ngermel*, meaning deep secret, and the verb for whisper, *mengelulau*. It takes us to the root of Palauan secretiveness, the whispers of kelulau, information that is carefully guarded from those not qualified to know it. Like all Palau's bai, it was highly decorated, with painted storyboards on its tie beams and paintings on its gables containing legends of the beluu. The klobak of Ngerdelolk takes its name, Ngaramelulau, from this bai. This translates as "We are the Ngermelulau."[24] The huge stone platform (odesongel) on which the bai sat survived the war; it is by far the largest Palauan-made object on Peleliu to do so.[25]

Figure 1. The Bai ra Ngermelulau in Ngerdelolk, 1936 (Kondo, Micronesian Expedition, Bishop Museum, Honolulu; CN 18835)

As explained previously, odesongel are of great symbolic importance in Palau. Those that served as burial platforms for titled elders were built next to the homes of leaders of kin groups. Many were built as stone foundations for important buildings. Burials in an odesongel that supported a bai were infrequent, but they were a means to honor a renowned village warrior. Just as olangch act as aides-mémoire for important stories, odesongel are the visual manifestation of one's past through the links to one's ancestors. Nero notes that such burials "are in a real way the material records of the clan and its interrelationships and are used to verify clan history."[26] Today most dead are buried in cemeteries, but high-ranking kin are still likely to be placed in the odesongel of the lineage.

The area where the Ngermelulau odesongel lies escaped the worst of the fighting in 1944. As a result, the precinct of this odesongel contains what for Peleliu is a unique concentration of surviving olangch. The odesongel itself, of course, marks the civic center of the old beluu of Ngerdelolk.

At one corner of the odesongel stands a vertical stone slab called a *btangch*, which is a backrest where the rubak sit when outside the bai. (Usually there are four of them, for the highest-ranking "corner post" titleholders.) This btangch has a smooth egg-shaped stone resting on its top. There are several versions of the story behind this object. One says that the men of Ngesias used to sneak into Ngerdelolk when its men were out fishing and ravish its women. One day the Ngerdelolk warriors hid behind this btangch, and when their tormenters appeared, they clubbed them down. Another version relates that whenever any person on Peleliu was threatened with exile he would be brought to this btangch, where the number three titleholder of Ngerdelolk, the Itpik, would determine the final sentence. Next to the btangch stands a very old tree named Barsakesau, which predates the Japanese era. Its common name is *beokl* (of the verbena family); its leaves make a highly valued medicine when they are boiled and the liquid drunk. It is forbidden to make noise under this tree. The important shrine Omuchel el Tekoi, home of the chelid Ngirabeliliou, stands close to the odesongel. Those who visit the shrine place an offering of money under the egg-shaped stone, and the obak uses the money for maintenance of the shrine.[27]

An elongated and stylized stone head visible in a 1936 Bishop Museum photo of the bai and odesongel, however, has disappeared. Hijikata states that knowledge of the histories, meanings, and functions of this and similar stones at the bai had been forgotten by the time of his research in the 1930s.[28] It was the same in other Peleliu villages. In Ngerkeyukl he attributes this waning of knowledge to the inhabitants' conversions to Christianity. Parmentier, however, cautions against a hasty conclusion that stones, as olangch, lack resonance in Palauan society today. He observes that evidence exists showing "stones continue to be highly valued repositories of magical, religious, and political power." The "casual indifference" some scholars found toward these stones could be "a profound unwillingness to discuss these objects with Westerners."[29]

Chad ra Beliliou often expressed intense regret to me over stones, odesongel, and other olangch that were lost in the war. The value placed in stones has clearly declined, particularly among adherents of the more fundamental sects of Christianity. Yet where olangch remain in the landscape, the people of Palau have the opportunity to retain their stories and meanings and the option to revitalize their relationships to them in the future. Where the olangch were obliterated, this option is denied to all future generations.

A large stone path bisected Ngerdelolk and ran to the village's landing place and pier, called Ngetkeuang, at the head of the channel that comes from the sea through the mangroves. This stretch of shore had been the site of a high stone wall from which the village warriors repulsed attacks from the shallow channel. This wall is reported by the English, in Keate's account of the ibedul's 1783 seaborne assault on Peleliu, to be 10 to 12 feet high, "thrown up across the causeway, which leads up to it" and having a "foot-bank of stone raised up behind, on which they could stand and throw spears at their enemy." The wall had disappeared by the time of Krämer's visit in 1909–10, but recent archaeological work discovered its remains.[30]

The rubak Sammy Ocheraol remembered an intriguing object that sat at the pier in his youth: a five-foot diameter stone disk of Yapese money, yet another olangch that disappeared during the war. The Japanese forbade long-distance canoe sailing, which ended the expeditions from Yap that had regularly sailed to Palau

Figure 2. Interior of the village bai in Melekeok, Babeldaob Island. Rekewis Kerai (right) explains the histories and legends painted on tie beams to his cousin, Colin Murray, son of Stephen C. Murray.

to quarry aragonite in the Rock Islands for their stone money.[31] Sammy speculated that this particular disk dated far back in time when Peleliu controlled the quarry sites, before losing them to Koror.

Sammy also related that several of the houses of Ngerdelolk had odesongel in which they buried their high-ranking members. There was also a public cemetery by Nan'yō times. Another olangch that survived the war lies close to the Ngermelulau odesongel, along the path to the old pier. It is a *diong*, a well or bathing place dug several feet below the surface. Its name, *diong ra kles*, means "the scraped diong." Its legend concerns a chief obak whose wife was grievously insulted. The obak took her to Angaur, and to entice him to return, the villagers dug this diong with a clamshell and had to pay the obak a piece of Palauan money. This money, another olangch, still resides with the women elders of his lineage, although it is not shown in public.

Smau Amalei Ngirngesang and Renguul Kelbasang Soalablai from Ngerdelolk described to me a political decision-making process from the past in which the chelid of Ngerdelolk would give word to the rubak of the village what needed to be done. The rubak's decision, which might decree construction of a new bai for example, would be passed down in order through the chiefs of the four lower-ranked Peleliu villages. The chiefs would check with the women to see if a taro crop sufficient to feed the laboring men was ready for harvest. If it was, the men would go fishing to provide this essential food, and then the construction could begin. The ewaul saus would bear most of the costs of the project, each paying for a particular section of a bai or pier. Each rubak would call together the members of his lineage to solicit contributions.

People from the other four villages demur at this notion of receiving direct orders from Ngerdelolk. Dilchuuch Ermang of Ngerchol, for example, described how before Japanese times the ewaul saus of each of the five villages would meet when an especially large project was in the offing. Susong Smau of Ngerchol remembered meetings taking place at the Bai ra Itoi in Ngesias, which was centrally located on the island. At such meetings the rubak of each village sat together. They would decide the appropriate contributions of labor and food from each of the beluu and then return to inform their villages. Such a decision-making process fits with the prewar independence of each of the beluu from the others and with the preference for decision by consensus in important matters.

Since the war's end, when residents of all five villages have lived together in the one community of Kloulklubed, the obak does seem to have gained influence since most public meetings now include residents from all five villages, where he will receive deference as the highest-ranking person. Residents agree that his ability to affect decisions involving the other four villages marks a significant change from the prewar situation. One reason for this greater authority is that, since the war, the two men who have held the title have maintained residence on Peleliu, while many chiefs from Peleliu and the other beluu have migrated to Koror. But like all chiefs today, he has to interact with a powerful state governor and an elected state legislature, who control public funds.

Ngesias

Ngesias ranks second among the five beluu. From the east it was reached by a stone path that ran from the pier of Ngerdelolk. Stone paths also connected Ngesias to Ngerkeyukl and over the mountains to Ngerchol. Like Ngerdelolk, Ngesias had access to the sea through the eastern shore mangroves; its boats set sail from one of the island's fine historic piers, named Ngebungel. Elders of Ngesias remembered 20 to 25 households, with perhaps 175 residents. The rubak bai of Ngesias was named Itoi; it lay on the flats near where the Japanese elementary school was later built. A second, older one was named Ngermeaus. Itoi had the storyboard tie beams standard in Palauan bai, on which were painted legends of the beluu. Youths would be taught these legends as they matured. Children were not allowed inside the bai, but one person remembered looking in as a child and his parents explaining what matters were under discussion by the klobak. For important events like intervillage social gatherings, sporting competitions, or public work projects, the chiefs would gather the people and lead the discussions that determined the actions to be taken.[32]

In a departure from standard practice, the klobak of Ngesias took its name not from a bai but from the portion of the island's mountain range that looms over the village to the north. Ownership of the range, which runs down the center of the island's main peninsula, is divided between kin groups from the villages of Ngesias, Ngerchol, and Ngerkeyukl. Different segments of the range have different names. The southwestern end is Rois Ngedechelabed (*rois* means "mountains"); a formation to its north is Rois Kar; and the southeastern heights, above Ngesias, is the Rois Omleblochel.[33] The klobak calls itself "Ngaromleblochel," "We are the Omleblochel." Some people recalled that the mountain valleys were used as sites for gardens of tapioca, sweet potato, and swamp taro. Others said that members of the Ngeskesuk lineage of Ngesias would grant permission to villagers to go into the range to gather breadfruit and small land crabs or to hunt pigeons.

The oral histories concerning relations among the five villages of Peleliu reveal that they fought each other frequently in the past but also maintained special alliances or friendships. The holder of the third title in Ngesias, Spesungel Ichiro Dingilius, told me that, despite the tensions between Ngerdelolk and Ngesias as the first- and second-ranked beluu on the island, they routinely provided each other with wives. Before German times Ngesias also fought with its other neighbors, Ngerchol and Ngerkeyukl. Probably because Ngesias had donated the land for the founding of the fifth village, Teliu, boatmen from the former were allowed to use Teliu's sandy beach to launch canoes. Teliu also made gifts of fish to Ngesias.

The limestone formations of the Omleblochel had many natural caves, one of which appears as an olangch in the most famous legend from Ngesias. This cave north of the village (now marked with signs for visitors) housed a fearsome man-eating giant named Meluadelchur. If villagers dared to cook their food he would see the smoke and come down to devour them. All residents fled to Desekel, on Koror, except one old woman who had two sons. They grew tired of always having to eat their taro and fish raw. They made a great spear and went to the Ngebungel pier, where they made a fire from two big logs that formed a bridge across part of it. When the giant attacked them, they killed him and laid his *delebekul* (gizzard) on a tray that they pushed out to sea. It floated up to Koror, and when the people there saw it, they asked if it was the gizzard of a fish or a pig. But when someone thought to ask if it came from Meluadelchur, it grew large, and by this sign, they learned the giant was dead and it was safe to return to Ngesias.

The Ngebungel pier was largely destroyed between the phosphate operations of the Japanese and the prolonged fighting around Ngesias during the war. Similarly, only a few stones of the Bai ra Itoi's odesongel remain. Tokie Morei did not remember individual houses in Ngesias having odesongel in which they buried their high-ranking members. Instead, Ngesias had a public cemetery. Disparities in memory were evident over this question of whether Peleliu beluu had burial odesongel for lineages (recall that odesongel for bai were not usually used for burials). Some elders remembered their existence, others insisted there were only public cemeteries. The answer may have been supplied by one of the eldest of the women I spoke with, Dilchuuch Ermang Ngiruous. She explained that burial odesongel did exist on Peleliu until the Japanese authorities prohibited them, apparently believing them to be unsanitary.

Ngerchol

Located on the northwest coast of the island, Ngerchol was one of the larger villages, with perhaps 30 to 35 households and approximately 225 inhabitants. Its boundaries reached to the northern portions of the central system of coral ridges and included the western beaches north of Ngerkeyukl. Krämer states that the village had originally been sited by one of the northern sets of hills, but it relocated closer to the western shore.[34] Its main rubak bai was the Bai ra Ibesachel, from which the klobak took its name, Ngaraibesachel, while two other bai were named Ngebiis and Oleal (or Oloch; memories differed). Like its counterparts in the other four beluu, the klobak of Ngerchol sat in an arrangement that distinguished the odd and even numbered titleholders. A messenger would pass back and forth between the two sides, the two odd-numbered rubak of the ewaul saus on one side, the even numbered on the other. Susong Smau remembered that these seating arrangements were adhered to strictly, as were prohibitions against women or children eavesdropping on discussions. Even with the prohibitions, women would congregate outside the bai when important village-wide matters were discussed.

Like elsewhere in Palau, the ten kebliil in Ngerchol would split into competing divisions of the five odd-numbered clans against the five even-numbered ones. Leaders were the first- and second-titled rubak and were called Obaklechol and Ngirakidel. Elders recalled that the Japanese did not interfere in the clan system or the structure of the klobak, though the chiefs lost much of their former governing powers. In early Nan'yō times, as Dilchuuch Ermang related, the Japanese were respectful when requesting assistance from the klobak. She noted, however, that Japanese officials were much pushier in their treatment of Ngesias residents when they wanted to begin mining the phosphate deposits. Besides managing the building projects already mentioned, the klobak of each beluu maintained social order in parallel with the Japanese police officer and assured that the village was kept clean. The Japanese authorities successfully channeled the energies that used to be expended on warfare into Palau-wide sporting competitions. Many elders recalled with Spesungel Ichiro how their villages and klobak spent much time organizing and training the village teams and celebrating victories with feasts and song.

Figure 3. Palauan house next to an odesongel, 1935–1936 (Micronesian Expedition, Bishop Museum; CP 127138)

All the five beluu practiced the same customs as those followed by Ngerchol. Prominent among them was the ocheraol, where a group would raise money for a house by providing a feast for those who donated money for the project; the *cheldecheduch*, a settlement of money and land at the time of the death of a spouse; and less frequently than today, the *ngasech*, a ceremony honoring a woman for the birth of her first child.[35] All these events involved preparation of food for those in attendance. The exchange of food among Palauan kin groups and friends remains today the most visible and symbolically important of the gestures that define social relationships. At occasions both formal and informal, food circulates in perpetual swirls and eddies of anticipation and satisfaction—food harvested, prepared, presented, displayed, consumed with gusto, discussed, marked in memory, then returned in reciprocation at the appropriate time.

More elaborate feasts called *mur* occurred at the installation of a new rubak of the ewaul saus (or a mechas of the four highest female titles). There were fewer of the great interisland feasts called *klechedaol*. They may have been rare on Peleliu, which was, of course, more isolated from other beluu than the many villages that ringed Babeldaob. One elder remembered a klechedaol occurring at the bai ra Oloch with a village from the east coast of Babeldaob. Smau Amalei Ngirngesang, an acknowledged historian of Peleliu (figure 16), described klechedaol from before Japanese times with the hamlet of Ulimang from Ngaraard village in northern Babeldaob. Ulimang's connection with Ngerchol traces back to the time when residents of the latter left Peleliu in a search for food and eventually settled in the new site. The visitors to Peleliu would sail in three huge canoes capable of carrying 100 people. They would stay overnight in Koror, then sail 12 more hours to reach Ngerchol, landing at the village's long stone pier named Kamosang. (As we shall see, Ulimang extended its hand to Ngerchol when the Peleliu village was forced to evacuate during the war.)

Smau Amalei described Kamosang, severely damaged in the war and then wrecked by a typhoon in 1964, as being 60 to 70 meters long, 7 wide, and perhaps 2 meters high. Built of stacked coral stones, its construction had been a major undertaking for the rubak of the Ngerchol bai, who bore its costs. Kamosang means "go take a look," fitting for the structure from which villagers watched for returning fishermen or, in the old days, a fleet of invading canoes filled with warriors. It had a canoe house and a bench for sitting.

Chief Obaklechol Ichiro Blesam confirmed that in former times Ngerdelolk and Ngesias held great power on the island. To some extent, he said, the four other beluu united against the dominance of Ngerdelolk, but at other times Ngerchol and Ngerdelolk maintained military alliances. I was told stories about how Ngerdelolk relied on Ngerchol's warriors to defend the northern portions of Peleliu—including Elochel, site of today's wharf and the offshore island of Ngedebus—from attacks coming from Koror or Babeldaob. It is said that Ngerdelolk compensated Ngerchol for these dangerous services by giving it tracts of land lying to the north and east of Ngerchol on the main peninsula. Today the two villages both claim these lands. At another time in the not-too-distant past, according to oral history, Ngerdelolk asked a great fighter from Ngerchol to train its warriors for battle with the Peleliu village of Chemiangel, then situated on these same disputed lands. As Ngerdelolk attacked Chemiangel, its inhabitants withdrew to the tops of hills, from which they threw boulders at their attackers. The men of Ngerchol rushed to burn the homes of the Chemiangel villagers, who then fled from Peleliu.

When Ngerchol moved down from the hills closer to the shore, many of its olangch were left behind at the old site. Christian and then Shinto beliefs made their inroads, casting doubts on those legends and olangch that recalled spirits, ghosts, or competing gods. Still, foreign religious influence may have been more attenuated on Peleliu than in other Palauan communities. People I queried gave much evidence for the continuing strength of the local beliefs, visible in the shrine to Ngirabeliliou in Ngerdelolk and in the shrine at Teliu that belonged to the revitalization movement of Modekngei, which will be described below.

The new Ngerchol village site lacked burial odesongel for high-ranking ancestors. One mechas recalled her clan elders saying that some deceased of high rank were buried near mesei. The burial structures remained behind at the old location, and by late Japanese times Ngerchol used only its cemetery. Since World War II this has served all the people of Peleliu, although some of the beluu also use their own prewar cemeteries. Ngerchol is now also the site of many monuments erected by Japanese visitors to honor countrymen who fell in the war.

Most footpaths within Ngerchol were of packed sand, but the main road (*rael*) running from Ibesachel over the mountains to Ngesias was entirely of stone. This rael Ibesachel carried foot traffic not just from the eastern parts of the island but also from the two villages to Ngerchol's south, Ngerkeyukl and Teliu. Matichau Ilemelong recalled that the terrain to the south of Ngerchol was swampy and very difficult to access; travelers to Ngerchol from the southern villages would either make the journey along the reef at low tide or at high tide swing all the way toward Ngesias to pick up rael Ibesachel. Semper walked this path in the 1870s and describes it as steep and very arduous, the sharp coral slashing his boots and feet (precisely as American troops would describe these ridges in 1944). Semper also found evidence of former habitation far up in the ridges—multiple paths, large paved squares, the monoliths associated with bai, and abundant fruit trees. His Ngerchol guide explained that they had in the past used the sites for protection while fighting Koror, but with the prolonged peace the area had been allowed to fall into decay. Semper describes the village of Ngerchol on the coastal flat as apparently depopulated, having only 8 to 10 houses.[36]

The five beluu maintained their distance from each other, figuratively as well as literally. People did not casually journey to another beluu. They went only when necessary, usually to see a relative or attend an event, and permission was required to enter village precincts. A man could take a wife from another beluu, which of course offered the advantage of creating affinal ties with a clan whose status or resources might be desirable. Many marriages were still arranged in the 1930s, although couples also married out of affection. The wife commonly moved to the village of her husband and took up farming on land belonging to his lineage.[37]

Ngerkeyukl

Fourth in the village hierarchy stands Ngerkeyukl, whose geography was unusual in several respects (see map 5). The homes lay vulnerably close to a long sandy beach (*chelechol*) named Chelechol ra Ngebedangel, which runs north–south, facing the western reef. The village appears to have kept and defended this location far back into the time of native warfare (unlike, for example, Ngerchol, which stayed close to the mountains until the warfare subsided). The village was divided into two halves by a coral ridge between 5 and 15 meters high that lies about 100 meters back from the beach and runs parallel to it for about 500 meters. This ridge, named Cheuatel, split the settlement into the upper village, Babelbeluu, and the

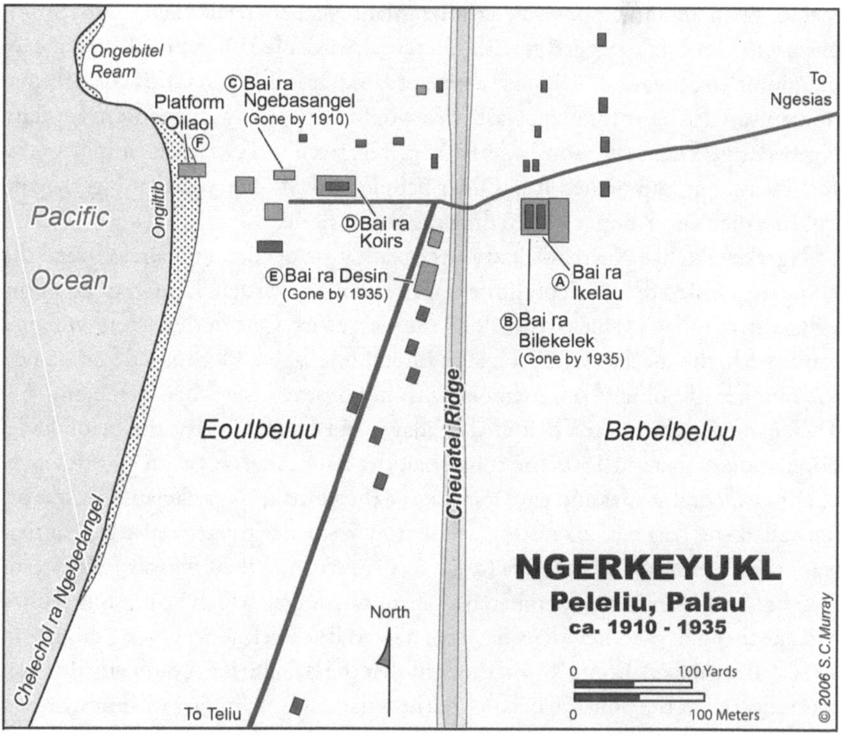

Map 5. The prewar village of Ngerkeyukl showing major structures and Cheuatel Ridge. "The Point" was the name imposed on Ongebitel Ream by American invasion forces.

lower village, Eoulbeluu, toward the shore to the west. *Cheuatel* is the term for a stone wall used for protection in war and often lies along a shore near a village. Ngerkeyukl's was a natural defensive bastion from which warriors could repulse attacks from either seaward or landward. The wall at Ngerdelolk in the 1780s was an cheuatel. Most were man-made, not natural.[38]

The village was further divided into northern and southern segments by the main path that ran from the shore over the top of Cheuatel and thence eastward to Ngesias. From the ridge to Ngesias it was made entirely of fitted stones. The path is gone now, but the cut through the top of Cheuatel is still visible, and just below it, to the west, can be seen the depression that is the remains of the diong named Desiu. The path terminated at the boathouse (*diangel*) on the beach, where there was also a stone platform named Oilaol, at which people could catch the breezes off the sea while they waited for fishermen to return. This small section of shoreline, the northern end of Ngebedangel beach, is named Ongiltib. It lies immediately south of a rocky promontory about 10 meters high that extends out into the reef for 50 meters and looks down the length of Ngebedangel beach.[39] This promontory, made of sharp jagged grayish-blue coral, was called Ongebitel Ream, meaning "dump site for *ream*," which is a type of weed. It is likely that this coral formation was used as a site for plant waste that would be applied as compost in gardens. Ngebedangel beach runs southward 700 meters from this site, then ends in an elevated coral outcrop named Iyai. Older people I asked observed that Ngerkeyukl lacked a pier, and Krämer's 1910 drawing shows none.

Ngerkeyukl, like Ngerchol, had a large plantation of coconut palms around the home sites and to the south of the beluu. The women's gardens lay to the east of the village, near today's vehicle road along the west coast. One of the oldest women I spoke with, the mechas Chobechad ra Eliou Song, aged 90, counted and named the number of homes from memory with her brother, Matichau Ilemelong, 83. They named eight in each half of the village, and estimated that the beluu had a population of around 130. The rubak bai, the Bai ra Ikelau, sat on an odesongel of chiseled coral stones and gave its name to the klobak, "Ngarikelau."[40] It was often called the "big bai," to distinguish it from a smaller traditional-style bai that was open to the public, the Bai ra Koirs. By Nan'yō times there was also a Western-style bai, and Matichau remembered a vacant odesongel, which he presumed once had another bai. (Krämer identifies a bai named Bilekelek as occupying this site in 1910.) The rubak Antonio Tewid thought that the Babelbeluu-Eoulbeluu division was reflected in the political balance of the village as well, in that the number two and three titleholders lived in the upper village while the number one and four rubak lived in the lower.

Ngerkeyukl's orientation is toward the west, toward the ocean and the setting sun. Indeed, the village's name means "on the west coast." From its shore Angaur Island is clearly visible to the southwest. Ngebedangel beach provided the people with easy access to the sea, and the reef flat was a reliable source of marine bounty, though the relatively small lagoon areas before Ngerkeyukl and Teliu immediately south meant that fish were not always plentiful there. People remembered having to eat a lot of fish soups to stretch the supply of fish. Residents of Teliu ate a lot of the plentiful small land crabs, *rekung*. The beach itself provided an abundance of *chesechol*, a small white clam that lies just below the surface and makes a delicious appetizer when prepared with coconut cream.

The beach also was the children's natural playground, day and night. Matichau re-created the children's fascination with the disappearance of the sun each evening when he described how he and others would dig a hole in the sand and lean over to listen for the sound of the sun as it fell into the ocean. The night of the full moon was a time for celebration throughout Palau, a night given to singing, dancing, and games. Children of Ngerkeyukl built huge bonfires on the beach from palm fronds and danced and sang into the small hours. They would have jump-

Figure 4. Matichau Ilemelong at the site of his village of Ngerkeyukl, 2003

ing contests to see who could leap highest over the fire. The youngsters of Angaur would answer Ngerkeyukl's fires with those of their own along their eastern beaches facing Peleliu. "We'd build ours higher, and then they'd do the same with theirs, trying to make theirs higher than ours. We'd signal each other this way throughout the night." Standing on Ngebedangel beach and remembering the fishing and farming, the patterns of life in the old village, and the children's games, Matichau grew quiet and gazed out at the ocean. "It was a good life," he said.

When asked about olangch from before the war, Matichau replied that during the conflict the village had lost a stone that he would give anything to recover. It was named Bibuiich el bad and was clear, like glass. He then told me this version of one of Peleliu's most famous legends, the story of Uchelkeklau and how Palau's fundamental political structure of the four corner post chiefs, the ewaul saus, came to be. It happened because four rubak of Ngerkeyukl tried to race the setting sun.

According to the story, the Bibuiich el bad ("shining stone," from *meliluich*, to glow) lay near the shore by Ngerkeyukl's boathouse and across the path from the stone platform Oilaol, at the stretch of beach named Ongiltib. Just several inches of the stone protruded aboveground, and it was about three to four feet on a side, large enough so four men could comfortably sit on it. Long ago, at a time when nobody yet had titles, four rubak used to sit on this stone, and they frequently spoke of their desire to voyage to the west to find out where the sun set. They decided to actually try. One morning as the sun rose in the east, they launched their canoe from the beach in pursuit of adventure, like so many heroes in legends around the world. They paddled powerfully all day toward the west. But they were slower than the sun, and the horizon kept receding, until the sun plunged into the sea far ahead of them. Finally, exhausted, they came to an island, which was the home of an chelid named Uchelkeklau. When they explained to him they were trying to chase the sun, Uchelkeklau said, "I have the sun," and he showed them an object that looked like the sun; they concluded that he must be the god of the sun and that he had control over it.

The men remained on the magic island for a long time. One day Uchelkeklau left them and warned them they must not open a *kim*, a giant tridacna clam, that he kept in his home. But the four were curious, so they decided just to take a peek. When they opened it they saw inside, to their surprise, their home village of Ngerkeyukl. They could see all the homes, the bai, the people moving around, all their children, relatives, and friends. (Matichau smiled here and observed that these were the first people of Palau ever to see television.) They all began to cry from homesickness. On his return, Uchelkeklau guessed why they had tears, so he agreed to send them back to their beluu.

He cut down a giant bamboo, large enough for a man to fit inside. As each man crawled within, Uchelkeklau gave him a dui (title). The first was given the title Aderkeroi, the first-ranked dui in Ngerkeyukl; the second became Adelbeluu, the second-ranked dui; the third became Edlach, and the fourth Uchelmekediu. Uchelkeklau then sealed the bamboo with a plug of the *kesuk* tree (croton) and placed it into the sea. It drifted back to the beach at Ongiltib, where the men's families joyously discovered the lost voyagers. The men explained how the village should now be organized in accordance with their new titles. In this way the institution of the ewaul saus came to Palau, and it has remained the cornerstone of the political structure ever since.

From their childhoods Matichau and his sister, Song, remembered four olangch related to the Bibuiich el bad legend: a section of bamboo that lay inside the rubak bai Ikelau, a huge tridacna clam shell that lay next to its odesongel, and a kesuk tree that grew next to a corner of this same bai. Water from the roof of the bai filled the clam shell, from which one could drink. Song agreed that the Bibuiich el bad was most unusual in its clear, crystalline quality—which would be particularly unusual on Peleliu, where there is only limestone, no crystalline igneous or metamorphic rock. I tried to obtain confirmation from other elders concerning the nature of this stone, but they either could not or would not discuss it. Krämer mentions the croton tree from the legend but not, identifiably, the shining stone. Hijikata mentions a flat stone that the English translation spells "Biyug el Bad"; but he does not describe the stone.[41] All four of the olangch associated with the story of the ewaul saus disappeared during the time of the airfield's construction and the ensuing war.

Teliu

Of the five villages on Peleliu, only Teliu was founded recently enough so its story lies almost within living memory. In the 19th century, just before German times (1899–1914), a group of about 20 people sailed to Ngerdelolk in order to escape warfare on Angaur. Offering hospitality to wayfarers is a fundamental imperative of Palauan social relations. By custom, when destitute persons arrive in a village, they become the responsibility of the high-ranking clans. The obak of Ngerdelolk, as leading chief on the island, took the Angaurese under his protection. At first they all lived in a cave.

According to the oldest person I interviewed, Obechad Tabelong Olkeriil, born in 1910, it was her ancestor, a mechas named Bosaol, who founded Teliu. From lands at the southwestern end of Peleliu she could see Angaur across seven miles of open water, a sight that made her and the others very homesick. These lands belonged to Ngesias. The Angaur obak asked the Ngesias chief, the uchelsias, to help them, and he agreed that they could stay in what is now Teliu so they could forever see their homeland. (Teliu is also called Bkulabeluu, meaning "village of the cape," for its location on the southwest corner of the island.) This story explains the special ties existing today between Teliu and its benefactors, Ngerdelolk and Ngesias. The ability of Ngesias to give up so much land suggests further the extent of the depopulation that had devastated villages by the mid-19th century. Ngerdelolk again accepted the people of Teliu as refugees after their lands were seized by Japan for the airfield.[42]

Palauan claims to lands and status often hinge crucially on assertions of priority of arrival to a site of settlement. Those families with choicest lands or highest rankings defend their positions, whenever possible, with stories of having arrived earlier than other settlers. Teliu's rank as a village on Peleliu—fifth out of five—reflects this late arrival to the island. Apparently more than one group crossed from Angaur. Matsko Tkel attributed the ownership of taro patches in Teliu to these groups' order of arrival. Those who had the best mesei prior to the war were those who had arrived first.

Teliu was the smallest beluu on the island, although elders disagreed on its number of households. One remembered 10, another 12, a third up to 25, which would imply a population of between 70 and 125. The highest-ranking chief is the renguul. Teliu's rubak bai, named Bai ra Brai, gave its name to the klobak, Ngarabrai. Obechad Tabelong recalled that among her clan's privileges was the right of its rubak, the third-ranked Ademesib, to bring children into the bai while the rubak were eating there. And only his clan could light the coconut oil lamps in the bai. Obechad Tabelong recalled another bai, Bai ra Sesemuch, that was for younger folk and for public occasions. It was built in a more Japanese style, with wooden walls and a tin roof. Matsko Tkel, who grew up later in Teliu, remembered a different number two bai named Meou, built in Japanese style, at which the younger folk learned to dance.

As in the other beluu, the ten rubak in the bai followed a division of odd- and even-numbered titles that determined where each one sat within the bai during meetings. The women had ten ranked titles as well. (In fact, the day after Dirasechedui Mellomes Shmull provided me this information, a mur feast was held to invest a new holder of the top female title, rukebai.) Neither Mrs. Shmull nor Matsko Tkel recalled a physical division of the village layout itself into two recognized halves. (Mrs. Shmull is the wife of the first chief of Ngesias during the early 2000s, Uchelsias Etibek Shmull.)

The village had a diangel at which the canoes were stored and a *yasumba* (bench) down at its long and lovely beach, Chelechol ra Bkulabeluu. Unlike Ngerkeyukl, Teliu had an entrance for small craft in its reef, which made the village the departure point for the voyage across the strait to Angaur.[43]

The paths running through the village were smooth-packed sand, lined with stones. Men and women had separate bathing places, the diong ra Brai for the men and another one, Olabed, for the women. These would have been large pools dug out of the sandy soils back from the beach, providing brackish water suitable for bathing. Dirasechedui Mellomes recalled that only a few old rubak still wore the breechcloth (*usakr*) by the early 1930s and most women had switched from the traditional skirts (*cheriut*) of hibiscus fiber to ones of cloth and Western design.

Both Obechad Tabelong and Dirasechedui Mellomes remembered the important Blai Lius in Teliu, which was a shrine for followers of Modekngei, a Palauan revitalization movement that was active during the Nan'yō era. Modekngei opposed Japanese institutions like schools and hospitals and sought to invigorate Palauan natives' ties to their ancient gods. Japanese officials considered it a subversive threat and imprisoned its leaders.[44] Blai Lius was a house entirely made of coconut trees (*lius*), whose construction was ordered by a spirit (chelid). All the Modekngei of Peleliu came to pray there, and about twice a year large ceremonies were held that brought people from all over Palau to the sacred site. Next to it sat a large round whitish stone, which the Modekngei ceremonially washed weekly with oil and a mixture boiled from tree leaves.

The world's history books do not recount the legends of Ngerkeyukl and their associated olangch, nor do they remember the native names of the shoreline's features, the range of mountains, the many bai, or the roles they played in the villagers' lives. In 1944 when American troops invaded Peleliu, Chelechol ra Ngebedangel was selected as an assault beach and given the code name White Beach. The beach of Teliu, Chelechol ra Bkulabeluu, was code-named Orange Beach and also invaded. The Japanese defenders heavily fortified Ongebitel Ream, the promontory that they called Iwamatsu ("stone pines"), which dominated the length of Ngebedangel and its reef flat. From its strategic vantage, their artillery and machine guns wreaked such havoc on the American landing troops as to threaten the success of the entire amphibious operation. The opposing forces engaged in two days and nights of slaughter for control of this vital site, which the U.S. Marines called "the Point." Japanese soldiers used Cheuatel ridge precisely as Ngerkeyukl's warriors had—as a stronghold against seaborne attack. From its crevices and heights they rained mortar and machine-gun fire down on marines struggling to advance off the beach toward the airfield. The beaches on Angaur, where its children had built bonfires to signal their friends in Ngerkeyukl, became the site of the American landings on that island two days after the assault on Peleliu. The natural caves in the Omleblochel Mountains of Ngesias and the ridges of Ngerchol, augmented by hundreds more dug by forced Palauan labor, sheltered Japanese troops so effectively that the battle for the island lasted 74 days and was remembered as one of the very worst of the Pacific War.

II

Peace, War, and a New Empire

3
Smiling Sky, Gathering Clouds

In the prewar decades up to the early 1940s, life on Peleliu revolved around subsistence fishing and farming that made the residents of the island almost entirely dependent on the sustained productivity of their lands and waters. They labored hard to wrest a living from the dangerous seas and the unfruitful soil. Their knowledge about these resources was broad and deep but focused on practical considerations of yield. They lived with the rhythms of the natural world, but the hard life does not inspire bucolic reveries even at the remove of six or seven decades. Their nostalgia for the years up to 1935 comes rather from their belief that up to that point the chad ra Beliliou lived their lives in the manner shaped primarily by their forbears and themselves, with minimal interference from outside forces.

As Smau Amalei Ngirngesang from Ngerdelolk and Ngerchol recalled, each of the five villages was autonomous and nearly self-sufficient. Relations among them were formal and restrained for the most part. Their inhabitants were segregated from each other by prohibitions against trespassing on other villages' territories or using their fishing grounds unless formal permission had been obtained from a chief. The first part of this chapter allows the elders to describe the patterns of their lives—how they fished and farmed, maintained their lands and waters, and passed down their heritage. The lifeways known firsthand to them by the late 1920s and early 1930s had already undergone significant change in the preceding century, but the fundamental subsistence patterns and most of the social structure were still very much intact.

The elders' reactions to the accelerating social and economic changes introduced in these years under Japanese rule were complex. The people of Palau welcomed certain of the earliest developments promoted during the Nan'yō era, like improved public safety and the opening of elementary schools for all children. Less popular were limitations placed on the traditional prerogatives of the chiefs and the persistent racism that Micronesians faced in their dealings with the Japanese government. The major prewar disruptions on Peleliu came in three distinct phases. First was the opening of mines to extract phosphate (*ringko*) in Ngesias, which marked the first taking of land by the Japanese authorities, the first large-scale settlement of foreigners on the island, and the introduction of wage labor among the islanders, which greatly expanded the cash economy. This was followed by the Nan'yō-chō's land registration program, the *tochi daicho*, which struck at the heart of Palauan society. It sowed seeds of confusion and disagreement that trouble Peleliu (and all Palau) to this day. Finally, disastrously, came the expulsion of two of the villages from the site the Japanese military chose for construction of the airfield in the late 1930s, presaging the doom that would befall the island in 1944.

Daily Life on Peleliu

Palau has a fairly strict division of labor between men and women. The ocean is generally, though not exclusively, the realm of the men as fishermen, sailors, and boat builders. Traditionally, the men provide the protein food, usually fish from the reef or deep sea. Even today, nothing contributes more to a man's reputation than to be acknowledged as an accomplished fisherman. Women are primarily responsible for produce from the land, as gardeners, gatherers, and stewards of this invaluable resource. Women provide the all-important taro, tapioca, sweet potato, or other vegetables and fruit that make up the bulk of the diet. A proper Palauan meal must contain these two complementary products, the foods higher in protein (*odoim*) obtained by the men, and the higher-energy carbohydrate foods (*ongraol*) produced by the women.

On Peleliu during the 1920s and 1930s, fishermen employed many different techniques, depending on the type of fish being sought and the number of men and boats involved. One or two men commonly went out in canoes for short distances in the lagoon, using spears, hooks and lines, or throw nets. The men of Teliu fished often on the reef in front of the village using lines and spears. Men of Ngesias could launch their canoes or bamboo rafts from their village pier then fish within the mangroves close to the village or sail out to islands like Ngebad on the eastern reef. They could also fish from the beach at Teliu, since this village had a special relationship with Ngesias. So purposeful was any trip to the reef that in the Palauan language "to go to the reef," *mora chei*, means to go fishing.

In the Nan'yō period sea transport within the archipelago was still made by native canoes. Matichau Ilemelong of Ngerkeyukl recalled that every rubak had a canoe of some sort, so there were many, of varying sizes. The smallest and most common was the *kotraol*, which carried three or four men. The largest was used when they cast the great nets in fishing grounds offshore of Peleliu and its adjacent reef flats. Only Ngesias and Ngerdelolk had one each of these great craft. Every village had one or more vessels about 20 feet in length used for longer trips, like to Koror or to villages along the coasts of Babeldaob when visiting relatives.

The absence of a channel through the reef at Ngerchol and Ngerkeyukl meant that a vessel from Angaur or Koror would have to transfer passengers to smaller boats of shallower draft that would bring them across the reef. Smau Amalei said the larger fishing expeditions of Ngerchol in Nan'yō years would launch five sailing canoes, each with a crew of three. If high tides allowed their canoes to traverse the western lagoon shallows and exit through channels to the north in the morning, and low tide occurred at noon, fishermen from the western villages could fish all day and then return on the flood around 4:00 p.m.

They would sail to small islands such as Ngercheu, Ngemelis, and Ngerechong, which lay three to eight miles to the north and northeast of Peleliu. The husbands would tell their wives whether they were going fishing to the west or east so the village would know where to look in case the crew did not return on schedule. One man steered the canoe while the other two fished, either with lines or spears. Sometimes they went as far as Ulong Island, 16 miles to the north, which was then the accepted boundary of Peleliu's waters. (Others maintained it ran all the way to Aimeliik, in southern Babeldaob.) The boundary is a sore point today because many of Palau's most famous tourist diving locations, like Blue Corner, lie in waters Peleliu claims as its own, yet most tourists stay in Koror hotels and use its diving shops.

Occasionally each man would sail his own canoe to the Rock Islands, but several would go in a group for safety. These northern fishing grounds inside the barrier reefs offered protection from heavy seas or strong tidal streams. The currents in the open seas around the southern end of Peleliu, and in the strait between it and Angaur, are swift and dangerous: former governor Yuki Shmull related how a full boatload of 27 islanders was lost in late Nan'yō times while crossing from Angaur to Peleliu.

Those who preferred to dive for fish used homemade goggles and hand spears. On trips lasting more than a day the men preserved their catch by smoking it once ashore; other methods of preservation included salting fillets and sun-drying. The wage labor that the phosphate mines provided in the mid-1930s had an immediate effect on fishing patterns since fishermen could stay out overnight only on weekends.

Turtles, abundant in the Rock Islands, could be speared from a boat or captured on shore. After finding a fresh path in the sand where a female laid eggs, fishermen would return in 15 days, knowing that she would come back in that time to lay eggs again on the same beach. They would let her lay her eggs, then capture her. (One of Palau's best-known legends describes how a boy from Peleliu and his girlfriend discovered this 15-day cycle, at new and full moon, while they met at Ngemelis Island for assignations.)

Elders enjoyed describing large expeditions of cooperative fishing, involving a fleet of boats, or an organized party employing a vast net along the reef. Scores of coconut palm fronds would be tied together and hung from a rope to form what was called a *ruul*. Known as a leaf sweep in English, a ruul was a long barrier of leaves that functioned like a net but was used to herd fish rather than snare them. The ruul was hauled in a large circle around fish in the shallows of the reef flat as the tide ebbed. Hanging below the rope in shallow water, the fronds touched the reef floor. The fish corralled inside would perceive the fronds as a barrier that they could not swim through. As the ruul was drawn tighter, the fish would be herded toward a mesh net at one end, where they were speared and piled aboard a bamboo raft.

A related technique was used to catch the prized *kelat*, the warty-lipped mullet (*Crenimugil crenilabis*), which spawns monthly on the reef according to the lunar cycle. A party of men would use nets to cover the channel entrances through which the fish swam during spawning. The nets would be drawn about the prey and the most skilled men would then use a kind of butterfly net made of coconut husk fiber (*suld*) to catch the trapped fish as they jumped in panic. One elder recalled occasions when all five villages would work together to make ruul, then sail to a sandy-bottomed area named "madechol," near Ngedebus, just north of Peleliu, to set them. Another described using this method in eastern grounds, where they would net kelat, *uluu* (diamond scale mullet), and other species. The kelat fishing could supply enough food for a week, at which point the men would stop their fishing.[1]

These methods are labor-intensive but they can be highly efficient. Even those with little experience or skill—children, anthropologists—can be helpful by holding a portion of the ruul and splashing water to frighten the fish toward the catch net. The rubak described the abundance of fish in these times and how all the collective methods amply rewarded the hard work involved. Chief Uchelsias Etibek Shmull remembered, "When we cast our nets and caught a school, we'd miss a second school while cleaning the first one out of our nets."

Matichau Ilemelong explained how the rubak of a village would gather the young fishermen together. A leader, called *melam miyoi*, would be selected to be in charge of the ruul. Everyone would get a turn eventually so all could learn the proper ways to fish. The melam miyoi had two primary responsibilities: first, to choose the proper time to close the ruul and spear the fish, and second, to keep track of the amount of fish speared from the net. If he determined that the catch was sufficient, then for purposes of conservation he ordered the ruul opened to release the remaining fish. If a fishing party returned with more fish than usable, the rubak would scold the men and the klobak had the power to fine them or compel them to perform community labor.

A regular theme in the elders' conversations was the extent to which people in the past shared their food, goods, and labor. When a fishing expedition brought the catch home it was shared with the entire village, a procedure known as *melatemang* (*temang* is a gift of fish). Chief Uchelsias remembered that upon landing, the men blew a conch shell to announce their arrival, bringing down to the shore one youngster from each household carrying a basket to receive its share. Smau Amalei said that they would pile the fish on shore together, count each house by roof, then divide the catch according to the number of people in each house. Matichau added that special consideration was given to a woman lacking a husband or sons to fish for her. Only then would the leftovers be divided among those who went fishing.

Peleliu's men also performed the many tasks associated with fishing. They built canoes and made the sails and rigging, made the fishing gear, constructed the village piers from coral rocks, and studied the lore concerning fishing grounds, techniques, marine species, and weather and astronomical patterns. Canoe building was usually a cooperative activity, led by a specialist boat builder. Men also constructed the family homes, the bai, stone paths through the village, and the odesongel. Ties that existed between certain villages were reflected in the ways they assisted each other in large projects. Ngerkeyukl, for example, helped its neighbors, Ngerchol and Teliu, with constructing bai.[2]

The building of family homes also involved shared labor, primarily among clansmen, with women providing food and drink for the men. While villagers on Babeldaob typically used a thatch made from *toechel* (Nipa palm), Peleliu had to rely on thatch made from *such* (pandanus), which grows in open grassy areas. The roof and walls were made of *such* hung on frames made of many kinds of mangrove trees and Palau's much-admired ironwood, *dort*. Flooring came from mangrove trees, *tebechel*, which were shaped and smoothed with an adze. The lineage and clan helped each member do the cutting, and they did most of the construction, but other people who were not busy readily helped out.

The favored staple crop throughout Palau among elders is taro, of which they use three species. It is this crop that is most identified with women as gardeners and producers of ongraol (starch staples), and until very recently a woman's reputation as a gardener was determined by the quality of the taro she grew.[3] The preferred species, *kukau* (*Colocasia esculenta*), is grown in deep muddy taro patches called mesei. Less prized but also common is the giant swamp taro, *brak* (*Cyrtosperma chamissonis*), grown in shallower wet ground called *dechel*. A distant third in favor is the wild taro, *bisech* (*Alocasia macrorrhiza*). On Peleliu, kukau can be planted in depressions containing water into which multiple layers of plant de-

Figure 5. Women harvesting taro at the Beches el Mesei, 2003

bris is added. However, given the absence of streams for irrigating mesei and the difficulty of preparing pits in the limestone, brak from shallower wetlands, produce from dry land gardens, fruit (bananas, mango, and papaya), and nuts provide a higher proportion of the diet on Peleliu than in the northern islands. Ngerchol has rather sandy soil, but if women clear brush then papaya and bisech (wild taro) will sprout and can be used to supplement the daily diet of fish. Peleliu was one of the few villages that regularly ate breadfruit. It was harvested in season, preserved by peeling and soaking it in the sea, and then dried in the sun. According to Dirribukel Ngirametuker, in Ngerchol it was stored in limestone caves in the mountains and if carefully cared for it would last until the next season.

Elderly chad ra Beliliou unanimously agreed that Ngesias had the best mesei on Peleliu. They were large, with the full water depths necessary for kukau. Brak was planted around their sides. The fertility of the mesei and soils of Ngesias was likely due to the presence of the phosphate deposits, which the Japanese government began to exploit in the 1930s. In 1873 Karl Semper described a fertile and agricultural abundance in Ngesias that is hard to imagine for those who know the island only after the war: "Elongated, swampy taro patches stretched out in the depressions between the hills. In the dry ground of the rocky hills, which only had a slight covering of humus, the sweet potato flourished luxuriantly. I had never seen anywhere else such large trunks on the [papaya] trees and such productivity, [bisech (wild taro)] spread its juicy leaves out to nearly a foot and mixed its shade with that of the ancient breadfruit trees. . . . Everything in the vicinity of the villages displayed the greatest fruitfulness of the earth."[4]

Ngerdelolk also had good mesei, and one resident remembered the village having quite good soil for garden crops before most of it disappeared in the war. The mesei in Ngerchol were extensive, but their kukau grew rather small; taro leaves, however, were used to make a nutritious soup. In the rainy season when the wind blew from the west (the *ngebard*) the mesei often flooded, so the women would gather nuts, bisech taro, and papaya to supplement their diets. The soil close to the beluu at the shore was sandy, so the gardens were placed closer to the hills (where they still are today). Ngerchol relied more on brak and a mixture of brak and tapioca (*diokang*) that is unique to Peleliu. Teliu's rather small mesei lay east of the village in nearby wetlands. Ngerkeyukl had a few mesei of its own, like the mesei ra Brai to the north; it also had dechel for swamp taro and gardens nearby. Through relatives, or from relationships established in the past, many women of Ngerkeyukl were granted access to mesei belonging to Ngesias.[5]

When possible, gardens were usually sited close to the cluster of village homes so they could be tended regularly. Housing and garden areas were cleared to be fairly open and food trees, like mango, breadfruit, bananas, and papaya, were encouraged. The soils around Tokie Morei's family home were so fertile that they could plant a crop of tapioca in one quarter and by the time they finished planting a full circuit around the home the first-planted crop would be ready to harvest. Dirasechedui Mellomes Shmull grew up in her father's beluu of Teliu. She remembered their soil being good enough to support continuous replanting, without having to lie fallow. Sammy Ocheraol's mother used to plant three varieties of mango and many papaya trees in Ngerdelolk. Sweet potato (*chemutii*) was mentioned by a few that I interviewed but seems not to have been important to the diet.

How the soils from before the war compare with those of today remains a heated topic for Peleliu's residents. Many, though not all, consider diminished fertility of farmlands to be one of the most significant impacts of the war. As a limestone makatea island, Peleliu generally lacked the fertility of the high islands in the archipelago, and elders from villages like Ngerchol and Ngerkeyukl described frankly the limitations of their prewar soils. Ngesias, with its phosphates and mesei, and possibly parts of Ngerdelolk and Teliu, seem to have been more favored by geology. World War II damaged the quality of soils and greatly reduced the amount of arable land on the island, when important tracts of productive land were lost entirely to the filling, grading, and construction of the airbase and associated facilities and roads.

But all of the women remembered that their responsibilities as farmers meant constant hard labor to clear land, fertilize it with leaves and mulch, plant and tend a wide variety of crops, bring in the harvest, and prepare the family's meals.

Figure 6. Tokie Morei of Ngesias, 2007

They could often work together in small groups, especially at the mesei or dechel, where their lands abutted. This presented opportunities for socializing and sharing knowledge on matters like crop varieties, soil preparation, and harvesting techniques, and helped maintain friendships among them. Women of Ngerchol recalled occasions when, on their way to the garden, a friend would stop them and insist they accept produce that she had already harvested. But memories were consistent in recalling the incessant toil that was vital to the maintenance of families and the society. As the men knew their business at sea, the women knew theirs ashore.

Children would learn the identities of the lands of their lineage and clan from their parents and relatives. They were taught the names and the stories connected to each garden plot, each taro patch, each home or burial site—all the parcels that their kinsmen claimed. Dirasechedui Mellomes remembered her father carefully teaching her the names, stories, and, importantly, the boundaries of all their lands. Boundaries were usually marked by natural objects like stones or trees. The ironwood tree (*ngas*, *Casaurina litorea l.*) was a favorite marker because of its longevity. She said all parents insisted that their children acquire this knowledge. Since Palauan practice was for the wife to move to her husband's village and work his lineage lands, married women would become conversant with the histories and ownership of these lands as well. Given the deep cultural importance of taro, women became particularly knowledgeable about mesei.

The elders spoke with feeling about their dependence on and connections to their family lands. Dilchuuch Ermang put it simply: "Our lives depended on the land. We had our gardens, the bai, boathouse, homes—all used the lands." Muchucheu Augusto Sengebau described how in Ngerdelolk all land parcels (*chutem*) had names and that families carefully passed down the stories. Like others I asked, he stated that no land on Peleliu was considered vacant or unclaimed. In the larger villages, and those with the most rugged terrain, there were lands that were unnamed but that were still claimed and "known."

Besides gardening, women also gathered wild foods like fruits and tropical almonds and the ubiquitous and tasty small land crabs, *rekung* (*Cardisome rotundus*). The meat of this crab, mixed with coconut cream and packed back into the body shell, makes a delicacy for which Peleliu is esteemed throughout Palau. Men commonly trapped the larger coconut crab, *katat*, and the mangrove crab, *chemang*, which looks and tastes much like the Dungeness crab of America's West Coast. Women and children regularly went gleaning on the reef flats, collecting large clams of the tridacna family, sea cucumber, octopus, trochus, and sea urchin. Men in turn had productive responsibilities ashore, such as the heavy labor of clearing land for farming or assisting in planting or harvesting.

The only significant cash crop before the opening of the phosphate mines was copra, dried coconut meat, which came from plantations begun during German times that were mostly located along the sandy western shore. Copra was man's work. Men and boys cleared the land, planted the palms, harvested and husked the coconuts, and dried and bagged the meat. In the early Nan'yō years the few Japanese nationals on Peleliu included village police, some teachers, and a handful of traders, who bought the copra and sold basic foreign goods like matches, sugar, and material for women's dresses.[6]

Nan'yō-chō: Japan Takes Control

Although not particularly visible on Peleliu, the Nan'yō-chō by the mid-1920s had nonetheless achieved total control over Palau and had begun transforming the people's lives beyond anything they had experienced under German rule. Japanese encroachment affected the native leadership the most by limiting its power. Many people on Peleliu, however, found their lot under the Nan'yō-chō acceptable, even attractive in certain ways. Families and clans were able to continue their basic patterns of social and political organization and of production. Japanese investment in Palau and Peleliu had ignited such a thriving economy by the mid-1930s that islanders' incomes increased substantially, even though their welfare was only an afterthought for the Japanese empire. Elders' memories of Japanese policies and the rulers' treatment of residents revealed a tangle of perceived benefits and losses, of kindness and brutality. Attitudes toward their former masters ranged from fondness and friendship to still-simmering resentment. Their ambivalence toward the Japanese officials from the Nan'yō era was found by both Peattie and Poyer et al. among the people of Micronesia generally.[7] The memories from these years would influence how the older generation responded to the Japanese who returned to Palau decades after the war. But up until the late 1930s, many on Peleliu recalled the island seemed to find a satisfying balance between the exciting modernity created by Japan and the comforting familiar patterns of Palauan life.[8]

The Japanese made it clear that the direction the Palau Islands would travel would be determined by colonial authorities, not natives. They replaced uncooperative chiefs, including the reklai and the ibedul, leaders respectively of the northern and southern moieties. Traditional leaders were reduced to passing down word of new laws from on high, collecting taxes, and providing laborers when required. Chiefs termed their meetings with Japanese officials "waisei conferences," since their only contribution was to nod and reply, *waisei* meaning "that's right."[9]

Under Japanese administration, all Palauan children were required to attend school for at least three years, with the most proficient students offered two additional years in Koror. The Peleliu elementary school was built in Ngesias since this village occupied the center of the island. Many elders expressed warm memories of their years in school: making friends with students from other villages, competing for prizes, learning something about the outside world that had always fascinated them. But like all its counterparts in Palau, the Ngesias school was strictly segregated. Japanese students attended separate schools and received eight years of education based on Japan's curriculum. The native curriculum taught only the most rudimentary "practical" skills. It emphasized the spoken Japanese language and "moral education" that was essentially indoctrination designed to acculturate students into Japanese ways and foster obedience. In keeping with the Nan'yō-chō's belief in the racial inferiority of the people of Micronesia, they were not trained to achieve leadership in any field. Theirs was education for servility, menial training for those who would permanently occupy the bottom rung of Nan'yō society.[10]

Everybody remembered with distaste the fixed racial hierarchy established by the Nan'yō-chō and the superior attitude assumed toward islanders by Japanese officials and immigrants. Palau's native inhabitants resented living their lives as targets of unconcealed disdain. There existed "a clear line between us, the islanders whom the Japanese called *tōmin*, and the Japanese," as Palau's ambassador to Japan, Daiziro Nakamura put it. Residents of Japan occupied the top rung. "Okinawans and Koreans made up the second class, with the Okinawans considered higher than the Koreans. The Palauans were at the bottom." Chief Obaklechol Ichiro Blesam added, "We were known as santō kokumin [third-class people]." Among the different ethnic groups Palauan natives were *kot el ngario*, the very lowest.[11]

The word *tōmin* carries a surprising load of emotional baggage in Palau so many years after the demise of the Nan'yō era. Among the young people in Palau today who are fluent in English, many consider it the equivalent of "nigger." In Japanese it means simply "islander." A former Nan'yō official told Wakako Higuchi that the Japanese "used it both consciously and unconsciously . . . to distinguish between themselves and the islanders." This is true but also disingenuous. Ambassador Nakamura is the son of a Japanese father and Peleliu mother (and is my Palauan brother). Japanese was the family's first language. He said, "Although the word *tōmin* was a neutral word . . . the Japanese could use it in a disparaging way when they wanted to. They would jeer at a Palauan as tōmin. This was true throughout Micronesia. [The Nakamuras] were looked down on by Japanese for being half-tōmin. In Koror we associated mostly with Okinawans and Koreans." Augusta Ramarui agreed that it was *how* the word was used that stung: "[It] was often used in a negative way."[12]

Many people commented on how strict the Nan'yō authorities were in dealings with Palauan natives; but they distinguish the bossiness of the earlier years from the far harsher treatment they endured as war approached the islands. Ungil Besul Matareklai and her sister Mesiou (figure 10) recalled having to abide by a curfew at night and that lying was punished by beatings. But all the discipline "made people try to get things right." There was, the women noted, far less out-of-wedlock pregnancy in those days. Cigarette smoking and alcohol were forbidden. Susong Smau, a titled rubak from Ngerchol, suggested that relations with the Japanese residents were easier for youngsters like himself than for Palauan elders. "For us younger kids, they were good to us, they taught us to speak and write Japanese; it may have been worse for the older people. If you did something wrong they punished you and sent you up to the jail in Koror. But at that time [the mid-1930s] you didn't see the Japanese using force a lot." Edelboi Ruul of Ngesias was more embittered. He stated frankly that he did not like the Japanese regime because in its hierarchy "Palauans were somewhere between animals and humans. They would speak like that to people: 'When we talk you'd better listen because you're like animals.' The Americans were much, much better, more polite."

On the other hand, a mechas, who preferred not to be named, said flatly that she herself had good relations with the Japanese immigrants and that her older brothers "worked under the Japanese and had many friends among them. Close friends and family. No bad things happened until the war broke out." While attending the Apprentice-Woodworkers Training School in Koror (the highest level of schooling available to Micronesian students and very selective), Spesungel Ichiro Dingilius became close to a Japanese family in the town. "The man was an officer with the Nan'yō-chō and always wore a spotless white uniform. I pumped the water up to the tank for the house, made a fire to warm it for baths, and raked the yard after school let out at 2 p.m. The wife made me nice clothes. Yet the [elementary] schoolbooks we used seemed to try to 'brainwash' the students about Japan, describing the Russo-Japanese war of 1905 and saying that Japan could never lose a war anywhere in the world."

Phosphates and Lands

Japan's presence on Peleliu and its intrusions into native life leapt dramatically when the Nan'yō-chō began exploiting the deposits of phosphates that the Germans had discovered on the island. The mineral—called ringko in Japanese—was valuable as fertilizer for agriculture. The much larger deposits extracted from Angaur consistently ranked as one of the most valuable exports from Micronesia. Peleliu's phosphates were concentrated in the Omleblochel hills and their bases, next to Ngesias. Surveyors appeared on the island in the early 1930s, and when their estimates came in at 200,000 tons, the Nan'yō-chō moved to gain ownership of the native lands. How the government dealt with the residents over the phosphates prefigured what lay in store for Peleliu under Japanese rule. The mining revealed Japan's readiness to strong-arm the island population to obtain commercial resources, brought the first destruction of village homes and lands on the island, forced the first significant populations of foreign workers onto Peleliu, and caused a permanent shift toward a cash economy.

The physical costs were very localized; Ngesias paid most of them. Chief Uchelsias Etibek Shmull believed the surveyors first came when he was about ten, in 1928. He said that Japan first got permission for the enterprise from the rubak of the beluu, and then negotiated with the landowners themselves. Imperial officials did not resort to threats, but residents from all the beluu insisted that the islanders were afraid to oppose Japan. Ungil Besul and her sister Mesiou, of Ngerchol, both believed that people agreed to these and later takings of land only out of fear and that they faced a great language and cultural barrier when dealing with Nan'yō authorities. Everyone remembered that Japan paid a very low price for the lands, one that all islanders considered unfair. As Tokie Morei observed, certainly nobody got rich from the sales. According to Ungil Besul, payments went to various chiefs but not to the persons who actually used the lands and suffered the most direct losses.

The lands taken were the most valuable and productive on the entire island: the rich mesei of Ngesias, where Peleliu's best taro was grown. Access to these mesei was prized by women from all the villages, and the ability to grant use to them constituted an important power for the chiefs of Ngesias. The mesei lay at the foot of the Omleblochel hills and in valleys between ridges—features that would become known to American military history as Death Valley, Wildcat Bowl, and the Horseshoe. Once the mining began, around 1933–34, these mesei pits filled with deep pools of water as the Japanese workers dug out the phosphates. (Several large pools can be seen today.) They also excavated open pits further inside some valleys north of Ngesias and mined within other portions of the hills and ridges above the village, recalled Mrs. Morei. The extractions left the already rugged landscape pocked even further with deep crevasses, coral spires, pits, ponds, and tumbled boulders. The terrain that made such an impression on the U.S. Marines when they encountered the southern end of the mountain system during the 1944 battle was no longer just a natural karst formation. It was a landscape out of science fiction, one which was both natural and human-made.

Families that lost their mesei were forced to rely more heavily on gardening, which provided ongraol that was considered inferior: tapioca, other types of taro, and sweet potato. Women from Ngesias and Ngerchol shared remaining mesei with these families as well, until the war intervened. Tokie Morei recalled that at least four or five households had to relocate their homes to accommodate the mining at the northern end of the beluu. The mining company built a small railroad through part of Ngesias to haul the phosphate to a pier that they built next to the village pier. Workers loaded phosphates from the hills into buckets, which were then emptied into the railway carts. At the pier the mineral was loaded into sampans and floated around to a drying plant erected at the north end of the island, from which it was shipped to Japan.[13] By 1938 the mines produced 30,000 tons per year.[14] Elders described the obvious disruptions to the village, and the many large pits that one could fall into if not cautious. Today one can find, amid the war relics, rails and cart wheels from this mining railway in two of the valleys north of Ngesias. At the north end of the one the American soldiers called Wildcat Bowl is an astonishing straight-sided excavation pit that appears 80 feet deep, with rails and rusted wheels alongside.

The first significant influx of foreigners that Peleliu experienced, Japanese and Okinawan laborers, came to work in the diggings and the drying plant. They were housed mostly around the plant, an area known as Elochel, near today's wharf at the island's north end. Men from all the villages seized the opportunity to work for wages at the plant and the diggings, and although the pay was poor, it provided a welcome boost to the cash earned from copra sales. There were also many jobs at Elochel working in Japanese stores or offices. A Japanese store opened in Ngesias, where locals could purchase valued imported items like sugar, cloth, kerosene, matches, small luxuries, and sweets at low prices that are remembered longingly today.[15]

Those who shared their memories with me left a clear impression that, except for those residents of Ngesias who lost lands or had to move, the mid-1930s were exceptional ones on Peleliu. Life went on very much as it had, as men and boys fished, women farmed, the villages retained a strong sense of community with

Figure 7. Diltpak Merkii Napoleon (left) and Dirribukel Ngirametuker, of Ngerchol, 2003

their political structures intact, and customary exchanges maintained social ties without imposing onerous obligations. The benefits attendant with Japanese rule seemed numerous: peace and order, increasing cash for imported goods, public schooling, better health care than ever before available, the bright lights and opportunities opening up in booming Koror, and for the lucky few, trips to Japan itself to view the wonders of the potent and remote metropole.[16]

Those who were young at the time could be expected to recall this period fondly since they did not know Palau before the Japanese era and they received the schooling that enabled them to interact with the Nan'yō overlords and obtain jobs. Most who spoke with me expressed the opinion that this period of the mid-1930s constituted Peleliu's banquet years. They knew well that, like all good things, it could not last.[17]

The interest of the Nan'yō-chō in land reached far beyond the phosphate deposits of Peleliu. Following the change from naval to civilian authority in 1922, Japan instituted a land registration scheme throughout the mandate that was intended to document ownership and allow orderly development of this most valuable resource. By targeting land, the core of Micronesian cultures, the survey was bound to disrupt the island societies. Most dramatic was the scale of Micronesian lands lost. Directives of the *tochi daicho* (*tochi* means record or registration; *daicho* is land) declared that any communal land that appeared unused or uncultivated would pass to the colonial government. During the surveys, government officials had villagers show them the extent of the lands they claimed title to, whether communally or privately. But, as Dr. Minoru Ueki told me, "not knowing that this would haunt them down to today," many clan and lineage leaders, especially on Babeldaob, marched the surveyors inland only as far as they could comfortably go in a short time and indicated boundaries of only those lands their peoples used most frequently for gardening.

From the Japanese viewpoint, the Palauan villagers did not claim ownership of the vast interior lands that were in fact historically apportioned to villages and used for hunting, wood gathering, logging, and as buffers between villages. As a result, by the end of the first round of surveys in 1932, the Nan'yō-chō declared 84 percent of Palau's lands to be government property, leaving 13 percent for Palauans as "private" and 3 percent assigned to foreigners. As corporate interests and Japanese and Okinawan immigrants flooded in to Palau during the 1930s, the government leased out vast tracts of its holdings to the new arrivals for factories, processing plants, plantations, farms, and homesteads. This amounted to "alienation" with a vengeance as native lands were snatched away by foreigners without compensation.[18]

The surveying and recording of the "private" lands was also fraught with problems. In Palauan custom, elder women had to be consulted by the male chiefs before any communal land could be alienated. Unsympathetic toward communal ownership and shrugging off the role of women in land tenure, Japanese authorities decreed that all lands had to be registered in the names of male individuals. Chief Obaklechol Ichiro described how this caused great distress among the women, but it was fruitless to argue with Nan'yō officialdom. In most cases it appears that, with communal lands, rubak heads of lineages or clans persuaded the surveying party to record the leader's name as mengkar, meaning "trustee." This indicated that the rubak did not own the land personally but oversaw it in his capacity as titleholder of the kin group. However, records did not always indicate whether the named individual was a mengkar or private owner. A bias toward individual ownership was planted, one that has grown successively under U.S. and Palauan administration since. The mechas Mesiou described the Japanese officials as being very strict during the surveys, but she gave them credit for being honest and for settling questions by consensus. As a result, she thought that disagreements over surveyed lands were settled in ways that were generally fair to the Palauan people. (By contrast, she believed that today's U.S.-inspired system allows greater corruption and unfairness.)

Another source of difficulty came from the Palauan use of natural features as boundary markers—trees, stones, a trench, a rivulet. Such objects marked the boundaries between villages (a massive boulder along the East Road still marks the boundary between Ngesias and Ngerchol) and also those between individual plots of land. Such markers are ill suited for permanent printed records, and almost none survived the 1944 battle and base construction.

Finally, the tochi daicho and the colonial administrations imposed in Palau took the resolution of land disputes out of the hands of the local peoples and placed it with court systems based on foreign models. Local familiarity with lands and families and the oral histories connecting them to their holdings were increasingly displaced by written records, names on lists and maps, and decisions made by jurists who had never seen the lands in question.

Because the tochi daicho was completed so late in the Nan'yō period, the survey's implications remained latent until peace returned and the United States assumed control under the UN trusteeship in 1947. American authorities treated the tochi daicho with great deference as an accurate record of ownership, and Palauan courts do so today. As will be discussed further, this has contributed mightily to the snarl of land problems and disputes in Palau.

Whatever their intentions, the tochi daicho and its successor land cadastre programs in the U.S. era drilled into the bedrock of the island cultures—their lands—to interfere with and ultimately to invalidate the islanders' conceptions of land, how they use it, the roles they invest it with in political arrangements and in personal and group identity, how they reckon and explain ownership, how they mark its limits, how they exchange and alienate it, and how they solve the inevitable disagreements over it. Japan and the United States imposed a framework based on their own notions of land—as a commodity in the capitalist economy they fostered. Under this system, land is owned by individuals who buy it, sell it, use it "rationally" to realize its "highest and best use," and the power to settle disputes over it is removed to an adversarial court system, which is deeply alien to Palauan conceptions of privacy and decision by consensus.

Japan's willingness to force the sale of land for phosphate mining and to usurp large tracts of land for itself were omens of even harsher treatment soon to come. As the mariners' phrase goes, "Red sky at morning, sailor take warning"; the dawns were indeed red. As the 1940s approached, the people of Peleliu received a stunning double blow. Their remaining lands were seized for use in a war that would obliterate their way of life. Then after years of delay, when they sought to rebuild their lives, they were required to sort out ownership of their lands under an American administration, using yet another unfamiliar language and another set of legal procedures dictated by the third colonial power to rule them in 30 years.

Handspike of Fate: The Peleliu Airfield

> "By heaven, man, we are turned round and round in this world, like yonder windlass, and Fate is the handspike. And all the time, lo! that smiling sky and this unsounded sea!"
>
> Herman Melville, *Moby-Dick*

The terms of Japan's mandate under the League of Nations prohibited it from constructing military fortifications in Micronesia. When it went to war with the United States in 1941, however, Japan launched naval and air attacks from powerful bases that by then lay strung all along the Micronesian island chains. The United States would expend nearly two years in destroying these installations and capturing selected island targets. Most American military planners and historians concluded that Japan had treacherously flouted the mandate's restrictions.

In Mark Peattie's history of the Nan'yō, he demonstrates that both Japan's construction of infrastructure and the closing off of the islands to outside interests during the 1920s and early 1930s in fact were motivated primarily by the desire to expand and monopolize commerce within the colony.[19] However, in the military debates back in the homeland, the Japanese Navy incessantly promoted its favored "southern advance" assaults to obtain the resources of Southeast Asia. This drew renewed attention to Micronesia for the potential facilities that could support these aggressive operations and then aid in defeating the U.S. fleet, the anticipated enemy. Palau's value in these schemes was its excellent harbor, the land mass of Babeldaob, and its proximity to the Philippines (550 miles east of the large southern Philippine island of Mindanao).

In the early 1930s Japan constructed in Micronesia communications and commercial facilities of equal value to civilian or military agencies. Koror's harbor, Malakal, was dredged and improved. In 1935 a seaplane base was completed on Ngerekebesang (Arakabasan) Island next to Koror. It was during the second half of the decade, after Japan withdrew from the League of Nations and while relations with the United States steadily deteriorated, that the Japanese Navy embarked on construction of major land, air, and sea installations throughout the mandate. Koror underwent another boom from all the construction and influx of servicemen; by 1941 it had become an important naval base.

Rapid strides in the design of combat aircraft made good quality airfields vital for modern warfare. For these, Japan's military surveyors sought terrain that was flat and open, requiring a minimum of grading or filling. This was not just a convenience, for Japanese civil engineering lacked the mechanized construction capabilities that, in the approaching war, would enable American Seabees to carve a functioning airfield from a jungle in less than two weeks. Japan was forced instead to rely on far slower human labor.[20] Although Peleliu lay 25 miles from Malakal and Koror and lacked a deepwater port, the broad, firm, relatively flat expanse at the southern end of the island offered the kind of terrain the navy sought. In a decision fraught with the most baneful consequences for the people of Peleliu, Japanese military engineers chose their island as the site for Palau's major air base.

Japanese documents state that the airfield was begun in June 1937 and completed in the "fall of 1939."[21] These dates appear to refer to the start and completion of initial construction.[22] Some chad ra Beliliou suggested that preliminary surveying may have occurred in 1936 and added that work to improve the airstrip continued through the early 1940s, as confirmed by testimonies in Ballendorf et al.[23]

The navy decided it would require land belonging to three beluu on Peleliu. Ngesias would lose farmland and mangrove lands near its southern borders, but the village settlement could remain where it was at the foot of the Omleblochel Mountains. Chief Uchelsias Etibek Shmull said that the lands taken for the airfield were not heavily used by the residents of the village since their gardens were closer to their homes. But the village had lost productive lands and mesei, plus some home sites, in its north for the phosphate mining; so now it was being compressed from opposite directions by two major Japanese projects.

Teliu and Ngerkeyukl, occupying the central and western portions of the flat lowlands, fared much worse. Elders recalled that Japanese military men abruptly informed the chiefs that the entire populations of the two villages were being expelled from their lands. They would have to move elsewhere within a matter of days. According to Chobechad ra Eliou Song, reared in Teliu, the chiefs were told simply that Japan was "preparing for war and needed their lands for an airport. . . . They said a war was coming someday." Dirasechedui Mellomes Shmull was born in 1925 and lived in Teliu. She remembered being 11 years old when her parents told her, "We have to move so Japanese soldiers can use the land." There was no indication from the Japanese authorities that the people might be able to return in the future. "They just said, 'You go, we need this island,'" Dirasechedui recalled.

This demand struck the villagers like a thunderbolt. It was incomprehensible that they would be uprooted from their homes, lands, beaches, and their entire way of life. As Chief Obak Isao Singeo of Ngerdelolk put it, "The people had no idea what was going on. They were being asked to sell the lands of their ancestors. They protested, 'It's the land of our mothers, so you can't buy it.' 'We're not, we're just paying for the crabs, plants, and trees,' the Japanese said." Antonio Tewid of Ngerkeyukl remembered that they "felt terrible" at the prospect of leaving behind their cemetery, odesongel, mesei and gardens, and all the old lands, and that they wondered "whether we'd ever be able to return." Former governor Timarong Sisior, also of Ngerkeyukl, said, "It was painful to be moved like that. We didn't want to stay in a village other than our own."

There were no means by which to resist the peremptory expulsion. Antonio Tewid said, "We were too scared." Dilchuuch Ermang remembered, "People didn't resist, because they were scared. Soldiers gave the orders. Men, women, and children cried. The people just cried and moved." "We felt awful (*mekngit a rengmam*). But we had to leave, we were afraid of being beaten," recalled Dirasechedui Mellomes.

Some people said they received no compensation from Japan, some that it was promised but not paid. Others remembered receiving token payments for houses and for public buildings but not for gardens or other lands. Ungil Besul and Mesiou said the Japanese authorities made payments for both the airfield and phosphate lands, "but the price offered was very cheap and people felt it wasn't fair. They feared the Japanese, though. They agreed because they were afraid of the Japanese."

More important was the question of where the displaced villagers would live. (I estimate the village populations at this time to have been, at the most, 200 for Ngerdelolk, 175 for Ngesias, 225 for Ngerchol, 130 for Ngerkeyukl, and 100 for Teliu, a total of 830.) Dirribukel Ngirametuker noted that they were not ordered to leave Peleliu. Nobody considered having individual households scatter throughout Palau. Such severing of ties to kin and beluu was inconceivable. But many recalled that the expulsions aroused deep compassion and local pride on the island of Peleliu. The chad ra Beliliou could not countenance their fellow islanders being forced off the island as refugees. Ungil Besul said that the obakdelolk (or obak) of Ngerdelolk called a meeting and asked all the people of the island to help. "We all survive together," he told them. Obakdelolk and his klobak invoked their ties with Teliu that dated to the founding of the latter beluu. Ngerdelolk, from its public lands, offered home sites and garden lands to the entire village. (Palauan villages had common lands that lay in the control of the top-ranked chiefs.) The obaklechol of Ngerchol met with his klobak and offered vacant land at the southern end of the village to their neighbors from Ngerkeyukl. Olikong ra Tikei Kokichi Ingas, who moved with his family from Ngerkeyukl, said that the Japanese authorities wanted the obaklechol to sign a paper documenting his decision to donate land. The chief refused to sign, saying "When I say this, that's all that's needed."

The relocations occurred quickly. Most families in Teliu were able to dismantle their homes and move them across the island to Ngerdelolk, using trucks provided by the Japanese officials. Some chose to leave their homes behind and rebuild in the new location. Sammy Ocheraol named 12 different families who brought their houses to Ngerdelolk. "They put their homes in a coconut plantation that was public. They were given empty land for farms, lands that clans made available to them." His mother got taro for the newcomers and shared her garden with Teliu folk, while he caught fish for them. "The people shared their mesei with them, and the *sers* [garden] land also. It was not permanently given to them, only to use, to live on, while following orders of the Japanese. Some of these people [among them Obechad Tabelong and her family] went to live on Ngebad [a small island on the reef near Ngerdelolk]; it was good for sweet potato and taro, also banana and coconut."

In what would have been an especially painful blow, the Teliu people were unable to save any of their bai, the political, historical, and emotional centers of their community life. "We were so rushed in getting our own homes and possessions moved in the time allowed that we had no time for the bai," recalled Obechad Tabelong.

The resettlement of Ngerkeyukl within Ngerchol proceeded in the same way. Dilchuuch Ermang said that, using trucks belonging to the Japanese government, most people dismantled their houses and moved the floorboards, frames, and walls to village land near today's new hospital. Antonio Tewid noted the trucks could not get to Ngerkeyukl's Eoulbeluu, the lower village nearest the shore, because they could not cross Cheuatel ridge. Homes from this half of the beluu were transported up the west coast by large canoes. Some families left the old homes behind and built new ones in Ngerchol. "We settled on public lands of Ngerchol, by the cemetery and hospital of today. At first we rebuilt the bai, which everybody stayed in, then rebuilt individual houses."

Governor Timarong Sisior aided his family in cutting down trees and clearing land for their home site. In the first weeks they could go back by canoe to bring food from their gardens in Ngerkeyukl. Mechas from Ngerchol gave them some mesei and land for gardens. Dirribukel Ngirametuker added that the refugees were given no support from Japanese authorities; the entire burden fell on islanders.

Ngerkeyukl received one consolation denied to Teliu: Ngerkeyukl was able to dismantle and bring its rubak bai, the Bai ra Ikelau, to a new site in Ngerchol. The other two bai were left behind. And the four olangch from the legend of the four rubak who paddled westward chasing the setting sun? "We left them all, the tridacna clam shell, the croton tree, the bamboo, and Bibuiich el bad, the shining stone," said Matichau. "We hoped we might return some day. We had no idea of how big the war would be." Obechad Tabelong of Teliu remembered their being able to return to their village in the first weeks to harvest crops, but soon everybody was forbidden to go into the areas set aside for the airfield. Most people said they never saw their villages again.

Antonio Tewid voiced the refugees' deep chagrin at being forced from their homes and becoming dependent on those from another beluu. "Although we became self-sufficient fairly soon, we felt ashamed at living in another village." The displacement of the two beluu, like the topic of wartime deaths, is a story of deep misfortune that the islanders discuss only with reluctance. Residents from Ngerchol and Ngerdelolk indicate modest pride at having warmly aided their neighbors but prefer not to dwell on the topic. It is an unhappy memory for the entire island. "We lived in Ngerchol for seven years, until 1944, when we left Peleliu and moved to Babeldaob [to avoid the invasion]," said Antonio.

To build the airfield, the Nan'yō-chō and the navy brought the second large influx of foreigners to Peleliu, hundreds of Japanese, Okinawan, and Korean laborers.[24] These workers cleared forests and plantations and leveled or filled terrain that extended from Ngesias all the way to the southwest coast. Muchucheu Augusto

Sengebau recalled that these laborers were housed in the middle of the eventual airstrip. The terrain was hilly in places, so they used dynamite to blow up higher areas, then carried the rubble by hand to use as land fill. They had no bulldozers or other earth-moving equipment. (Muchucheu Augusto noted that the U.S. Navy Seabees later took fill from the mountains of Ngesias to use for road surfacing and land fill. Photos in the Peleliu museum show the Seabees carving out the large flat on Hill 300, where the Marine Corps monument and Shinto shrine stand today.)

The Japanese filled in the mesei of Teliu. "We lost all of them," said a mechas who preferred to remain anonymous; Obechad Tabelong confirmed that their mesei and gardens were filled or leveled. Tokie Morei described how the Japanese laborers dug up the bones of a public cemetery in Ngesias and then filled it in with crushed coral. Some of the land taken was unfarmed scrub forest or mangrove swamp, but all of it was valuable as a source of wild plant food, wood, materials, crabs, or medicinal plants. There is general agreement that along with the loss of homes, villages, and mesei, many acres of gardens disappeared under the runways, hangers, and other installations.

Chief Obaklechol Ichiro believed about 50 men of Peleliu worked along with what he estimated were 500 Korean and 1,000 Okinawan laborers. The Korean workers built most of the buildings and radio towers, while the Okinawan laborers worked on the runways. Mrs. Morei's husband, Judge Francisco Morei, said the site "was very secretive, and even Peleliu people were not allowed to see what was going on."[25]

This sealing off of the military sites prevented residents of Ngerkeyukl and Teliu from returning to their villages for even brief visits after the first weeks, a regret voiced frequently by elders. It also helps explain certain confusions one encounters over which changes—e.g., roads, causeways, landfills, and paving—were due to Japanese construction and which to American activity after the invasion. Few residents saw firsthand the full extent of the transformation of the southern half of Peleliu until their return from Babeldaob after the war, by which time the U.S. Navy had vastly expanded the base the Japanese military had built.

During the airport's construction the villagers of Ngesias continued to live in their homes, and the village school remained open. Spesungel Ichiro of Ngesias got to know many Okinawan children as he learned some of their language. He recalled that many men were injured during the airfield construction by mishaps with dynamite. Edelboi Ruul remembered occasional scuffling between Okinawan laborers and Palauan villagers. Tokie Morei observed that while imported laborers did the heavy construction, the Japanese authorities also extracted what she called "forced volunteer" labor from Palauan natives. Like others I spoke with, she spent many days clearing brush and cutting grass along the sides of the new runways, where she witnessed the first planes landing and taking off. Elizabeth Emilian of

Ngesias cut grass on the field as a schoolchild, uncomfortable in the strong light reflected off the coral runways. She and her classmates received their lunches at school and a small wage as payment.

Both the displaced villagers and their hosts accommodated themselves to their new circumstances as best they could, but their lives had taken on an air of uncertainty and foreboding. They witnessed a steady flow of military men to the island as the airfield became operational. Susong Smau saw their numbers grow in the early 1940s; unlike the laborers, who lived near the field, these *soldau* lived all over the island. Tokie Morei's youth group weaved cigarette cases for the Japanese soldiers and danced to entertain them at their compounds. "We would always give them gifts, but we never received any in return."

4
War

The Palauan community felt little threat during the first two years of the Pacific War. The main theaters were far away, and Japan used the islands primarily for the transit of forces on their way to the battlefields of the South Pacific. But Japan made increasing demands on Palauan land and labor, and some loyal natives volunteered for duty in the war zones to the south. The conflict reached Palau suddenly in March 1944 when the United States staged a devastating aircraft carrier raid on the archipelago. Peleliu's airfield received heavy damage. When Japanese authorities warned that further attacks were likely, the chad ra Beliliou removed themselves to the nearby Rock Islands, where they lived precariously for five months. In late August 1944, just two weeks before the United States invaded Peleliu, the Japanese military evacuated the people to Babeldaob. They would not see their island again until 1946.

The need for land-based airfields in the island-hopping strategy adopted by the United States in the Pacific War made Peleliu a prime target in the preparations to return to the Philippines. Here Peleliu's characteristics as an island—its marine, terrestrial, and human environment—acquired yet another cast: as obstacles or defenses in perhaps the most specialized form of warfare, amphibious assaults. The battle for the small island unexpectedly turned into one of the fiercest and most prolonged struggles of the island war. The Japanese commander used Peleliu's caves to protect his troops and delay the invaders. The American commander hurled his men against the defenders in wasteful attacks that would cost him his career. Peleliu, when won, would prove to be of such limited value to the United States that it became mired in historical controversy, viewed by many as a symbol of mistaken military judgment. The remains of 11,000 Japanese dead preserved in the caves would draw both relatives and unrepentant imperialists back to Peleliu from the 1960s onward; eventually American veterans would begin to stake their claims to war memory as well.

Blood-Dimmed Tides: Micronesian Islands and Amphibious Warfare, 1943–1944

Even as the Japanese Pearl Harbor attack crippled much of the American Pacific fleet, other imperial forces attacked objectives in the central and western Pacific. From Palau sailed a fleet with 30 transports, carrying the troops that would make three of the six landings in the Philippines. Other units sortied from the Nan'yō to seize the American base at Wake Island and the British possessions of Tarawa and Makin in the Gilbert Islands (now Kiribati).[1] By mid-1942, after inflicting an unbroken series of humiliating defeats on American, British, Australian, and Dutch forces, Japan's empire stretched from Burma in the west through the Netherlands East Indies, along the north coast of New Guinea, down the Solomon Islands chain, across vast reaches of the central Pacific, and north to two outposts seized in Alaska. The American possessions of Guam and the Philippines were swallowed up as well.

From the time of Japan's arrival as a world sea power in 1905 with its victory over Russia, Japanese planners anticipated a future war against the United States for control of the western Pacific and east Asia. Japanese naval officers foresaw that if Japan expanded south, its capture of the Philippines and Guam would force the American fleet to cross the ocean and do battle, where they hoped to destroy it in a single decisive engagement.

American naval strategists envisioned basically the same scenario, with opposite results of course, in their War Plan Orange. This called for the American garrison in the Philippines to hold out long enough for the fleet to arrive from Hawaii and engage the Japanese Navy in what U.S. planners also expected to be a decisive battle. Japan's seizure of Micronesia in World War I greatly complicated things for the United States since these islands lay astride the course the American fleet would have to sail. In 1935 the naval planners added a provision to War Plan Orange calling for the capture of islands in the Marshall and Caroline chains in which to construct bases to support the advance westward. This change was at least tacit recognition that a war with Japan would take years, not months.[2]

Japan, with its limited material resources, could not hope to withstand the industrial potential of the United States in a protracted struggle. Japan's leadership "gave virtually no serious thought to how the conflict might be terminated." But they expected that widespread conquests, coupled with the destruction of the American fleet, would force the United States to negotiate a settlement that would leave Japan in control of its Greater East Asia Co-Prosperity Sphere. This hope was dashed when, in June 1942, the U.S. Navy dealt the imperial fleet a catastrophic defeat off Midway Island. Next the battle for Guadalcanal Island in the Solomons was lost in early 1943 after six months of costly air, sea, and land engagements into which Japan poured its men and machines to no avail. Japan found itself trapped in the war of attrition that it could not win.[3]

Interservice rivalry between the U.S. Army and Navy complicated the strategy for pushing the Japanese forces out of the South Pacific. Army general Douglas MacArthur favored a route through New Guinea and the Philippines as the shortest road to Tokyo. But the navy clung to its belief that War Plan Orange, with its advance through Micronesia, offered the fastest means of subduing Japan. In early 1943 the navy won approval for this second route of attack. What the United States called the Central Pacific Campaign would bring the scourge of war to the islands and people of Micronesia. Palau, westernmost of the Micronesian archipelagoes, possessing the finest harbor in the region and the airfield at Peleliu, figured prominently in all American plans.[4]

Prior to World War II, many strategists had concluded that modern firepower rendered impossible amphibious landings against a fortified shore because struggling troops could never gain a foothold before being pushed back into the sea.[5] But the U.S. Navy was confident that it had developed, for the first time in the history of warfare, the capacity to assault distant and heavily defended islands from the sea, which Joseph Alexander calls "the most complex and perilous of military operations."[6] The very features that invest tropical islands with such fascination for outsiders—small wisps of land, remote and isolated, ringed by coral reefs and fringed by sandy beaches—make warfare waged over them extremely difficult. And given the way the American and Japanese forces prosecuted the war in Micronesia, this island fighting proved exceptionally destructive.

The remoteness of Micronesia—Tarawa in the Gilberts lay 2,100 miles from Pearl Harbor, Peleliu 4,600—meant that the American fleets and armies would be fighting a war where distance was a major obstacle. The navy would have to strike targets far beyond the reach of the nearest American airbases, then support and supply all the ground forces put ashore.[7]

The limited size of the Micronesian islands meant that each one had to be taken by a direct frontal assault, what a Japanese officer termed "storm landings," in which U.S. forces hurled enormous firepower against the Japanese positions and then sent infantry attacking into the teeth of their defenses.[8] As Samuel Eliot Morison writes, when the American attackers invaded an island in Micronesia "either they must exterminate the enemy within a few days or be thrown out. Every blow struck in the Central Pacific had to be swift, sure and powerful."[9] The isolation of the islands also meant that once an American fleet cut off a Micronesian objective by seizing control of the air and sea around it, then the Japanese defenders were doomed. There was no escape and no hope of resupply.

Coral reefs—rich gathering and fishing grounds to the islander and underwater gardens to snorkelers—pose a most difficult obstacle to an amphibious assault.

This is particularly true of fringing reefs like Peleliu's, which create shoals with enough water to float landing craft at high water but strand them at lower states of tide. The "reef problem" remained one of the most vexing for American commanders throughout the war.[10]

The requirement to land thousands of men and vast amounts of equipment within hours meant invasions would have to storm ashore on sandy beachfronts. The assault troops were at their most vulnerable while crossing beaches, and for most of the Micronesian campaign, until the battle for Peleliu, Japanese doctrine called for counterattacks to prevent the American assault troops from gaining a toehold on the shore. For both invaders and defenders, beaches were the killing grounds of the central Pacific war.

The character of the war in Micronesia, however, was not determined solely by unique geographical factors. The antagonists fought these battles with violence and hatred that are unpleasant to contemplate decades later. American forces returned the treachery of Pearl Harbor with a war of vengeance that had heavy racial overtones.[11] The U.S. amphibious troops, the marines, were trained in what Craig Cameron calls an "exterminationist warrior ethos."[12] American science and industry exercised fearsome ingenuity to produce, in boundless quantities, weapons that could subdue nature itself and any living creature. American troops went ashore on Micronesian islands with both the technological capacity and the will to lay waste to anything in their paths.

Japanese military training expressly forbade surrender under any circumstances.[13] The commander of Palau's defending forces, Lieutenant General Inoue Sadae, said during postwar interrogation, "It was not even considered by me or by local garrison commanders that the garrisons would surrender, no matter how hopeless the situation."[14] This grim doctrine contributed greatly to the sheer horror of the island fighting; every invasion became a battle of annihilation, and the island landscape suffered proportionately. With the Japanese troops unable to flee and unwilling to surrender, the contending armies wreaked their havoc over every foot of the islands, until the last defender was dead.

To assault island strongholds the U.S. Navy and Marines developed two primary innovations: aircraft carrier task forces that could remain at sea for months and long-range amphibious operations that were capable of withstanding fierce opposition.[15] The newly built mobile carriers, by mid-1943 steaming into Pearl Harbor in numbers Japan could not hope to match, allowed the navy to project air and sea power across vast distances. The fleets could seize control of the air and sea around a targeted island while daring the imperial navy to issue forth to do battle. For crossing coral reefs the United States developed specialized landing vehicles, including "amtracs" that, using tank-like treads, could power themselves over a reef, float like boats over the shoals of fringing reefs, and run up on a beach to drop their cargoes.[16] A vast "sea train" of logistics ships would then supply the naval and land forces, while carrier aircraft and naval vessels protected them from counterattack.

The first phase of the central Pacific campaign attacked the atoll chains of the Gilberts (Kiribati) and the Marshall Islands in November 1943 and January 1944. The invasion of Tarawa in the Gilberts resulted in unexpectedly high losses; but the leadership in Tokyo recognized the Micronesian campaign for the lethal threat it posed to Japan's position in the Pacific. Radio Tokyo warned the nation that the war was turning "from one of self-existence to one of self-defense."[17] Invasions of Kwajalein and Enewetak (formerly Eniwetok) in the Marshalls early in 1944 went more smoothly and at lower cost for the American military.

In mid-February 1944 U.S. carriers raided the largest Japanese base in Micronesia, at Truk (Chuuk), causing massive damage and effectively eliminating this installation as a threat. Just before the U.S. Navy's arrival the major ships of the Japanese fleet fled to Palau. Sailing over 5,000 miles in total from its base at Majuro atoll in the Marshalls, the U.S. fleet then staged a similar raid on Palau the next month, heavily damaging the airfield at Peleliu, sinking many support ships, and chasing the imperial fleet to harbors back home and along Asia's shores.[18]

These powerful attacks in Micronesia forced the Japanese high command to hurriedly transfer army units from China and Manchuria into the remaining Nan'yō outposts to erect defenses.[19] But where would the next blow fall? In June 1944, the U.S. Navy stunned the Japanese leadership by bypassing all of central Micronesia in order to assault Saipan, Tinian, and Guam in the Marianas. Saipan was a key bastion in the empire's inner defense ring, compelling the imperial navy to engage the American fleet in its defense. The Imperial Japanese Navy endured a crushing defeat, and when Saipan fell on July 9, so did the government of Prime Minister Tōjō Hideki.[20]

War Reaches Palau

In Palau the Japanese authorities announced with fanfare the opening of hostilities with the United States in December 1941. The imperial forces' confidence in ultimate victory impressed the Palauan people. After living under the Rising Sun for nearly 30 years, most responded with loyalty and enthusiasm, donating small amounts of money and laboring hard for the cause. Ambassador Daiziro Nakamura, who lived in Koror, recalled that every day at school the students looked to the north and chanted "We are Japanese citizens!" "The Japanese officials tried especially hard to build our spirit when the war came. It was propaganda, but at this time they weren't truly harsh with us." Spesungel Ichiro Dingilius said that he wanted Japan to win the war and assumed it would.

Although the battlefields of the Pacific War remained remote, military activity in Palau picked up steadily. The islands were used primarily for training and for staging troops, ships, and planes southward. Dilchuuch Ermang said that by 1943–44, significant numbers of Japanese soldiers on Peleliu lived in tents that "went all the way around the island." The islanders agreed that the attitudes of the Japanese troops hardened under the exigencies of wartime. Naval officers became stricter and demanded ever more Palauan labor. Subris Sabro said that the Japanese "became more pushy and cruel. This was because [Palauans] had to work harder because of the war," which they did not like.

Large numbers of Palauan men were conscripted for work on the Peleliu airfield. Meltel Kodong of Melekeok, on Babeldaob, brought 100 Palauan laborers to Peleliu to help with continuing construction and improvements. Koshiba Basiou said that almost all Peleliu males eventually worked on the airstrip as he himself did for four years.[21] Governor Timarong Sisior, in his early teens, worked with the Japanese surveyors of the fighter airstrip that was begun on Ngedebus Island, off the north tip of Peleliu.

At first Japan refrained from seizing any property beyond that initially taken for the airfield. Families continued to be able to feed themselves. But for all the preparations on Peleliu, the war seemed distant and the Japanese forces overwhelmingly powerful.

On the morning of March 30, 1944, when many fighter planes suddenly filled the sky around Peleliu and Angaur, the islanders assumed they were fresh Japanese squadrons. Quickly, however, the residents realized something was wrong. Planes swooped low over the island and made repeated passes at the airfield, dropping bombs whose explosions resounded in the villages. Japanese aircraft rose to attack. Moiling dogfights occurred, from which smoking planes spiraled down into the sea. The dock and phosphate plant at Elochel were hit and began burning, and the new fighter strip on Ngedebus was struck. The attacks continued throughout the day, until dark columns of smoke rose from the airport and no more Japanese planes challenged the attackers. The American planes returned the next day, fought with Japanese aircraft that had been flown in during the night, then resumed bombing the airfield. The war had finally come to Palau. *Sangatsu Kūshū*, Japanese for "the March Air Raid," has remained indelible in the memories of those who lived through it.

Japanese shipping was the primary target in Palau, but as at Truk the major Japanese combat ships escaped before the planes arrived.[22] Nonetheless, the Americans sank 36 ships, mostly transports and oil tankers. Peleliu's air groups were destroyed and its field made inoperable. Malakal Harbor's facilities, the two seaplane bases on Ngerekebesang by Koror, Angaur's phosphate works, and the new, still-inoperative airfield begun in Airai on southern Babeldaob were all heavily damaged.[23]

"We were terrified," said Dilchuuch Ermang of the raids. "People ran into the hills [near Ngerchol]; some had houses there, many hid in caves. We could hear the bombing and saw flares dropped, and could see that the airfield was bombed that night. We saw many Japanese airplanes destroyed. We watched the dogfights, where all the Japanese planes were shot down. The Japanese had taught us how to fight fires with water and sand, and mop the fire out. We thought they would want our help, but they didn't."

Diltpak Merkii and Dirribukel Ngirametuker (figure 7) also remembered the fear and the eerie flares at night. Like others, they said that Palauan homes suffered very little damage and that no islander was killed. Tokie Morei confirmed that homes in Ngesias, closest to the airfield, survived intact. Elizabeth Emilian recalled running to the high mountains to shelter in caves above Ngesias; from there she could see the whole airport. "From behind a tree I saw the U.S. fighters shoot planes on the ground and in the air. After the attacks a Japanese soldier gave us canned fruit that was burned from the bombs. He felt sorry for us; there was no place for us to go. He didn't mistreat us."

Chief Obaklechol Ichiro Blesam very nearly lost his life on the first day of the raid. The Japanese had taken him and about 12 other young Palauan men to Makassar in Sulawesi (Celebes) Indonesia for a four-month course in operating small boats. On March 30 they were returning to Palau in a vessel of 300 tons that was steaming about three miles off Angaur Island when the raid began. The passengers saw a Japanese plane attempt to take off from Peleliu but get shot down. Immediately afterward American planes attacked the ship. Its fuel tanks were set afire and it sank rapidly. Obaklechol and six Indonesian crewmen began swimming for their lives toward Angaur. When a plane strafed them in the water, four of the Indonesian men dove under the waves with Obaklechol, while two did not. Those two disappeared. Obaklechol was wounded by a bullet, but managed to reach Angaur, and then spent ten days in the hospital in Koror recovering from his injury.[24]

Once again foreigners had shattered the world of the chad ra Beliliou. Peleliu was in grave danger, a likely target for more bombing and even an amphibious invasion. Reeling from the shock of the attacks, most residents abandoned their homes and sought shelter in the many natural caves scattered in Peleliu's mountains. Reiko Kubary, a young child at the time, remembered hiding in a cave with her parents, who told her that war had begun. They were unable to light fires for fear of attracting planes.

The Japanese authorities assured Dilchuuch Ermang and her family that reinforcements would come. She saw none arrive while she remained on the island, though after her departure in May the army transferred a reinforced infantry regiment to construct defenses against an invasion. Fearing more air attacks, the people stopped fishing during the day. They trapped mangrove crabs and harvested taro and garden crops at night. Japanese officers urged villagers to move to Babeldaob, saying they would be safer there than on Peleliu. Throughout the spring families reluctantly loaded their home furnishings and possessions into canoes and sailed not to Babeldaob but to Ngercheu Island, which lay three miles to the north (see map 2). About one mile long by one-half mile wide, Ngercheu was flatter and more spacious than most of the Rock Islands; it offered the best nearby refuge for the hundreds who would eventually abandon Peleliu.[25]

Japanese authorities were severely shaken by the success of the Sangatsu Kūshū. Palau was considered so secure within the inner defense ring of islands that few fortifications had been prepared and few troops stationed there. Since all hands were needed to meet the now-perilous future, good relations with the natives suddenly became urgent. Spesungel Ichiro and Muchucheu Augusto Sengebau both remembered an official pronouncement made to the Palauan people. From now forward, they were informed, the old three-level racial hierarchy was abolished. Spesungel related with a wry smile how the islanders were assured, "We are all Japanese now."

Desperate for manpower to help construct defenses, the Japanese Army forced many of the younger men of Peleliu to remain on the island from April through August 1944. The Japanese plan was to protect supplies and inflict maximum damage on American landing forces by going underground, so the army ordered the Palauan men to join other laborers digging shelters, storage spaces, and caves in the mountains. Judge Francisco Morei (the husband of Tokie Morei) dug underground shelters with a Palauan crew from March to July. He described excavating U-shaped caves with two entrances and proudly related how his Palauan crew could dig these twice as fast as their Japanese counterparts.[26] Working 12-hour days, the Palauan laborers had become, as one man put it, "like slaves."

The Japanese troops took over the homes left vacant by the residents who had fled. Chobechad ra Eliou Song's family had lost their ancestral home when the Japanese expelled them from Teliu. They lost their new home in Ngerdelolk as well when Japanese forces seized it to use for storage. When Chief Obaklechol Ichiro returned to Peleliu after recovering from his wounds, Ngerchol was still mostly intact, but it was entirely occupied by soldiers. His parents were living in a cave in the ridge.

A second wave of carrier attacks struck Palau in late July 1944. Susong Smau recalled that these caused far more damage to Ngerchol than the previous raid. Many elders described the massive explosion of an underground bomb storage bunker. Its stunning shock wave and spectacular roar buffeted the refugees all the way out on Ngercheu, while its fires lit up the sky. More islanders who had stayed behind now fled to Ngercheu. Ungil Besul Matareklai said that an chelid, a Palauan spirit, warned her parents to leave Peleliu. Eventually only a stubborn remnant of the population of Ngerchol remained on the island. An elder who asked to remain anonymous related what happened: "A Japanese officer came to us with a Ngesias man translating. We were told to take all our light belongings to [the wharf at] Elochel. He said they would get two boats, which would take us to any Rock Island if we wished, or elsewhere. He was harsh. He had a sword and said, 'If you stay behind you'll be considered a spy and killed.' We took what we could to Elochel, and went to Ngeroblobang [a beach on the east side of the island Mecherechar, north of Peleliu]. We were only Ngerchol people. [That is, there were no refugees from the other four villages of Peleliu.] We felt good being the last to leave Peleliu, as if we'd kept watch over it for the others." (Confusion by foreigners has led to many charts and maps giving the name Eil Malk to this island of Mecherechar. Today it is best known for its tourist site, Jellyfish Lake.)

On a boat trip past Mecherechar, James Beluong pointed out to me several other beaches where chad ra Beliliou took refuge. These beaches did not serve as entrances onto broad and open islands offering space, resources, and some safety from air attack; rather, they were the narrowest of footholds at the base of a typically steep-sided and forested Rock Island.

From April onward the hundreds of refugees on Ngercheu stoically organized themselves into a functioning community. They built huts from local materials and planted gardens where possible. They even built their own school. "Not a real one like the Japanese one, but ours," said Dilchuuch Ermang. Lacking all medical care of the sort that had become available in the Nan'yō era, they reverted to relying on Palauan plants for medicines. Fearful of the return of the "small planes" of the carriers, which could swoop low and strafe, the men fished exclusively at night, using lines and nets. Fortunately Ngercheu lay in one of the most bountiful fishing grounds in the Palau lagoon. Its own reefs also provided plentiful protein foods, *odoim*. Rice and garden produce, ongraol, was obtained by sailing canoes back to their villages on Peleliu, usually at night.

Spesungel Ichiro related how his fellow villagers of Ngesias carried food out to the first evacuees on Ngercheu using canoes and rafts. During one such daylight trip Spesungel and a group of men were caught in the open sea when a U.S. plane spotted them. One of the rubak ordered all the men to take off their shirts, to show that they were Palauan and not Japanese men. It worked, as the pilot flew off without shooting. Women of Ngesias told a similar story about how an American plane that circled a group of women from their village who had gone to Peleliu to collect taro during the day. "They dove into the sea and prayed but saw it circle more when they came up to the surface. They [then] saw the plane shoot a Japanese [soldier] who was just coming up close to a part of Ngercheu, so we think the U.S. pilots could recognize the difference between Japanese and Palauan [people]."

The seven families of Ngerchol villagers who were removed to Ngeroblobang lived even more precariously than those on Ngercheu. A mechas described their time on Ngeroblobang: "Life was difficult there. We [only] had crabs and fish, and coconuts, but didn't go to Peleliu for [more] food; we were afraid of airplanes. We saw a plane shoot and sink a Japanese ship, and from this we got biscuits that we found floating in the sea. The dry ones were distributed first. For the wet ones, the women wove baskets, squeezed out the salt water, and dried them by wrapping them in *duubch* [young coconut sprouts]. We put the biscuits over a fire and ate them. We never came to Peleliu for food as did those on Ngercheu."

Remarkably, only one Peleliu native lost her life during the terrible period between the March attacks and the evacuation from the Rock Islands in late August. The young girl was killed in July when a bomb exploded on Ngercheu, burying her under the sand.

Evacuation to Ngaraard

With Koror vulnerable to carrier raids and B-24 bombers based in New Guinea, General Inoue decided to move his headquarters to Ngatpang on Babeldaob. The remnants of the Nan'yō-chō and many Palauan residents of Koror established themselves in Aimeliik.[27] This settlement became known as "Dai nichi Koror" or number two Koror. From what the Palauan people believe to have been a mix of humanitarian concern and military convenience, the authorities finally decided to evacuate the civilians of Peleliu and Angaur to Babeldaob as well. Several assumed they were moved because the Japanese military feared they would reveal to the invaders the Japanese defensive positions on which they had worked for four months.

Palauan elders said that the military administration had called a great meeting in Koror with the chiefs of Palau and asked them which ones could take in the refugees from Peleliu and Angaur. Mad ra Ngebuked, the highest-ranking chief of Ngaraard, a large village in northern Babeldaob, volunteered to accept everyone from both islands, nearly 1,000 in all. According to Chief Uchelsias Etibek, between August 27 and August 30, 1944 many Peleliu families loaded their belongings into sailing canoes and began sailing north through the Rock Islands to Aimeliik.

Without advance notice, on what Dilchuuch Ermang remembered as August 28, a number of Japanese diesel-powered boats appeared at Ngercheu, and those islanders who had not yet left were ordered to get aboard. They hastily bundled together belongings but did not have time to prepare a meal for the journey. Ungil Besul said that the families at Ngeroblobang did not want to leave, that they preferred to die there, but the obak of Ngerdelolk persuaded them to go. All the residents I spoke with agreed that no chad ra Beliliou remained behind on Peleliu.

The B-24 bombings made the trip in open boats dangerous. "But the B-24s came regularly, every day at noon, so we hid the boats in the Rock Islands until they left. Then we'd start up again," said Spesungel Ichiro. Chief Uchelsias described his sailing canoe getting becalmed in the islands, so that by the time he reached Aimeliik the diesel boats had already departed for Ngermeskang, in the beluu Ngaremlengui.

Abandoning their home villages and island for an uncertain future and leaving behind everything known and cherished caused everyone deep pain. People feared that Peleliu would suffer a dreadful fate during their absence. Former governor Yuki Shmull was five years old at the time. As his boat passed near Ngerekebesang Island near Koror, "We could see very thick black smoke over Malakal. The mechas aboard the boat cried at this because they foresaw that this would happen to our home island. 'If this is what happens to a secondary target like Malakal, then what will happen to Peleliu, the primary target?' We all knew Peleliu was the main target, having the main airfield."

What lay in store for them was also unpredictable and disconcerting. Babeldaob was like a foreign land in many respects. Today, people move rapidly about the archipelago by car and speedboat, but the stories told by the evacuees remind us how different life was seven decades ago. The beluu were far more isolated from each other than now because travel was slow and risky, difficult either by foot or by canoe. People simply did not visit other villages or islands often. While many evacuees had made the 25-mile trip through the Rock Islands to Koror, few had ever continued north to Babeldaob, and almost none had ever lived on the large island. Peleliu was not only their home, it was their world.

The village they were being taken to was unfamiliar in many ways. Ngaraard lay only about 50 miles northeast of Peleliu, accessible through sheltered waters. But Babeldaob was a volcanic island, not limestone. Peleliu lacked the larger island's tracts of savanna grasslands, its more fertile soils, its rolling terrain and streams, and its vast numbers of productive mesei from which the residents obtained plentiful kukau. Farming techniques and tools were different. Fishing techniques were similar, but the chad ra Beliliou lacked the local knowledge that makes fishing productive.

Most of the people came to Ngaraard as homeless and landless supplicants. Only those who had relatives there would, through them, enter with a local identity and a claim to local lands and fishing grounds. Almost as bad as losing Peleliu was having to accept charity from another beluu. It was a blow to the people's pride, exacerbated by the low status accorded Peleliu and Angaur in the hierarchy of Palauan villages.

The army boats carried the islanders along the west coast of Babeldaob and then entered what few had ever seen: a freshwater river, at the mouth of which stood a Japanese pineapple-canning factory that had been damaged in the air raids. It was the Ngermeskang River, whose winding channel the boats followed further and further inland. They finally arrived at their destination, a government-sponsored agricultural community named Asahi-mura, one of five that the Nan'yō-chō had promoted for colonization in Palau.[28] The hamlet's Palauan name is Ngermeskang, in the center of Ngaremlengui. The Japanese soldiers dumped them off and turned around. "We arrived at 6:00 p.m., as it grew dark. It was raining and we were very cold and hungry. We'd left our food and even most of our cooking things back on Ngercheu. We found some houses left by Japanese farmers, so we slept there," recalled Dilchuuch Ermang. There were no Japanese officials, no local villagers there to offer help or guidance, and no vehicles for transport. Their ultimate destination in Ngaraard lay over 15 miles to the north, part by crude road, part through high savanna.

For all the miseries the people suffered, the timing of the evacuation proved fortunate. The American fleet appeared again in early September, this time to deliver the preinvasion bombardment of Peleliu and Angaur. Peleliu was invaded on September 15, 1944, Angaur two days later.

War without Limits: The Battle for Peleliu

By late summer of 1944, General MacArthur was ready to make his long-anticipated return to the Philippines, with the southern island of Mindanao as the target. The American joint chiefs felt that Palau could provide useful support for operations in the Philippines if its excellent harbors and the airfield at Peleliu were held by American forces.

As noted earlier, the Japanese military had not been idle in Palau. In the flurry of redeployments that followed the reversals in the Gilberts and Marshalls, Imperial General Headquarters sent the tough and experienced 14th Division of the Kwantung Army of Manchuria to Palau to prepare its defenses. It arrived in the islands in late April 1944, three weeks after the American carrier raids had chased out the imperial fleet. Its commander, General Inoue, expected invasion of the entire archipelago and accordingly stationed the bulk of his forces on the largest island, Babeldaob.[29]

U.S. commanders, however, decided to invade just the two southern islands, Angaur and Peleliu. The latter already had the Japanese airfield, and the former was judged a good site for building a larger field capable of handling four-engined bombers. The First Marine Division, veterans of Guadalcanal and Cape Gloucester, was assigned the assault on Peleliu; the army's 81st Wildcat Division would then seize Angaur as soon as the marines had the situation on Peleliu under control.[30]

Then occurred an event that has stirred controversy and colored American memories of Peleliu ever since. Admiral William Halsey sailed the U.S. fleet on strikes against targets throughout the western Pacific during the first two weeks of September. He found the Japanese resistance in the Philippines so unexpectedly weak that he radioed an audacious proposal to Admiral Chester Nimitz in Hawaii: cancel the Palau operation entirely, and bypass Mindanao in favor of an invasion into the central Philippines. The joint chiefs approved the recommendations regarding the Philippines, but Nimitz ordered the operations against Peleliu and Angaur to go forward as planned.[31]

Events ultimately suggested, however, that Halsey was right. New Japanese tactics turned Peleliu into a brutal struggle that delayed its capture until it was able to play no significant role in supporting MacArthur's October 20 landing in the Philippines. The Pacific War then moved on so rapidly to the north that the expanded base on Peleliu contributed little to the American war effort. Peleliu became an instant backwater. (Luzon and Manila were invaded in January 1945, Iwo Jima the next month, and the climactic battle in the Pacific, Okinawa, began in April.) The navy's semiofficial historian of World War II, Samuel Eliot Morison, concludes his chapter on Peleliu by saying, "It would take more arguments than this writer can muster to prove [Peleliu] was worth the cost. Admiral Halsey had the right idea; [Palau] should have been bypassed." Nathan Miller is blunter: he calls the decision to invade Peleliu "Nimitz's major mistake of the war."[32]

This issue of whether the battle for Peleliu was a costly blunder continues to trouble its American veterans and the national memory. The discussion seldom points out that the loss of 11,000 Japanese lives was equally needless. Still less does it consider the benefits to the inhabitants of Peleliu and Angaur had their islands been spared.

By the summer of 1944 Tokyo formulated directives that sought to prolong the war in order to gain time to perfect defenses in the most strategic areas, rebuild the naval air arm wiped out (again) in sea battles off the Marianas, and continue the hope that the American public would balk at a protracted war with mounting casualties. Island commanders were directed to organize a defense in depth away from the shoreline. The object now was not to defeat an invasion but to delay the American attackers and sell each island for the highest possible cost in lives. The battle of Peleliu became a brilliant but horrible success in this effort.[33]

General Inoue placed one of his ablest officers, Col. Nakagawa Kunio, in charge of constructing Peleliu's defenses. Nakagawa had approximately four months to prepare before the invasion occurred, using the 11,000 men at his disposal—including conscripted Palauan labor, although all Palauan civilians were removed from the island just prior to the invasion. Nakagawa succeeded in turning Peleliu into "the most heavily fortified small island in the Pacific War outside of Iwo Jima."[34]

Nakagawa intended to inflict maximum damage as the U.S. Marines came ashore, when they were most vulnerable. On the reefs, obstacles and mines of every description were deployed, while beaches were heavily mined and strewn with barbed wire. Antitank ditches were dug close to the beaches. Casemates and bunkers of steel-reinforced concrete were sited where their weapons could rake the reefs and beaches. The coral outcrop lying at the north end of Ngerkeyukl's Ngebedangel beach (named Ongebitel Ream by the residents and Iwamatsu by the Japanese military) and the smaller coral outcrop at the beach's southern end both received a heavy concentration of bunkers with heavy cannon, machine gun pits, and infantry positions. All beaches and reefs were sited in by mortars and artillery situated in the high ground inland and north of the airfield.[35]

In every account of the battle it is the subject of Peleliu's land—what both militaries invariably describe as "terrain"—that dominates the story. An army views terrain with none of the emotional ties with which Palau's natives view their islands and their lands—their gardens or villages, their beaches or reefs that provide them with their livelihoods, identities, and histories. An army considers terrain for the way it will affect military operations; it greatly influences how a battle will unfold. Is the land flat and solid, making it easy for tanks to support infantry? Is it swampy or steep and mountainous, forcing men to fight without heavy vehicles and equipment? Does it have much high ground that allows those who hold it to dominate the terrain below? Peleliu's flat limestone platform at its southern end was ideal for the air base. But the extensive limestone ridge system of the main peninsula provided Nakagawa with the site for his main defensive positions. Here lay jagged cliffs, narrow valleys, and sharp-spined ridges, all pocked with hundreds of natural caves. Though nowhere higher than 300 feet, this karst formation commanded all the low ground on the island. "It was this high ground which made Peleliu so perfectly adaptable to defense-in-depth" notes a marine who fought there.[36]

The natives of Peleliu applied different names to different portions of this ridge system. The southeastern section was the Omleblochel Mountains, which belonged to Ngesias. Its klobak or council of elders took its name from them, "Ngaromleblochel," "We are the Omleblochel." The Japanese surveyors called the system the Momiji Plateau. U.S. histories use a corrupted version of the Palauan name, Umurbrogol Mountains, and erroneously apply it to all the central range. But the marines who took such terrible punishment from Nakagawa's forces gave the mountains one of the most memorable names from the Pacific War: Bloody Nose Ridge.[37]

Nakagawa's insight was that he could best survive the preinvasion bombardments and delay the capture of the island the longest by preparing a vast network of underground positions in the ridges. Between April and September 1944 he directed mining engineers and thousands of Okinawan, Korean, and Palauan laborers to improve Peleliu's many natural caves and dig hundreds more, until the island had 500 in all. He carefully arranged their fields of fire to be mutually supporting when attacked by infantry.[38]

On the day of the invasion he vigorously contested the landing and sent counter-attacks against the invaders. But after that his forces withdrew to their caves and tunnels, turning the battle into a grueling 74-day struggle between two armies, one of which fought above ground, the other below. Nakagawa's tactics, faithfully executed by disciplined troops, forced the American invaders to scale the ridges and destroy the defenders in the caves one by one. In five weeks the First Marine Division suffered such casualties that it had to be withdrawn. The bloodletting consumed the full resources of the 81st Army Division for five more weeks when it took over from the marines. For American military strategists, Peleliu marked a new and ominous phase in the island war. A fierce dispute would flare among American forces over what naval intelligence had learned about the island's highlands from photo reconnaissance made in July 1944. The existence of the deadly ridges caught marine commanders and the ground troops by surprise. After the battle the marines complained that they had again been let down by the navy, and the dispute simmers to this day.

All this lay in the future as the Americans made their plans for invasion. The commander of the First Marine Division, Major General William Rupertus, a veteran of Guadalcanal and Cape Gloucester, felt optimistic that Peleliu would be a rough but quick campaign lasting four days at most.

Coining a pleonasm, Dorothy Richard describes how an "unexpected windfall of information concerning the number of Japanese troops in the Palaus fell into American hands on Saipan," so that Rupertus knew within a few hundred the precise number of his foes on Peleliu. The final estimate was 10,700, of whom 2,200 were naval labor personnel, many presumably forced conscripts from Okinawa and Korea. For landing, two beaches on the western coast were chosen, code-named White and Orange. They were precisely the kinds of beaches that the U.S. military preferred: broad, firm coral sand with rapid access to the airfield.[39]

These were the beaches that fronted the two Peleliu villages of Ngerkeyukl and Teliu, the same communities that the Japanese authorities had forcibly removed for construction of the airfield. What American planners dubbed White and Orange Beaches had always been known as Chelechol ra Ngebedangel and Chelechol ra Bkulabeluu to the villagers. Except for one opening at Teliu, their reefs lacked passes for small craft, so the villagers had to transfer at the reef's edge from larger craft to smaller ones of shallower draft. The American assault troops would do much the same thing. The first few waves would ride all the way ashore in amtracs, but other waves would approach the reef in flat-bottomed craft, from which men and supplies had to transfer into the tracked craft. It is not possible to know just how much of the two villages remained seven years after the residents' departure but not much registered with the American planners. Most maps prepared before the invasion show only three villages: Ngerdelolk, Ngesias (shown as "Asias"), and Ngerchol (shown as "Garekoru"). Only coconut groves appear on the shoreline where Ngerkeyukl and Teliu stood. One map, printed in McMillan's *Old Breed*, also shows Ngerkeyukl, but no map shows Teliu.[40]

The Fates had once again turned their backs on the unlucky inhabitants of these villages. What for the Japanese military was a strand to defend with mines, obstacles, and bunkers and for the American military a beachhead to bombard and wrest from the enemy, was to dozens of Peleliu families their ancestral homeland.

The American fleet arrived off Peleliu on the morning of September 12 and began three days of preinvasion bombardment. Safe in underground shelters, Nakagawa's men were little affected and held their fire in order not to disclose their positions. The sheer weight of the munitions expended, though, blasted the vegetation from the ridges and transformed the island's surface "into a barren wasteland," as one Japanese soldier phrased it in his diary.[41]

On the morning of September 15 the crescendo of bombardment from U.S. ships and aircraft as the landing craft approached the shorelines of Ngerkeyukl and Teliu transformed them "into a continuous sheet of flame backed by a thick wall of smoke," recalled one marine. Another wrote that the beach "was smothered in black vapor and flying spray and sand" and that "it didn't seem possible that anybody could live under such a shelling."[42] At Guadalcanal and Cape Gloucester the First Marine Division had enjoyed "landing luck," encountering negligible opposition in both landings. That luck was extinguished at Peleliu. Once the assault troops crossed the reef, they were engulfed in a maelstrom of deadly fire from Japanese positions concealed along the beaches and in the mountains. Carnage ensued on the reef flats and along the shore. A marine interviewed by *NBC Dateline* 50 years later remembered that "the water was red for four feet out [from the water line] and as far as you could see in both directions."[43]

The division landed three regiments abreast on the beaches of Peleliu on D-day. Each regiment—the First, Fifth, and Seventh—had about 3,200 men, and the total number in the reinforced division, many of them support troops, was about 28,500.[44] Elements of these regiments would fight on the island for 34 days, until mid-October, when the U.S. Army took over completely. The horror of the first of these days is indicated by the fact that fully one-sixth of the total casualties the division suffered occurred on D-day, the day on the beaches.[45] No figures exist for Japanese losses that day.

Inexplicably, Ongebitel Ream, the powerfully fortified coral outcrop that commanded the north end of Ngebedangel (White) Beach, proved largely untouched by U.S. naval gunfire. Its antiboat guns and machine guns, housed in reinforced concrete bunkers and pits dug into the solid coral, sprayed enfilading fire down the entire length of the beach and reef flat, mauling the landing force. The American military planners had recognized this dangerous feature from aerial photo-

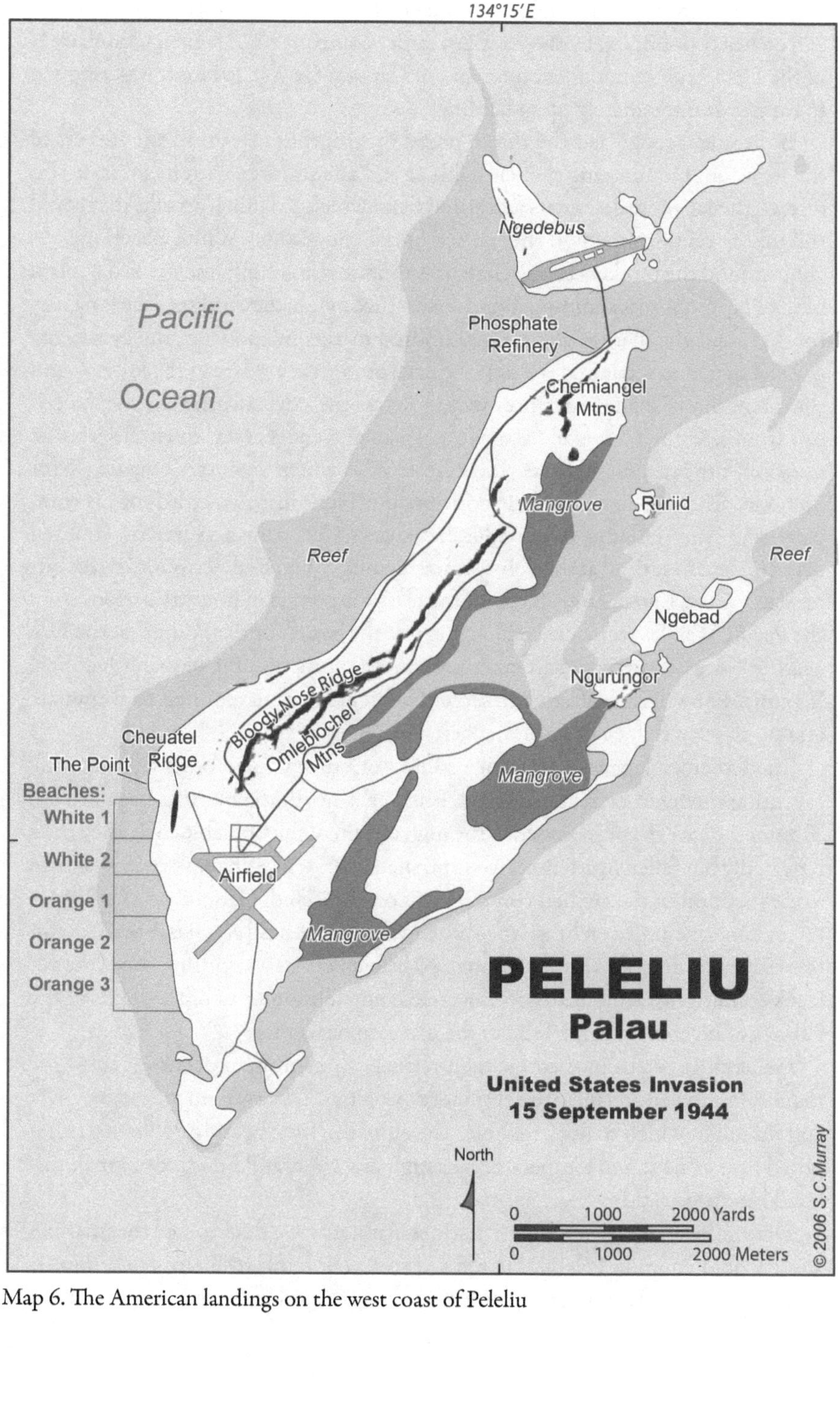

Map 6. The American landings on the west coast of Peleliu

graphs prior to the invasion. It was dubbed "the Point," and was supposed to receive a heavy pounding by the navy. An entire company of 235 men, Company K of the First Regiment, under command of Captain George P. Hunt, was assigned to capture it immediately upon landing.

Both sides recognized the threat posed by Ongebitel Ream to the success of the invasion. Dominating the left flank of the assault force with its guns, it also offered the Japanese defenders a position from which to launch attacks that could roll up the tenuous toehold the United States clung to on White Beach. By circling around the bunkers to attack them from the rear, Hunt's men seized control of the Point soon after landing. But the existence of Cheuatel ridge—the long narrow coral height that lay about one hundred meters inland from the beach, ran parallel to it, and separated the upper village of Ngerkeyukl from the lower—and the strength of Japanese defenses within it was the next surprise for the American troops. Using Cheuatel precisely as Palauan warriors had, to repel seaborne invasion, the Japanese fighters threw hundreds of men against Company K for 36 hours. The marines held their position, but Hunt lost two-thirds of his company—157 men killed or wounded—in two days. Company K's survivors counted over 500 Japanese dead at the Point and its vicinity.[46] Hunt's description of this bitter fight, *Coral Comes High*, is one of the classic accounts of infantry actions from the Pacific War. So tactically challenging was the battle for the Point that the U.S. Marine Corps constructed an exact replica of it at its training base in Quantico, Virginia. For a decade afterward, second lieutenants were required to formulate assault plans to reduce its fearsome defenses.[47]

The ferocious Japanese resistance could not prevent U.S. forces from quickly capturing the main prize, the airfield. But to the north the marines began to encounter the caves honeycombed in the high terrain of the Omleblochel. They tried repeatedly but failed in attempts to climb sheer cliffs while under withering fire. In a rare mention of the civilian communities on the island, Garand and Strobridge tell of a marine unit reaching "the ruined village of Asias [Ngesias]" on September 18. Gailey describes action through Ngerdelolk but says nothing about the village's condition.[48] American accounts make no mention at all of remnants of the villages of Ngerkeyukl and Teliu at the invasion beaches.

General Rupertus pushed his men relentlessly as those units assigned to the mountains slowed and incurred ever more casualties. There was no protective cover and no soil in which to dig a foxhole. The equatorial sun beating down on the exposed limestone raised temperatures as high as 115° F, and hundreds of men suffered heat prostration.[49]

Despite heavy losses among the marines, Rupertus was determined that marines alone would conquer Peleliu. He refused to accept reinforcements from the Army's 81st Wildcat Division until ordered to by his superior, General Roy S. Geiger.

Figure 8. U.S. Marines coming ashore on Ngebedangel (White) Beach, September 15, 1944 (National Archives and Records Administration, U.S. Archives 127-GW-704-095256)

American forces then were able to sweep around the main Japanese defenses in the central hills and seize the smaller groups of ridges at the north end of Peleliu; they next made a short overwater assault on the island of Ngedebus. (American accounts call the island "Ngesebus.")

The main Japanese garrison in the central mountains was now totally isolated, both within Palau and within Peleliu. Their island was lost in the sense that their enemies had seized everything militarily useful. But their cause was not lost because they clung to their determination to delay the American capture and force them to pay dearly for the rest of the island. Whatever the precise balance between compulsion and resolution, the men of the 14th Division held their ground and fought to the bitter end.

By the start of October the American infantry had the surviving Japanese troops completely encircled in an area about 900 meters long by 500 wide that they called the Umurbrogol Pocket—"a cave and ridge fortress suitable to a fanatic and suicidal defense" as Gayle, who fought there, puts it.[50] At its heart lay Nakagawa's underground command post. Each cave became its own distinctive battle, in which the

American soldiers inched forward under artillery fire and bazooka rockets aimed at the mouth, until close enough to immolate the defenders with flamethrowers or blow them to pieces with grenades or satchel charges, or, if one were flushed out of his shelter like a game bird, shoot him down as he tried to run. Many of the valleys were so narrow that caves on one side could pour fire upon infantry trying to engage caves on the other wall. Once they entered one of these death traps, the marines endured mortar, machine gun, and small arms fire from ahead and from both flanks. Clearing the caves was slow, dehumanizing battle, which took an enormous toll on the attackers. One by one, the marine regiments were torn to pieces.

The First Marine Division was finally withdrawn from Peleliu in mid-October. During 34 days of fighting it had sustained roughly 6,800 casualties, of whom 1,300 were killed. After combining forces with the marines for a month, the Army Wildcats took over full responsibility on October 20. Their commander, Major General Paul Mueller, acknowledged what the marines' Rupertus had refused to admit: that the struggle for the Pocket had long since devolved into a siege that required siege tactics. The army slowed and intensified—if that was possible—the attack on the determined resistors, making even more liberal use of artillery, flame, and air support.[51]

Since the war fighting methods that the American and Japanese forces employed at Peleliu had such bearing on the damage they inflicted on the island and thus on what the islanders found remaining when they returned from their exile on Babeldaob, it is worth considering these tactics in more detail. Keep in mind that the island is a total of five miles square. Consider first the sheer weight of munitions the United States expended against Peleliu. American carrier forces had raided Palau in three major operations lasting two to three days each prior to the invasion; in each attack Peleliu with its airfield was a primary target. High altitude bombers also raided Palau numerous times in the spring and summer. During the invasion itself, Garand and Strobridge state that naval guns fired nearly 6,000 tons of munitions, while navy carrier planes dropped 620 tons of bombs between D-day and September 28. Marine air squadrons operating from the captured airfield dropped 186 tons of bombs. Isely and Crowl describe a marine squadron dropping twenty 1,000-pound bombs in a target area of 100 yards on a side. The most astounding figures are those McMillan provides for the munitions of all calibers fired by the First Marine Division during its month on the island. It expended almost 16 million rounds of ammunition, including 13.3 million of 30 caliber from rifles and machine guns, 1.5 million of 45 caliber, 98,000 rounds of 60mm mortars, 116,000 hand grenades, and 65,000 rounds of 75mm pack howitzer. McMillan then calculates that if 10,000 Japanese were killed, it required 1,589 rounds of all sizes to kill each one.[52]

McMillan's calculation became one of the most oft-cited statistics of the amphibious war, and many authors imply that it fully measures the scope of the struggle. But none of these figures includes the enormous volume of munitions expended by the Japanese—the opposing army—in their fierce defense, which continued 40 more days after the marines were withdrawn. And they exclude the ammunition used by the U.S. Army's 81st Division, whose men fought on the island for nine weeks. I discussed the volume of American munitions with a marine veteran of the campaign, Rich Gettell. "The idea was, 'whatever it takes,'" he recalled.

The Japanese infantry was not the only enemy the American forces faced. Peter Schrijvers and Eric Bergerud describe convincingly how American forces in the Pacific warred against what they saw as an alien and hostile nature, a disease-ridden tropical landscape of impenetrable jungles, oppressive heat, and exotic animals and natives, which concealed a wily foe within.[53] (The landscape and people in Europe were far more familiar to Americans.) Peleliu fit this pattern, from the reefs treated as natural obstacles to overcome to the willingness to obliterate the landscape in prosecuting the battle. The naval bombardment blasted away the vegetative cover of the island and demolished any structure, Japanese or Palauan, above ground. Once ashore the marines used light mortars "to clear all vegetation from small objectives and routes of advance." On a limestone island like Peleliu there is no reserve of deep soil. Vegetation grows in pockets where previous leaf litter has decayed. With massive burning the cycle was broken and recovered only slowly. Nor were the landforms themselves immune. "Troublesome sections of certain cliffs were literally demolished by direct fire, and the rubble [bulldozed] into a ramp for tanks to climb toward better firing positions."[54] Some of these ramps are visible today deep in the reforested mountains.

But it is the American forces' use of fire that best represents the readiness to employ, in a war of extermination, the most terrible weapons. Flamethrowers were used extensively against the caves and fortified positions. The marines also developed a vehicle-mounted flamethrower, used on amtracs at Peleliu (see figure 9). Forested areas that concealed Japanese positions were burned off systematically with amtrac flamethrowers that moved into range on the ramps of rubble.[55]

Napalm—jellied gasoline dropped in belly tanks from airplanes—was used experimentally on Tinian in July 1944 but came into its own at Peleliu. It was released from the treetop level, sometimes with instantaneous fuses, then more commonly without, as in the case where 14 tanks of it were dropped to saturate a target area, which was then set alight with white phosphorous mortar shells.[56] Napalm brought a new kind of hell to the earth's surfaces, but like high explosives, its usefulness when dropped from aircraft against the underground Japanese enemy was marginal. The 81st Division found a way to use it more effectively. Troops ran hoses into the hills from a roadbound gasoline truck, allowing them to shoot napalm hundreds of feet ahead into Japanese defensive areas.[57]

Figure 9. Flame in the battle for the ridges, c. October 1944 (National Archives and Records Administration, U.S. Archives 127-N-098260)

Another fiery munition widely used at Peleliu was white phosphorous, in every size from hand grenades to heavy artillery rounds. When it landed on flesh it burned steadily down to the bone. Japanese infantry were said to be particularly fearful of this munition. "WP" left a white residue that contributed to the stark whiteness of Peleliu so frequently remarked on by the natives when they returned home.

Thermite is a different chemical composition that was equally grisly in its effects. On the first night the marines were ashore, George Hunt's men caught Japanese attackers trying to flank the Point along the beach. They were repulsed with thermite hand grenades. The Japanese soldiers "caught fire and screeching horribly, with the ammunition in their belts exploding like strings of fire crackers, ran into the water and rolled over and over attempting to extinguish the flames which clung to them relentlessly." They burned in the water, "crackling human bonfires that lit up the night."[58]

Certainly the most unlikely weapon employed against the Japanese foe was one that the island itself supplied: beach sand. The limestone ridges lacked any topsoil into which the infantry could dig foxholes to avoid enemy fire. Rear echelon men filled bags with sand from the beaches; the bags were then passed hand to hand up the ridges. The infantry would inch the sandbags ahead of them, repeatedly piling up a protective wall as they assaulted each cave.[59] Here the many different ways beaches were perceived and used by those who came to Peleliu calls forth a memory from tragedy. One imagines three chelid, ghostly spirits of Peleliu, waylaying Colonel Nakagawa within the blasted crags of the Omleblochel and assuring him that his mountain fortress would not fall until the beaches of Peleliu came to the cliff tops.

The inevitable end came on November 24, 1944, when the colonel radioed a final coded message to Koror, "*Sakura, Sakura*," meaning "cherry blossom," a flower associated with the samurai for its brief life of splendor. In World War II it became "the supreme symbol of young patriots perishing in modern warfare."[60] The message indicated that resistance had ended and Nakagawa would burn the regimental colors. He and Major General Murai Kenjiro then took their own lives. Infantrymen from the 81st Division pushing into the final valley from the north met their comrades coming up from the south on November 27, in the area close to Nakagawa's last command post. Seventy-four days had elapsed since the marines had come ashore.

Nakagawa and his men fought an innovative, skilled, and courageous defense of Peleliu; it anticipated the tactics employed by Japanese commanders at Iwo Jima and Okinawa. The Japanese fighters on Peleliu maintained extraordinary discipline. U.S. forces captured not over 300 of them, and of those just 19 were regular Japanese military; the rest were Korean and Okinawan labor troops.[61] The imperial garrison's undeniably brave and stubborn fight against impossible odds would form the heart of the Japanese memory of the battle.

The chaos of war renders any final count elusive, but the last published figures from official U.S. sources say the First Marine Division suffered 1,336 killed, 5,450 wounded, while the U.S. Army on Peleliu lost an additional 278 killed and 1,381 wounded, a total of 1,614 dead and 6,831 wounded. Japanese sources give the empire's losses as 10,022, which includes 6,632 army and 3,390 naval personnel, with 446 men presumed captured. Most American accounts estimate 11,000 Japanese soldiers died.[62]

These heavy losses would form an important component of both the American and Japanese memories of the battle. The extraordinary severity of the struggle was widely recognized by those familiar with it. Generals and admirals declared that the battle for Peleliu was the toughest in the entire Pacific campaign, smaller but no less difficult than Iwo Jima. Yet there remains the nagging question of the quality of the American field leadership, whether many more troops died than necessary.

The quick sacking of General Rupertus, the marine commander, by the commandant of the Marine Corps, General Alexander Vandegrift, strongly suggests that the top echelons in Washington, D.C., believed he had wasted lives.

Vandegrift, in his memoirs, caught another painful element of the battle by calling it "one of the least publicized but most difficult campaigns of World War II." That the battle so quickly slipped from the nation's memory became an enduring disappointment to those veterans whose own memories were seared by their experiences on Peleliu.[63]

The American victors rapidly rebuilt and expanded the military installations on Peleliu. Reefs, beaches, forests, terrain, and the previous human landscape were altered as necessary to fulfill the mission assigned to Peleliu. Using coral dredged from the reefs and limestone from the hills, they lengthened the airstrip, built more roads, and filled terrain, covering former garden lands in the process. They gouged out a harbor at the western invasion beach, and erected hundreds of Quonset huts and tents for housing and offices. An odesongel, the foundation of the main bai for the village of Ngerdelolk, was the lone Palauan structure to survive the war largely intact.

Several marine air squadrons based on Peleliu flew suppressive missions against the rest of Palau for the remainder of the war. As described in chapter 5, many of the most vivid memories the Palauan people retain from World War II stem from this year of constant and indiscriminate attacks from the air. As a naval base Peleliu became a forward supply depot, site of a base hospital of 600 beds, and home to infantry and tank units, service battalions, and the usual array of construction and maintenance units. Casualties from the Philippines were treated on Peleliu before being flown back to U.S. hospitals.[64]

For all this seeming activity Peleliu, like the bomber base constructed at Angaur, played a very minor role for the United States for the remainder of the war. The historian Harry Gailey concludes that Peleliu made no vital contribution to either the Philippine operations or even to the neutralizing of Palau, which had already been accomplished by U.S. control of the seas in the central Pacific.[65] Peleliu lapsed into rear echelon status so promptly that it seems as if the American military bypassed their own base.

For American veterans and almost all their countrymen who have written on the battle, Peleliu represents a noble victory in the Pacific campaign. But painful issues dog the national memory: the necessity of the invasion; intelligence failures regarding the terrain; the extreme severity of the battle and unexpectedly high losses, due in part to ineptitude of the command; the limited utility of the island base; and the conflict's quick decline into historical obscurity.

What Peleliu represents in memory and history to Japanese visitors of today depends on the beliefs they bring from home concerning Japan's role in the Pacific

War. The perspectives they hold and the agendas they follow on the island reflect their disparate personal experiences from the war and their underlying political and ideological commitments. Pacifists believe Peleliu illustrates the futility and inhumanity of war. Resolute conservative Japanese governments have memorialized it cautiously, while the nation's patriotic Right presents it as a struggle of heroic sacrifice.

For Peleliu's native residents, the meaning of the war is brutally straightforward: it brought them environmental and social catastrophe. It is the obliteration of everything that sustained them and everything they had built that primarily shapes their memories and judgments of the conflict.

5
Exile, Fear, and Hunger
Ngaraard, Babeldaob, 1944–1945

In the last days of August 1944, two weeks before the invasion of their homeland, the people of Peleliu found themselves alone in Ngermeskang, a hamlet of Ngaremlengui on the western coast of Babeldaob. Japanese military craft had dropped them there after plucking them off their refuges in the Rock Islands. Cold, wet, and hungry, they took shelter in houses left by Japanese immigrant farmers from the agricultural community of Asahi-mura. They knew the village of Ngaraard, to the north, had offered them their next refuge.

The next morning men from Ngaraard arrived to guide them the 15 miles to the village. There were no motor vehicles, so those too old or weak stayed behind temporarily in Ngaremlengui until other transport could be arranged. Over the next few days most families began the trek to Ngaraard.

They were a bedraggled, dispirited lot. They had progressively lost their few possessions during the escape from Peleliu to Ngercheu and then the abrupt transfer to Ngermeskang. Now they could bring only what they could carry. Women strapped babies to their sides and lifted heavy loads onto their heads. Chief Uchelsias Etibek Shmull remembered that for much of the trek there was no path, forcing them to walk through unfamiliar tall elephant grass, *bokso*. Tokie Morei (figure 6) recalled, "We were so poor and pitiful (*chebuul*) then. Recently I saw on television pictures of refugees in Somalia. I called to my grandchildren to come watch and told them, 'That's just what we looked like walking to Ngaraard.'" The Japanese officials provided no food, but sympathetic Palauan villagers along the way brought them food and drink and helped as guides as they passed small settlements in the interior of Babeldaob.

Some, like Chief Uchelsias and most of the rubak Susong Smau's family, sailed their canoes up the coast of Babeldaob to Ngaraard. The majority walked, which took two or three days. Finally the chad ra Beliliou arrived at the village of Ngebuked, home of the chief Mad ra Ngebuked, the highest-ranking chief in Ngaraard. They moved into the Bai ra Ngaruau.

Ngaraard is a large and influential beluu in Palau; it is one of the 16 states of the Republic of Palau. Straddling the narrow neck of Babeldaob Island, Ngaraard has long coastlines along both the island's east coast, which is called Despedall, and its west side, which is called Keyukl. Ngaraard, like Peleliu, contains five distinct villages, each of which has its own ruling council and bai. Its constituent beluu are Chol, Ngebuked, Chelab, Ulimang, and Ngkeklau. All five of the settlements lie on the east side of Babeldaob, Despedall. As they do today, Ngaraard's large and carefully tended mesei produce one of the most bountiful crops of taro (kukau) in all Palau. The chad ra Beliliou told me that the Mad ra Ngebuked agreed to accept the residents of Peleliu because, of all Palau's beluu, Ngaraard was best able to feed and house them.

Ebilrairung Ilebrang Soaladaob of Ulimang said that the people of Ngaraard had received a prophecy of the impending war. A woman of the village, Diraiterrir, could foresee the future by looking at the shapes of clouds. On one occasion she saw clouds shaped like a herd of horses, from which she predicted that war would come to Ngaraard. When Japanese soldiers arrived in the village, their officers were mounted on horses.

Residents of Angaur Island had also been evacuated to Ngaraard. The people decided their community had a better chance of surviving if they split up, so one portion let the Japanese authorities remove them to Ngaraard. Many others deliberately delayed on Angaur until American submarines made departure impossible. Along with an estimated 35 non-Palauan Micronesians, they sheltered themselves in caves when the American forces invaded the island. After three weeks of battle, Richard reports that 182 islanders, of whom 147 were from Angaur, surrendered to U.S. troops. Lorenza Pedro recounted to me that five natives of Angaur died during the invasion (and two others gave birth). The 1946 census reported by John Useem counted 316 natives of Angaur; this implies that about 160 came to Babeldaob in 1944.[1]

Households in Ngaraard took in their kin from the displaced villages. Chiefs, responsible for the welfare of guests, took the largest numbers. Those arrivals lacking relatives were assigned households according to a scheme that matched beluu of Peleliu to beluu of Ngaraard. Chief Beches Iluches Reksid, of Ulimang, and the Ngaraard historian Andrew Shiro remembered the division this way: Teliu was assigned to Chol; Ngerkeyukl to Chelab; Ngesias and Ngerdelolk to Ngebuked; Ngerchol to Ulimang; and those of Angaur to Ngkeklau.[2] Chief Uchelsias Etibek of Ngesias explained that those who found relatives in Ngaraard felt the least awkward. "But it was hard to start relationships with people you were assigned to when you didn't know them. . . . It was hard to open up to each other."

There was no chance to integrate the newcomers into the routine living patterns of their hosts. The American military invaded Peleliu and Angaur on September 15 and 17, respectively. U.S. forces considered all of Palau to be a war zone.

Every structure and every person throughout the archipelago was considered a legitimate target. Once Peleliu's airfield was seized and made operational, Marine Air Groups (MAGs) flew strafing and bombing missions over Babeldaob regularly every day and often during full moons.[3] High-altitude bombing continued as well. The residents were forced to abandon their villages and seek shelter in caves and under cover of forests and mangroves.

This, then, would be the situation in Palau for 12 dark and terrible months, from September 1944 until hostilities ceased on August 15, 1945. While roughly 150 natives of Angaur remained on their island, all other islanders were gathered on Babeldaob, Palau's largest island at 128.5 square miles (334 square kilometers). They were concentrated in Ngaraard and in Aimeliik but spread throughout the island's villages. Expecting an invasion of Babeldaob to follow those of Angaur and Peleliu, General Inoue Sadae had concentrated his army on the big island. A conservative estimate of the populations stranded there as of September 1944 would include the following: 29,700 Japanese Army and Navy troops; approximately 14,300 foreign civilians (a mix of Nan'yō-era immigrants and Okinawan, Korean, and other Asian conscripted laborers); 5,500 Palauan natives; and 200 others from Micronesia. This made a total of 44,000 Japanese and other foreigners, and 5,700 from Micronesia, or 49,700 altogether. The foreigners outnumbered the Palauan natives by nine to one. But Inoue was completely isolated from the Japanese war effort in the Pacific. The overwhelming sea and air power of the United States effectively cut his command off from Peleliu (except for radio contact with Nakagawa's headquarters) and from reinforcement by Japanese forces.

For the duration of the war the Japanese forces and the Palauan natives marooned on Babeldaob lived off whatever supplies the army had stockpiled and from the island's natural resources. Japanese troops were concentrated in certain areas considered likely invasion sites but many, along with the natives, were also scattered together across much of the island. Hostile ships cruised offshore while deadly aircraft patrolled the skies; Babeldaob was effectively under siege. Nobody knew how long the ordeal would continue. Everyone faced a daily struggle for survival and feared the possibility of an American invasion, although once the United States landed in the Philippines (October 20, 1944) Inoue realized the American forces had no reason to invade Babeldaob, and they never did so.[4] The people of Peleliu lived with two other anxieties: What was happening to their beloved homeland during the prolonged battle being waged there? And how could they minimize the strain they inevitably placed on their hosts in Ngaraard?[5]

Life under Siege from the Air

Once a Peleliu family joined its host family in Ngaraard, the refugees came under the protection of an established household and gained access to that family's gardens and mesei. The demands on these and other resources, however, would have been extraordinary even under peacetime conditions. It was common for a host family of perhaps 8 to 12 persons to take in two or three families of equal size. Dilkerrai Kebor's father held the second title of Ulimang, although the family lived in Ngebuked at this time. They found relatives of her father among the Peleliu refugees, so they told them to join their household. I asked her how many of these relatives there were. She smiled and replied, "38." The 12 members of the family of rubak Melobchechelild Ngirmekur Ngirchorachel accepted two Peleliu families, with 15 people. Beches Iluches and his wife received 48 evacuees from Peleliu.

The Palauan refugees were unable to remain in the five villages of Ngaraard, where they could have used established homes and gardens and maintained a semblance of ordinary social and political life, because these villages, which faced beaches along the eastern side of Babeldaob, Despedall, came under gunfire not only from airplanes but also from U.S. ships that could steam in close to the fringing reef. The best shelter lay on the western side of the island, Keyukl, across the steep ridge that runs down the narrow neck of Babeldaob. More forests grew here, and the long barrier reef offshore of Keyukl, with its lagoon miles in width, kept the naval vessels at a safe distance. The different groups, each led by a Ngaraard family, separated in order to build crude shelters under the canopy of forests growing below the grassy ridge crest. Some stayed behind on the Despedall side and made homes in the jungles at the foot of the hills behind the villages. Although riskier locations, they had the advantages of being near the existing gardens and mesei and familiar shorelines and reefs.

Kebor's group of about 50 people crossed to Keyukl and found a patch of forest in an area named Desengong. Here they built three thatched homes for themselves, structures typical of the type that almost everybody erected. They had floors of bamboo or mangrove poles but were open sided. They were called diangel, the word used for boathouse. Melobchechelid Ngirmekur explained that for safety they made these diangel as small as possible, so they could not be seen from the planes, and they dispersed them over the largest possible area.

On a research trip I climbed the central ridge with Melobchechelid so he could show me where his 27 people had hidden. From the top we looked down on the Keyukl side as he pointed out to me four areas of forest in which people found shelter. The view is breathtaking, with rolling savanna ridges giving way to tall stands of forest that dip toward the sea. The deep azure of the great western lagoon lies framed within the distant white ribbon of breakers that marks the barrier reef. Except for the new road that rings Babeldaob, there remains little sign of human habitation as one looks southward along miles of coast toward Ngardmau. It is a traveler's dream landscape, and there was something profoundly dissonant to listen to this rubak describe the precarious lives endured by these island peoples, trapped within a war brought to their world by foreigners.

His group and others from Ngebuked and Peleliu stayed in a forest in an area named Ngeskii, to the immediate west along a hill. Ten Japanese lookouts lived in the forest as well, to watch for signs of an invasion from a nearby hilltop, but they lived away from the Palauan natives. A second forest to the south, Ngirmeai, hid people from Peleliu and Ngaraard and another 20 Japanese lookouts. The third, in Elobel, had residents from Ulimang and Chelab villages. The fourth, in an area named Klou el Taoch (great channel), was closer to the western coastline. Two future governors of Peleliu lived here, Timarong Sisior and Yuki Shmull, along with Antonio Tewid. Melobchechelid made sure I understood that people had hidden in many other areas; these were simply four readily visible from our vantage point. It bears remarking once again how an island landscape—this one thickly forested and, to an outsider, seemingly primordial—is, for the local people, subdivided and named and charged with human history.

The three families with whom Melobchechelid lived all worked together, seeking food and sharing whatever they were able to obtain. There was nobody else nearby, so, as he put it, "We were a survival unit." They were so busy finding food, and people were so dispersed, that they seldom traveled to visit others in hiding. He described how every day at 3:00 a.m. he and other men would come out of the forest and swim along the coast for a distance of about two miles, using bamboo floats. When the sun came up they could then see to gather clams or whatever else was available, but they had to hurry and remain watchful of the planes.

Customary rituals, public and political activities, and even the most basic ceremonies like funerals had to be relinquished. No schools or hospitals functioned. People were truly reduced to survival units. To avoid attracting planes, the Japanese military advised people not to build cooking fires during the day and to cover lights during the night. Chobechad ra Eliou Song demonstrated to me what it was like to eat at night by closing her eyes and fumbling with her hands outstretched before her. Any activity that could be observed from the air during daylight hours carried high risk. For the most part, then, fishing, gathering, farming, hunting, or any form of travel was confined to dark. Fishing was most hazardous of all, since there was no place to hide if attacked except beneath the water's surface. Life under the trees was not pleasant for anyone. Particularly near streams it was dank, tenebrous, and by Palauan standards, chilly: "Every day and every night we were cold and hungry and afraid," said Susong Smau.

In recalling these times, people from all over Palau most readily talk about the hunger and the struggles to obtain food. In a sense this is the easiest thing to discuss from the war. Everyone faced hunger and even starvation; it was the shared experience of them all, and it became central to the postwar collective narrative. The people of Palau are deeply reluctant to discuss misfortunes, either their own or those of others. Talking about hunger allows them to avoid remembering the more painful events, like the deaths of fragile elders and infants, the strafing of fishermen, or the brutality of Japanese soldiers. But also, in a people for whom food—its production, consumption, and its exchange in a multitude of private acts and ceremonies—looms so large in cultural life, the hunger of wartime remains the single most powerful and evocative symbol of the misery and deprivation of that era.

High-value, high-carbohydrate garden produce, the ongraol normally grown by women, was the key to survival. Most families living on Keyukl would cross the ridge to work at night in the gardens and mesei of their Ngaraard household. Dirribukel Ngirametuker said that many Peleliu families also built new gardens and even mesei that were closer to their hideouts. Governor Sisior described how his family was one of three that stayed with a Ngaraard family in the Klou el Taoch shown me by Melobchechelid. They made farms near their homes and could begin working them in the late afternoon when the planes stopped patrolling. They would also go out in the moonlight to clear land and weed the gardens.

Dilkerrai Kebor recalled a life of unrelenting labor, necessary to feed the large numbers who depended on her family. During the day she would stay by their mesei, working as best she could between flights of planes, hiding in tall grass as necessary. She would harvest taro and put it in baskets that she had woven; others would come to collect them around 6:30 p.m., just after dark. Most nights she and other women worked in their gardens planting, weeding, and harvesting tapioca and sweet potato. Her younger brothers would use blowguns to shoot a small crab in the mangroves called *senges*. Villagers from Ngarchelong also lived under the trees in Desengong with her group, as did a camp of Japanese soldiers.

The protein foods (odoim) normally provided by men were particularly difficult to obtain since it was so dangerous to be out on the water. Babeldaob has no real land-dwelling game. A favorite target was the pigeon, *belochel*, shot with blowguns, enjoyed for its dark and strong-flavored meat. Men scoured the mangroves for the senges and for the larger mangrove crab, chemang. They gleaned on the reefs when possible. Boys also caught fish that "didn't taste good" in the freshwater streams recalled Gov. Yuki Shmull. Parties would fish at night with lines and take chances casting nets when patrols were unlikely, in the very early morning or late afternoon just before dark. Everybody remarked on the shortage of odoim and of salt, which could not be distilled from seawater because of the danger of smoke attracting planes.

Those families able to hide on Despedall had a somewhat easier time than those who crossed over to Keyukl. The former were closer to their settlements' mesei and gardens and could more easily expand them if needed. Beches Iluches took his 50 people to hide in a forested area named Ngerkesang that lay back from the beach and the flat of Ulimang village. Each of the families functioned largely on its own once the division of mesei and gardens was made. Ebilrairung Ilebrang and her family also stayed on Despedall. She remembered their efforts to share their food with those in Keyukl: "We couldn't always share, but when we could we sent young men at night with food around to those of Ulimang who were hiding on the other side of the ridge, and to their Peleliu dependents."

The U.S. Marine air patrols flying from Peleliu were a constant menace throughout the day. For them Babeldaob was a free-fire zone for most of this period. Melobchechelid Ngirmekur recalled, "The planes flew in two pairs usually, up to Ngarchelong, and if they saw someone they would radio each other and all four begin making strafing passes. People would lie still so not to be seen." Ambassador Daiziro Nakamura was nine years old in 1945. Like many other boys, he learned to play daredevil with the pilots. "People were always running away from the sound of the engines, and [you] could hear the bombs drop. Kids would run, like chickens with their mother. Young kids would climb mountains and watch it, but the elderly were scared. You could see the pilot as he banked the plane, but you could jump in a small hole for protection before the plane could get around facing head on to shoot. You never ran away from the plane, always toward it or into a ditch or trench." Large bombers, usually B-24s from the new bomber field on Angaur or bases in New Guinea, also continued to bomb Palau. Daiziro Nakamura saw the Japanese antiaircraft batteries in Ngerekebesang and Airai shoot down three of these planes, whose crews bailed out while flying toward Kayangel atoll, which the United States occupied.[6]

Reiko Kubary, eight years old at the time, remembered that "no matter what else you were doing, you had to constantly listen for the planes." People had many stories of close calls. Reiko's grandmother was almost hit by a bullet as she wove a basket. A bullet struck inches away from Andrew Shiro as he stood in a doorway. Beches Iluches received a wound in his leg as he dove out of the way of a stream of bullets. The family of Ngedikes Tmodrang still owns a table that they had brought by canoe to the cave in Airai where they sheltered for over a year. They had piled belongings on top of it where it sat near the cave's mouth, yet a 50-caliber bullet left a visible dent in its surface. (After Ngedikes's family evacuated from Koror, as ordered by the Japanese Army, American bombing destroyed their Japanese-style home and everything they could not fit into a single canoe, including the sewing machine that provided Ngedikes with her livelihood as a dressmaker.) Andrew Shiro said so many shell casings littered the slopes of Ngaraard following the war that foreigners collected them for scrap. The other fear always lurked in the background too: "Invasion is a powerful word. You don't forget it," said Ambassador Nakamura.

I also heard stories of American pilots who refrained from shooting when they recognized people as Palauans. Spesungel Ichiro Dingilius believed that he and

Uchelsias Etibek were spared while fishing near Aimeliik when a fighter pilot, who circled them three times, saw they were not Japanese. There are, however, many more stories of indiscriminate strafing. The largest number of Palauan people killed in a single incident of which I am aware occurred in Ngaraard when a plane caught a group of men fishing in the open. One of the men killed was the younger brother of Judge Francisco Morei and of Muchucheu Augusto Sengebau. Muchucheu told the story this way: "My younger brother [Mosang] went fishing by Klou el Taoch on Keyukl, with some men from Ngaraard, Ngarchelong, and Peleliu. They were walking near the mangroves; they were not in boats. Some planes had been bombing Babeldaob and were returning to Peleliu when a rubak named Ngirablosch threw a net that caught the attention of the pilots, so they came and strafed. Three Peleliu men and some from Ngarchelong, a total of six, were killed."

Many in Palau still resent how American planes strafed and bombed them indiscriminately for an entire year. In Karen Walter's dissertation on the years 1944–51 in Palau, she says that pilots from Marine Aircraft Group (MAG) 11 were told in briefings that Koror and Babeldaob were one large Japanese base, holding numerous Japanese military installations. The archives of these air groups reveal no concern for the safety of the native population, and there is no evidence that they were told to avoid Palauan or other civilians. This recklessness toward civilian lives contrasts markedly with the air raids of March and July 1944 against Peleliu and Angaur: the villages were carefully avoided and no Palauan villager was killed on either island, although the young girl was later killed on Ngercheu. Near the war's end, Walter writes, as some Palauan people escaped to Peleliu and were interrogated, the United States did try to identify where Japanese supply dumps and troop concentrations were and avoid communities known to house islanders.[7] American planes dropped leaflets written for the natives urging them not to fear the American flights, but how could they have found safety? The Japanese military punished them for reading such leaflets. Other leaflets urged Japanese soldiers to surrender since they were eating "rats' leftovers," but these were ignored.

Japanese vs. Palauans in the Struggle to Survive

Particularly in the early months, both the Japanese military and civilians lived apart from the Palauans; each community largely took care of itself. This did not mean, however, that the army's demands for Palauan labor waned. Dilkerrai Kebor said that they spent most of their time in the forests trying to obtain food, but the Japanese military would still frequently order chiefs to supply labor. Both she and Governor Sisior worked without pay as porters for the army, carrying goods and equipment at night between Ngaraard and Ngardmau and Ngatpang to the southwest. Governor Sisior also made coconut oil and cooked for the military. Japanese officials could be vicious toward chiefs who failed to muster the required number of men. Judge Francisco Morei described how they beat a chief of Ngaraard with hardwood clubs when only one-half the number of men demanded showed up. "Many years later he was still hurting from these beatings." JeRome Temengil, the author of several compilations of Palauan legends, described a beating his grandfather Blailes received, and more beatings appear in the history textbook used in Palauan schools.[8]

The army had stockpiled rice for its forces in case of invasion. (In most operations the Imperial Army expected its forces to live off the land, but in recognition of the distinctive environments of the small Micronesian islands, Tokyo sent rations sufficient for six months to one year with the defending garrisons.) Presumably the forced laborers were also fed from these stocks.[9] As the months passed, however, supplies dwindled, and by early 1945 famine stalked the Japanese communities. Daiziro Nakamura said that his father, conscripted as a boat builder by the army, was paid in precious rice, which he brought to his family. Gov. Yuki Shmull pointed out that the stores of rice came to be reserved for high-ranking officers' daily needs, so that the junior officers and enlisted men had to forage for their food. They knew nothing about growing crops or fishing, so required instruction from the Palauan natives. Inevitably soldiers began to pressure them for the food they were better able to produce.

The living situation for everybody on Babeldaob steadily deteriorated. Harvest cycles for sweet potato, taro, and tapioca ranged from four months for the first to six months to a year for the others. The sweet potato, chemutii, highly nutritious and with a relatively short growing cycle, rapidly became a favorite crop for everyone—natives and soldiers. But all crops for the many newcomers in Ngaraard would take time to mature. The Palauan natives supplemented their diets by eating a variety of wild plants and roots and by resorting to two famous "famine foods," available wild in the mangroves, where they could be harvested under the shelter of the tall trees. *Denges*, the oriental mangrove (*Bruguiera gymnorhiza* [L.] Lam.), is a long shoot that is cut and then chopped; it must be placed in a stream for 24 hours to wash out its bitterness. *Belloi*, a bitter type of yam, grows on a vine. Ebilrairung Ilebrang would cook and peel it, then cut it up and put it into a basket lined with leaves, which was then submerged in a stream for up to a week. The reward for all this labor was a tasteless sodden mush of limited nutritional value. Almost every elder mentioned denges and belloi; they came to symbolize the hardships the Palauan people suffered during their year of hunger and fear. Both appear in a song written down for me by Miako, wife of Andrew Shiro of Ngaraard. (The eight-line song appears first in Palauan, followed by the English translation.)

Chulekum e ngotiall a tekoi,
Mak ngunguchii Ngiramekemad
Me ngongelil a mekemadil
E le sechelei kid a kukuoi choremang.
Chelebuul er a chereomel ma,
Sengerengoi uoi meketketang
E le bosech a mlei el omosech
Ma kikola denges ma belloi.

We wish we could retrieve the ancient wisdom,
So we could pray to the god of war,
So he could make the war magic,
Because friends, we are suffering terribly.
We are impoverished in the deep forests,
And have been starving for a long time,
This time of privation has caused famine,
And reduced us to eating denges and belloi.

The words and concepts in the first four lines are powerful old ones. In the past, Palauan chiefs would seek a prophecy from the god of war, Ngiramekemad, on whether to engage in a war and ask him to make his magic to assist them in battle. The first three lines in particular lament that, because the people did not participate in the decision to engage in this war, they were unable to propitiate Ngiramekemad to obtain his aid and protection.

Ambassador Nakamura cited two important advantages the Palauan natives had in the struggle to survive as compared to the Japanese and other Asian populations on the islands: "We Palauans knew how to live in the jungle and get food; we could live for several years if we had to. The Palauans on Despedall were better off than where our family was, in Aimeliik [which had fewer mesei]. Still, nobody starved, though they did suffer. And Palauans share what they have; it's an important part of our culture, so those in need could always get help." Karen Nero observes that since sharing food was a primary way to define social relationships in Palau and throughout the Pacific, the refusal of the Japanese soldiers to share and their stealing food from the islanders radically altered many Palauans' attitudes toward their longtime masters.[10]

Conflicts with Japanese soldiers increased as they became more desperate in their search for food. Sometimes people were able to shame them, as when Governor Shmull's father scolded some Japanese soldiers for taking his family's crops. When a Japanese soldier barged into Dilkerrai Kebor's home and stole a cooking pot, she complained to an officer, "My father is the second chief here; if you need anything you only have to ask." They brought the soldier to the house and he apologized. Andrew Shiro remembered watching some Japanese soldiers catching lizards and snakes to eat.

Ngedikes Tmodrang found a sickly and very emaciated Japanese man, presumably a soldier, wandering in the forests eating roots. The islanders called these people by the Japanese term *tōbōsha*: fugitives or deserters. Ngedikes took him in to their shelter and gave him soup; but he was half mad, and though they nursed him for days, he died.

Often, however, the soldiers simply took what they wanted. They had the guns. There are many stories of soldiers fencing off a mesei or garden plot for themselves as the crops ripened, ordering the Palauan gardeners away, or simply stealing the crops. Governor Sisior recalled villagers coming to Ngaraard from Ngarchelong to get taro and land crabs but having to go home empty-handed after the military snatched away what they had obtained. The troops also waylaid Palauan fishermen returning with their meager catches, and grabbed their fish. Ebilrairung Ilebrang's husband Soaladaob and another man once caught a large number of chemang (mangrove crab). "They shared them with a few families that lived by a stream, and with other families isolated in the forests of the Keyukl side. But the Japanese punished them for failing to offer some crab to them. They were made to stand facing the sun, looking at it with open eyes, for an entire day." The stealing of coconuts irked the islanders but gave them a grim satisfaction too, for one racist taunt the Japanese officials had flung at them throughout the Nan'yō years was that they smelled like coconuts (*bul a lius* in Palauan). As one Peleliu rubak, Tkel Simeon, told me in the 1960s, "When they got hungry enough they began eating any coconuts they could get. Then *they* smelled like coconuts."[11] Occasionally the islanders struck back. Governor Sisior tells how some of them peeled an inedible type of taro; when six Japanese soldiers seized it and wolfed it down, they became violently ill.

Beches Iluches pointed out that of course not all Japanese soldiers were overbearing or cruel. "Some were good, and they would admit that the U.S. would win the war because they were so powerful. So they advised the islanders to take care of themselves." Despite the mistreatment, most Palauan natives retained sympathy for certain Japanese populations on Babeldaob. Several Palauan natives told me that no group suffered more than the Japanese civilians, who struggled to survive in unfamiliar surroundings far from home. They had been cut loose by the military authorities to fend for themselves after the March 1944 air raid but, unlike soldiers, lacked both stocks of rations and the weapons to take food forcibly. Those families left from the Nan'yō administration were particularly miserable.

Ambassador Nakamura told a poignant story of the family of a Japanese immigrant who had been principal of his elementary school in Koror. "He was being sent to New Guinea, so he asked [the Nakamuras] to care for his family. The woman, who had two beautiful daughters aged 14 and 16, didn't want to mingle with the Palauans, whom she considered tōmin [islanders]. One day, after we had gone to Aimeliik, I saw a woman with long hair walking bent over, with a straw rope for carrying heavy loads. With a shock I realized she was the principal's wife." The ambassador's mother, Aliil, gave the woman some sardines. "The woman was very hungry, she ate ravenously. She was an arrogant, high-class woman, and now she was eating like a starving beggar." Both her daughters had starved to death. The ambassador's brother, former president Kuniwo Nakamura, agreed that of all groups stranded on Babeldaob the Japanese civilians had the worst time. "Palauans knew how to fish, gather, and farm. The civilians knew none of these things."

One cannot discuss this period with Palauan elders without having the name Morikawa-san come up. This near-mythological figure, Morikawa Yoshiyasu, was a 24-year-old captain in the Imperial Army. As directed by headquarters, he walked all over Babeldaob dressed in a white uniform, meeting formally and informally with Palauan natives, imparting information, soothing relations between them and disorderly and abusive soldiers, and urging them to produce as much as possible from their farms. His dignified manner, considerate treatment of Palauans, personal bravery, and mysterious powers gave rise to the most imaginative speculations.

Chobechad ra Eliou Song described him this way: "He walked alone on the *ked* [open grasslands] and on the ridges. He wore white clothes and a scarf, and a white *hajimaki* [headband]. There was a second person also, named Masei, from Ulithi [an atoll northeast of Yap]; he also walked in Babeldaob, was very courageous, and was never shot. He spoke Palauan. They would talk to the women in the sers [gardens], urging them to plant food and prepare for war. The U.S. planes stopped shooting women in the mesei because of Morikawa and Masei and stopped shooting fishermen. This is why we thought they were spies who could communicate with the American forces. Also, we didn't know how they arrived in our village, and they left at night, maybe on a submarine." Her belief that Morikawa caused the reduction in strafing is a common one.

The pillar supporting Morikawa's reputation in Palau is the widespread belief, repeated to me often, that, as the food supplies dwindled, the Japanese army planned to massacre the entire native population in a cave located in the village of Ngatpang. Morikawa is credited with preventing this genocide by convincing his superiors that the native people were more useful to them alive because they could grow crops for themselves and the Japanese forces. Mark Peattie found similar stories of impending slaughter on many other Micronesian islands. Actual massacres did occur on Ocean and Nauru Islands before Japan capitulated.[12]

What has gone unremarked is that Morikawa was not just dealing with isolated cases of friction between troops and the islanders. When headquarters cut off rations to its forced laborers and lower ranks, discipline among these thousands of starving men dissolved. They formed marauding bands, the tōbōsha who harried the Palauan natives constantly for their food, while Inoue and his officers used their ranks and privileges to save themselves. Morikawa's story, however, constitutes a rare memory among the Palauan people of decency and respectful treatment from the military overlords during the crisis of war. Spesungel Ichiro remembered that while dancing the *matamatong* women sang a song in which Morikawa was praised as "a good leader who was very kind and strong."

There is a darker side to the Morikawa story that many Palauan natives do not know, yet others can describe in detail. A program begun by Morikawa and the Imperial Army on Babeldaob has been shrouded in disagreements between its Palauan participants and the Japanese officers who ran it concerning its intent. In 1944 and 1945 the army forcibly conscripted 80 young Palauan men into what those youths testified was a suicide attack force, called *Giyu-Kirikomi-tai*, or Patriotic Shock Corps. They insist that they were trained for guerrilla missions against U.S. forces: to counterattack Peleliu, to help defend Babeldaob, but primarily to sink American vessels anchored in the lagoon several miles northeast of Peleliu. The youths were to paddle wooden boats alongside the ships at night, then attack them with crude gasoline bottle bombs or attach canisters of explosives to their hulls. (These craft were the boats that Daiziro Nakamura's father, Zenhitsi, built for the army.)

Matichau Ilemelong was adamant that the purpose of the training he received was combat. "The plan was for two or three men per canoe to carry a mine to attach to the ship with magnets." He indicated a countertop coffee maker as the size of the mine. "We were told to die with the mine. Sacrifice ourselves to kill many. For us [the operations] would be suicide runs." There is no question that the Palauans—expert swimmers, divers, and boatmen, equally effective at night or day, who knew intimately the islands, waters, and reefs that the boats had to traverse from Babeldaob—were ideal as guides or participants in such missions. At least seven raids occurred, but just one of them is documented after the youths completed their six-month training; so we know of only one Palauan man who joined actual attacks. American vigilance at sea, destruction of the boats by air patrols, and the decline of the health and morale of Inoue's command as starvation and disease ravaged it, all combined to snuff out the Kirikomi-tai runs.

Decades after the war, Captain Morikawa disputed the Palauans' memories, arguing instead that the purpose of the corps was merely to suppress possible "rebellion" among the Palauans or to teach the young men self-defense.[13] New findings, however, strongly support the testimonies of the Palauan participants and their dismissal of Morikawa's version.[14]

Figure 10. The sisters Ungil Besul (left) and Mesiou Matareklai, of Ngerchol, 2003

Through the endless months on Babeldaob the Palauans were disoriented, terrified, and insecure. They could find no explanations for how the fates treated them. As exiles in Ngaraard, the chad ra Beliliou bore a particularly heavy psychological burden. Chief Uchelsias Etibek explained, "Since we were the ones expelled from our homes, we felt we were bringing our suffering to others, and forcing on them a responsibility to feed us." The mechas Ungil Besul said, "We did not understand the politics behind the war, what they were fighting for. We thought the gods of Peleliu were punishing us, so we received this war and misery for things we had done wrong. We prayed every night, trying to keep hope. We hated to be bringing suffering to others in Ngaraard." Andrew Shiro struck a note that sounds often when the islanders discuss their role in the war: "When I was older, after the war, I heard elders say that the Japanese and Americans had their reasons to fight each other, but we Palauans weren't involved, and shouldn't have been put into the middle of it."

Another source of torment for the exiles from Peleliu was the excruciating uncertainty of what was befalling their homeland during the invasion. "Every single day," said Susong Smau, "we thought about our beluu and what was happening to it, how it was being damaged." Ungil Besul said the lack of information was depressing. "We couldn't find out what was happening back home, and we ourselves were caught in this war [on Babeldaob]." They could look south at night to see bright flares and explosions over Peleliu and black smoke rising above it during the day. Karen Walter quotes Fumio Rengiil as saying that these sights convinced them that "Peleliu was no more."[15]

As the weeks turned to months, many Peleliu islanders without relatives in Ngaraard chose to strike out for other Babeldaob villages, ones where their kin resided or where they might find more food or greater safety. In December 1944, while Tokie Morei's husband remained in Klou el Taoch, she walked from Ngaraard to the village of Ngiwal in the cold and mud at night. On December 20, she gave birth to a son. In Ngiwal her kin had very little odoim to eat, making due with occasional mangrove crabs: "Crab soup was a feast." But there was enough ongraol in the form of brak (giant swamp taro), coconuts, and tapioca.

According to Chief Beches Iluches, constant foot and boat traffic moved up and down both coasts of Babeldaob, mostly at night. Dilchuuch Ermang said that eventually Peleliu residents dispersed to every village in Babeldaob as they sought relatives. When Ngaraard ran short of food, she also left for Ngiwal. Her brother Remeliik, father of the first president of Palau, Haruo Remeliik, came up from Ngchesar to visit her there. But when her son grew ill she returned to Ulimang in Ngaraard. The son passed away and was buried in Ulimang. Frequently younger boys and girls had to attend to sick relatives in other villages. Mesiou Matareklai went to Ngaraard with her sister, Ungil Besul, but when their father's relatives weakened in Ngaremlengui she had to return there to care for them. They faced severe hunger, having few gardens and no odoim; they depended on denges and belloi to survive.

The long darkness that seemed endless and inescapable lifted abruptly. The Japanese surrender, announced on August 15, 1945, came as a stunning surprise to the Palauan people. Reiko Kubary learned of it from leaflets that American planes dropped over Babeldaob. Spesungel Ichiro learned through an announcement from the Japanese military. "The message did not say that Japan had lost, just that the fighting was stopped." Judge Morei learned from Lieutenant Hachisu, who was training his group of Kirikomi-tai. "I was awakened at 4:00 a.m. 'The Japanese emperor announced the end of the war,' Hachisu said. Everybody was happy." Summoned by High Chief Ibedul, Morei walked from Ngaraard to Koror. "Along the way the Japanese said, 'Onegaishimasu' (Please take care of us). Our positions were now reversed."[16]

The steady decline in relations between colonizer and wards prompted by the military buildup of the late 1930s had accelerated under the oppressive and brutal behavior of the armed forces during the war. Yet until almost the end the islanders had remained attached to their colonial rulers. "Palauans were not enemies of the Japanese. We were loyal to them and they knew that," said Ambassador Nakamura. Scores of Palauan men willingly served in the war effort in locations as scattered as Indonesia and New Guinea. At least 19 of these volunteers gave their lives in this service; their names are inscribed on a monument at the site of Koror's once-great Shinto shrine, the Nan'yō Jinja.[17]

Many of the Palauan people were saddened when the United States shipped all Japanese nationals back to their home islands following the official surrender on September 2, 1945. But many were also relieved to see them go. For decades Japan had drilled into the islanders the conviction that the empire was all powerful and that their proper role was obedience to authority and gratitude for blessings received. Giving up their lands and ways of life, they had been told, was their small contribution to the glory of the empire and its god-like leader. They had been assured that Japan could never be defeated in war, and that Palau was fortunate to assist in the inevitable victory. Now they felt betrayed and even foolish for having been duped by such cant. They had seen their overlords dressed in rags, crawling on the ground to catch snakes and lizards to eat.

In the end Japan's great Pacific adventure brought Palau destruction, starvation, misery, and death. While the geopolitics behind the war, its strategy and tactics, might have remained a mystery to many Palauans, they had no trouble concluding that it was Japan that brought the scourge of war to their islands and was now leaving them to face a cloudy future as dependents of yet another foreign power—the fourth in 60 years. As time passed, they would distinguish the benefits brought by the Nan'yō era from the horrors of the war, separate their good times with kindly Japanese colonists from their humiliations at the hands of thugs. In talking with them, I encountered subtle and nuanced and often ambivalent memories. The sharp contrast between the bustling modernization of the Nan'yō period and the 25 years of cataleptic administration that followed America's victory contributed to a nostalgia for Japanese rule that lingered into the 21st century. But in late 1945, as Judge Morei remarked, the world had turned. The confident, often arrogant rulers who claimed the islands in 1914 were unceremoniously booted out as defeated and impoverished refugees. Beches Iluches observed, "The Japanese had no farewell words to us at the end of the war."

How many Palauan natives died in the 17 months of hostilities following the March 1944 air raid? This question is extremely sensitive to the islanders since it involves family misfortunes, which are tightly held as kelulau, whispers, but they did not suffer the wanton bloodbath that some have asserted. They were far better equipped to survive on Babeldaob than any of the Japanese or foreign populations. My collaborators consistently replied, as did Kokichi Ingas, that everybody had been hungry but only a few were killed or died of illness. Similarly, Chief Beches Iluches was emphatic in saying that, despite all the suffering, only small numbers actually died. Three elders shared with me the numbers who perished in their villages of Peleliu, Angaur, and Ngchesar. From this sample and other data, I estimate that out of a population of approximately 5,650, which includes the 147 on Angaur, between 150 and 225 Palauans died within the archipelago from all causes in this period. To these figures must be added the 19 known to have perished while serving abroad. A reasonable estimate, then, is that between 175 and 245 Palauan citizens died during the hostilities. Approximately 65 of these would have been natural deaths, so that the war was responsible for the deaths of between 110 and 180 natives of Palau.

Other populations on Babeldaob fared far worse. Japanese sources document that 5,000 Japanese soldiers and sailors died. A terrible toll also occurred among the Japanese, Okinawan, Korean, and other Asian civilians on Babeldaob: possibly another 5,000 men, women, and children, for a total of 10,000 out of the 50,000 besieged. Starvation and disease caused 80 percent of the deaths in both groups. When the 12,500 Japanese soldiers killed on Peleliu and Angaur are added to that, the 17 months of warfare bring a total of 22,500 Japanese and other Asian deaths in the lost cause of defending Palau. General Inoue should have acknowledged his powerlessness and accepted the American offers of surrender, despite prohibitions against this in Imperial Army doctrine.[18] Certainly the 20,000 Palauan and Asian civilians were bound by no pledge to fight to the death. The 14th Division's command put 50,000 people at risk of annihilation if the war had dragged on to late 1946 or 1947, as many Allied planners expected.[19]

Besides the deaths they suffered, the people of Palau had other losses to reckon as well. The five villages of Ngaraard had suffered heavily from naval shelling and air attacks. Most houses were damaged or destroyed. All the old bai were wrecked, taking with them their pictorial histories and centuries of memories. Stone walkways, bridges, and piers had been smashed. Koror, the once-beautiful capital of the Nan'yō colony, lay in ruins. The infrastructure that had been built under Japanese rule and the numerous enterprises had collapsed. Like victims of the war around the globe, the people of Palau faced the prospect of slow, expensive rebuilding. The major economic and political decisions affecting them, however, would be out of their hands. Americans, a people they knew nothing about and whose language only a handful could speak, would determine Palau's path from now on.

Yet nothing could dampen the relief at being spared. "We had a huge party, with dancing, singing, and feasting," recalled Tokie Morei. Her husband brought her 50 pounds of salt, a treasure. Families reunited and took stock of their situations while nervously waiting for the Americans to appear and assert their wills as the victors. In a few cases Palauans avenged themselves on Japanese individuals. Andrew Shiro believed that Palauan natives killed a small number of them after the fighting stopped, and Kokichi Ingas told me they definitely beat some out of vengeance.

Brotherhood and Gratitude

In scores of my conversations with the elders of Peleliu concerning the Nan'yō era and the war, certain memories almost invariably arose: the fondly remembered and deeply rooted village life involving klobak councils, social occasions, fishing, and farming from the late 1920s and early 1930s; the mixed blessings of the cultural and economic impact of the Japanese presence; the equally mixed attitudes toward these able but haughty rulers; the dislocations caused by the seizing of lands; the unexpected arrival of war, bringing terror, flight, hunger, and misery; and, again and again, the deepest, most sincere gratitude to the other Palauan villages, whose people jeopardized their own survival to offer the chad ra Beliliou shelter and relief. Foremost among these, always, stand the people of Ngaraard. "They are our brothers," Chief Obak of Ngerdelolk told me. Uchelsias Etibek said simply, "We are like one beluu." His wife, Mellomes, recalled that her parents told her "never to forget that the people of Ngaraard were the only ones to take us in when we needed a place to stay."

According to Chief Beches, when lives had settled into the routines of peace, the Peleliu islanders returned to Ngaraard to celebrate their relationship with a great intervillage feast, a *klechedaol*. This word comes from *mengedaol*, meaning to bless and commemorate, to make something holy; these feasts are an explicit form of public commemoration. The two villages gathered at the site of the Bai ra Ngaruau in Ngebuked village for an important act of collective memory. Here they erected a stone marker, an olangch, to evoke the gratitude of the chad ra Beliliou for the salvation offered them by the inhabitants of Ngaraard. They inscribed on it the date 1945 and the legend "Odesangel Bad," the stone of Odesangel, using the ancient name for Peleliu. This unimposing stone, the remaining stone platforms of the vanished bai, and the stone paths of the old village now constitute a protected historic site of the Republic of Palau.[20]

The klechedaol continues at five- to ten-year intervals, alternately hosted by each beluu. Nero describes a klechedaol in Peleliu from 1985.[21] These ceremonies provide the occasion to renew friendships, recall the past and compare experiences, and teach history to the younger generations. Lasting for two or three days, they feature historical reminisces, feasting, dancing, and singing. New songs and chants are composed and performed for each of the celebrations. One occurred on Peleliu in 2006 on the anniversary of the invasion, September 15. Iyechang Isaac Bai of Ngaraard explained that the five chiefs of Ngaraard each brought two baskets of betel nut and ten of kukau as gifts to the people of Peleliu. And they brought two things more—olangch: five coconut plants, *lius*, as a symbol of the five villages of Ngaraard and Peleliu, and a basaltic stone. Village historians related their

Figure 11. Julius Temengil points to the inscription on the Odesangel Bad in Ngebuked village, Ngaraard, 2003

respective experiences, chesols (chants) were sung by each beluu, and dancing and feasting lasted throughout the night. The five lius were planted the next day and the stone set in a temporary location, as new olangch to reaffirm relationships and teach those too young to have experienced the war.

That Peleliu villagers interred their relatives in Ngaraard during the war is highly significant to both beluu. An essential part of Palauans' attachment to place, to the matriline's lands, stems from the presence there of ancestors who are buried in the odesongel or other burial grounds. Nero observes that "by burying the dead of another clan, a host clan acquired a close relationship to the descendants of the deceased." Parmentier prints a postwar song from Peleliu that praises Ngaraard and cites the graves of ancestors there as the motivation for the friendship.[22]

Elders from both beluu remembered many songs and chesols being composed after the war to tell its harrowing tales. The great majority of these seem to have faded away, along with the men and women who experienced the war firsthand. The mechas of Peleliu sang one of these songs, dating to the 1940s or 1950s, as they danced at the annual Ochelotel Fair in Koror in October 2003. As a Palau-wide dancing competition, it was the ideal setting for Peleliu to once again express its thanks to those who stood by the island in its time of need. (The Palauan lyrics appear first, followed by their English translation.)

Odesangel

Odesangel a silechel bad, e chelecha eng mesisichang, loikab el tukekla chimal, le
Belau a silisichii.
Erenguul ma Belias a mlei, Ngotel ma Ongedechuul, ma Imeiungs ma Ngerbungs a mlei, tulekisak el smisichak.
Melekeo re chedam a di mekedung e di medenge chelebuul, Oldiais e ma Kiueluul a mlei, me te ngilsukak e smisichak.
Kerradel ma Rteluul e ma Ngedebuul ma Edeaur a mlei, suliu re ngak a diak kubes, er chelechal mo remedad el rak.

Beliliou (Odesangel) was very ill and bedridden, but now she is getting stronger. She can brace her arms and raise herself out of bed because the whole of Belau made her strong.
Koror (Erenguul) and Airai (Belias) came; Ngatpang (Ngotel) and Ngardmau (Ongedechuul), Ngaremlengui (Imeungs) and Aimeliik (Ngerbungs) came, and they woke me up and gave me strength.
Melekeok (Melekeo, Ngetelngal), your people are virtuous and know what it means when others are suffering. Ngchesar (Oldiais) and Ngiwal (Kiueluul) came. They helped me and made me strong.
Ngaraard (Kerradel) and Ngerchelong (Rteluul), Kayangel (Ngedebuul) and Angaur (Edeaur) came. I will never forget your care for me, from now and throughout the future, forever.

6
An Island Desolated, a Trust Betrayed, 1946–1994

The Devastation of Peleliu

On September 2, 1945, the same day Japan formally surrendered to the Allies aboard the USS *Missouri* in Tokyo Bay, Lieutenant General Inoue Sadae, the Japanese area commander of Palau, surrendered his forces on Palau and Yap to Brigadier General F. P. Rogers, U.S. Marine Corps, the island commander of Peleliu. Inoue surrendered approximately 24,900 military men and 9,750 Japanese and Asian civilians in Palau.

Dorothy Richard writes, "Crops already planted on Babeldaob were used to feed the captured garrison. Displaced Palauans whom the Japanese had held captive on Babeldaob were removed to their home islands during September. The occupation problem was complicated by the fact that large numbers of Japanese desired to remain in the Palaus." These were probably from the 6,600 surviving residents who had come to prewar Palau as Nan'yō officials and immigrants. Some did leave their children behind with Palauan families.[1]

Expulsion of all Japanese military and civilians in Palau began in October. Daiziro Nakamura said that when his mother, Aliil, decided the entire family would accompany their father to the homeland, their ship, possibly the last one, left in February 1946. Four years later Aliil secured permission from MacArthur's office in Tokyo to return to Peleliu with the father and all the children.

Because Peleliu was still a functioning naval base, its residents were not allowed to return home, despite their frantic desire to learn what had happened to the island during the battle. In early 1946 the U.S. Navy took 60 men of Peleliu to the island to have them prepare living quarters for the return of their families. Chobechad ra Eliou Song said that these men sent word back to Ngaraard describing the extent of the disaster on Peleliu and warning the people that they would have to rebuild everything.

The residents remaining on Babeldaob gradually gathered at a compound, established by the American authorities, at Renrak, a portion of Airai near today's Koror-Babeldaob bridge. Dilchuuch Ermang recalled arriving at Renrak on April 24, 1946, over eight months after the fighting stopped. The American medics were giving shots of penicillin so exuberantly that people joked that they dared not bend over without first assuring that there was no medic behind them.

More men were sent to work on Peleliu during the spring of 1946, and then finally the women and children were sent home in what people recalled as three separate waves, in June, July, and August 1946.[2] The U.S. Navy had established settlements for everybody at the north end of the island, the largest one being Kloulklubed, by the former site of Ngerchol village. Every family was given a Quonset hut to live in, but nobody was allowed to resettle on the sites of their former beluu, and because the base was active, at first residents were not permitted to even visit the sites of Ngerkeyukl and Teliu. Only those working for the military were allowed to travel to the southern and eastern portions of the island. Chief Obaklechol Ichiro Blesam recalled, "Before the war we lived all over the island, but the U.S. banned us from moving around or living elsewhere on the island. They were saving the land for their base, so they restricted people to the north."

Once they arrived home, the chad ra Beliliou were stunned at what they encountered. Peleliu was transformed beyond recognition, from two separate causes. First was the furious battle, in which tons of munitions and extravagant use of flame had defoliated great tracts of the island's landscape and destroyed almost every structure that had existed before the battle. Second were the massive construction projects the U.S. Navy had embarked on to create a multipurpose military base from which to continue the war. Bergerud observes that on larger islands in the South Pacific the war had been localized; natives who lived 15 miles from a scene of heavy fighting might have scarcely known anything was amiss.[3] But the war's impacts were immense throughout the Palauan archipelago, especially on the two invasion sites, Peleliu and Angaur. Aerial photos of Peleliu (figure 12) show vast areas stripped of vegetation, especially the mountains where the battle raged the longest. They also show U.S. facilities covering the entire southern half of the island: an expanded airfield, hangars, warehouses, roads cut through forest and farms, Quonset huts laid in rows, the new harbor dredged through the reef of Teliu. The American military had appropriated whatever they wanted of the island's land, beaches, reefs, and waters for their purposes, without regard for anything that had been there before.[4]

Ungil Besul Matareklai of Ngerchol came home in the second wave of families. Her reaction was typical: "We simply could not recognize Peleliu from all the damage it had received. There was no forest left, only white coral; everything looked burned over. All the plants and trees were gone. All the homes had been leveled,

Figure 12. The U.S. Navy base on Peleliu, June 1945, looking southeast. Invasion beaches and a boat harbor cut through the reef on the right. Military construction has obliterated the sites of Ngesias, Ngerkeyukl, and Teliu. (National Archives and Records Administration, U.S. Archives 80-G-346234)

with only some Japanese buildings left. Everything was white, crushed coral. We came up to Kloulklubed but didn't recognize the area, we couldn't find our homes. We eventually found some sers and mesei and did some planting. But we had to rely on the American *haikyu* (charity, handouts), American food, like Spam."

Chief Uchelsias Etibek Shmull of Ngesias debarked at the new harbor, which the United States had gouged out of the reef fronting Teliu, called today Camp Beck. "As we passed along the shore of the island we couldn't see any trees; we could see across the island to the mountains. Because all the trees were gone, we could see all the way to Angaur from Elochel [the northern tip of Peleliu]. There was no more food on Peleliu, no gardens. But we had houses, the Quonset huts from the Americans, so we felt glad for that."

Spesungel Ichiro Dingilius said that when he arrived on Peleliu "the island was all white, like a dinner plate; you had to wear sunglasses. They took me to an American supply room, where a soldier gestured toward a bin of sunglasses, and so I took a pair. He smiled and grabbed a handful of them and told me to take them all. But my village of Ngesias was totally destroyed. The bai of Itoi was beautiful, but it was destroyed in the war." Koichi Wong compared the whiteness to snow, which he saw when he later attended college in the United States. Reiko Kubary's vessel steamed down the eastern side of the island. "There wasn't a single tree; the mountains were so white you had to wear sunglasses. All the mechas and rubak were just quiet at seeing their motherland so torn up, all bare, with no vegetation. Yet they were so glad to be back in Peleliu, their home beluu. So people were crying, trying to find their old home sites, yet relieved too."

It is not strictly true that not a single tree remained, of course. Many I spoke with used the same Palauan phrase ("Ng kmal diak a tal kerrekar") not as literal truth but for emphasis. Richard Gettell, a marine who had fought in the battle and then stayed on the island until September 1946, recalled that the deforestation was "a lot worse in the southern half of the island than in the north, though it occurred everywhere to some degree." Aerial photos confirm this. Similarly, the statement that Angaur was visible from Elochel occurs so often that one suspects that it was repeated until it was incorporated into the collective memory of the war.

Chief Obaklechol Ichiro, who had survived the sinking of his vessel in the air raid of March 1944, walked over the site of what had been his village of Ngerchol. He could find nothing. The site was flatter than it had been, its low hills gone; its topography had been leveled by bulldozers. He tried to locate the village's symbolic heart, the odesongel of the rubak bai Ibesachel. Before the invasion he had seen Japanese soldiers using stones from various odesongel for their own fortifications and using the bai for living quarters. Now he could find no remnant of the odesongel of Ibesachel. "I couldn't tell if they had removed it or destroyed the site or buried it; there was just nothing left. Everything was flattened, just sand and a few big trees; most other vegetation was gone." Dirribukel Ngirametuker recalled, "We wondered at first where we actually were. People felt sad at losing their mesei; it was terrible to lose their homes and lands. We didn't even have bathing water so we had to bathe in the mesei that were left." This sense of disorientation, of being unable to locate home, village, and burial sites, was particularly troubling to people who had known the geography of their island so intimately.

I asked Diltpak Merkii Napoleon, sister of my Palauan mother, Aliil, whether people had felt angry at what had happened. As a relative, she was less constrained in discussions with me than were other Palauans. Her reply exhibited the one flare of impatience I encountered from anyone I spoke with in all my interviewing. She snapped, "Of course we were angry. You people destroyed everything we had!"

Dirribukel, sitting with us, sought to soothe things: "Most of us felt angry because the Japanese started the war and didn't know how strong the Americans would be; [their miscalculations] wrecked our island."

Many elders shared the reactions that Reiko Kubary described above: shock and bewilderment at what had befallen their island but simultaneously deep relief that they were no longer dependent on the charity of villages on Babeldaob. People felt genuine gratitude toward the beluu that accommodated them during the war, but they also described the discomfort and frictions that built up during the year of terror and hunger. Chief Obaklechol Ichiro recalled how awkward it had been to live a prolonged time in other beluu with differing customs and ways of life (apparent even during wartime). People from Peleliu inevitably felt like interlopers, he said, of a lower rank, eating others' food during a time of extreme shortages. "For reasons like this, we were glad to return home." A mechas said of the return, "We felt happy and sad at the same time. Sad at the devastation, but happy to be on our home island again, finally." Ungil Besul recalled, "We gave thanks to the gods for our return to Peleliu and for having the nice homes that the U.S. gave us. This was so much better than the terrible year on Babeldaob."

When allowed, people fanned out across the island to survey their villages, homes, beaches, and gardens. Everywhere they found desolation and military construction smothering their most precious sites. All five villages with their bai, homes, and boathouses had completely disappeared. Cemeteries and burial odesongel of the homes of ranking kin members had vanished, taking with them the living connections individuals and kin groups felt with their ancestors. If the identity and strength of a lineage ultimately rested on its long-validated claim to certain lands, which were valuable in specific Palauan terms—for their productivity, for their location in the heart of the village or along the shore, for the myths attending them, for the ancestors resting within them—then what did it mean when those lands were cratered, burned, buried under roads of crushed coral, covered by strange buildings, when no sign remained of the village of which they had been a vital part?

Dirasechedui Mellomes Shmull said the people of Teliu had been restricted from seeing their village while the soldiers were still active, but they were eventually allowed to make a short visit. They cried at what they found. "Where are our houses? *Chedil, chedil*, there's where our house was, everything is scraped off. How can we come back and live here? There are no trees, just buildings all over our lands. All the odesongel and cemeteries, gone, wiped clean." The important sites of the Modekngei religion, the blai lius and its stone, had disappeared.

The one significant object left nearly intact from Peleliu's 3,000 years of Palauan occupation was the odesongel of the bai Ngermelulau in Ngerdelolk village. It was damaged, but the villagers restored the large platform to its former size. Elsewhere, olangch of every description, including burial odesongel, carved stone figures, and man-made and natural objects of every kind, had vanished. Surprisingly, a few small house odesongel remained identifiable beyond Cheuatel ridge in Ngerkeyukl. But the clam shell, croton tree, bamboo, and shining stone—the olangch for the legend of the four rubak who brought Palau its political structure of four corner post chiefs—were never found. When Matichau Ilemelong told of searching for them after the war, I mentioned the havoc American naval shelling had brought to the Ngerkeyukl shoreline. Research colleague Bouwel Iekar found the perfect word for their likely fate: "They must have been pulverized," he said.

The olangch with the strongest emotional grip were the burial odesongel. "We felt very bad because the houses had the odesongel, with our ancestors, but now we couldn't even find them," said Dirribukel Ngirametuker. "Now there are no more odesongel on Peleliu. The young don't even know what they are. We feel we lost something that we knew used to be there." Mesiou Matareklai concurred: "You couldn't even tell where important things were. The odesongel that could tell the stories are gone, except for the one in Ngerdelolk." Susong Smau explained, "When we lost the odesongel of the house or of the bai, it separated us from our ancestors. So now we have trouble talking to our children, because there's nothing to show them any longer. We can talk about the past, but it's not the same. The bai is gone."

On D-day the marines on the beaches had great trouble orienting themselves to their maps. The shelling "had leveled everything along the beach. Landmarks had disappeared."[5] The olangch that performed the most practical function for villagers had been those stones, trees, and mounds that marked the boundaries of people's lands. These were Palauan metes and bounds, just like the European method of marking boundaries with stones, a practice the Pilgrims brought to Massachusetts Bay.[6] The elders' despair arose from both the shockingly unrecognizable landscape and their inability to orient themselves through the boundary markers. One of the major causes of the land disputes that bedevil Peleliu to this day is the war's obliteration of these landmarks.

Knowledge of the ancestors and the skill to decode the layered stories of other olangch were an important source of power for titled elders. The loss of lands and olangch, these physical correlates of histories, abruptly cut people off from large parts of their pasts. The battle, then, had been not just the newest stratum of history laid down on the previous 3,000 years' worth. Instead, the war abraded much of the history that had come before. The islanders retained what they had brought back to Peleliu in their memories, but they had lost the way of life in which their connection to specific sites and objects made those memories richly meaningful. The war had stolen from them their sense of continuity with their forbears and the expectation that they would preserve that shared life and pass it down intact to their children.

It was not only the human landscape that was ravaged. As people surveyed the natural environment they grew somber, for they realized that they had lost most of the means of livelihood on their tropical island. The Japanese and American militaries had burnt forests, scraped away the fragile topsoil of gardens and paved them over, filled and paved mesei, littered beaches with mines and debris, and massively damaged reefs. The flat limestone areas of Peleliu not developed as part of the airfield were typically capped with crushed limestone. On Peleliu and Angaur "practically all level land was utilized for various operations and for storage and encampment."[7]

Peleliu—an island, described by scientists as among the most fragile of environments, the most vulnerable to disturbance—had suffered ecological catastrophe. Cato the Elder exhorted the Roman Senate for years to crush Rome's rival, the city-state of Carthage. "Carthago delenda est," he declared repeatedly: "Carthage must be destroyed." When Rome's legions finally conquered the city they burned it to the ground and plowed salt into the soil so that it could never recover. Japan and the United States did not intend to treat Peleliu in the same way, but in fact they did, right down to the poisoning of the soil—*and* the coastal waters.

One mechas described how, after arriving, they anxiously awaited the opportunity to check their gardens and mesei. When they finally reached them, they were crestfallen to find many of the mesei paved over for roadways, and many others severely damaged by explosives. Some of the craters, visible to this day, rendered the mesei "too deep to plant brak, kukau, or anything." Teliu's mesei no longer existed, buried beneath the runways. Those of Ngesias by the Omleblochel Mountains were ruined by the fierce fighting in that area. But military construction brought one unintended benefit to Peleliu's women: the causeway carrying the road through the swamp between Ngesias and Ngerdelolk created a large wetland in which brak, although not the choice kukau, could be planted. Women from all over the island now use this Beches el Mesei, new mesei (see figure 5).

Whether Peleliu's garden soils have recovered their prewar fertility remains contentious today. Peleliu, as a raised limestone makatea island, was never very fertile. Most plant life grows within a thin layer of topsoil created by eroded limestone and leaf litter. Many elders insisted that Peleliu had quite good soils, at least in some places. Others were less enthusiastic about the prewar situation. But all agreed that what they found in 1946 was a disaster for a people whose survival depended on horticulture. Most gardens were simply gone, scraped away and built over. Tanks and vehicles had flattened whatever farms and forested areas had survived the shelling and burning. Visitors can still see tread marks across the island's hard limestone surface. In many locations the vegetative cycle had been broken. The trees and plants, with their seeds, were now removed, and the litter that sustains seeds was burned or buried under crushed coral.

The much-remarked whiteness of the island derived from two distinct phenomena. One was the stripping away of vegetation, revealing the barren limestone that forms the geologic platform of Peleliu. The other was the ubiquitous residue left by white phosphorous munitions. Karen Walter writes, "Nothing was green but instead was powdery white. White phosphorous from incendiary shells and flares coated everything." The narration of the American video *The Bloody Ridges of Peleliu* states, "The landscape was burned free of vegetation and scarred white by thousands of phosphorous shells. One Marine thought it must look like 'the face of the moon.'" White phosphorous, "WP," had been used profligately by the American forces for flares during nighttime (which the Palauan refugees had seen over the island from Babeldaob); for smoke screens to cover daylight assaults; and as yet another form of incendiary munition.[8]

It is the harshest of ironies that Japanese enterprises had gouged phosphates out of Peleliu's hills and shipped them to Japan for fertilizer, while the American invaders returned a different form of the chemical to the island as a scorching weapon and a thick sediment that polluted soils and water. It must have been detrimental to human health if contacted regularly. "WP," however, was just the most visible of the many pollutants and toxins that coated Peleliu. A short list would have to include petroleum products ranging from napalm to fuels and lubricating oils; high explosives; solvents, paints, and thinners; massive amounts of DDT mixed with diesel oil;[9] herbicides; and vast quantities of lead from bullets. All industrial chemicals would have been used and disposed of with the carelessness that war encourages.

Then of course, the residents had to learn to live with the tens of thousands of rounds of unexploded ordnance that littered the island. The United States did try to remove the largest and worst of the munitions in the immediate aftermath of the fighting. But a truly comprehensive, island-wide cleanup has never been made. Residents succumbed to the temptation to use leftover explosives for fishing, resulting in many accidents that maimed or killed. Munitions became unstable as time passed, making them even riskier to move. Oyama Ngiraloi of Ngerkeyukl and Ngerchol complained that there is still much ordnance lying on people's lands today.[10]

Robin DeMeo, a resource conservationist with the U.S. Natural Resource Conservation Service, surveyed Peleliu during the drought of 1998. Wildfires blazed on the island, and she heard what she thought was gunfire. She then realized it was wartime ammunition baking off. She asked the U.S. military what it would cost to clean up Peleliu and Angaur (and all of Palau for that matter). The reply was that the military would perform site cleanup as necessary—meaning that if a hotel were planned, its immediate site would be scoured. She contends that both Japan and the United States still have the obligation to perform a better cleanup of Palau. Her report states that, despite the nitrates and phosphates left on Peleliu from explosives, by the late 1990s the levels of these chemicals fell within ranges for similar soils elsewhere.[11]

Chief Uchelsias Etibek said that the war's biggest impact was its effect on fishing grounds. "It destroyed the area [where] the kelat (milkfish) spawned, along with many beaches and reefs. Before, our nets would catch all we wanted, right close to the beach. The channel by Ngercheu was a good place where we would cast nets, get one school, and end up missing a second school while we cleaned the first out of our nets. After the war this never recovered. The beach changed and I think the food of the fish was depleted, so their numbers never recovered."

Postol Remeliik, former Speaker of the Peleliu Legislature, comes from Ngerkeyukl. He said, in contrast, that fish were generally plentiful in the postwar. "But certain areas of fishing grounds, around Ngerkeyukl and Teliu, eating the fish from there would make you sick, especially the fish closer to shore. This was not true of the deep-water fish, just the reef fish. They made people nauseated, but we didn't know why." The reefs off these two beluu, of course, were those that bore the brunt of the amphibious invasion and its immense volumes of shelling and boat traffic.

Several who shared their recollections, among them Chiefs Obaklechol Ichiro and Obak Isao Singeo, Fuanny Blunt, and Oyama Ngiraloi, said that a fundamental change occurred to the reefs off Peleliu's shores. Prior to the battle the reef flats were white sand; but afterward the bottom changed to a dark, muddy silt, and a type of seaweed began to grow thickly. The species of fish changed and their numbers declined. (But some men remarked that overfishing *since* the war has led to declines in populations as well.) It is possible that the sediment on the reefs resulted from soils and debris washing off the denuded landscape during rains. Older men also pointed out that, with the forests shattered as they were in 1946, they could find no trees large enough to use for making canoes. The men had no alternate means of going to sea to fish. They could only fish from inshore.[12]

Navy Time

The U.S. Navy, meanwhile, regarded the islanders as refugees who had to be fed, clothed, and housed, but whose presence could not interfere with the functioning of the naval base, which still had a "sizable contingent of troops, probably larger than that on Angaur," according to Rich Gettell. The Americans' generosity in attending to the needs of the population, and their respectful treatment of everybody, went far in salving the psychic blows that buffeted the despondent islanders as they surveyed their losses, and left warm memories of what is recalled as "Navy Time."

There is not much to laugh at in considering the lives of the chad ra Beliliou from 1936 to 1946, but it is truly entertaining to see the enjoyment (and self-deprecation) with which they describe their reactions to the great waves of material goods that washed over them when they became wards of the navy. Six decades later people still expressed astonishment and amusement at the undreamed of quantities of houses, food, clothing, vehicles, tools, materials, medical care, jobs, and movies that poured out of the cornucopia of the American war machine. The impact was all the greater for its contrast with the destitution and starvation that had been their lot for the previous two years. "They lived like kings," Spesungel Ichiro told me with a grin.

Unwittingly, the Americans touched the core of Palauan social relations, food exchange, by providing them with copious amounts of food.[13] The navy fed the entire population three meals a day in the mess hall, all they could eat of every item, with buckets of ice cream for dessert. A people whose diet normally consisted of fish, with the occasional piece of fatty pork a rare treat, gorged themselves on unlimited quantities of foods they had never heard of: potatoes, spaghetti, fruits, vegetables, beef, and lamb. Throughout Micronesia, the introduction to Spam, that dietary blight of Oceania, occurred at this time. "Not those little cans you see today," one man told me, "but like this"—he couldn't suppress a smile as he extended an arm out horizontally and marked the length to his shoulder with his other hand, the method Micronesians use to indicate the length of a *really* big fish. Laden as it was with fat and salt, Spam must have tasted like ambrosia after the scarcities on Babeldaob. The handouts of clothing and personal items, from pants and shirts to shoes and hats, from toothbrushes to mirrors, followed the pattern Spesungel Ichiro had encountered with the dark glasses: do not take only what you need or can wear at one time, take handfuls, stacks, multiples of everything. People became giddy with surfeit.

Most seemed to like living in the Quonset huts. They had been assigned according to village, as people preferred, and the families appreciated the comfort and privacy after the months of dependency. "We were glad to have a place to stay of our own and glad for the plentiful U.S. food after all the hunger," one mechas observed. But the chad ra Beliliou had never before all lived in one community like this; it was a new and disconcerting experience and served to remind them every day that they had not truly returned to their home beluu. Smau Amalei Ngirngesang pointed out a subtle loss from the months of mess hall meals. In the beluu the preparation of food and its consumption had provided the opportunity for families to speak together, and for elders to explain clan matters and important news to the young. The prepared food and the lack of privacy in the mess halls discouraged family discussions at a time when they were badly needed.

People's initial reactions to the Americans included amazement at their height, the size of their feet, and how they sunburned "like lobsters." Overall the Peleliu residents' relations with the new rulers ran smoothly. Men had ample employment on the base, and many women found jobs as maids for the wives of officers. Navy personnel treated the islanders with far more respect than they had received from all but a few colonists under Japanese rule. One mechas played tennis with the woman she worked for on the courts built, of all places, on the Point, Ongebitel Ream, in Ngerkeyukl. Not surprisingly, romances flourished. "There were lots of love affairs once we got to know Americans," said another. "That's why that one beach is called Honeymoon Beach."

As they had done during the Nan'yō period, many islanders admired the power of the new authority, and many embraced the abundance and novelty of the new life. In John Useem's report on Palau published the year of the return, he took pains to explain to military officials how the Palauan people feared losing the advances they had enjoyed during the Japanese era: "The people of Palau are impatient to resume the historic process of change so successfully directed by the Japanese. . . . There is anxiety that [America may abandon Palau] and . . . Palau [will] revert to conditions which prevailed prior to the coming of the foreigner. Palau people are not only eager to progress, but to do so more rapidly than other island groups in Micronesia."[14]

As broad and "essentializing" as Useem's observations sound today, few in Palau would dispute their accuracy: the natives *were* interested in acquiring the benefits of the modern world, and their competitive nature was well-known.[15] Thirty years of exposure to Japanese development and education had whetted Palauan appetites for the outside world. That the United States could overwhelm the all-powerful Japanese made the new rulers all the more attractive. The Peleliu islanders take pride in having been the first to establish close friendships with the conquerers of the once-mighty Nan'yō and to acquire the trappings of the new American-style modernity. The island's goodwill toward the United States is caught by a popular song of today, "U.S.P.," which stands for "The United States of Peleliu." It refers to its dancers as "soldiers" and, in contrast to the humility of the song of gratitude sung by the women at the Palau fair, "U.S.P." boldly asserts that Peleliu as a village has raised up the rest of Palau.

Tokie Morei's troubled recollection of this period revealed the difficulties people grappled with after the war. "We'd had a great struggle and so much hunger during the year on Babeldaob. But when we returned we got beds, plates, things we'd never had before. And we got caught up in all this; everything was new and attractive. But we missed the old life where we could plant tapioca and taro in our yards easily." Although this was not the first time they had faced change among opportunities brought from outside, the magnitude and the abruptness of the disruptions the chad ra Beliliou had endured since the building of the airfield were staggering. By 1948, not only was their island painfully foreign, their roles as social beings were reversed: they were now guests in their own home, dependent on the hospitality of people who, however friendly and generous, had taken over Peleliu as theirs.

While it remained open between 1946 and May 1948, the U.S. Naval Base at Peleliu dominated life on the island even as its forces were reduced to about 110 men and 35 dependents. The chad ra Beliliou lived in their Quonset huts, received their three meals a day, and were prohibited from visiting much of the island. Many retained jobs and enjoyed the income that allowed them to purchase the consumer goods still available in the PX. They were, however, in Fran Hezel's phrase, strangers in their own land.

The quiet routine was shaken in April 1947 by the discovery of a group of 34 Japanese stragglers who had hidden within a swamp along the western coast for two and a half years. The men—22 from the army, eight from the navy, and four civilians—had raided American supplies and occasionally skirmished with U.S. naval guards, but had maintained remarkable discipline under an army lieutenant, Yamaguchi Ei. U.S. authorities knew that a few Japanese holdouts remained at large. Richard Gettell, who was stationed on Peleliu for a year after the invasion, said that when a U.S. serviceman disappeared it was assumed he had been killed while souvenir hunting. Lieutenant Yamaguchi agreed to surrender after a Japanese seaman presented him with letters from Japan assuring him the war had ended. A sign along the west road today marks the men's hiding place.[16]

As the navy wound the base down, the bulk of the surplus materiel was turned over to a scrap company that employed civilian Chinese workers. Many islanders, who argued the residents better deserved the tons of equipment, vehicles, and supplies, believed it was shipped off to Chiang Kai-shek's Chinese Nationalist forces. In 1947 the United States exhumed the bodies of American soldiers from the Orange Beach cemetery and returned them to the men's families or reburied them, many at the lovely American military cemetery in Manila. Many Palauans expressed disappointment to me that the bodies were removed. From the Palauan perspective, their presence on the island represented a special bond with the United States, like that formed with Ngaraard.[17]

Strategic Trust

Immediately after the war the possibility that Micronesia might become a U.S. territory was very real. The power of the triumphant United States now stretched unchallenged across the Pacific to Asia's shores, and as the Cold War deepened American vital interests were defined to include Japan (occupied until 1952), Korea, Taiwan, and the Philippines, who would be granted independence in 1946 but would cede basing rights to the United States. This was an empire in the time of the United Nations, enforced less by the jingle of spurs and the crash of boots than through immense economic influence and a near-monopoly on military power. The language of security alliances and economic stability, however, never quite masked how the power arrangements invariably served the interests of the United States.

The strategic value of the Micronesian islands was obvious. Walter McDougall writes that the new Pentagon expected to swallow the entire central Pacific. "Had 'these atolls, these island harbors,' said Admiral [Ernest] King, not 'been paid for by the sacrifice of American blood'?" Robert Kiste calls this the "blood in the sand" argument. He quotes a naval officer who said about the Marianas, "Military control of these islands is essential. . . . [Development of their few] inhabitants should be subordinate to the real purpose for which these islands are held."[18] This resolve concerning the military value of Micronesia would anchor American policy in the region throughout the many unpredictable turns of the postwar decades.

The era of decolonization had dawned, however, so in 1947 the United States allowed Micronesia to become one of 11 trust territories established under the auspices of the United Nations. The people of Micronesia were not consulted; they were given no more say in self-determination in 1947 than they had been in 1919. The United States became the administering authority of this U.S. Trust Territory of the Pacific Islands, (USTTPI, or commonly, TT).[19] The United States pledged "to promote the political, economic, social, and educational advancement" of the Micronesian islands and to lead them toward self-government or independence, as chosen by the islanders. However, uniquely among the 11 trusts, the TT was a "strategic trust." America was allowed to use the islands for any military purpose it deemed necessary for international peace and security and to close off the islands for security reasons. The TT's affairs were handled not in the U.N. General Assembly like those of the other 10 territories, but in the Security Council, where America had veto power. And, uniquely, the trust agreement, including termination, could not be altered without the consent of the United States. Although American officials strenuously denied it, like the Japanese Mandate before it, the TT was a colony, lightly camouflaged. For most of the trust's 47 years, American administrations, whether Democratic or Republican, would manage it as if the United States were both the trustee *and* the beneficiary.[20]

Even before establishment of the TT, a heavy military burden had fallen on certain parts of Micronesia. Islands—small, distant from population centers, easy to seal off, containing insignificant populations themselves—made perfect sites for military experiments or clandestine activity. From 1946 to 1958 the United States held 66 nuclear tests on Bikini and Enewetak (Eniwetok) Atolls in the Marshalls and built Kwajalein into what it remains today, a test site for antimissile development. A secret CIA base for training Chinese nationalists to return to mainland China operated on Saipan until 1962. Otherwise the Pentagon did not construct facilities in Micronesia but maintained a firm policy of "denial": no other nation would be allowed military access to the Trust Territory. Micronesia was closed to civilian traffic as well.[21]

Robert Kiste writes of U.S. administration in the TT, "Except for strategic concerns, there was no overall policy." The inattentive trustee administered the islands with an annual budget ceiling of $7.5 million, unmoved by the frustration in Micronesia as years, then generations, of stagnation piled up.[22] Initially the Americans vaguely promoted economic "self-sufficiency," a return to subsistence farming and fishing with some handicraft production. Palauans and the Chamorros of the Marianas, both of whom had most deeply participated in the Nan'yō's wage economy and sought connections to the outside world, particularly disliked this policy. The TT did have its successes: schools and hospitals were built, scarce government jobs opened in capital towns like Koror, all districts offered 12 years of education through at least one free public high school. The Micronesian people were steadily given positions of administrative authority; they had held no office higher than policemen in the Japanese era. Nor did the United States permit the waves of foreign immigration that had swamped the Micronesian islands in the Nan'yō years. But far into the 1960s infrastructure deteriorated and no economic development worthy of the name occurred. The most valuable export from Palau remained scrap metal from the war, sold mostly to Japan. The government offered a tiny number of highly prized college scholarships, which went exclusively to men. Elizabeth Nakamura pointed out, "My husband [Tosiwo Nakamura] and his brothers were sent to universities in Hawaii and the Philippines. I was trained to be a telephone operator." Micronesians had no access to outside assistance: tourists were not permitted entry until the mid-1960s; Micronesia was not opened to investment from the United States until 1962, nor from other nations until 1974.[23] Early Peace Corps volunteers to Palau were caught unawares by the many complaints about the Americans' failures to rebuild Koror or create an economy offering jobs for the people of Palau. Contrasts with the vigor of the Nan'yō period were explicit.

Few natives of Micronesia were aware that their futures were being decided in the Pentagon and at the United Nations. The worries of the chad ra Beliliou were much more immediate in the wake of the closing of the island's naval base. The island that had little value to the United States even during war now had no value at all. In a stroke the islanders were deprived of the food, jobs, and imported bounty they had depended on since their return in 1946. The navy had forbidden reconstruction of their villages and made no efforts to rehabilitate their farmlands. No systematic island-wide cleanup of unexploded ordnance had occurred. There would be no Marshall Plan for the ravaged islands of Micronesia. Embittered Palauan observers have skewered Western assumptions that in Europe war destroyed priceless treasures of civilization, while in the Pacific it wrecked only a few thatched huts. In 1948, even meager war reparations lay 25 years in the future. Now the moment Peleliu's residents dreaded had arrived, when they would be thrown back on the diminished resources of their island, in a Palau that was experiencing precisely what John Useem had foreseen: a reversion almost to pre-Nan'yō-era levels of economic activity and public services.

Yuki Shmull, a former governor of Peleliu, remembered, "As kids we weren't aware of the seriousness of the situation on the island. Like elsewhere in Palau, the people felt they had assurances from the Americans that the U.S. would do well by them. Meanwhile, we stayed at Kloulklubed at the urging of the Americans, who said it was convenient for administration." The prewar gardens were damaged and fishing was disrupted—certain species were gone, the reef flats were changed by sea grasses, fish from the invasion beaches tasted bad. "Both the fish and animals were reduced in numbers by the war," said Renguul Kelbasang Soalablai. As mentioned, fishing was made the more difficult since the large trees used to build watercraft had been burned.

Postol Remeliik recalled, "When the U.S. left, then came the worst time, when we had to make it on our own. The soil was poor, the land cleared of topsoil; plants didn't grow well. We were all just getting by, struggling. People were hungry. Food was scarce. Papaya and bananas and chemutii [sweet potato] grew, but only one time, then we had to let the soil recover." Several women discussed the dangers gardeners faced from the unexploded ordnance. Another blow landed when the copra crop was devastated by the coconut beetle.[24]

The chad ra Beliliou badly hoped to return to the sites of their former villages. Postol explained the problems: "Those of Ngerkeyukl, Teliu, and Ngerdelolk wanted to move to their old homelands, but no buildings were there. The buildings were all here in the beluu [Kloulklubed].[25] They didn't seriously consider returning to the homelands until Typhoon Louise [November 1964] brought a chance to move, they thought. Every Quonset in the village was destroyed by this typhoon. People talked of moving, they said this was the time. But [TT officials] came and persuaded them to stay, saying it made it easier to give them water, electricity, etc." In fact, the generating plant and water system left by the navy had long since ceased functioning, casualties of the penurious budgets that characterized the Trust Territory in its first 20 years.

Renguul Kelbasang believed that the biggest impact of war was disruption of the former village life and the residents being concentrated into one locale. "After so many years they've become accustomed to being [in Kloulklubed]," he said. I asked if they were losing connections to their land and past as a result. "The elders were very sad, and it has affected their connection to their roots, to relatives who are buried there," he replied. "The younger generations don't have the same understanding and feeling. I myself feel strongly about the past and would like to be out there."

The Tangle of Land

The most serious obstacle to returning to the old village sites was not simply the need to rebuild everything from scratch. It was the fundamental question of who owned the land on which the villages lay. As the successor to Japan's mandate, the U.S. TT administration claimed all those tracts that Japanese interests had bought or seized on Peleliu for phosphate mining or military operations. As a result, the TT asserted ownership over much of Ngerchol, most of Ngesias, and all of Ngerkeyukl and Teliu. Fortunate Ngerdelolk remained largely intact in the hands of its clans and lineages.

By the mid-1950s, however, some in Palau had begun successfully challenging the TT's land claims. During the early 1960s the TT began what it called a homestead program, under which it eventually returned to Micronesian islanders huge portions of the lands that Japan had seized. In some parts of Palau and Micronesia persons obtained land in true homestead style, by staking claim to government land and improving it. In Peleliu, though, the program simply tried to return lands to the rightful owners.[26]

Exactly what happened with this homestead program is murky and has fallen prey to the sorts of confusion and high emotions that attend most dealings with land in Palau. Two elder chiefs, Obaklechol Ichiro Blesam and Uchelsias Etibek Shmull, said that the TT failed to consult with the rubak of each village concerning how best to return the lands. Postol Remeliik believed that to speed the process the village councils asked that the lands be returned collectively, to the ewaul saus, the four corner post chiefs of each of the five beluu. After that, said Postol, the plan was for individuals and lineages, who owned most of the lands, to sort out claims among themselves using the Japanese land survey, the *tochi daicho*. Balkuu Kumangai, of Palau's Department of Lands and Surveys, said that the TT quitclaimed lands to certain clans and lineages, giving it not to individuals but to the chiefs by their titles as trustees (mengkar). But nothing went smoothly after that.

Wilhelm Marsil, also of the Department Lands and Surveys, pointed out that the surveying of the homesteads was rushed and contained numerous errors, many due to the war's obliteration of the native boundary markers. Further, the tochi daicho often assigned clan lands to a single male elder, without distinguishing whether he was an individual owner or a trustee for those lands. The tochi daicho records for most Palauan beluu, including Peleliu, survived the war and have been considered valid documents in land disputes by the TT and the Republic of Palau. Courts give it less standing in Peleliu since the survey was never completed, and people were never given the chance to contest its results.[27] Finally, sadly, some ewaul saus on Peleliu simply got greedy. Chief Renguul Donald Haruo of Teliu said that some, instead of acting as mengkar, made land claims for themselves based on the tochi daicho.

The TT administration insisted that the numerous disputes over land be adjudicated within the territory's American-style legal system. It never completed its own program to survey and certify lands in Micronesia. Today the republic carries on its own national program to certify ownership of lands. Like all 16 Palauan states, Peleliu has many parcels still to be reviewed. Unresolved disputes—the great majority—go before the courts. An adversarial court system is antithetical to traditional Palauan ways of resolving disputes. In courts families are forced to reveal publicly their deepest secrets, their kelulau, regarding their histories, genealogies, migrations, adoptions, and relationships to other clans of long ago. Judges, whether Palauan or American, are unfamiliar with the lands on which they must rule. The advantage lies with the wealthy, who can afford to hire lawyers for long periods of time. Elders, frustrated with the system, nodded ruefully when I described the cartoon of the lawyer asking a prospective client, "How much justice can you afford?"

On Peleliu the certification process has proceeded furthest at the north end of the island, around Kloulklubed and Ngerchol. In the meantime, one takes great risk in building a home or business on land to which he lacks clear certified title: lose the court case, lose what you built.

While discussing the land tangle, Susong Smau reminded me that the chad ra Beliliou "have kept many important aspects of Palauan life down to today. The structure of clans and lineages, the titles, the chiefs, and so forth. The ranks for men and women are the same, and the *ocheraol* [an event for raising money for a home] and customs are going on." (He could have added that age-ranked men's and women's clubs still function.) Families take pains to teach the young the names of land parcels and the stories attached to them, to keep alive the foundation beneath these institutions. Residents described family gatherings for the purpose of visiting sites and reviewing the lore. Others expressed fears that despite their best efforts, knowledge and histories were inevitably being lost. "If we lose the stories we lose part of the culture, and land is a fundamental building block, so the whole culture could crumble," said Kent Giramur.

Seventy years after the end of World War II the fundamental issue of who owns what land on Peleliu remains in protracted, enervating dispute. The great number of disagreements is evidence itself of the loss of knowledge, as Fuanny Blunt observed. People spoke in sorrow of how so many of the well-informed titleholders, who knew the stories and the conflicting claims from the past, have gone to their graves. The uncertainty of tenure poses the ultimate obstacle to the rebuilding of Peleliu's five traditional villages. The day rapidly approaches when anyone who actually lived in one of them, who remembers what they looked like and how life functioned in them before Japan and the United States changed everything, will be gone.

Reparations, Aid, and Independence under the Compact of Free Association

Not until 1969 did the United States and Japan sign an agreement to provide reparations to the citizens of Micronesia for loss of life, physical injury, and property damage resulting from the hostilities of 1941–45. The Micronesian people were not party to the negotiations. Each country was offered $5 million as ex gratia grants, meaning they were given out of goodwill, not as a matter of right. To this the United States added another $20 million for claims arising during its military administration from 1944 to 1951. The compensation for loss of real property was set at $50 per acre per year. In the end Palau received $5.75 million from the Micronesia Claims Commission, in response to claims valued at $47.7 million.[28]

Reparations became another sore memory from the war. No one on Peleliu was satisfied with the method of payments or their amounts. "The words *ex gratia* are used to duck responsibility, as if we give you money out of goodness," complained Ambassador Daiziro Nakamura. Opinion was uniform that the amounts received were inadequate. Oyama Ngiraloi called them "*bai me kesai*" (far too small). "My father, Itpik, claimed for the Ngisiliong clan of Ngerdelolk," he went on. "He got $88,000 for the whole clan, which he divided among the lineages." Each household would have been lucky to get a few thousand dollars. Regarding the war claims, Chief Obaklechol Ichiro complained that people seldom got even one-third of what they had claimed. Dirasechedui Mellomes brought up the issue before I asked. She called the payments "*ongesonges*," (insufficient). "You couldn't buy anything with it; it wasn't just."[29]

It was also in 1969 that the Congress of Micronesia, a TT-wide legislature of representatives from each of the six districts, opened discussions with the United States on the future political status of the islands. American negotiators revealed that full independence was not what the administering authority had in mind for its strategic trust. The Pentagon was calling the shots. When it announced the lands and waters that it wanted within Palau, the requirements were *potential* access to the Airai airfield, Malakal harbor facilities, and a large area on Babeldaob for troop maneuvers. Peleliu and Angaur, for which the United States had spilled so much blood and treasure in World War II, were ignored. (The United States has exercised none of its options in Palau but has expanded its military facilities on Guam.)

The Marianas split from the rest of Micronesia and accepted status as a commonwealth of the United States in 1975. The Marshalls and Palau also decided to negotiate separately with the United States government, leaving the remaining island groups to form themselves into the Federated States of Micronesia (FSM). In 1979 the Republic of the Marshall Islands (RMI) and FSM formed constitutional governments, followed in 1981 by the Republic of Palau (ROP). All three continued negotiations with the United States for compacts of free association, under which the small republics would grant the Pentagon its demands, deny military access to other states, and be defended by America. They would run their own domestic and foreign affairs. In return they would receive generous payments from the United States.

Palau's constitution models its national government on that of the United States. It has a bicameral legislature, the Olbiil Era Kelulau (OEK), with a House of Delegates and a Senate; a president who heads the executive branch with its various ministries; and a Supreme Court. The main beluu became states, 14 in the main archipelago and two in the Southwest Islands, Sonsorol and Hatohobei. As one of the states, Peleliu has an elected state legislature and a governor exercising executive authority. Power of the purse rests with elected government officials, not the councils of chiefs. In keeping with the traditions of village independence, the 16 states maintain a great deal of autonomy relative to the central government of the ROP; it has been disinclined to lock horns with the states over their traditional prerogatives.

The 1981 constitution contained a clause prohibiting the transit or storage of nuclear materials within Palau. American negotiators demanded this restriction be removed before agreeing to a compact and pushed Palau relentlessly. Large sums of money flowed secretly, while at the same time Palau became an entrepôt for the international drug trade. Finally, after eight plebiscites, Palau signed a compact acceding to the demand and granting the Pentagon options to the lands and waters it had identified.[30] On October 1, 1994, Palau became a sovereign nation freely associated with the United States for 50 years. In the first 15 years, to 2009, Palau would receive payments totaling $602 million.[31] Like the Marshalls and FSM, which negotiated their own compacts with the United States, Palau is a sovereign voting member of the United Nations.

At the request of President Kuniwo Nakamura, of Peleliu, the U.S. Department of Agriculture surveyed the soils of Angaur and Peleliu. The report, mentioned previously, concluded that Peleliu's thin top soils had probably returned to the same quality as before the war and that the forests had regenerated quickly after the fighting, although "the diversity and maturity of the forest and agro-forest ecology took longer to recover."[32] The report's author, Robin DeMeo, explained to me that there is no known scientific study of the quality of the soils or composition of the forests prior to the war and so there was no reliable baseline. As noted previously, however, the issue for horticulture on Peleliu today is not merely the quality of the remaining soils. It also includes the *quantity* of usable soils and taro fields that remained after the massive loss of these subsistence assets from the phosphate mining, the construction of the airfield, the battle, and postwar paving and construction.

Economic activity in Micronesia lagged far behind political developments. The TT was roughly awakened from its 1950s slumber by the U.N. visiting mission of 1961, sent to assess whether the United States was meeting its obligations under the trusteeship. The mission's scathing report embarrassed the United States into raising the annual appropriations from $7.5 million to $60 million by 1971.[33] Yet there was little in the way of recognizable economic development. In Peleliu farming gradually improved as the vegetative cycle recovered, but the island experienced a steady drain of population as people moved to Koror for school or the few wage-paying positions in the government.

In the mid-1960s the United States gradually began opening Micronesia to the outside world, ending 20 years of imposed isolation. Peleliu soon found itself hosting an unexpected, but mostly welcome, flow of visitors from, of all places, Japan. These were not holidaymakers eager to visit tropical paradises, however. They came for a more somber purpose: to visit battle sites where they had lost loved ones, and to collect the remains of their dead in order to give them proper burials. They were the first of the *Ireidan* (ee′-ray-don), visitors who would play a significant role in the lives of the chad ra Beliliou for decades to come.[34] And in the 1980s the number of Japanese tourists who started visiting Palau for recreation, especially its superb scuba diving, climbed steadily.[35]

Once the constitutional government of 1981 was formed, Palau could deal directly with foreign nations. The government of Japan was therefore able to provide direct foreign assistance to Palau (and to the two other sovereign Micronesian states). It proved an eager contributor. The Japan International Cooperation Agency, JICA (rhymes with "mica"), has funded over $200 million worth of projects in Palau. Major projects have included $40 million for electrification of Koror and Babeldaob, $31 million to replace the bridge between these same two islands that collapsed in 1996, and $5.25 million to upgrade the wharf at Elochel in Peleliu.[36]

In Wakako Higuchi's thoughtful article on Japan's war reparations in Micronesia, she raises a number of issues concerning Japan's relationship with the former Nan'yō. She decries Japan's refusal to accept its share of responsibility for the war and sees its cooperation in Micronesia as trying to bury the past rather than confront it. She also asks whether Japan's now generous aid to Micronesia is intended as a form of apology or a form of reparations, as many Palauan people and Japanese officials themselves suggest. She rejects the contention: "The generosity of Japan's [assistance] is admirable but it cannot be interpreted as a substitute for war reparations unless that is publicly stated and accompanied by a sincere apology."[37]

Could Palau reopen the matter of reparations with Japan now that it is independent? Policy makers did not think confrontation would work. Former president Kuniwo Nakamura explained that Japan looks on its aid as gifts, much as Japanese individuals exchange small gifts as tokens of friendship and esteem. Temmy Shmull, a long-serving minister of state, is the son of Chief Uchelsias and Mellomes Shmull. He believes Japan regrets many of its actions in the past and that the aid is sincerely offered. It "comes out of their hearts," as a way of making up for the past. Palau had raised the issue of reparations once, which Japan rebuffed by saying that the issue had been settled under the 1969 agreement. Many natives I spoke with agreed that public shaming of Japan would be counterproductive. At the personal level, however, several said they remind Japanese friends that Japan remains in debt to Palau for damages from the war.

Current and former ROP officials offered carefully considered assessments of Palau's relationship with the two Pacific superpowers, Japan and the United States. As Daiziro Nakamura put it, "Most Palauans recognize that the U.S. and Japan are their main allies." In the postwar period, Japan used "its economic might" to become a dominant state in Asia and the Pacific Islands. Its tourists are one of Palau's two largest markets, and the people of Palau praise them as considerate visitors and careful divers who are sensitive to the islands' ecological fragility. President Nakamura noted that Japan expects from Palau support in certain international arenas, like in the United Nations and the whaling commission, and on fishing issues. "They are appreciative and they reciprocate," someone else told me.

Policy makers are keenly aware of American security concerns in the Pacific and where Palau fits in to those concerns. They argue that Japan and the United States need each other in the Pacific to achieve their goals and that the Micronesian islands remain valuable as possible basing sites close to Asia. One official contrasted the two nations in a way that recalls Henry Kissinger's comments on Americans as cowboys: "The U.S. acts like a powerhouse still. Palau understands this; it likes to beat others at baseball and then strut. The U.S. still has the attitude in Palau that it has bigger things to do, it seems unwilling to take time. It's adventurous, it moves on." The more patient Japanese, however, look for ways to cooperate. "They live with you and blend in more."

Today Palau is a multicultural society, a striking contrast with 40 years ago when the population was entirely made up of natives with a smattering of American TT employees. The compact payments and growth of tourism in the 1990s produced the largest economic boom Palau has experienced since the heady days of the late Nan'yō period. Business opportunities have been concentrated in the urban center of Koror, although the newly completed Babeldaob ring road will open that island to unprecedented development. Most investment comes from Taiwan, Japan, and China. Much of the labor is provided by Asian workers.[38] The United States is relatively underrepresented as an investor, a source of tourists, or even as a governmental presence. "The U.S. lets Palau know what subjects really interest it," as former president Nakamura told me (these have included terrorism and money laundering in recent years). Palau's connections to America, however, remain strong. Taking advantage of terms of the compact that allow ready entrance into the United States, thousands now live, work, and attend school in Guam, Saipan, Hawaii, and the U.S. mainland.

Critics of the compact complain that its flood of money has ignited greed, fostered corruption, and undermined the traditional system, as people ally themselves with profit-driven foreign business partners. In important ways money has indeed acted, in the words of Lionel Trilling, as "the great solvent of the solid fabric of the old society." Many in Palau have sought wealth more as individuals than as members of a corporate lineage or clan. High office in the elective government requires financial backing, tying wealth to power. New elites overshadow the old ones, with traditionalists arguing that the former lack the sense of responsibility for the welfare of one's people that guided chiefs in the past. Attitudes toward land are changing as it assumes the role of a productive asset in business. Elderly titleholders can view offers to sell land as a quick route to riches for themselves, although at the expense of their relatives and descendants. Such pressures on land have been confined mostly to Koror, but with Babeldaob opening up and the Palauan people eager to improve their living standards, tempting opportunities will migrate to the more rural areas.

One could argue that life on Peleliu today is no different from how it would have evolved if the invasion had never occurred. The economy of today is like that of other outer-island beluu, an opportunistic mix of activities. People fish and farm for both subsistence and to sell in markets in Koror. Income also comes from small-scale tourist enterprises (three small resorts oriented toward diving and a fluctuating number of homestays), jobs in the state government, shop keeping, and cultivating marijuana. Peleliu has not yet succeeded in obtaining the share of marine-oriented tourism that it would like, but as discussed below, by the 1970s its battlefield attracted enough visitors to boost the island's economy to some extent. Most homes today are built of cement blocks, have metal roofs, and are hooked up to Kloulklubed's electricity and water system. Local and international telephone service is excellent, and the Palauan people are avidly connected to the Internet. Almost every family has a car or truck for travel on the island's excellent roads, a lasting legacy of the war. A well-furnished new dispensary opened a few years ago. Private speed boats and the village's public boat provide regular communication with Koror.

Like others in Palau, many on Peleliu receive remittances from employed family members living in Koror or abroad. Palau's best business opportunities continue to cluster in Koror, the center of government, education, and tourism, where 70 percent of the archipelago's population now lives. Throughout Palau, once youngsters finish the eighth grade they move to Koror for high school, then on to Palau Community College, jobs in Koror, or work or college off-island. With so many living in the urban center for school and work, Peleliu is typical of the beluu in the way its resident population tends to be very young—attending grade school—and elderly, with relatively few residents between 20 and 50 years of age. The 2000 census showed Peleliu had 571 residents in 135 households; by 2005 there were 702 persons living in 191 households. This increase may reflect the progress in sorting out land titles that has occurred. But in 2005 there were also 1,600 persons whose mothers were born on Peleliu (remember that descent is reckoned matrilineally), and many more women who consider themselves chad ra Beliliou would have been born in the hospital in Koror in recent decades. With 1,600 Palauans living on Guam and Saipan, perhaps 1,000 in Hawaii, and up to 3,000 living on the U.S. mainland at any given time, there may be 1,800 to 2,000 chad ra Beliliou today.[39]

Despite its similarities with the other beluu, Peleliu's history remains significantly different from most of them. Except for Angaur and parts of Koror, the other villages of Palau retained their physical layouts, infrastructure, and sociopolitical and ecological integrity at war's end. Thus, in ensuing decades they were better able to control the degree and pace of change that they accepted. They gradually reduced their subsistence farming and fishing as the young departed to Koror for school and work and the cash economy expanded. They have let mesei and farmland go out of production, but unlike Peleliu, they did not lose huge portions of their home sites and farms to wartime construction. The Babeldaob villages were able to make deliberate decisions that affected their appearance and way of life, such as choosing whether to turn stone village paths into roadways for automobiles. Some rebuilt traditional style bai; most have not.

The chad ra Beliliou never had the chance to participate in such decisions for themselves. The departure of the U.S. Navy in mid-1948 led to a precipitous decline in the residents' standard of living, as they suddenly had to survive on their own but barely retained the means to do so. Reconstructing the lost villages was hampered in many ways. Even if the TT had promptly returned the lands it held—about half the island's total—the villages could not have been rebuilt easily given the scale of damage to their sites and farmlands and the postwar lack of capital and materials. But the naval administrators squelched the best opportunity the people had of rebuilding and recovering what they had lost. Right after the war, with motivation high and knowledge of the old ways secure, the islanders might have been able to lay out the prewar villages to the extent possible and work out among themselves the uncertainties involving land boundaries and ownership. They could then have exercised better control over the surveys for the homestead program. Opposition from military, then civil, administrations, however, spilled the wind from the villagers' sails, sapped their determination, and allowed the confusing and alien legal system to assert its authority in deciding who owned what.

III
Pursuing Memory

7
Retrieving the Dead

> Oh! ye whose dead lie buried beneath the green grass; who standing among flowers can say—here lies my beloved; ye know not the desolation that broods in bosoms like these. What bitter blanks in those black-bordered marbles which cover no ashes!
>
> Ishmael, musing on marble cenotaphs (tablets naming sailors lost at sea) in a whalemen's chapel, New Bedford, Massachusetts.
>
> Melville, *Moby-Dick*, ch. 7.

This chapter begins the portion of the book that examines the return of Japanese and American servicemen and civilians to Peleliu to commemorate their experiences from World War II. The discussion compares their memories of the battle with each other and with those of the chad ra Beliliou. Peleliu provides a tightly focused setting to follow James Young's suggestion that historical inquiry should combine study of "both what happened and how it is passed down to us."[1] Close observation of the monuments, relics, ceremonies, and activities of visitors attracted to Peleliu for its wartime past reveals much about the three people's disparate memories and how they conceive of the war.

The earliest visitors to Peleliu were Japanese Ireidan (visitors for commemorative purposes), who came to retrieve the bones of their nation's 11,000 dead. Initially most Ireidan were relatives of dead soldiers, but many did, and still do, arrive with political agendas. The diverse ideological and political demands of the Ireidan, pressed insistently for decades, have been the primary force shaping commemoration on Peleliu.

Not until 40 years after the battle, and 20 years after Ireidan had begun excavating caves, did U.S. Marine veterans erect their first monument. These veterans quickly claimed primacy in defining the interests and official memory of the United States on Peleliu. They found support from the U.S. government when the National Park Service began exploring the feasibility of a formal battlefield park on Peleliu in the 1980s—an effort that came to naught but that has been revived in a form more acceptable to the islanders. As the more accessible bones have mostly been retrieved, and American veterans have passed on, Japanese and American tourism on Peleliu has gradually modulated. The younger generations, who arrive for day tours, lack the fervor or grief that motivated their elders. The notable exceptions are zealots of the Japanese nationalist Right, some determined to comb the island for the very last bone, some intent on surreptitiously turning Peleliu and Palau into memorials to the lost days of imperial glory.

This array of visitors has made it impossible for the chad ra Beliliou to put the war behind them. They have had to accept, host, and negotiate with an endless stream of foreigners, even as these foreigners treat them and their wartime past with slight regard. The observation of Peleliu resident Kent Giramur captures the situation. "The war is still going between the Japanese and Americans but in another way. You see them racing to put up monuments, racing to give us assistance, so they're still trying to compete against each other, to conquer Peleliu's heart. It's better, far better, than using a rifle or bayonet. But both always come here for their own reasons."

Japanese Memories of World War II

Among the major combatant nations, Japan is widely viewed as having made the least progress in coming to grips with its role as an aggressor in the Second World War. Even as the 60th anniversary of the war's end approached in the spring of 2005, Japan was fiercely rebuked by China and South Korea for what these neighbors saw as its continuing refusal to accept its responsibility for instigating the war or to acknowledge its brutal wartime behavior.

On this occasion, two hot button issues relating to Japanese war memory were involved. First was release of a new set of government-approved school textbooks that critics argued sanitized or obscured Japanese aggression and atrocities. (For decades Japan's textbooks have oscillated between editions that acknowledged Japan's role as aggressor and those that avoided the topic or denied blame.) Second was another visit by the prime minister, Koizumi Junichiro, to Yasukuni Shrine in Tokyo. Yasukuni is a Shinto shrine where the nation's war dead are not only honored but worshiped—including those convicted of war crimes and executed by the Allies after the war. Yasukuni was the head shrine of the prewar militaristic imperial cult of State Shinto, which glorified the emperor as divine. Asian nations that suffered under Japanese colonialism, particularly China and Korea, have protested every such visit by a prime minister.[2]

Other sources of tension between Japan and its Asian neighbors include Japan's refusal to compensate the "comfort women," Asian women used as sex slaves by Japanese armed forces; the tiny amounts paid as reparations to foreign nations; and the perceived failure of the national government to offer a clear, heartfelt apology for Japan's wartime actions—failures made all the worse when contrasted with Germany's many symbolic and practical acts of sincere contrition.[3]

After some years of quiet, the election of Abe Shinzo as prime minister in late 2012 again threw open the bag of winds of Asian war remembrance. Members of Abe's radically nationalist cabinet advocated revising textbooks to deny most of Japan's wartime atrocities and reconsidering apologies Japan had previously made for its aggression and abuse of comfort women. In late 2013 Abe visited Yasukuni Shrine, provoking denunciations from China and Asian neighbors, and even a public rebuke from the United States, which badly wants its allies in the region unified against Chinese expansion. A Japanese government unrepentant over its wartime behavior makes such unity much harder to achieve.

These diplomatic uproars suggest that the Japanese people uniformly refuse to confront their wartime past. This is most certainly not the case. The Japanese public actually exhibits a wide range of attitudes toward World War II and debates them frequently and vigorously.[4]

John W. Dower, considered the dean of American scholars of 20th-century Japan, singles out five kinds of war memory shaping popular consciousness in Japan. The first denies Japan's aggression by reviving wartime propaganda that asserted the country fought only to defend the homeland and expel Western imperialism from Asia. A second stream evokes moral (or immoral) equivalence by emphasizing examples of Allied cruelty, like the dropping of the atomic bombs—"as if," Dower observes, "the transgressions of others exonerate one's own crimes."[5] Third is an acute sense of victim consciousness for having suffered the firebombing of 64 cities and the atomic destruction of two more. The fourth highlights the active participation by the United States in scrubbing away many Japanese war crimes when Japan became valuable as an ally in the Cold War. For example, when the American occupation astonished the Japanese people by leaving Emperor Hirohito on the throne, the sovereign, the wartime supreme military commander, became the symbol of *non*responsibility.

Fifth, however, are popular discourses that do acknowledge war guilt and responsibility. Public discussion opened up further after Hirohito's death in 1989, and Japan's expanding relationship with China forced confronting the imperial "debaucheries" of the China War. Jane Yamazaki demonstrates that Japanese government officials have also offered sincere apologies for the nation's conduct, only to have them undercut by actions of the Diet or visits to Yasukuni Shrine or threats from successor governments to withdraw the previous apologies.[6]

Franziska Seraphim points out that, again in contrast to Germany, the Japanese government has failed to provide leadership in public discussions of Japan's role in the war. Because of this vacuum, Seraphim writes in her illuminating study, the "making and negotiating of public [war] memory took place largely on the middle level of the political process"—at the level of citizens' groups, most of which organized as special interests.[7] The debate over the war goes on actively and heatedly among these special interests, which vie for government favor and support. She examines five such civic groups, whose political positions range from the reactionary Association of Shinto Shrines to leftist pacifists.

One of the most influential of these organizations is the *Nihon Izokukai*, the

Japan Association of War-bereaved Families. It lobbies the government for pensions for those who lost family in the war and for state-sponsored (instead of private) ceremonies for the war dead at Yasukuni Shrine. It has opposed "categorical" or "unequivocal" apologies for Japan's aggression and atrocities.[8] It also collects remains of Japanese war dead from foreign battlefields and conducts ceremonies in their honor. This group has been active on Peleliu since the late 1960s.

Seraphim explains the connections between the location of pressure groups in the Japanese political spectrum and their attitudes toward the war. The Left is often pacifist and wants the government to apologize clearly and compensate victims in Asia. In the center, the Japan Teachers' Union wants school textbooks to forthrightly acknowledge the wartime aggression. The Right (including Nihon Izokukai) denies that Japan was an aggressor or owes redress to its victims; it wants the nation's dead to be remembered as heroes and Yasukuni to be publicly funded. At its extremes, the Right dreams of a reversion to an emperor-based polity where he is again worshiped as a Shinto god. Right-wing principles have received sympathy from the national government during the long postwar dominance of the conservative Liberal Democratic Party.

Core principles of the nationalist Right today include considering the emperor a semisacred figure, the parent of the national family; elaborating the prewar religion, State Shinto, in which the nation itself is an object of worship; and promoting notions of a Japanese racial purity and exclusive national identity. Rightists vehemently deny events like the Nanjing Massacre, reject victims' claims for restitution, and resist calls for formal apologies. The Right has developed intimate links with organized crime (*yakuza*) and professional corporate extortionists (*sokaiya*) and engages in "extortion, intimidation, and political corruption under cover of legal protections afforded to political organizations."[9]

Japan's many discordant views of World War II have been exported abroad, and, once familiar with common topics and idioms in Japanese war memory, the observer can discern these clashing opinions in the memorials and activities and ceremonies performed on Peleliu.

Bones

No tourists of any kind were allowed into the Trust Territory by the American administration until the mid-1960s. In 1965 Funasaka Hiroshi became one of the first Japanese citizens allowed in Palau since World War II. When he was there, he visited the battlefields on Angaur and Peleliu. He was a former sergeant in the Imperial Japanese Army who was severely wounded in the battle for Angaur and captured by the American troops. On his return to Angaur, 21 years after his unit was annihilated, he tells what made him weep: "It was the bones, bones, bones—left just as they had fallen during the fierce fighting."[10] His comrades' dying requests were that their bones be returned to the homeland so their spirits could dwell at Yasukuni Shrine. Funasaka returned to Palau many times and says that he collected over 1,300 remains with the help of islanders. He was the first of the Ireidan to visit Peleliu and influenced Japanese tourism to the island for many years afterward.

John Dower captures the emotional difficulty facing Japanese regarding the two million men who died fighting for Japan, so vivid in Funasaka's anguish. In Dower's Pulitzer Prize-winning history of Japan's immediate postwar, *Embracing Defeat*, in a chapter titled "What Do You Tell the Dead When You Lose?" he writes, "Where the victors focused on Japan's guilt vis-à-vis other countries and peoples, the Japanese were overwhelmed by grief and guilt toward their own dead countrymen. The victors could comfort the souls of their dead, and console themselves, by reporting that the outcome of the war had been great and good. . . . Triumph gave a measure of closure to grief. Defeat left the meaning of these war deaths . . . raw and open."[11]

Mark Peattie describes how after the war others from Japan, like Funasaka, found a solution for the tens of thousands of skeletons of war dead scattered across Micronesia, "made imperative by the Buddhist tradition of setting at peace the souls of the dead by appropriate funerary ceremonies and cremation of human remains." With support from Japan's Ministry of Health and Welfare, starting in 1968 the Nihon Izokukai sent annual missions, composed mostly of relatives of those killed and Buddhist priests, to Micronesian sites to collect and burn the remains. The "melancholy task went on, until all the known sites were sifted, the souls of the dead set at rest."[12]

If the searches have concluded in most of Micronesia, on Peleliu the hunt for remains continues to this day because of several factors unique to the island. One is the great number of undisturbed caves, littered with skeletons, which lay hidden in the mountains behind dense jungle. Many of them were sealed by U.S. bulldozers during the battle. Fearful of the spirits of the unburied dead, few islanders entered any caves in the decades after the war. Peleliu is also distinctive for its lack of urbanization since the war. In contrast, population growth and rapid development of facilities for mass tourism transformed the battle sites of Guam and Saipan in the 1970s and 1980s.[13] (Of the other Micronesian invasion sites, Kwajalein in the Marshall Islands is closed to the public as a U.S. missile testing base. Enewetak has been unattractive to tourists since the United States used it for atomic tests after the war. Tinian's battlefield was thoroughly disrupted by the American airfields constructed for the B-29 campaign against Japanese cities.)

The distraught search for remains does not go unchallenged by other Japanese individuals or organizations, some of whom, as discussed below, argue that it is time to stop, to let the past go. Peattie's eloquent summary also leaves out today's

Figure 13. Site of the village of Ngerkeyukl, 1968

complex relationship between Japanese visitors and the islanders. On Peleliu, residents have several times withdrawn permission for Ireidan to remove bones, which has strained relations and prompted efforts by the highest levels of Japanese officialdom to influence Peleliu's leadership.

Dr. Minoru Ueki, son of a Palauan mother and a Japanese father, explained that two main groups began coming in the 1960s. One was soldiers (mostly survivors from Babeldaob) who had been repatriated to Japan from Palau; the other was relatives of the dead on Peleliu and Angaur. Prominent among the latter were *Izokukai* organizations from the prefectures that were home to most soldiers of the 14th Division—Ibaraki, Gunma, and Tochigi. Dr. Ueki began a tourist service to assist these early Ireidan. Ueki said about Funasaka, "Like all the people, he was curious to see where he'd been in the army and what had happened to Palau since. The visitors developed the idea to collect bones after they saw all the caves filled with them." The Japanese government obtained permission from the TT to begin regular trips into Micronesia. "They came quite regularly after that. . . . After the first few groups they negotiated the bone collecting, and then planned to build memorials for those who died. They took the bones to Japan from both Peleliu and Angaur."

In 1967 the Japan Youth Group to Collect the Remains of the War Dead was formed. It worked in tandem with the youth section of Izokukai and the Health and Welfare Ministry. Their first trip outside Japan was to Peleliu in 1968. They visited many other locales subsequently in the Pacific Islands and Asia.[14]

Mayumi Keibo provided lodging for the Ireidan who came to Peleliu. She remembered that the first group of Ireidan "were high officials from the wartime, and they knew what battalion had been located where on the island during the fighting, so they helped the relatives locate the probable sites where their men would have been fighting." She said that Funasaka first came to Peleliu in 1965, after which he started regularly escorting groups of Ireidan, mostly Izokukai, to the island. They collected bones, which, if not taken directly to Japan, were burned at the cemetery. The ashes were either returned to Japan or placed in memorials at the cemetery.

Other Japanese and Okinawan tourists also began returning to Palau, civilians who had lived there as immigrants under the Nan'yō. As of 2014, the *Nihon Kikanshikai*, or Okinawan Repatriation Organization, still visits every September. Its members hold several days of ceremonies and festivities in Koror and visit Peleliu to pray for the dead. Okinawans, who are Japanese nationals, appear to have made efforts at collecting remains separate from those led by Funasaka and the early pioneers. One does not hear much about Korean tourists coming to Peleliu or Palau for commemorative purposes, although recently they have become far more visible in this regard; 19,000 traveled to Palau as tourists in 2012.[15]

For the Ireidan, then, Peleliu was not an alluring tropical island or even a curiosity of former empire in the South Seas. Its beaches, reefs, and waters held little interest. Peleliu was, rather, the most poignant of sacred ground, the place where loved ones went to their doom in valiant defense of the emperor and nation. On such a small island (Guam is 40 times larger, Saipan 17), with the 11,000 dead concentrated in hidden but unmolested caves, bereaved families pleaded with American authorities and the residents of Peleliu to allow them to climb the tangled slopes so they could release their sons and fathers to their eternal rest.

In the stagnant economy of Peleliu in the 1960s and early 1970s, the Ireidan became the primary source of income and the most visible connection to the outside world. Some chad ra Beliliou voiced concern that if the Japanese took away all the bones, then they would end their visits, which would curtail the tourism and with it the best source of cash the island had seen since the closing of the naval base.

Dr. Ueki explained: "The older ones on Peleliu would allow taking bones and building monuments; they became friends with the Japanese who came. But the young officials and governors had it in mind that if they take all the bones away they won't come back to visit. So leave them here and allow them to come visit frequently to develop tourism. The old people understood, in Palauan culture if you die abroad we bring you home to bury in our own land. The young had a different motive, not that they didn't understand the cultural need, but the elders knew these Japanese come to pray. They allowed them to build the monuments so they could pray there."

Olikong ra Tikei Kokichi Ingas of Ngerkeyukl told me the important story of what unfolded as a result of these competing views. "The Peleliu state legislature passed a law sometime in the late 1960s prohibiting the taking away of bones from the island. The state government then had a meeting with Japanese [officials] about being allowed to come collect bones. The Japanese said to the people of Peleliu, 'These are the bones of our sons and brothers, we must take them back to Japan.' The people replied, 'No, they fought and died here and their bones should remain here.' The Japanese replied, 'Let us take the bones. Their blood will always remain behind.'" (Here is the "blood in the sands" argument from the Japanese perspective.)

"In 1970," Kokichi continued, "a member of the Japanese Diet, Nakamura Kishiro, came to Peleliu and invited a delegation of Peleliu's leaders to Japan." Chiefs of each beluu accepted, along with the respected Peleliu magistrate Saburo Ngirablai. Kokichi represented Ngerkeyukl. All spoke the Japanese language, Saburo the best of all. They were given VIP treatment in a trip that lasted 22 days.

At the visit's climax they were ushered before a high Diet official whose intention was to plea for removal of the prohibition against repatriating remains. But, for the first time, the Peleliu leadership had a chance to confront high officials of the Japanese government as their equals. The interview got off to an embarrassing start. Kokichi recalled,

> Kishiro introduced us to him but he asked, "How can I talk to these people?" assuming we couldn't speak Japanese. So he was surprised to learn all of us could speak it very well. Saburo asked him a straight question, not a silly one: "I wasn't here so I don't know, but did you Japanese and Americans get an invitation from us to come fight on our island of Peleliu? You destroyed everything and then went away and left us with nothing." [The official] took a long pause, then said, "It was not my decision, it was the Japanese government and the U.S. But Japan went to Palau and that's why the war came to Peleliu." Saburo said, "We on Peleliu are very poor now because of the war. When it was over and we went back, there was no more tapioca, taro, anything. So we had to eat American food like soldiers, but when they left we had nothing, because when the Chinese came they took the food, the equipment, and everything."

The chiefs gave the official a huge turtle shell with their names written inside, and received a gift of $10,000 for Peleliu.

The visit failed to resolve the deadlock over bones. There has never been a definitive resolution to the matter. During the period of my research Governor Timarong Sisior, who grew up in the Nan'yō era and labored for the army, allowed the Japanese to collect and burn remains on the island. The ROP's Historic Preservation Office has entered the fray, objecting to opening caves because they are historic resources. Yet in 2007 Japan's chargé d'affaires, Nakamura Kunio, bluntly told me that his country's overriding interest in Peleliu was recovering wartime human remains. Chad ra Beliliou know they walk a fine line in their dealings with Japan. They do not want their countrymen to accuse them of jeopardizing the goodwill and generous support the republic receives from this important ally.

The Ireidan numbers grew steadily in the 1970s and 1980s. Some groups reached 50 or more. Many women came to Peleliu, widows or mothers of lost soldiers. Sympathetic mechas of the island established friendships with these visitors, particularly those who came multiple times. And as Palau slowly grew wealthier, Palauan women's clubs were able to make reciprocal visits to Japan.

While few residents drew distinctions among the Ireidan, in fact they were a mixed lot politically. Many had no particular political bent but wanted to walk the ground where their loved ones had lost their lives. Many were members of the conservative pressure group Nihon Izokukai. Some were committed pacifists. Organizations of the far Right were attracted to the island and made generous gifts to the villagers to preserve access. Eventually, agents of Japan's Ministry of Health and Welfare (H&W) objected to these private efforts to control Japanese relations with Peleliu and to define Japanese war memory on the island. Ministry officials insisted that the only proper relationship was one of government to government. The greatest friction, according to well-informed Palauan sources, arose between H&W and Ireidan of the extreme Right. One resident of Peleliu described a furious argument that broke out between a Japanese official from H&W and Namekawa Yuji, the leader of the very active and reactionary Shintoist organization that calls itself Seiryusha. The official insisted that Seiryusha should cease its activities and defer to the leadership of the government. So fiercely did Namekawa reject this claim that the two men almost came to blows.

Mayumi Keibo described how Namekawa and Funasaka Hiroshi made a documentary showing vast amounts of bones in Peleliu's caves after H&W personnel had announced that all accessible remains had been gathered. She said that the film caused an uproar and worsened relations between the Right and the government over Peleliu. Olikong ra Tikei Kokichi remembered Funasaka as trying to establish himself as the national leader of the Ireidan and Izokukai trips to Palau. Perhaps because he was accused of shady financial transactions, the Japanese government also asserted its rights with him in the recovery of remains. "The government representatives pointed out that the men who died there did so for Japan, for its government." In response, Funasaka reduced his activities. It is a measure of Funasaka's politics that Mishima Yukio, the renowned ultranationalist author, wrote the introduction to *Falling Blossoms* (*Eirei no Zekkyō*), Funasaka's memoir of his fighting on Angaur.

An uncomfortable divide separates some of those in Palau who descend from a Japanese father or grandfather from those who do not. (Palauan elders recalled only a single instance in which a Japanese woman married a Palauan man.) Those of mixed ancestry are more likely to maintain knowledge of the Japanese language and to follow Japanese customs or cultural elements like patrilineal descent. Language facility is a key. Few Japanese tourists speak English, the second language of all Palauans under age 70. These families of Japanese descent were best positioned to establish business relationships with Japanese investors and tourists who arrived in the 1960s and 1970s. Some on Peleliu complained that the Japanese visitors who came to the island were monopolized by families that have such ancestral ties.

In September 2003 work parties spruced up the island before a visit from an advance party of Japanese officials, who were surveying possible sites for Emperor Akihito to visit in Micronesia. Some residents told me they refused to work on behalf of the Japanese who "were so mean to us" and "who were planning to kill our grandparents in Ngatpang in that big hole." One woman told me, "Some made fun of the half castes, saying, 'He's your *Tennō Heika* [emperor], you clean up the village.'" In their first visit to a foreign battlefield, Emperor Akihito and Empress Michiko visited not Palau but Saipan in June 2005, where they paid tribute to Japanese, American, islander, and Korean dead. The stop at Saipan's Korean memorial was an unscheduled addition to the itinerary, probably in response to the protests of that spring and to ease pressure from the island's Korean community. At this stop, no photographs were allowed. As we shall see, to the delight of many, the emperor and empress did come to Peleliu a decade later to pay their respects to the war dead there and on Angaur.[16]

When American veterans and tourists began coming to Peleliu in the 1980s and 1990s, different local families, more comfortable with speaking English and less friendly to Japan, sought to cater to them. Meanwhile, the island also developed small diving and fishing resorts to try to capture a share of the main tourism to Palau, those who come for diving. But Koror has remained the center of what is now Palau's economic mainstay, foreign tourism.

Stones of Memory

To those individuals and nations who participate in war, battlefields become, as Edward Linenthal notes, sacred ground.[17] They can induce a powerful attachment to place, as the site where the veteran fought bravely, where family travels to remember a lost relative, or the state honors men who sacrificed on its behalf. On

Peleliu, this proprietary sense among foreigners collides with that of the islanders who live there and trace their past far beyond the events of World War II.

Neatly groomed cemeteries and memorials avoid the obvious fact that the dead perished while dealing death to others. Battlefields cannot ignore this, so attention turns to the heroism of the fighters, to their loyalty and sense of duty. Knowledge that their lives were cut short elicits the need to believe they did not die in vain.

Most war commemoration occurs within a nation's boundaries and reflects its domestic debates and priorities, and the outcome of its competitions for public voice. Usually combatant states vigorously attempt to mold war memory for their purposes, using monuments as particularly emotional and potent symbols. The government of Japan has declined to take the lead in either defining a national memory of World War II or erecting memorials at home or on Peleliu. Yet it has constructed more memorials on the island than has its American counterpart. The Republic of Palau (ROP) does not see itself as custodian of Palauan war memory, but it strives to accommodate the interests of its two influential allies.[18]

Monuments are erected by those who hold the power and resources to do so. Levinson's study *Written in Stone* examines "how those with political power within a given society organize public space to convey (and thus to teach the public) desired political lessons."[19] Monuments represent the *politics* of memory in a high-stakes contest to see whose version of events will prevail. They can therefore be sources of virulent disagreement: witness the Vietnam Memorial in the United States. Frequently made of stone, monuments are literally lapidary pronouncements, meant to last the abrasions of time. If Pacific people are "primitive" in their historical markers—trees, stones—what is the atavistic impulse that goads people everywhere to employ stone to mark a place as sacred?

The primary function of monuments is to consecrate, to honor, and thus to offer consolation. They are unlikely to be pedagogic as well. As Buruma puts it, "In a memorial, ceremony and analysis simply don't mix."[20] Context and explanations must instead be sought in books and museums. Monuments thus offer striking examples of what is *not* said. Their inscriptions are reticent, guarded, often evasive. At Peleliu, silences are notable on who bears responsibility for the war and this battle, on the taking of native lands, and the destruction of the local way of life. The texts admit of no close examination of the war, not its geopolitical, diplomatic, or economic contexts, nor its morality or the manner in which it was fought. Monuments' eliding of unpleasant truths serves the purposes of both adversaries. Their inscriptions in fact share the brevity and tendentiousness of Palauan history telling, which, as observed previously, is "partial" in both senses of the word.

Memorials' invocations of emotions like grief, pride, and vengeance also drive away historical analysis or searches for cause and effect. They dissuade us from asking probing questions. What arrays of power and ambition brought two nations to commit bloodshed on this scale on such a remote and tiny island? What were the consequences for *all* those affected by the conflict? What are the lessons for us who view the stones and plaques generations later? Ideally a memorial should serve as an inspiration to seek broader explanations and deeper interpretations—exactly how olangch function in Palau, intended to send the viewer off to find the knowledgeable persons who can decode the symbol and provide meaning.

Japanese Commemoration on Peleliu: Freedom of Maneuver

With war memory so controversial in Japan, attempts to build a museum or memorial within the home islands dedicated to the war era frequently ignite opposition to the interpretive stance proposed for the structure. Political forces on both the Left and Right are quick to mobilize and complain. Xiaohua Ma writes that museums have been more bitterly contested within Japan even than have history textbooks. Peace Osaka, a museum devoted to presenting an open-minded view of Japan's wartime aggression and commemorating its victims in Asia, opened in 1991 and begat a nationwide boom in peace museums. Nationalists, however, angrily objected to what they considered a "masochistic" view of history and in time managed to trim some of Osaka's exhibits.[21]

The peace museums and almost all other activities commemorating World War II in Japan have been funded by private organizations or by local governments. After erecting a memorial to Japan's Unknown Soldier in the 1950s, the central government remained on the sidelines for decades. So when it finally proposed to build the Shōwa-kan, a national museum dedicated to Japan's wartime experiences, the project received intense scrutiny. (Shōwa is the name given to Emperor Hirohito's reign, 1926 to 1989.) Liberal groups criticized the role Nihon Izokukai played behind the scenes to define the museum's mission as honoring Japan's fallen soldiers and their bereaved kin. The outcry forced repeated revisions of content and design, so by the time the facility opened in 1999 anything controversial had been excised. The watered-down message became one of victimhood and suffering, shared by Japanese and Asian populations alike.[22]

The most visible storm of World War II memorial politics in the United States occurred in 1994–95, when the Smithsonian Institution was forced to cancel its proposed exhibit on the Hiroshima bombing after conservatives, veterans, and members of Congress objected to the plan to display the bomb's effects on the people on whom it was dropped.[23]

Japan's central government built its first war monument on Peleliu in 1967 and a second, the island's largest, in 1985. There are several reasons why both public and private Japanese organizations have favored foreign sites for commemoration. Memorial activities on a remote battleground like Peleliu faced little threat of the crossfire from domestic activists that greeted controversial projects at home. Nor, in the Pacific, did the government face the stern protests from increasingly assertive China and South Korea that greeted the prime ministers' provocative visits to Yasukuni Shrine or maladroit comments on war-related issues back home.

Palau offered its own set of advantages regarding memorial activities. Although Peleliu's policy on collecting human remains has fluctuated across the years, the island has had no policy at all concerning memorial ceremonies or monuments. Neither the ROP nor the Peleliu state government has interfered with the purpose, size, design, location, or message of any structure erected on the island. The people of Palau are usually friendly toward Japanese visitors, and some are even nostalgic for the Nan'yō days. This is decidedly not the case on Guam, for example, where the Chamorro natives deeply resent the abuses suffered at Japanese hands during the 33 months of occupation during the war.[24] Palau's residents exhibit both their customary sympathy for anyone seeking to bury his dead and their customary reticence toward the private actions and stories of others, which means tolerance for public or private ceremonies and for the messages on stones or plaques. This freedom to speak to a select audience and to build contributes significantly to Peleliu's attractiveness to Ireidan. Because of this freedom, Japanese activities and memorials on Peleliu are also unusually revealing.

Despite the passage of 70 years, Peleliu has no formal battlefield park and has just begun taking steps to protect its major wartime historical resources. The small museum opened by the islanders on the 60th anniversary of the invasion in September 2004 contains rusted and worn relics from the battle sites, fascinating photos and letters donated by visitors, but has no interpretive exhibits. For now, the most visible and tangible aid to memory on Peleliu is the island's impressive array of monuments. Most are of modest size, the great majority built by Japanese interests. The Japanese government has built only the two described above. The U.S. federal government has erected only one, a plaque from 1985 declaring the entire island to be the Peleliu Battlefield National Historic Landmark. All the other monuments on the island were erected by private groups or individuals, of both nations.

A close look at the "material leavings" of the Japanese visitors to Peleliu reveals much about the memories of the nation that lost 11,000 sons here in 1944. Of particular interest are the competing interpretations of the historical meanings of the battle and the Pacific War that one can discern within the texts of different monuments, which reflect underlying conflicts along the Left-Right divide within Japanese politics.

The earliest Japanese monuments were placed in a section of the native cemetery that lies in Ngerchol (see figure 14). The two oldest monuments on the island are a large metal tablet that Funasaka Hiroshi erected in 1967 and, next to that, a stone put up by the Japanese government at the same time.[25] Funasaka's plaque has three large Japanese characters above a long inscription inscribed in the metal. The three characters are *I* = consoling, *Rei* = souls, *Hi* = monument. The text says in part, "We pray for the repose of the defending soldiers in Peleliu who bravely fought for noble [*totoi*] peace, and we honor and give thanks and respect for their contribution." It goes on to identify Funasaka and says he financed the monument with the royalties from his book about the battle of Peleliu, *Sakura Sakura*, and also with contributions from bereaved families and wartime comrades. Today its base is often used by Japanese tourists for making offerings of incense.

Next to it stands a badly worn, blackened stone. This is one of the two monuments on Peleliu erected by the Japanese government. It says, "A memorial for all the Japanese who died here." The date is curious. It reads Shōwa 28, or 1953, which is 14 years before it was actually emplaced on Peleliu. This is the date, however, that the first Japanese expeditions were allowed to search Guam for remains; perhaps this stone was one of several created at this time in anticipation of being placed on Micronesian islands.

Funasaka's text captures a common attitude in Japanese memory of the wartime deaths: that the men died fighting for peace. Statements like this occupy a safe but evasive middle ground in Japanese war memory, a way out of the "moral and psychological dilemma that the victors did not have to confront": honor the dead but devote Japan to a new order of peace and justice, which is what the dead believed they were fighting for.[26] Neither inscription contains notes of repentance or regret. Neither provides an English or Palauan translation. Most Japanese memorials raised in following years, however, would contain English versions of their texts.

Next to Funasaka's memorial sits a black tablet dated 1986. Here the Association of the Peleliu Tank Battalion writes, "For the repose of the *eirei* of the tank battalion." Its back side contains a history of the tank battalion in Manchuria and relates that it came to Palau in April 1944 and to Peleliu the next month. The annihilation of this battalion in its counterattack against the marines on the afternoon of D-day is a highlight of most American accounts of the invasion.

The seemingly innocuous message of the battalion is in fact significant for calling the fallen soldiers *eirei*, which is a highly contentious term in Japan and a key word in the idiom of the ultranationalist Right. *Eirei*, or "spirits of the glorious/honorable/heroic war dead," as Seraphim defines it, became official terminology during World War II. As Herbert Bix explains, today it implies "a positive attitude toward the imperial state and a negative evaluation of the postwar values inscribed in the constitution." Newspapers avoid it in favor of the more neutral *senbotsusha* (those who died in war).[27]

The largest memorial in the cemetery is a white pyramidal structure with a large

Figure 14. Stephen C. Murray (right) and Professor Iitaka Shingo in the Japanese section of Ngerchol cemetery, 2003. The Funasaka memorial and white pyramid stand behind.

black sphere on its top. Its three Japanese characters incised in granite read *Mi Ta Ma*, meaning dead souls. Next to these is the name of a minister of Health and Welfare, Saito. It says it was constructed by the Peleliu Mitama Association, whose head was a congressman from the Diet, Nakamura Kishiro. This is the man Kokichi Ingas spoke of, who invited the chiefs to Japan. Dating apparently from the early 1970s, it is dedicated to "those officers and men who died in World War II" and offers prayers for the repose of their souls. At its back is a door to a chamber for holding ashes of the cremated.

Not counting the Shinto shrine, which is discussed further on, there are five Japanese memorials in areas where the battle occurred. One is a sign south of the cemetery on the west coast, which marks the area where Lieutenant Yamaguchi and his 33 stragglers remained hidden until their surrender in 1947. There are two memorial stones in the mountains, a third in Ngerkeyukl near the invasion beaches; the island's largest war monument, the Peace Park Memorial, is located at the southern shore.

The Japanese monument at the base of the Five Sisters peaks, the original Bloody Nose Ridge, is dedicated to the Peleliu Sector Defense Command and lists its constituent army and naval units. It's a four-sided stone approximately four feet high set in the earth, with brass tablets on two sides containing inscriptions in Japanese and English. Like the other monument in the mountains, this one is usually ringed at its base with war debris and souvenirs that people find in nearby caves: canteens, mortar shells, Japanese helmets, and rifle magazines. The English version reads:

> Battlefield Monument
>
> In defending this island against the overwhelming American landing forces, the Japanese Peleliu Sector Defense Command fought the most fierce and courageous battle to the very last soldier extending for over two months from 15 September to 24 November 1944.

Engraved next on the monument are names of all the units deployed under the Sector Defense Command. The monument's text ends:

> Their heroic dedication to the country should be told forever from generation to generation.
> The Peleliu Sector Defense Command
> Commanding officer Colonel Kunio Nakagawa

Nine Army Units and eight Naval Units are then named, and the monument text ends:

> February 1989
> 2nd Infantry Regiment Peleliu Island Memorial Monument
> Promotion Association

The following translation of the Japanese text was made by colleagues Iitaka Shingo and Kido Ichiko:

> Monument of Honor
> The following defense forces in Peleliu, commanded by Regimental Commander Nakagawa Kunio, moved to this island at the end of April in Shōwa 19 [1944] and prepared a meticulous (defensive) strategy with the Navy unit already arrived here. On September 15 of the same year, the United States military with its superior war power landed on the island. They [the Defense Corps] held out for two long months to accomplish their duties. But with their fighting capacity exhausted by Nov. 24, Commander Nakagawa committed suicide. The other soldiers turned to guerrilla warfare and died heroically for their homeland [*sokoku*]. This place is a battlefield where it is fitting for us to appreciate the souls of the eirei who died bravely praying for peace, and honor their distinguished military service.

Like most later Japanese monuments, this one contains an English translation. The inscription is like that written by Funasaka in its direct tribute to the heroic fallen fighters. It captures that strand of Japanese war memory that may or may not openly consider the fighting men heroes but definitely values their sacrifice and sees them as victims. In eulogizing only the fighters, it is directly comparable to its American counterparts on Peleliu, which were erected by military units or individual veterans, not by historical or peace groups. With the focus on the fighting men there are no expressions of regret for the war or hopes for perpetual peace as appear on other memorials. The Sector Command stone was placed five years after that of the American First Marine Division, which is a short walk away. The Japanese stone's praise of defense may be a deliberate echo of the marines' praise for their attack.

Both versions of the Sector Command's message strike a note that will reappear in Japanese accounts of the battles for Palau—the overwhelming material superiority of American forces as the explanation for defeat. But the differences between the Japanese and English texts, as provided by the builders themselves, are noteworthy. The one in Japanese describes the heroism in more detail and uses the provocative word *eirei* for the soldiers, who, again, died "praying for peace." The Japanese language plaque, but not the English one, has a prominent row of engraved cherry blossoms, sakura. (Recall that sakura are associated with the short, heroic lives of samurai.) The Japanese text, but not the English, reveals that Colonel Nakagawa committed suicide. Readers of Japanese are assured that the surviving fighters engaged in guerrilla warfare before dying honorably. American histories of the battle, to the contrary, brush off the resistance after November 24, including the harassment from Yamaguchi's 34 stragglers, as a minor nuisance.

Most conspicuously, the Japanese text does not exhort the reader to tell future generations of the soldiers' dedication to the country. Citing "the country" as their devotional aim obscures what had been inculcated into both soldiers and the populace throughout Japan's 15-year war: that they fought for the emperor, the personification of the nation and empire, in whose name Japan had gone to war. The variance in the Japanese language version suggests there is a parallel at work here. Just as builders of memorials on Peleliu can write messages without fear of the criticism they would face at home, so the inscriptions in different languages can be subtly shaded to comfort Japanese readers (soldiers were eirei, Colonel Nakagawa admirably took his own life, survivors fought as guerrillas) while concealing these same terms and events from the audience that reads only English.

Nearby the Sector Command's stone lies the Last Stand or Last Command Post monument, erected at the same time and by the same group. The Last Stand marker sits at the end of a path that runs along a line of caves in the ridge. It is a low stone with worn brass plaques in English and Japanese. It attracts more offerings of military relics than its neighbor.

When I first saw this site in 1999 I realized with eerie discomfort that these were the very caves that I had explored in my first visits to the island in 1967. At that time there were no footpaths on the heavily wooded slopes, and the caves were extremely hard to find since the forest was thick and the cave openings were very small. My friends and I thrashed about this hillside for several hours and gradually realized that these caves lay in a row, all at the same elevation. On a visit to Peleliu in the summer of 1967 it had appeared that nobody had entered them since the U.S. military souvenir hunters of the 1940s, since they were filled with skulls, skeletons, ammunition, rusted helmets, cooking gear, gas masks, boots, and corroded rifles and bayonets. The leather boots were dried and cracked, and when we turned them over, foot bones rattled out onto the earth. Today these caves stand emptied of all their war debris.

The English text on the monument reads:

> The site of the last stand
> by the soldiers of
> the Peleliu Sector Defense Command
> of the defunct Imperial Japanese Army.
>
> This is the spot of the command post of Colonel Kunio Nakagawa, commanding officer of the 2nd Infantry Regiment, concurrently with the Peleliu Sector Defense Command of the Imperial Japanese Army was located when the defenders fought desperate fight [*sic*] to the last man. The 2nd Infantry Regiment, one of the elite units of the defunct Imperial Japanese Army, saw its end, and Colonel Nakagawa committed suicide right here after having destroyed by fire the regimental color[s] on 24th November, 1944.
> February 1989
> 2nd Infantry Regiment Peleliu Island Memorial Monument Promotion Association

What is peculiar is that this is *not* the site where Nakagawa and General Murai maintained their final command post. The actual cave is known to lie in a valley to the west, deeper inside the last pocket of resistance. Eventually I learned why this seeming error exists. In 1989 the location of the command post had not been definitely rediscovered; that occurred around 1994, at the time of the 50th anniversary of the battle. Peleliu leaders decided to put the marker in this other location because, with a new road up the side of the ridge and a footpath leading to them from the nearby Peleliu Sector Command stone, these caves are the most accessible for tourists making a short day tour.

A Peleliu guide, Tangie Jesus, told me that on the occasion of the 50th anniversary Colonel Nakagawa's mother (others say it was his widow) made the arduous journey to Peleliu and deep into a valley to see where the colonel had actually died. Upon reaching the cave where he had taken his life she became hysterical and had to be carried out through the forest.

Thus on Peleliu there exists a two-tiered collective memory for one of the most important sites from the battle. Casual tourists, both American and Japanese, are shown the Last Command Post stone and the row of caves associated with it. Dedicated tourists who are willing to spend more time on the island are taken to the actual site, a fantastical formation of huge vertical slabs of stone surrounding a small bowl, at the bottom of which lie the two vertically connected caves where the colonel and general took their lives. It appears the well-intentioned Last Command Post stone will misinform generations of visitors to Peleliu.

Located at the far southwest corner of Peleliu on the seacoast, the Peleliu Peace Park Memorial was erected by the Japanese government in cooperation with the Republic of Palau in March 1985. The second and last memorial raised by the Japanese government, it is the largest of the war monuments on the island. It's a simple tall stone-and-mortar trilithon, whose two vertical posts topped by a slightly curved lintel recall a torii gate. The English plaque reads: "In memory of all those who sacrificed their lives in the islands and seas of the West Pacific during World War II and in dedication to world peace."

This is the only monument in Palau that provides its message in the Palauan language as well as Japanese and English.[28] This statement from the Japanese government deliberately includes *all* those who lost their lives in the war and expresses the wish for peace. Such wishes are common when people of Japan reflect on the war; most are sincere, and they can help foster reconciliation, as Chris Ryan observes. John Dower writes that even among Izokukai some are pacifists, many antimilitarist. "Their memorial services to the Japanese dead almost invariably involve appeals for peace. . . . Unscrupulous right-wing politicians routinely exploit these sentiments, and non-Japanese routinely condemn them."[29] The message also exhibits how commemorative stones and tablets must be brief, an advantage for those for whom the history is awkward or for whom it is simple celebration. Yet alone among foreign memorials on Peleliu, this one recognizes that islanders suffered too and should be able to read its message in their own language.

Near the former site of Ngerkeyukl village and next to the Peleliu museum stands a memorial that commemorates Japan's singular experience as the only nation to have suffered atomic bombings. Placed by a peace group from Hiroshima, of all

Japanese statements on Peleliu it exhibits most clearly the Japanese Left's ethos of victimization, pacifism, and antinuclearism. Politically it stands well apart from Peleliu's memorials raised by the Right, to honor the imperial era and the fighters, or by the government, with their carefully elided admonitions.

The monument was erected in 1999, although its plaque says 1991. It provides this English translation of its Japanese text:

> Atomic-bombed Stone Pledging Peace
> Message from Hiroshima
> August 6, 1991
>
> This granite [roadway] slab . . . witnessed the horrible nuclear blast which killed hundreds of thousands of citizens in one of the worst tragedies in human history . . . .
>
> *Learning lessons from the calamity we suffered and the sense of guilt we feel toward other nations concerned in World War II, we have pledged in our Constitution never again to conduct aggression toward foreign countries* (emphasis added).
>
> We should like to present these slabs to the peoples of the world, hoping that all mankind will share our common wish for world without war by possessing a memento of the atomic bombing of Hiroshima as a reminder of the importance of peace.
> Stone for Peace Association of Hiroshima

The paragraph I have italicized is unique in Palau for its admission of aggression and its expression of Japanese guilt over World War II—although the exact reasons for the guilt are not elaborated. This phrase does not appear in the Japanese version of the message. The paragraph in Japanese says, "We learned much from the tragic experience of WW II and pledged in our peace constitution after WW II that we will never invade (*shinryaku*) other nations." Iitaka Shingo believed that the authors probably feared criticism if they used the word *sumi*, guilt. "The Right would never use it," he told me.

He explained further that the Right would also vehemently object to using the word "invade," *shinryaku*. This word periodically gets excised from textbooks in favor of locutions like "Japan advanced (*shinsyutsu*) into China"—locutions that invariably provoke loud protests from China and South Korea.[30]

Like the Peleliu Sector Command inscription, then, the Hiroshima Stone displays the greater freedom of expression available to private organizations that go abroad—being forthright about "invasion" as a cause of war—and also the freedom to alter the message within the translation—adding "aggression" and "guilt" to the English text. But the two memorials address very different audiences: the Sector Command stone speaks primarily to conservatives from Japan, the Hiroshima Stone to the foreign nationals of the 185 countries where it was to be erected. Both also speak from opposing political and historical stances. So where the Sector Command memorial conceals Rightist idioms and values from those who read only English, the Hiroshima Stone conceals Leftist criticism of Japan's responsibility for the war and its guilt for atrocities from those who read only Japanese.

This monument is the strongest antiwar statement on Peleliu Island. The peace constitution it lauds is the same one that Prime Minister Abe vows to amend. However, by introducing Hiroshima into the war history of Palau and Peleliu, the stone inserts Japan's ultimate assertion of war victimhood into the memory and meaning of this island conflict. John Dower describes some of the complications surrounding Japanese memories of Hiroshima this way: because of the atomic bombs, "the recent war itself became perceived as fundamentally a Japanese tragedy. Hiroshima and Nagasaki . . . [fixated] Japanese memory of the war on what had happened to Japan and simultaneously [blotted] out recollection of the Japanese victimization of others."[31]

The stone can be read to imply that the nearly 17,500 Japanese soldiers who died in Peleliu, Angaur, and Babeldaob sacrificed themselves not just to defend the homeland but also to shield their countrymen from atomic catastrophe. Alone among the monuments erected by the two belligerents on Peleliu, the Hiroshima Stone provides a bit of historical context for the battle that consumed the island. However, having raised the fact of aggression, its message tends to exonerate Japan from the very colonialism and aggression that brought its troops to their deaths on Peleliu. It asks the reader to focus his vision 2,000 miles to the north, on Japan as victim, not on the people of Peleliu or Palau or Asia who suffered so grievously.

For many years the most visible and active Japanese organization in Palau has been a right-wing Shinto group named Seiryusha, which means "clear stream organization." From the time of the Meiji Restoration in 1868 until 1945, the Japanese government promoted a form of State Shinto, whose central tenet was worship of the emperor as a god and the embodiment of the mythohistoric Japanese state. Shinto was ultranationalistic, inextricably bound as the religious element in the complex of race, throne, religion, power, and gain that drove Japan's sense of mission to expand and rule in Asia. The U.S. occupation disestablished State Shinto and forced Emperor Hirohito to renounce his divinity in 1946.[32] But radical Shintoism has continued to fester within the far Right.

According to a knowledgeable Palauan colleague, Seiryusha has been led for over 25 years by Namekawa Yuji. One islander who was willing to discuss the organization thought Funasaka Hiroshi might have been a founder of Seiryusha and definitely was a member. Most Ireidan make gifts to Peleliu and Angaur in cash, like support for the elementary schools, or in kind, such as donating used bicycles. I was told that Namekawa, however, has been munificent in his gifts over the years, including a large motor vessel each to Peleliu and Angaur to improve their transport to Koror. Such generosity has won him friends on both islands.

In recent years, Seiryusha comes to Palau in force at the time of Independence Day celebrations, October 1. For years it came as a guest of the Palau government, but this honor has recently been removed. In the early 2000s it dropped the name Seiryusha in favor of calling itself the Japan-Palau Cultural Association. It pays for an elaborate display of fireworks said to cost $300,000.[33] Most people in Palau know Namekawa, in fact, only as the *chad ra hinabi*, the fireworks man. Seiryusha's *mikoshi*, a Shinto palanquin carried by Palauan youths, and a float that it sponsors represent Japan in a multicultural parade, and its dancers perform traditional Shinto dances. Its leaders dress in combat uniforms and boots, looking much like a militia of the sort raised by the reactionary writer Mishima Yukio.[34]

Several of my Palauan informants were familiar with Namekawa and his organization. Given the sensitivity of the topic, they asked to remain anonymous. They were aware that Seiryusha and Namekawa occupied the extreme fringes of Japanese politics and were, in the words of one, "radical Shinto" and "imperialists." Another termed them "politically extreme, different from normal Ireidan" and noted that "Palauans don't know who they are, they think of them as 'philanthropists,' but Japanese people know them." Due to their antigovernment stance in Japan, he went on, the local Japanese embassy is "wary" of them and of Palau's cozy relationship with them.

While one thought their activities were inspired more by "nostalgia" for the Nan'yō era, another demurred: groups like Seiryusha "use Palau to collect money more than to [promote] nostalgia." They extort funds from businessmen by telling of their plans to build monuments in Palau "in honor of the soldiers who died so you can now safely run your business." Of the resulting "donations," 80 percent never reach Palau, he asserted. Instead, they go to finance political activities within Japan.[35]

Namekawa and Seiryusha have erected one Shinto shrine each on Angaur and Peleliu and revived the highest-ranking Shinto shrine ever built outside Japan, Koror's Kampei Taisha Nan'yō Jinja. This Great South Seas Shrine, dedicated with solemn panoply in 1940 on the 2,600th anniversary of Japan's imperial house, was the symbolic apogee of Japanese colonialism in Micronesia.[36] Palauans dismantled much of it after the war, but Seiryusha has rebuilt part of it, added memorials and features, and holds elaborate Shinto ceremonies there during its annual visits. It holds identical ceremonies at the shrines it built on Peleliu and Angaur.

Seiryusha has erected a tablet at the Nan'yō Jinja whose text appears only in Japanese. It translates as:

> The purpose of reconstructing the old Kampei Taisha Nan'yō Jinja: The Meiji restoration . . . stimulated the advance [shinsyutsu] of Japanese all over the world. Now one hundred years have passed since Japanese immigrants prospered in [*hanei*] foreign countries and the second and third generations are now living in these countries. In order to reside in such lands we . . . [had] to respect *kami* [spirits, gods] and worship ancestors with a full heart.
> The place where such kind of spirit is focused is the shrine. But, because of the setback [*zasetsu*] in the Great East Asia War, we were forced to withdraw the Nan'yō shrine temporarily. As a new time has come, the interested persons of Japan and Palau reconstruct it in accordance with the proper historical purposes of the shrine and pray for divine protection of the ancestors' souls and souls of dead soldiers [eirei], and make [this place] a cardinal point of development and peace of the Nan'yō, and hope that we contribute to the development of world civilization.
>
> Heisei era 9 [1997], October[37]

The inscription clearly reveals nostalgia for the days when Japan ruled the Nan'yō and its immigrants were dominant in the islands. But it invokes an era when the Palauan minority were third-class citizens in their own homeland, when they were educated for servility, when their natural resources were harvested and mined for the benefit of foreigners, and when the colonizer's ambitions brought Palau the ruin and suffering of war. Notice that the war's dead were "eirei," and its results were a "setback" that forced withdrawal of the Shinto shrine "temporarily." Seiryusha implies that, as the shrine was a necessary spiritual center for Japanese immigrants previously, so its rebuilding is a precondition for renewed assertiveness by their descendants, with help from interested parties from the homeland.

A few years earlier Seiryusha had placed a large granite structure in the shape of a Palauan bai, also at the top level of the Nan'yō Jinja's steps. Its English text reads: "Enshrined in the Nan'yō Jinja are gods of ancestors and fallen soldiers World War II [*sic*]. The pride of Japan and Belau. On the other side of this monument are inscribed the names of the brave men of Belau. (Built Nov 24, 1994)." On the back, under the legend "El Mlad Ra Mekemad" (Palauan for "Those Who Died in the War") are listed the names of 19 Palauan men who died while serving with Japanese forces in New Guinea or Indonesia. At the end of the structure Namekawa's name appears as one of the donors. Near the bai, carved on a pedestal supporting a stone lion and dated 1986, are the three Japanese characters of "Seiryusha."

The date of dedication is notable: November 24, 1994, marked the 50th anniversary of the defeat of the Japanese troops on Peleliu. On September 15 of that year, the Palauan government, American veterans and armed forces, and the people of Peleliu held large celebrations commemorating the 50th anniversary of the day of the U.S. invasion. In subtle protest of the Palauan and American celebration, Seiryusha and the Right acknowledged the event that resonated with them.

Honoring the 19 Palauan dead earned Seiryusha and Namekawa a resolution of thanks from the Palauan congress, the OEK, dated September 8, 1994. The Palauan officials, as usual, were too polite to remind either of the antagonists that the 19 were only a fraction of the Palauan citizens who died from the war. Nor did anyone mention that the 19 would have been worked like slaves by the Japanese Army as laborers, porters, and stevedores, then abandoned to their fates when the enemy appeared.[38] But the resolution does point out that "many young Palauans were ordered to serve in the Japanese Imperial Forces," that surviving "Palauan War Veterans" still remember the "emotional trauma" of their service, and that after 50 years neither the Palauan nor Japanese governments had officially recognized this service.

In 1982 Seiryusha built in Peleliu a Shinto shrine dedicated to the Japanese dead. Palauans removed this shrine some years ago to make that location into a rock quarry, but Seiryusha, in efficient secrecy, worked out a means of erecting a new larger one on the slopes of Bloody Nose Ridge, right next to the monument of the U.S. First Marine Division. With its flights of steps, torii gate, stone lions and lanterns, sacred structures, and stone tablets, it is the largest Japanese structure erected on Peleliu.

The new shrine was dedicated on Independence Day, October 1, 2002. Its stone tablet reads:

> Peleliu Shinto Shrine
> This Shinto shrine was constructed in May 1982 (Shōwa 57 nen) by Seiryusha, which is organized by youth [*sic*] Shinto priests and others. Here is the place to repose and pray for all the dead souls of army or navy soldiers and also private citizens who died here in the battles to protect our homeland, Japan.
> The memorial service for them will be held every year to pray for the peace and security of our homeland and for the peace of the world.
> On an auspicious day in July, Heisei 13 [2001]
>
> Seiryusha

What meaning does a reactionary organization like Seiryusha attach to these revived Shinto rites? The longing for empire is obvious beneath the anodyne statements of the tablets. Also disturbing is the veneration for the relationship between Shinto, the state, and emperor worship, the "proper historical purposes" of the shrine from the era of the Nan'yō. The idiom and the symbols Seiryusha em-

Figure 15. The 2002 Shinto shrine and the U.S. Marine Corps monument (behind flagstaff) on Bloody Nose Ridge, 2003

ploys hearken to the days of Japan's belligerent expansion throughout Asia. The name Seiryusha, "clear stream organization," deliberately evokes purity, which John Dower calls the "central concept" in the Japanese racial thinking that developed in the 50 years after the defeat of China in 1895. As the "Yamato race," the people of Japan were held to be the "leading race," distinctive for the purity and homogeneity that they inherited through association with their deified emperor, expressed in the mythic and religious (Shinto) traditions that had grown up around the throne. "This was blood nationalism of an exceptionally potent sort," Dower writes. During the crisis years of the 1930s and 1940s, he continues, purity lay in identification with the militarized imperial state and readiness to sacrifice oneself in war.[39]

Seiryusha carefully masks its political stance, and even changed the name it uses in the islands to cover its tracks. It excludes Palauans from its core activities. Not a single Palauan native attended the lengthy Shinto ceremony I witnessed at the Nan'yō Jinja. Seiryusha's decades of success with its hidden agenda and secretive activities are the outstanding example of the lack of constraints Japanese organizations encounter in Palau while engaging in their memorial programs.

8
Remembering a Painful Victory

> Old men forget; yet all shall be forgot,
> But he'll remember with advantages
> What feats he did that day.
>
> Shakespeare, *Henry V*, Act 4, Scene 3

American memory views the Second World War as "the good war," in which the men of the "greatest generation" fought a necessary war against treacherous and brutal adversaries to defend freedom and democracy.

This widely accepted orthodoxy stands in marked contrast with the way Japanese war memory remains a matter of spirited dispute domestically and internationally. Historians of the war do raise disturbing questions, but the American public seldom considers them: how isolationism let tyranny prosper; how clumsy diplomacy and embargoes provoked Japan into an avoidable war; how light U.S. losses were compared to all other major combatants; how the Allies soiled their victory with terror bombing and with the alliance with Stalin's Russia, which cost much of Europe its freedom despite Hitler's defeat; how America fought in the Pacific with a racial fury that we still try to repress. The designers of the Smithsonian display on the Hiroshima bombing discovered just how unprepared most Americans are to confront such sharp-edged subjects.[1]

Philip Beidler argues that the representations of the war that flooded into popular culture after 1945 typically reinforced Americans' sense that they fought with noble purpose and clarity. He notes that although many works are candid about the war's "hardships and follies," they nonetheless "keep faith with its truly heightened sense of collective moral enterprise." Books, films, plays, musicals, and photographs became "a canon" that eventually became "enshrined themselves as forms of history and memory." Many serious novelists avoided the large moral issues by taking an approach that was "consciously microcosmic, with the emphasis on individual units, the small heroism and cowardices of average men." Meanwhile, all the media operated to render the "subtext of horror largely irrelevant."[2]

On Peleliu, American veterans of the battle have played the central role in what remains a limited effort at commemoration. U.S. memorials tend to sound similar themes; they lack the variety of voices jockeying to speak for the dead or the political divisiveness evident among Japanese texts. Veterans are, however, like the

Ireidan, a very intense interest group with deep convictions about the fighting and what should be remembered. They often assert primacy for their experiences and hence for their interpretations of their battles, but this creates problems. An infantryman had only a narrow perspective on the fighting, limited to what one survivor of Peleliu, PFC Fred Fox, called "My Ten Foot Circle of Space." Allowing veterans of either side to define history can also displace the war experiences of others: "Powerful images of veterans re-living traumatic memory may promote the 'forgetting' of other victims, and threaten to supplant historical analysis."[3]

American Commemoration on Peleliu: Triumph over Adversity

When American veterans finally began to organize visits to Peleliu in the mid-1980s, the chad ra Beliliou welcomed them and offered the same warm hospitality as given the Japanese Ireidan. The residents understood and sympathized with the motives and emotions that brought the visitors from so many thousands of miles away. The islanders noticed how the victors did not erect a site at which to offer prayers to the dead. But otherwise the islanders granted the newcomers the same tolerance for their activities and the same freedom from oversight concerning designs and texts of their monuments.

Like the Japanese tourists, the U.S. visitors tended to focus on their own agendas and most recognized that they were guests on a foreign island. Their sporadic visits and the few modest markers they constructed did little to change the dynamic the Ireidan had long established. Americans gravitated toward local families that catered to them with lodging and English-language tours. As the Ireidan had before them, the vets made personal contacts with guides or hosts on the island, who then helped arrange with landowners a site for a stone or plaque; American markers too had a way of popping up without previous notice. If Ireidan and an American party did bump into each other on the island, awkwardness and language remained significant barriers to conversation. Year after year islanders, defenders, and invaders each went about their business with little overt friction among them but even less mutual exchange and understanding.

Willard Smau and Tangie Jesus frequently guide U.S. servicemen and their families on the island. Both described how American marine veterans felt that the local population of Peleliu did not understand "the truth" about the battle. This truth lay in the fighting experiences of the U.S. soldiers, and the vets set about teaching the details of the combat to the two guides. Tangie was brought all the way to Camp Pendleton and San Diego to learn how the Marine Corps views the history of Peleliu.

PFC Fred Fox, who fought on the Point at Ngerkeyukl with George Hunt's Company K, was probably the first American veteran of the Peleliu invasion to return to the island. He came back on the 20th anniversary of the invasion, September 15, 1964. Like Funasaka, Fox became a pioneer for his countrymen visiting Micronesia, Palau, and Peleliu. But the trickle of American visitors to Peleliu did not develop into a substantial stream of veterans, war buffs, or tourists until the 2010 HBO television miniseries, *The Pacific*, produced a noticeable, although likely temporary, boost. It is a curiosity of Peleliu's history as a battlefield that the side that won came back to the site only slowly and in small numbers. America seemed to ignore its men and their sacrifices—eliciting "a surge of fury" from historian William Manchester when he saw the lone visible American memorial on Peleliu in 1978, a stone obelisk on top of the Omleblochel hills, Bloody Nose Ridge, whose metal letters were rusted and deteriorating.[4]

The losing side, however, had returned in a rush once the TT opened the gates in the mid-1960s. The primary reason for the disparity lies with the disposition of the remains of the dead. Izokukai, the bereaved families, lived in torment while 11,000 of their loved ones lay in the limestone caves of Peleliu, unburied and forgotten by the nation. The approximately 1,060 American dead within the cemetery at Orange Beach (Chelechol ra Bkulabeluu), by contrast, had been exhumed and either sent home or interred elsewhere, according to the families' wishes. The American dead had been individually identified, honored, and buried beneath green grass and marble. Japanese families were denied such consolation; they had only Ishmael's "bitter blanks . . . which covered no ashes."

The long distance and high cost of travel to Palau from the United States, as compared with the relatively inexpensive flights that come down to Micronesia from Japan, also reduce American tourists. Yet even many veterans who could afford the trip have chosen not to come. E. B. Sledge, author of a masterful memoir of the battle, declined to join the ceremonies for the 50th anniversary. He wrote to Professor Dirk Ballendorf in reply to an invitation, "I think it is perfectly fine to have such events of commemoration. But I couldn't attend, ever" (Ballendorf, pers. comm.). Almost all the 7,000 American tourists who come to Palau annually, like today's young Japanese visitors, are attracted by the scuba diving and make their base in Koror.

Like the Ireidan, the U.S. veterans and their descendants who do visit Peleliu come to pursue the role the individual family member played in the fighting. They come, that is, on personal quests. The island's identity is that of a battlefield, one that breaks down into a series of terrains crossed under fire: reef, beach, flatland of the airfield, ridges, cliffs, and the caves that lie within. Lands killed over, lands where friends or relatives were killed; the island is sacred ground.

Often the quest involves the need to find one particular place on the battlefield, for memory is indeed tied to landscape. Minister of State Temmy Shmull of Peleliu drove around the island with a group of veterans during the invasion's 50th anniversary in 1994. "You could see in their eyes when they reached certain sections, they would change, they'd flash back. 'This is where my buddy was lost; this is where I was almost killed.' Their memories came back very strongly."

The experiences and understandings of the islanders, meanwhile, seldom register with visitors. The villagers are not very visible to day tours, which concentrate on sites south of Kloulklubed. As with the Ireidan, guests who stay overnight have to work to overcome the language and cultural barriers in order to engage their hosts in meaningful discussion of the past. Although the new village museum has relics, photos, letters, and flags from both combatants, it lacks displays depicting the war's impacts on the chad ra Beliliou and how that calamity changed their lives.

Willard Smau, who guides both American and Japanese tourists, said that his American clients want to hear about the battle itself and are fascinated by the relics scattered about the island. The Japanese day visitors, on the other hand, "come mostly to pray and pay their respects. They see and hear, then forget. They are much less interested in the battle and its history. Most young Japanese on Peleliu ask no questions, while the Americans will ask many questions, trying to learn."

Tokie Morei offered a more sympathetic view of Japanese tourists. She and her daughter Olympia observed that the U.S. veterans are interested only in seeing the American monuments, then return to Koror the same day. In the 1970s and 1980s, Tokie's female friends among the Ireidan would stay for two days at least and make contributions to the elementary school. The chief of Teliu, Renguul Donald Haruo, is unusual among the postwar generation for having been educated in Japan. He expressed regret that although many Japanese Ireidan have erected private monuments and parks on the island, the United States has failed to do so to the same extent. "Things are not balanced on Peleliu," he told me. "There are many more Japanese shrines and visitors to the island than there are U.S. memorials or visitors. Where is the U.S. on Peleliu? The U.S. needs more of a presence." In another conversation he noted that the Japanese tourists come with spiritual motives, to pray for the dead and to grieve. "The Americans don't pray or mourn. They just look at sites and relics."

The Americans built monuments of stone at three sites immediately after the battle. By the 1960s the only one visible was the aforementioned obelisk of coral stones erected on the top of the Omleblochel ridges. Reaching it required a difficult scramble up the precipitous slope. On my first climb, in 1967, I reached for a handhold on a ledge and found a rusting American hand grenade. The column's metal letters had badly deteriorated even 11 years before Manchester saw them. The legend says simply:

> Lest We Forget Those Who Died: 323 Infantry, U.S. Army, 1944

The letters have since been refurbished, and in the 1980s the American Seabees in Palau constructed a stairway up to the marker and surrounded it with an attractive wooden deck. This platform provides visitors with the best available view of the heavily forested island.

Chief Obak described to me how, some years ago, the men of Peleliu located and cleared away the growth from the paired American monuments at Chelechol ra Bkulabeluu (Orange Beach). (Peleliu's residents have picked up this beach's code name and pronounce it "orengee." They have not picked up the name for White Beach to its north.) These two identical stone markers stood at the U.S. cemetery that held the American dead until late 1948. A plaque on one says:

> 81st Infantry division United States Army
> This monument is dedicated to the lasting memory of those members of the Wildcat Division and attached troops who fought and died on Peleliu Island between 20 Sept and 27 Nov 1944.

A small pillar that honors the army's 321st regiment in Kloulklubed was also overgrown and damaged but has been reconstructed. Its inscription, dated December 1944, bears mention: "In Memory of Heroic Dead," a phrasing that recalls the Japanese term *eirei*.

Only three further memorials were erected to American forces prior to 2005, all of them by private parties. Not until 1984, 40 years after the invasion, did the First Marine Division finally obtain a memorial dedicated to its men. That year its association of veterans erected a four-sided peaked structure made of local stones on a flat beneath the slopes of what the marines remember as Bloody Nose Ridge. About five feet high, it has tablets on each side (see figure 15).

The plaque on the north side carries the text of the Presidential Unit Citation awarded the division for the battle. It is worth quoting in its entirety:

> For extraordinary heroism in action against enemy Japanese forces at Peleliu and Ngesebus from September 15 to 29, 1944. Landing over *a treacherous coral reef* against hostile mortar and artillery fire, the First Marine Division, Reinforced, seized a *narrow, heavily mined beachhead* and advanced foot by foot in the face of relentless enfilade fire *through rain-forests and mangrove swamps* toward the air strip, the key to the enemy defenses of the southern Palaus. Opposed all the way by thoroughly disciplined, veteran Japanese troops heavily entrenched in caves and in reinforced concrete pillboxes which honeycombed the high ground throughout the island, the officers and men of the Division fought with undiminished spirit and courage despite heavy losses, *exhausting heat and difficult terrain*, seizing and holding a highly strategic air and land base for future operations in the Western Pacific. By their individual acts of heroism, their aggressiveness and their fortitude, the men of the First Marine Division, Reinforced, upheld the highest traditions of the United States Naval Service (emphasis added).

The language of this citation, dating from the time of the war, highlights a point made previously: the Americans' sense of being at war in the Pacific with an alien and hostile nature. I have italicized pertinent phrases. The citation also seeks to grant Peleliu a strategic value that almost no veteran or historian believes it actually possessed. The language displays the narrowest possible military perspective toward Peleliu Island. Its every natural feature—reefs, beaches, mangroves, hills, caves, climate—is presented in military terms, invariably as an obstacle. The text conjures an exotic island whose significance derives from the battle waged upon it by American forces, who eventually prevailed over a vicious and skilled foe. History on Peleliu began on September 15, 1944, and ended one month later. The events of that month sanctified the island.

This text was written by American officialdom for consumption by the home front, and as Paul Fussell, who fought in the war, observes, this kind of prose was designed to conceal the real war from the civilians. Fussell insists that bromides like these do not fool the veteran. This exalted and sanitized war is not the one he fought and lived through; these were not his thoughts at the time, and they are not his memories now.[5]

A second plaque lists the eight marines who won the Congressional Medal of Honor for their actions at Peleliu. The division won 19 total in its four engagements in the Pacific War—Guadalcanal, Cape Gloucester on the island of New Britain, Peleliu, and Okinawa. None of the texts on the monument is translated into Japanese or Palauan. There are no hopes for peace, no expressions of sympathy for Japanese losses.

Along the west side of the ridge system lies one of the more dramatic relics from the battle, a U.S. Sherman tank that was blown over on its side by a land mine, killing all its crew. Veterans erected a plaque whose inscription presents an object lesson in what can go wrong when there is no review or regulation of such displays. After naming the four crewmen killed in the explosion, the plaque says:

> Men of the 1st Platoon Co. A 710 TK died here 18 October 1944 after hitting a land mine. Having saved two navy airmen the tank, upon returning to fire into the Jap held caves, was hit. Capt. H. W. Jones, 1st Marine Division, was also killed.
>
> Erected by veterans of the 710 Tank BN
> Dedicated 18 October 1997

Old habits and old hatreds die hard. I accompanied a Japanese tour group to the site and watched as they read the message. A woman told me how insulting she considered the word *Jap*. It is regrettable that the authors of the inscription disregarded the instructions Admiral Nimitz sent his fleet immediately after the surrender in 1945: "The use of insulting epithets in connection with the Japanese as a race or as individuals does not now become the officers of the United States Navy."[6]

On the other hand, a private memorial can be created that exhibits great tact and honesty of feeling. In 1999 Fred Fox, the former marine PFC., again returned to Peleliu, this time to place on the Point a tablet honoring Captain George P. Hunt, his commanding officer during the two days and nights of fighting to hold the north flank of the invasion beaches. Fox installed the tablet next to one of the Japanese bunkers dug into the coral. It contains a photo of Hunt and text that describes his resolute leadership in defending the Point against Japanese assaults, even when his command was cut off and reduced to a handful of men. It notes that after the war Hunt became managing editor of *Life* magazine. It ends:

> Capt. Hunt was a leader of valor, cool under pressure, with personal courage, determination, and respect for each of his men. Each of us who served under him at Peleliu knows, if ever a combat infantry officer deserved the Congressional Medal of Honor it would have been George P. Hunt. (Died July 6, 1991).
>
> In lieu of this honor we of K-3–1 who have survived these years dedicate this plaque to Capt. Hunt and all of our comrades who have gone before. Semper Fidelis.[7]

This act of respect for Hunt so many years after the conflict reminds us of the bonds formed in combat between skillful officers and the men they command. Fox's belief that Hunt deserved the Medal of Honor was widely shared. Hunt did receive the Navy Cross, the next-highest award in the naval services.[8]

In consigning memories to stone on Peleliu, the Japanese have thus far outstripped their opponents, just as Renguul Donald Haruo observed. In the Ngerchol cemetery Japanese visitors have installed dozens of signs and markers alongside the larger ones described previously. There are no U.S. markers in this cemetery. In an ironic twist, all across Peleliu the nation that was defeated is winning the contest for public memory through the same tactics by which the American victors won the battle—employing an overwhelming preponderance of material resources.

Neither side forthrightly confronts the underlying reasons of power that brought them to bloodshed on this distant island. Yet the Japanese memorials, reflecting the ongoing debates over the war back home, offer more varied points of view on the war's historical meanings for today, a more somber reckoning of the lessons it teaches. Their translated messages are accessible to visitors from the United States and, in one case, to the local inhabitants. Some include mention of all those lost in the conflict, a gesture that embraces a more tragic view of the vast Pacific War.

No American memorial yet translates its text or commemorates anything other than the actual combat of 1944. The fighting, the victory, and the fallen are remembered. In their narrow focus the U.S. markers are like the earliest of their Japanese counterparts. The U.S. inscriptions lie comfortably within the accepted national memory of World War II, in which Peleliu is one painful but necessary rung on the ladder to the final triumph. Written by or for soldiers, they place the emphasis on the soldiers' experiences—capturing the emotion of the event, yet missing the broader view and even a modicum of historical interpretation. The brevity and limited perspective of monument inscriptions in general remind us of the need for other formats, ones that can better express histories that are more complete, more nuanced, and more easily revised as new information becomes available and opinions change over time.

Patterns of Memory Today

The chad ra Beliliou celebrate August 15 each year as Liberation Day. Exactly what the day honors is a bit vague. The name may come from events of this same name in both Guam and Saipan. It seems to recall the end of hostilities in 1945, though some islanders believed that the third and last flotilla of refugees returned from Babeldaob on this day in 1946. September 15, the anniversary of the invasion, is recognized as Veterans' Day on Peleliu. School is closed, but otherwise it is a quiet holiday with no public celebrations. For Palauans, the most important ceremonies have been those that remember the bond between Peleliu and Ngaraard in traditional Palauan ways: the raising of the olangch Odesangel Bad, and the holding of klechedaol, explicitly commemorative feasts, which occur around one of these two dates.

Forty years elapsed before a small group of American veterans returned to Peleliu for their first formal commemoration of the battle. It was during this three-day visit in 1984 that they dedicated the monument to the First Marine Division, in a ceremony attended by many residents of the island.[9]

The most elaborate ceremonies ever held to remember the battle occurred in Palau for the 50th anniversary of the invasion, in September 1994. Organized under the auspices of the government of Palau, it marked the first time that the national government recognized the battle as a historical event, and the first occasion in which Palauan citizens from throughout the archipelago gathered to share their wartime experiences as a people. (It was a busy month for Palau and its administration: the sovereign Republic of Palau came into being just two weeks later, on October 1.)

From September 6 to 9 an international conference was held in Koror: "The War in Palau: Fifty Years of Change." Speakers from Palau, Japan, the United States, and other nations examined the war, the colonial eras, and postwar economic and political developments. For the first time, Palauan elders who lived through the Nan'yō era and the war were granted the opportunity to speak publicly of their experiences.[10] They described life under the Nan'yō administration, service with Japanese forces in New Guinea, the terror of the March 1944 air raids, the year of hiding in dugout shelters on Babeldaob, and surviving the invasion of Angaur in caves. They are testimonies of fear, hunger, confusion, and loss.

Approximately 30 American veterans and their families traveled down to Peleliu the next week for ceremonies held on September 15. In front of the elementary school a navy band led a parade with two color guards, one composed of Palauans dressed as soldiers. A man dressed as a traditional Palauan warrior carried the Palauan flag. Smau Amalei carried the American banner wearing a marine uniform, and another resident dressed as a Japanese soldier carried Japan's flag. The American veterans marched, as did Palauan elders. Palau's president Kuniwo Nakamura, born on Peleliu in 1943, spoke to the crowd about Peleliu's history and difficulties after the war. Later the American visitors gathered at the monument to the First Marine Division, where it was rededicated and a 21-gun salute fired.

A very few Japanese veterans attended the events. They were recognized but were not an integral part of the program arranged by the Palauans and Americans. Some marines objected to their presence, but their former officers reprimanded them and there was no public fuss (Dirk Ballendorf, pers. comm.). Most islanders I spoke with said that there was little interaction between the former foes, but that relations were civil. Minister Temmy Shmull said that although not many Japanese veterans came, "all the former soldiers came together not in war but in peace."

On Peleliu in 1994 Seiryusha seized the opportunity to represent Japan by performing a Shinto ceremony at the shrine that has since been relocated to the slopes of the Omleblochel hills. Palauan elders say that some of the Japanese veterans expressed surprise at how tall the trees had grown. Smau Amalei told me that some Japanese visitors apologized to Chief Obak for bringing the war and forcing the people out of Peleliu. They asked how they could help the residents.

A far smaller contingent of veterans and their children returned for the 55th anniversary in 1999. There were no formal events planned, but the men and their American guide toured the island for several days. They, too, concentrated on finding specific locations from the battle, among them a fortification on Ngedebus that E. B. Sledge writes of in his memoir. For the 60th anniversary in 2004 Palau organized a formal ceremony in Koror with speakers representing Palau, Japan, and the United States. A rear admiral presided for the Americans. Fourteen American veterans attended and three Japanese veterans, among them Kurata Yoji, a survivor of Angaur. They then went down to Peleliu to lay wreaths at the monuments. The people of Peleliu formally opened the war museum in Ngerkeyukl, housed in a massively constructed Japanese fuel storage bunker that had withstood many direct hits from naval gunfire.

The U.S. Congress sent a message that was appreciated in Palau even though it singled out only the peoples of Peleliu and Angaur. It said, "You too experienced the horrors of war and the tragedy of losses of innocent loved ones once caught in the crossfire of battle. Let the memories of the Battle of Peleliu and World War II serve as reminders of the need for peace in the troubled parts of our world."[11]

The number of Ireidan visiting the Peleliu battlefield peaked in the 1970s and 1980s. The chad ra Beliliou welcomed both the chance to meet foreigners and the economic stimulus the tourists gave the tiny local economy. Many did not readily forgive the Ireidan for Japan's past racism and exploitation, but in the tradition of island hospitality, nobody forced confrontations. Palauans told me of their sympathy with Ireidan for the deaths of their relatives and their need to put the souls to rest. The Ireidan for their part generally treated the people of Peleliu with dignity and friendship, putting colonial attitudes behind them.

Like many women of Tokie Morei's generation, she made friends with the women's groups among the Izokukai. One group came every year for 15 years, into the mid-1990s, and made donations to the village school each time. "We have very good rapport with the visitors, we have a lot in common and a lot to talk about. We paid visits back to Japan, where our hosts had a big dinner for us and gave us gifts. We want to keep these memories alive and teach the children the stories about the Palauans and the Japanese, who will always have those close ties. Especially those from Peleliu, because a lot of Japanese died on Peleliu." These relationships among the women—among the mothers, wives, and daughters of the fallen Japanese and the women of Peleliu—constitute the most thorough exchanges that have occurred between any of the combatants and the natives of the island.

Daiziro Nakamura remembered a visitor who was convinced he had found a piece of his father's bone. Most Japanese tourists have settled for much less. While visiting Gunma Prefecture, home of many soldiers of the 14th Division, Governor Yuki Shmull joked to his hosts that the only bones remaining on Peleliu were probably American. "That doesn't matter," they replied. "We just want some small memento from the island." Obviously many Japanese and other visitors took souvenirs from the caves over the decades: there are few relics left in most of them, very different from the large quantities of military debris with which they were littered in the 1960s.

Tour guides and owners of diving shops with whom I discussed Japanese tourism uniformly agreed that the vast majority of Japanese visitors to Palau since the 1990s have come only for diving and recreation. They are in their twenties and thirties, show little interest in the war and rarely know of Palau's colonial past under Japan. "Almost nobody goes to Peleliu for the battlefield, compared to the interest in diving," said one operator. "The grandchildren of former [Japanese] residents or soldiers may come once, but not again." The chad ra Beliliou themselves speak freely of this generational change and the decline in visitors.

"The young Japanese like to forget about the war," said Dr. Ueki. "They say, 'The war is not our business, we don't like war.' . . . To be reminded what their country lost . . . doesn't appeal to modern thinking." Some will tour Peleliu but without enthusiasm, "although they will be *curious* if they're told Peleliu was a bloody battle."

Occasional groups of Ireidan numbering 20–30 arrive on Peleliu, but the great majority of visitors are day-trippers from Koror taking a four-hour battlefield tour. Some Koror-based divers come into the harbor for lunch and opt for a quick one-hour land tour. But Des Matsutaro, owner of Peleliu Adventures, believes that the daily average hovers around 20 tourists.

Three small tour companies are active on Peleliu. The tour buses pass through Kloulklubed but seldom stop to purchase anything, although there is little to purchase other than snack foods and drinks. There is no tourist shop with souvenirs or other knickknacks, no cafe. One hears complaints that the three operations monopolize the contacts with Koror businesses.

The tours typically make about ten stops around the island to see the primary monuments and the most interesting relics: a rare 200-mm Japanese cannon, a smashed Japanese tank from the counterattack on D-day, several American landing craft. Among the best preserved is the U.S. Sherman tank blown up by a Japanese mine. A downed U.S. Avenger aircraft, of the type that was flown by future president George H. W. Bush over Palau, lies nearby. Groups also visit battered concrete buildings erected by the Japanese Navy, now consumed by jungle and becoming unstable. Visits to the false Last Command Post set of caves prove an emotional experience for many Japanese tourists. The guides occasionally take Japanese clients to the Shinto shrine, but it appears to be too political for the typical tour group of today.

Japanese visitors whom I observed on Peleliu showed genuine interest on their tours. One group of youthful divers stopped at the cemetery to make offerings and burn incense that they had brought from Koror. Older women seemed particularly affected by the battle stories of the late guide Nakagawa Tsukane, who had grown up on a government farm in Palau before the war. Several visitors commented on how little they learn of World War II in Japanese schools. But these day tourists have almost no contact with the residents of the island and so learn nothing of the islanders' wartime experiences and sufferings. Whatever interchange occurred 35 years ago at the height of the Ireidan visitations has not been sustained.

Just when it seemed as if Japanese awareness of Peleliu would fade from memory, a new member of the Right arrived to spade over the earth that most residents of Palau thought had been tamped down. Tōjō Yuko, the granddaughter of wartime prime minister (and executed war criminal) Tōjō Hideki, visited Peleliu five or more times between 1999 and her death in 2013. She was a vocal ultranationalist who denied that Japan's wars in Asia constituted aggression or that the Imperial Army had enslaved Asian women within brothels that served frontline troops. She called the Nanjing Massacre, which killed possibly 300,000 Chinese, "a lie." In 2007 she ran for a seat in the Upper House of Japan's Diet but lost.[12]

Tōjō Yuko showed particular interest in excavating caves that the U.S. forces sealed during the fighting. Murai Masami, the son of General Murai Kenjiro, who died with Colonel Nakagawa, once accompanied her. In one visit she clashed with the Palauan Historic Preservation Office, which wanted caves left sealed as national historic resources. In a later visit she and 17 companions, most wearing camouflage uniforms, collected and burned seven bags of bones, then took the ashes to Japan.

Kurata Yoji, now in his 90s, immigrated to Micronesia at age 14. In Palau he received training as a naturalist. He fought for the Japanese battalion on Angaur, in a different company than Funasaka, whom he knew. He survived a severe wound and was astonished to encounter Funasaka alive in the POW stockade on Peleliu. He returned to Palau in 1973 as a tourist, naturalist, "and as an Ireidan to pray" and settled there in 1996. An admiring writer has published his life story.[13]

Years ago in Tokyo, Kurata met Namekawa Yuji, the head of Seiryusha. At Namekawa's office he saw many young men who looked like yakuza, members of organized crime rings. Kurata told me that Namekawa "has different political opinions than I do" and that he and his people still have "strong emotions" regarding the war experience.

Kurata encountered Tōjō Yuko during one of her trips to Palau. He told me, "She is trying to gather bones but they are difficult to identify, and it's impossible to collect them all. She seeks to remove the dishonor from her grandfather's name. She was especially interested in digging for bones in an old anti-tank ditch [along Chelechol ra Bkulabeluu, Orange Beach on Peleliu]. . . . Japanese soldiers had dug that trench using small hand shovels," he continued. "But ultimately the U.S. used it as a mass grave for about 200 Japanese bodies as the fighting moved on." He paused then said with a wan smile: "We dug our own graves."

He went on, "I told Tōjō Yuko that if she digs there, then she should stop hunting for bones. It's time to focus on things other than the war—like the natural environment and the welfare of the island people." She did not object to his statements, he said, but in later visits continued her attempts to open sealed caves on Peleliu.

Kurata has worked with the people of Angaur to establish the Angaur State Nature Park, which encompasses the entire island. He hoped to attract ecotourism to the island and simultaneously reinvigorate the local populace's understanding of its natural environment by having them direct the appreciation of nature and their history through the park. He told me that "the over-emphasis on the war history is not a good draw for ecotourism. The lands were Palauan originally, and Japan and the U.S. came and fought on them. It's a mistake to think about the war only." He mentioned a museum that he helped establish on Angaur: "I have no strong feelings about the U.S. [as a former foe]. I want to place wartime memories in the museum, try to present the facts in a neutral way. The war is only one aspect of the history of the island, so it shouldn't be overdone." He agreed that the chad ra Beliliou should tell their story of the battle in their museum.

The people of Peleliu were both fortunate and unfortunate, he said. "Fortunate because they were moved off the island before the invasion, and the behavior of Japanese soldiers was very bad at the time. They stole the food of Palauans, commandeered their homes as barracks, even killed a few babies perhaps. But they were unfortunate in that they lost their land. It was destroyed. And so both the U.S. and Japan need to contribute to their welfare now. Both are responsible here."

Rival Pasts, Rival Futures: The Plans of the National Park Service and Japan International Cooperation Agency for Peleliu's Development

In the early 2000s Peleliu's residents were considering two competing plans for expanding tourism on the island, offered them by government agencies of the United States and Japan. The proposal of the U.S. National Park Service (NPS) to establish a large Peleliu Battlefield National Historic Park twisted together the three strands of war, memory, and land, which are examined throughout this book. Since 1991 the NPS had been in sporadic conversation with Palau about implementing the park, described in a draft report.[14]

In 2000 the Japanese national aid agency, Japan International Cooperation Agency or JICA, completed a study for economic development of Palau. The report recommended massively increasing tourism infrastructure on Peleliu to create a "New Tourist Center, Large Scale."[15]

The rival visions of growth promoted in these publications were rooted in profoundly different estimates of Peleliu's possibilities as a site for tourism. These in turn derived from the gulf between the attitudes toward the war on Peleliu held by these two agencies and their governments. What the reports share are heavy-handed top-down approaches to "development" and fundamental misunderstandings about the native people, their war experiences and memory, and their complicated existence in the early 21st century.

In the late 1970s the U.S. Congress authorized the NPS to identify sites relating to the war in the Pacific that could be made into historic parks. In 1986 an NPS team spent five days surveying Peleliu. The team's draft report, issued in 1991, marveled at the island's battlefield, which "has retained a remarkable degree of historic integrity—perhaps more than any of the other battle sites of the Pacific campaign of World War II" (1991 Draft:15, 11, 57).

The report proposed to incorporate three areas of central, southern, and eastern Peleliu into a battlefield park, which included land, beaches, mangroves, and reefs. The park's 1,310 acres of dry land equaled 43 percent of Peleliu's land surface.[16] The three proposed areas encompassed almost all of Ngerdelolk, Ngesias, Ngerkeyukl, and Teliu, running from the reefs and beaches of the latter two and upslope to include most of the central ridge system.

The surveyors found that although "small portions" of the battlefield were being used for food crops, "most of it remains unused and untouched since the GI's pulled out more than four decades ago." They learned that Peleliu "is still divided into five traditional villages," but "the lands which these villages encompass are today uninhabited" (1991 Draft:11–12, 58).

The report concludes that incorporating the three areas into the proposed park "would have minimum impact on existing land uses. None of the resident population would be affected," except for one elderly chief who resided in Ngerdelolk. The report describes the beaches of the park as not suitable for "agricultural, commercial, or residential purposes." The taro growing they noticed "may not necessarily be incompatible with an historic park" (66). The surveyors displayed total ignorance of the role land plays in this society, why the people were still clustered in Kloulklubed, and how strongly the residents hoped to return to their ancestral villages.

The report maintained a mysterious silence on many vital issues. What roles would be played by the NPS and the Republic of Palau (ROP)? Who would own the park? Who would pay for it? Who would manage it and pay the operating costs? Palau's leaders raised these and more questions in the years following the publication of the report. In time the NPS clarified that Palau would have to purchase the lands and the Park Service could help manage the park. Where the ROP would find the funds was hard to imagine.

The landowners of Peleliu were troubled by their own questions. Why was so much land needed? How could a park be built when the kin groups of Peleliu themselves did not yet know who held legal title to the tracts? Could people farm or build homes on lands placed in the park or remove those lands later if their needs changed?

By 2002, discussions among the NPS, the ROP, and Peleliu's state and traditional leaders had sputtered along for over a decade. In June 2002 Peleliu leaders sent a letter to the NPS office in Honolulu. It asked the NPS several questions: Could the NPS send a representative to Peleliu to discuss these problems? Could the park be reduced to just Bloody Nose Ridge and drop from consideration the historic village sites, shorelines, and flat farmlands? Could the park include only particular locations where historically valuable features lay?

The NPS reply, dated July 8, 2002, was written by the superintendent of the Honolulu Pacific Islands Support Office. He agreed to abandon areas of the central and eastern flatlands, and somewhat reduce Area 1, to 635 acres of dry land, 21 percent of the island's surface (SRS: 16). Area 1 still included almost all the central ridges, and most of the western villages of Ngerkeyukl and Teliu and all their shorelines and reefs. The letter rejected limiting the park to just particular features, saying Area 1 was the "minimum area required [for] feasibility," which requires an area "of sufficient size to ensure sustainable protection" of its resources. The letter also stated that residential housing would be incompatible within the park, but that farming, if done for "traditional subsistence uses rather than for commercial purposes," may be compatible (SRS: 34–37).

Expanding tourism in Peleliu has strong support among many residents. Tourism is the economic hope for the island, and a park of some sort can contribute to that, they said. But if homes and gardens were not permitted inside it, then residents who sold to the park, or whose chiefs did so, would have no alternative places to live. "Where are we supposed to go?" a mechas from Teliu asked me. "Into the ocean?" Haruo Esang, one of the authors of the June 2002 letter, told me, "If we give up all the land then we can't move back to the old villages." In a painful re-enactment of history, the people of Teliu and Ngerkeyukl, forcibly expelled by the Japanese authorities for the airfield in 1937, would lose their villages once again if the NPS park were established.

Former governor Yuki Shmull, coauthor of the 2002 letter, argued the case for a smaller park. "The NPS should be more specific. They need to come and tell us why [a particular site] is important to the war. But they can't connect one area of interest to another across a large area of no interest. Peleliu is such a small place." The NPS letter brusquely rejected the notion of selected and separate sites. But Guam's War in the Pacific Park, a U.S. National Historic Park administered by the NPS, consists of seven distinct "units" strewn along nine miles of Guam's west coast. Some units are invasion beaches, others lie one and a half miles inland. The Piti Guns unit is a few acres on a hillside with three Japanese coastal defense guns. Together the seven units total 2,037 acres, or 1.4 percent of this U.S. territory.

The July 2002 NPS letter had an uncompromising message and an impatient tone. The Park Service refused to come to Peleliu until agreement had first been reached "on size and location" and property owners had agreed "to allow the use of their property for historical park purposes" (SRS: 37). That is, the NPS would not come to the island to learn the residents' concerns, answer their urgent questions, and negotiate a compromise solution. American officials would come only after the islanders had granted their every demand. The rubak Smau Amalei expressed the local willingness to discuss a park with the American officials: "If the NPS would come and explain the details, talk and negotiate, then it might work. But their standoff attitude, send a map and make demands, is upsetting."

Without further discussions having occurred, the NPS wrote the SRS in January 2003. It declared the park "not feasible at this time" since Honolulu interpreted the Palauans' June 2002 letter as saying the landowners wanted to continue land uses that were incompatible with a park (SRS: 1). Palauans did not learn of this decision until the SRS was released in January 2004.

In the end, the battlefield park plan wound up as a case study in differing assumptions, misunderstandings, and poor communication. Peleliu's lands were entangled in a snail-paced legal process to determine clear title. This fundamental problem and the many uncertainties and doubts that arose during village meetings held with Palauan staff from the Historic Preservation Office were not adequately relayed to Honolulu.[17] The NPS was vague on critical matters like allowable land uses within a park, whether lands had to be sold outright, and who would buy them. No landowner that I interviewed understood that the park would be set aside "in perpetuity." The 1986 surveyors thought they had received agreement for a park from their brief consultations with chiefs and residents. But the report containing the maps showing all the land that the NPS wanted was not published for five years and was never distributed widely. In the 16 years following the survey, the NPS never returned to Peleliu in a concerted effort to deepen its understanding of life and land there, present its case in person, or listen directly to the people's misgivings about the size and terms of the proposal.

A major impediment that NPS personnel missed is that Palau has no tradition of parks that permanently remove land from productive use. The closest traditional analogue is the *bul*, which is a declaration by village chiefs that bans *temporarily* the use of certain public resources until they regenerate. Bul are almost always confined to marine resources.

Many Palauans questioned whether a battlefield park would attract many tourists. Haruo Esang observed, "[The Ireidan] are now getting very old. The young generation doesn't care as much. They are like Westerners, [the battle] is nothing to them. They come instead to dive; they like beaches." Of Peleliu's visitors Kent Giramur argued, "Eighty percent come for scenery and diving, fishing and sightseeing, and 20 percent for the war sites." If interest in the battlefield among Japanese and American tourists is low, among Palau's second-largest market, vacationers from Tawain, it is zero. In a good month Peleliu's battlefield attracts perhaps 600 to 700 day-trippers, most on packaged tours from Koror, who pay only a three-dollar entry fee. The NPS itself never addressed who would visit such a park; its definition of "feasibility" left out the entire question of economic viability.

It takes time to learn to read Peleliu's landscape, even superficially. An island that seems vacant and unused to outsiders, with uninhabited village sites, does not appear that way to its owners. The hand labor agroforestry practiced there does not look like cornfields in Iowa or even a backyard garden in Oregon. Plots are small and shifting constantly because of poor soil, and the food plants blend in with the forest cover. The emotional ties to lineage and clan lands, and to the past, mean the villages do exist, but in memory; they just have not been rebuilt yet. The brochure that Peleliu gives visitors has on its cover a map showing what Peleliu looks like to its residents: the island and its five traditional villages displayed proudly. Kloulklubed, where they have all lived for over 65 years, does not appear.

Residents of the island repeatedly expressed the need to retain lands to which their descendants could return to build homes. Matsko Tkel of Teliu explained that she and her husband have 16 children and grandchildren, each of whom eventually could return to Peleliu seeking land to live on. This right to traditional land is what it means to be a Palauan citizen. Even the park confined to Area 1 was not feasible if the people of Ngerkeyukl and Teliu were not willing to surrender the lands of their ancestors. Land is not a fungible commodity in Palau, not yet. If people lose their personal or lineage lands, they indeed have no place else to go except into the ocean.

Underlying the NPS plan was the assumption that the island of Peleliu matters to history, or to anyone, solely because of the battle of 1944. This is the same view held in orthodox American collective memory, and by political conservatives in Japan. Great portions of Peleliu's scarce land would be devoted to preserving the 74 most violent days in its 3,000-year history, violence wreaked by foreigners on each other, which obliterated the native way of life. The people of Peleliu do not share this opinion of their island's worth.

In recent years the NPS has worked in partnership with the local residents to create a different model for protecting cultural and historic resources. The Park Service funded a study that recommended establishing a heritage area on the island. This would involve a "lived in landscape," where lands, beaches, and waters remain inhabited and actively used for traditional sustainable economic purposes, while historic resources are also preserved. Heritage lands can be owned privately, or portions can be controlled by a public entity through long-term leases, easements, donations, or purchase. Landowners grant the public access to historic sites but also protect those sites from degradation caused by economic activity.

The Peleliu Legislature has created a Peleliu State Historical and Cultural Preservation Commission with broad powers to designate, acquire, and protect all the island's historic resources—not just those of the battlefield but also those of the Palauan natives and of the Japanese and American colonial regimes. The NPS supports the commission in many ways. It has funded the most thorough archaeological survey ever taken of the battlefield (and its dangerous unexploded ordnance), helped fund ethnographic research by Palau's Bureau of Arts and Culture, and offered technical assistance.[18] The commission's more difficult tasks will include enforcing professional standards of excavation in the remaining unopened caves and trying to bring order to the erection of monuments. Still, the commission and the heritage area concept should greatly aid Peleliu's people in finding a balance between their own needs for lands and resources and those of the foreign visitors drawn to the island for both its present and its past.

In 2000 the Japanese foreign aid agency, JICA published the results of its comprehensive study on economic development in Palau. Aware that U.S. Compact funding was scheduled to expire in 2009, the report's authors recommended that Palau expand its tourism development, which was seen as the primary engine for the archipelago's economy.[19]

The report recommends diversifying the diving and marine-based tourism in Palau by establishing tourist bases outside of Koror. It suggests constructing one in Ngarchelong on Babeldaob and the other in Peleliu, which would become the tourist base for the "Peleliu and Angaur Zone." The report correctly notes (on p. 32) that "Peleliu Island is located in the midst of the most attractive diving and fishing field in Palau" with most of these attractions in the Rock Islands and along the western reef, within a 30-minute speedboat ride of the island. The study makes very optimistic projections of future tourist arrivals in Peleliu and calculates the infrastructure needed and its costs. It makes no mention of having consulted the island's population. It is a classic top-down development scheme proposed by outside experts who know best what the target locals need.

The maps for Peleliu's two proposed Tourism Promotion Zones display how starkly different from the NPS was JICA's notion of the island's tourist attractions. For the West Coast Area, JICA proposes seven hotel lots, lined shoulder to shoulder—down the entire length of the White and Orange invasion beaches. The seventh lot abuts an otherwise undescribed "historical marker," which is the former U.S. cemetery. Three more hotel lots are proposed for the nearby South Coast Area. Lot nine is adjacent to a not-further-elaborated "memorial park"—the Japanese government Peace Park trilithon, the largest war monument on Peleliu.

The JICA report, in fact, contains not one single mention of the 1944 battle for Peleliu Island. Although the charter of the survey team was to identify the island's potential for economic growth, members of JICA did not even examine the military past in order to reject it as a possible contributor to tourism. The Japanese government's aid agency simply ignores the war entirely.

Accurately reflecting their respective governments' approaches to remembering World War II, the American NPS strives to commemorate the war, while JICA appears determined to forget it. The differences in their resulting proposals are stark:

the invasion beaches that the NPS wants to preserve in perpetuity, JICA foresees as a western Pacific Waikiki, devoted to hotels and water sports. JICA intends Peleliu to cater to Asian tourists, for whom the fascination of islands lies in the leisure they provide. For JICA's economists, Peleliu's reefs are now valued as coral gardens teeming with marine life to enchant foreign tourists. Where the four rubak set sail to chase the sun and landing craft crossed the reef to disgorge young men onto beaches smothered in fire and smoke, launches will glide across cerulean waters to drop passengers on sandy palm-lined beaches fronting air-conditioned hotels. The ten hotels will have their backs to the rest of the island: to its farms, its mangroves and mountains, to its caves and wartime past—and to its native residents. The hotels would not just ignore the sites of battle, they would demolish the scores of important ones on and behind the invasion beaches.

We have seen how the people of Palau avoid confronting Japan over its wartime depredations, in return for which Japan donates generous aid. Japan gets to avoid explicit discussion of the war era, just as it prefers at home and elsewhere in Asia. JICA's silence on the war history of Peleliu is consistent with this modus vivendi. In fairness, the silence may also derive from JICA's pragmatic assessment of what attractions bring most tourists, especially most Japanese tourists, to Palau in the first place: diving, boating, fishing, but not battlefield history. Even so, JICA's mission was to identify opportunities for Peleliu's economic future, and the agency itself advocated making the island a southern tourism center. It seems unconscionable that JICA would completely ignore the potential for a battlefield to attract the interest of some portion of the 22,500 visitors it projected by 2010 (45,000 by 2020), even if every one of them initially chose the island for marine recreation.

Renguul Kelbasang Soalablai, a state legislator, advised me that the legislature had not approved the JICA study, so it remained moot. He thought the scheme was too grandiose. Several residents were similarly wary of Peleliu's being brought full throttle into the global tourist industry, where, as they saw it, foreign investors and market forces would make all the decisions. JICA anticipated 1,350 jobs created by the 45,000 visitors of 2020 (vol. 2:37), but it was silent on the nature of those jobs and who would fill them. International tourism is notorious, of course, for shuffling locals into only the most menial of service jobs—jobs that Palauan residents have largely refused to take in Koror, leaving them for foreign workers. Peleliu's doubters had reason to question the benefits to their island.

In the early 2000s, JICA's plan stood as the major rival to the National Park Service's vision for Peleliu's future, the huge and exclusive battlefield park that so disturbed the Palauans when they learned its details. It is a pungent irony that along with all its other difficulties, the American plan encountered sub rosa resistance from an alternative conception proposed by a Japanese development agency. (The JICA plan was known primarily to various elites of Peleliu. When someone assured me that the western beaches were too valuable for tourism to devote to the battlefield park, the JICA influence seemed apparent.) The proposals of both agencies betrayed the same fundamental ignorance about the lives and values of the island's residents. The NPS at least initially made good faith efforts to obtain agreement and cooperation from them. JICA could never be bothered; its experts knew better what Peleliu needed than islanders could ever know. From the agencies' shared ignorance, they then parted ways to produce two incompatible designs that stemmed from diametrically opposed attitudes toward the war, and from conflicting answers that the agencies assumed to questions that they never explicitly posed—to themselves or to the islanders. What "value" does Peleliu possess? What do its features like seas, reefs, beaches, shores, farmlands, village sites, and hills mean to its residents? How do they use them now, and what are *their* plans for them in the future? Where do foreigners fit into this island society and landscape today? Do the chad ra Beliliou have an independent history? Does it matter?

9
Parallel Histories

Three Peoples' Memories of War and Loss

> I would not have the anniversaries of our victories celebrated, nor those of our defeats made fast days and spent in humiliation and prayer; but I would like to see truthful history written.
>
> Ulysses S. Grant, *Memoirs*, ch. 12.

In thinking of the three peoples whose lives were altered by the battle for Peleliu—the chad ra Beliliou and residents from each of the two warring powers (Japan and the U.S.) that participated in the fighting, lost loved ones, or study and commemorate it today—I am tempted into a geometrical metaphor that seems incoherent: their memories intersect at Peleliu, yet those memories seldom, if ever, *touch* each other. It is more accurate to say that their memories share the battle of Peleliu as their substance, but as emphasized throughout this book, each of the three groups views that event, and the island itself, in distinctive and mutually exclusive ways. Their memories, then, travel in parallel; they travel alongside each other, but even at the horizon, out where the four rubak of Ngerkeyukl chased the sun, they fail to converge. The three peoples almost never interact in ways where their memories can be exchanged and broadened and revised.

The failure here is most egregious among the foreign visitors, few of whom stop to consider that the people whose only home was Peleliu suffered immeasurably during the war, while their ancient and settled way of life disappeared in that inferno. The Izokukai and U.S. veterans come to Peleliu because of the loss of life itself that they experienced. For these foreigners and their descendants the emotional trauma and the long trip to Peleliu, which may be the climax to decades of anxious expectation, limit their readiness to look beyond their own concerns. Differences in language, culture, and history—and residual enmities among some—continue to divide most tourists. These also impede them from filling out the missing portions of their experiences and possibly finding acceptance and peace within the shared tragedies of their pasts.

The chad ra Beliliou, although accused of ignorance about the battle, comprehend very well the essentials of the war experience for their visitors. Japanese soldiers died in large numbers defending the Nan'yō, and their relatives or countrymen come to mourn, to pray, or to search for the bones of their dead. Americans come to visit the island they or their countrymen fought over (and to mourn in ways less apparent to the Palauans). Both raise memorials to their losses. Residents of Peleliu know relatively little of the context of the battle or how it was conducted operationally. They do not consider these to be elements of *Palauan* history. Many also keep a certain distance from both Japanese and American Ireidan, believing it is not their role to force contact where none seems wanted.

American and Japanese Accounts of the Battle

A close reading of monument texts can be revealing, but, as we have found, they are necessarily limited in their purpose and their space and are neither comprehensive nor analytic. In order to explore further the memories that travel in parallel, we must add a review of representative postwar historical accounts produced by the two combatants. In the discussion of the works that follows, several themes emerge: the advantages accruing to the victors in writing the history of the battle; the narrow focus, deliberate silences, and lack of critical analysis shared by official government accounts on both sides; the role played by overwhelming American material might and Japanese attempts to counter it with superior spirit; the painful truth for both foes that the Peleliu battle served no military purpose worthy of its death count; how U.S. sources have obscured the failures of the marine commander, while his Japanese counterpart performed superbly; and the valuable contributions to the record of the Peleliu campaign and the Pacific War by memoirs and works from both sides that included personal testimonies of infantrymen. The discussion will also include what the two adversaries have to say about the people on whose island the drama played out (when they are considered at all); and present in turn what the chad ra Beliliou say about their foreign visitors, their war, and the quests that bring them to Peleliu.

In war's immediate aftermath, ignoring, forgetting, or dissembling serve the useful purpose of helping people surmount residual pain and shame. It has been over seven decades since World War II ended. Much truthful history has been written about this terrible cataclysm. Yet, with few exceptions, both combatants from Peleliu still produce constricted narratives of this battle, touting national and individual virtues that are designed to offer pride and solace but that fail to incorporate the perspective that the passage of so much time should have provided.

Except for George McMillan's well-regarded history of the First Marine Division (1949), which devotes one chapter to Peleliu, and Stanley Falk's illustrated account of the Angaur and Peleliu battles (1974), for the first 40 years after the war the only comprehensive English-language accounts of the battle were official U.S. government histories.[1] These placed Peleliu within the American narrative of the Pacific War. It was significant as "a stepping stone towards the ultimate objective" of defeating Japan, a duty forced upon the United States by the attack on Pearl Harbor.[2] American armed services performed heroically and won a well-deserved victory. The American official historians—and most others who followed them—produced versions of "victors' history," a privileged history like that described by John Dower in chapter 7: consoling accounts reporting that "the outcome of the war had been great and good," in which "triumph gave a measure of closure to grief." But as A. C. Grayling reminds us, "Victory tends to provide absolution for all wrongs since the victor is the judge and jury in his own behalf. . . . The victor nations of the Second World War have allowed their victory to excuse them from self-examination over some aspects of their behavior. But that is a wrong in itself." (He is primarily concerned with the morality of the aerial bombing of civilians, the central subject of his important study.)[3]

The landmark official history, Frank Hough's Marine Corps monograph, *The Assault on Peleliu*, was published in 1950 and reprinted in 1990. Thorough, with fine maps and useful information about the Japanese side, it remains an indispensable source. Robert Smith's official army history first appeared in 1953 and was reprinted in 1984, and Garand and Strobridge covered the battle in volume 4 of the official history of Marine Corps operations in the war (1971). These works examine the American strategy, planning, and conduct of the battle in fine-grained detail, and they dominated the historic record until the mid-1980s. Their narrow focus, however, raises a central concern about Pacific War history: if the scope of relevant history is defined as preparation for battle, its execution, and the immediate aftermath, then the struggle occurs in a historical vacuum, devoid of context that explains what brought the participants to blows in such remote locations and what resulted from the conflicts not just months but decades later. So too, the native people will be, by definition, irrelevant. For all the differences in their accounts of the battle for Peleliu, Japan and the United States have shared this blinkered perspective toward the event. To this day, their official histories ignore or discount their colonial ambitions, the impact of their warfare on the island's inhabitants, and their failures toward the Micronesian people during their respective periods of colonial rule before and after the war.

The single most important Japanese publication on the fighting in Palau is contained in the 104-volume official government history of the war, commonly referred to as the Senshi Sōsho, war history series. Volume 13, published in 1968 and still not yet translated into English, covers Peleliu, Angaur, Babeldaob, and Iwo Jima.[4] For the Palau operations it draws on such sources as Funasaka Hiroshi's *Eirei no Zekkyō* and *Sakura, Sakura*, diaries of soldiers, interviews with survivors, electronic communications, and many U.S. publications. Most valuable was a large set of documents brought back from Palau by an army colonel, Nakagawa Ken. These provided records of preparations, dispositions, tactics and strategy, and the progress of the battles. The volume also contains excellent maps of Japanese military activities throughout the Palau archipelago, several of which, along with tables, provide crucial data on numbers of troops and civilians at the three main sites of Peleliu, Angaur, and Babeldaob.

The historian Mark Peattie describes the Senshi Sōsho as "the most detailed, most complete, most authoritative record of the plans, organization, armaments, strategy, and tactics of the Japanese armed forces in the Pacific War." But as he and coauthor David Evans observe elsewhere, it has serious shortcomings, chief of which is the "lack of any interpretive or critical approach to the subject treated."[5] The compilers accumulated vast amounts of information but failed to stand back and ask larger questions of their material. They also seldom criticized wartime commanders, some of whom the writers had served under. With its focus on tactical and operational details, its lack of broader context, and its reluctance to criticize the wartime leadership, the volume on Peleliu shares the weaknesses of its official U.S. counterparts.

Japanese historiography of the Pacific War faced other limits as well. After its defeat Japan rejected military concerns, and its scholars exhibited indifference, even hostility, toward operational history.[6] Scholarly studies, as a result, have been few, which left the field open to memoirs from nationalistic veterans like Funasaka or to biographies like the one about Kurata Yoji, another veteran survivor of Angaur.[7] Japanese popular accounts of the war in Palau have therefore been dominated by histories written by veterans, their memoirs, biographies of them, journalistic works, and one excellent fictional rendering of the battle for Peleliu. Some of these same men pursued war commemoration within Palau as well, so their impact on Japanese memory of Peleliu and Angaur has been pronounced.

The American official histories reflect the orthodox opinions of the Pacific War and do much to define the particular versions that apply to Peleliu. They portray a battle of extreme ferocity, dominated by the arduous process of rooting the Japanese infantry out of the caves. Like the text of the plaque on the Marine Corps monument, the books emphasize how U.S. forces considered themselves at war with both a stubborn and incomprehensible human foe and a hostile and alien environment: reefs that were "treacherous," swamps that trapped the unwary, razor-sharp coral, perpendicular cliffs, exhausting tropical heat, dehydration mocked by drenching downpours. All were obstacles that could be overcome only with tenacity and courage.

And against all of them the United States applied its unprecedented industrial might and unlimited force, with the determination recalled by a marine veteran: "Whatever it takes." In David Kennedy's Pulitzer Prize-winning book, he explains that in World War II it was American national policy to minimize its casualties, to fight instead a "war of machines," in which America's primary contribution to the Allied cause would be its productive capacity, not the lives of its citizens.[8] Total U.S. ground forces, for both Europe and the Pacific, numbered 90 divisions. By contrast, in 1942 Germany had 183 divisions on the Russian front, and 3 in Africa. Japan had 56 divisions at home and 167 divisions abroad as of August 1945; these latter were concentrated in China, Manchuria, and Korea. At Okinawa, the climactic battle of the Pacific War, the United States employed 7 divisions, with 1 more in reserve. But they were supported by 1,200 ships, including 40 large and small aircraft carriers with over 2,000 aircraft, 18 battleships, and 200 destroyers. Kennedy notes that in the final 18 months of the war a U.S. combatant in the Pacific could draw on four tons of supplies; his Japanese opponent had two pounds. The U.S. national policy worked: 405,000 American service personnel lost their lives, equivalent to three-tenths of 1 percent of the 1941 U.S. population of 142 million; proportionately this was the smallest loss of any major combatant. Japan lost 3.1 million war dead, 2.3 million servicemen and 800,000 civilians, or 4.2 percent of its population of 73 million.[9]

Funasaka Hiroshi, the survivor of the battle for Angaur and early Ireidan to Palau, wrote several books about the battles for these islands. One, the story of his experiences fighting on Angaur, where he received severe wounds and became a prisoner of war, was translated into English as *Falling Blossoms*.[10] The Japanese original is *Eirei no Zekkyō, Scream of the Eirei*; recall that *eirei* is a politically sensitive term for dead soldiers.[11] His account of the Peleliu battle, *Sakura, Sakura*, takes its name from the final coded message sent by Colonel Nakagawa as he prepared to take his own life.[12] A third book tells the story of the war in Palau through 600 messages to and from General Inoue's headquarters, which, Funasaka explains, were smuggled to Japan at war's end.[13] Its title, *Gyokusai*, literally means "crushed jewels," another heroic term for soldiers who seek an honorable death rather than surrender.[14] It is the term used in the Senshi Sōsho to identify all the garrisons in the central Pacific that were annihilated, including Peleliu and Angaur (e.g., vol. 13, Attachment Table 1).

Like most American histories, *Falling Blossoms* restricts its focus almost exclusively to the battle. The Japanese Army soldiers fought, Funasaka avers, for a vital cause, to protect the empire of Japan. For this they were always willing to lay down their lives. "The Americans cannot be allowed to get any nearer to Japanese soil. We cannot let the enemy take this island!" he remembers thinking as he awaited the invasion of Angaur. The marines, he believes, fought only in hopes of staying alive and being rotated back home.[15]

After the war many people in Japan attributed their defeat to the superior wealth, science, industry, and organizational skills of the United States, as symbolized ultimately by the atomic bomb. This disparity in material and intellectual resources became central to Japanese memories of the conflict.[16] In both *Sakura, Sakura* and

Falling Blossoms Funasaka writes with deep feeling about the technological superiority of U.S. weaponry and the overpowering quantitative advantages enjoyed by its military. In the latter book, American tanks are "giant" and terrifying as they approach his men, who have no weapons beyond clutching a bomb as they allow the treads to crush them. The American bombardment is a "waterfall of fire that flowed without pause, painting a layer of red just above our heads." Funasaka peers down at the well-lit American tents in a secured part of Angaur: "That sea of electric lights was a powerful silent commentary on their 'battle of abundance.' They had everything material while we had nothing but our strong determination." Even on the first day of the invasion the attackers having landed 22,000 men to the defenders' 1,200 meant "we'd already been defeated, overwhelmed by a superior abundance of material resources we could never have imagined."[17]

The text of the monument raised by the Peleliu Sector Defense Command makes this same point about opposing "overwhelming American landing forces" while fighting "the most fierce and courageous battle to the very last soldier." The sad irony here is that the immense industrial potential of the United States was precisely what knowledgeable Japanese leaders like Admiral Yamamoto most feared when contemplating war and why they pinned all their hopes on a decisive naval victory forcing a quick negotiated settlement. What struck Funasaka and his foot soldiers with such awe had been understood but ignored within a haze of wishful thinking at Imperial Headquarters. In 1937 America's share of world manufacturing output was 32.2 percent, Japan's was 3.5 percent. In a joint Army-Navy conference in August 1941, Imperial General Headquarters had received a detailed presentation demonstrating that American industrial war potential was, in aggregate, ten times that of Japan.[18]

As one defeat followed another in 1944–45, the high command invoked the self-sacrifice of gyokusai to make heroes out of men killed in a lost cause. But gyokusai also deflected blame downward onto the ordinary fighting men and the suffering civilians: Japan was losing its war of survival not because of Imperial Headquarters' disastrous ignorance and fantasy-based strategy but because of the soldiers' and citizens' insufficient spirit and effort.[19] It is unfortunate that the Senshi Sōsho perpetuates the use of this dishonest term. Peleliu and Angaur represent the price paid by common soldiers for the countless failures of the military and civilian elites in the war they started. It was young men dying for old men's mistakes. Although not meant to be, Funasaka's books and the plaque on Peleliu, in the way they impel the careful reader to consider Japan's catastrophic miscalculations, are pointed rebukes of the nation's wartime leadership.[20]

The indomitable bravery of Japanese soldiers forms an important part of the memories on display at Peleliu and Angaur, although the fatalism that accompanied the courage remains a puzzle to many Americans. Even more than their former enemies, the Japanese tourists who come to Palau have to confront the question of whether their men died without purpose. Defeat could haunt survivors even after half a century. One Japanese soldier tells the camera in *Tears of Peleliu*, "I can't be proud of myself because we lost the war. If we'd won, I'd be proud despite the suffering. We lost, so we suffered in vain."[21]

Funasaka, though, is curt with doubts raised in the postwar, "when one could often hear one-sided criticism directed against the military, as if to say that the victims of the Pacific War died a dog's death in vain. But these were always the words of men who had failed as soldiers, riding on a trend of intellectualism. The most earnest desire of us young men was simply and innocently to 'die for our homeland.'" He reports a lieutenant who, when his men exhausted their ammunition, ordered a *banzai* charge, exhorting: "Now's the time to realize every man's dream. Meet you at Yasukuni Shrine!"[22]

The official and semiofficial American histories of Peleliu skirt or dismiss possible topics of controversy. Yet eventually reevaluations were published that took a more critical stance toward U.S. strategy in mid-1944 and toward the planning and conduct of the invasion. In the 1990s journalists brought new voices into the record by adding the reminisces of veterans, who provided vital personal details of the combat but also expressed longstanding doubts about the tactics employed, the quality of American leadership, and the utility of the island as a base.

Some of the American amphibious operations in Micronesia went very smoothly, resulting in victories at low costs. Tinian is the outstanding example, Kwajalein perhaps the second. But from the first hours of fighting on Peleliu it was clear to many that something had gone terribly awry in the planning and execution of the invasion. In the past 25 years Peleliu has joined Tarawa in the way it is remembered more for its historical controversies than for its success as an amphibious assault.

Most troubling for American memory is whether the invasion was necessary in the first place, given the air base's limited usefulness after its capture. The first official American account of the battle, by Major Frank O. Hough under the auspices of the Historical Division of the U.S. Marine Corps, appeared in 1950. It includes a discussion of this subject—an indication that from the outset it bothered historians. Hough states, however, that doubt about the strategic importance of the seizure "is unfortunate to the memory of the men who fought and died there." But memories of struggle and loss are irrelevant to the separate question of necessity. Three years later army historian Robert Smith was more forthright, saying that from the vantage of hindsight the invasion should have been skipped, but what the commanders knew at the time suggested proceeding. The semiofficial naval historian Samuel Eliot Morison concludes the gains had not been worth the cost; yet the marine history by Garand and Strobridge dismisses the question as "a matter of unproductive speculation." This American debate over needless losses never includes the 12,500 Japanese who died defending Peleliu and Angaur or what the battles cost these islands' natives.[23]

Only as the 40th anniversary of the invasion approached did Harry Gailey, a professor of history, publish *Peleliu 1944*, the first independent, full-length study of the battle intended as a *critical* study of the leadership, planning, and conduct of the campaign. In its thoughtful, sharp, but fair assessments, Gailey's small volume, though out of print, remains the best guide to the battle.[24]

He argues that by the summer of 1944, when the Imperial Navy had been chased out of the western Pacific and its air arm destroyed during the Marianas invasions, seizing Palau was no longer required. Thus commanders should have altered the plans even before Halsey's 11th-hour discoveries of enemy weakness in the Philippines led him to recommend aborting the landings in Palau. Gailey skewers military historians' attempts to dismiss questioning of Peleliu's usefulness as "largely an apology for the upper-echelon Navy and Marine officers who did not use effectively the intelligence reports available to them. American possession of [Peleliu and Angaur] had little influence on General MacArthur's campaign in the Philippines and played only a minor role in subsequent actions in the Central Pacific."[25]

As to why Peleliu became so little known despite its terrible severity, Gailey blames marine commander Major General William Rupertus for his open hostility to the press, which discouraged many reporters from following the campaign. Rupertus told the press before the landing that it would be over in three to four days, convincing many reporters that they should find more newsworthy stories to cover. Publicity given operations in Europe and the Leyte landings in the Philippines on October 20, 1944, also conspired to push Peleliu into the shadows. In the 1995 *NBC Dateline* episode on Peleliu a bitter veteran says of the battle's obscurity, "It was a classic military mistake, and was . . . covered up. You can interview a hundred people on the streets of the U.S. and I doubt you'll find a one of them who knew what it was." One can only sympathize with his frustration, but Peleliu was never covered up. The fact is, as Montaigne reminds us, few battles from any war gain lasting fame.[26]

Gailey wades into the controversy over whether the navy's aerial reconnaissance had recognized the formidable ridges and provided warning to the marines (who insisted they had not been properly alerted). Gailey criticizes both Morison's and Hough's accounts for repeating the marines' claims.[27] In the archives he found both photos and maps that show the ridges clearly, despite heavy forest cover. It appears the intelligence centers recognized the mountainous terrain, but awareness of this dangerous high ground failed to percolate down to the lower echelons that most needed it.

Despite the Japanese sense that they were crushed by overwhelming force, Gailey argues that the United States assigned insufficient troops to the invasion, so that the same exhausted men had to make repeated assaults up mountain slopes until their units ceased to exist as organized forces. Again General Rupertus deserves blame for this unimaginative straight-ahead hammering. The most recent of the official histories, Brigadier General Gordon Gayle's pamphlet for the 50th anniversary, does confront the American failures to some extent. Gayle was a battalion commander at Peleliu, so like many of the compilers of the Senshi Sōsho, he writes about the performance of men under whom he served. He criticizes Rupertus for failing to adjust his preinvasion plan to the realities of Peleliu's mountains but obscures how General Geiger had to order Rupertus to accept help from the army. On the question of Peleliu's usefulness Gayle concludes, "The holding was a convenience, but not a necessity."[28]

While works like Gailey's try to carefully evaluate the battle's necessity, a high-profile television program misrepresented the subject in a tawdry display for dramatic effect. An August 1995 episode of *NBC Dateline* mixed footage from the battle with interviews of veterans and film taken on Peleliu at the time of the celebration of the invasion's 50th anniversary the previous September.[29] Other documentaries about Peleliu—*The Bloody Ridges of Peleliu* or *Peleliu 1944: Horror in the Pacific*—had presented the battle and its main issues in chronological order and with responsible accuracy. One, *The Tears of Peleliu*, interviewed elderly chad ra Beliliou at the time of the 50th anniversary who voiced thoughts much like those I obtained concerning their losses from the war.[30] However, *Dateline*'s Tom Brokaw—beginning his "Greatest Generation franchise" at this time—and Jane Pauley sought to wring every possible drop of emotion from veterans and the audience. They did so by manipulating the facts and the men who survived their month of hell on the island. *Dateline* states the United States thought there were only 3,000 Japanese defenders. This is utterly false; the numbers were known with precision from captured Japanese documents. The inadequate naval bombardment and ignorance of the Omleblochel hills, however, are correctly depicted, as is the racial hatred that animated the soldiers. No native of Peleliu is interviewed. A few island women are shown as they greet the veterans arriving at the island's wharf, and a few more residents are glimpsed during memorial ceremonies.

The script tries to imply that Peleliu's lack of usefulness in the war became apparent to the veterans only upon their return to the island in 1994. Well into the program Brokaw asserts, "It would be many years before the survivors of Peleliu would learn a terrible secret about the island so many fought for and died for," while Pauley assures us that their memories "turned bitter when they began to discover a terrible truth about Peleliu." Only here does *Dateline* reveal Admiral Halsey's recommendation two days before the landing to abandon the Peleliu operation. Cut to Peleliu in 1994, where an aged veteran is prodded into tears by an NBC interviewer as he refuses to accept that his buddies died for nothing. It is shabby and meretricious stuff, and E. B. Sledge, whose memoir on the battle is discussed below, gives the lie to it by telling the camera that he and his fellow marines knew, when the invasion of Leyte occurred *while they were still fighting on Peleliu in 1944*, that the island would play little if any role in the return to the Philippines.[31] It was no dark secret; the survivors had lived with the knowledge all their adult lives. When I described this episode to marine veteran Rich Gettell, he replied, "That sort of thing does a disservice to the men."

The Japanese antiestablishment writer and pacifist Oda Makoto wrote a moving fictional account of a battle for a Pacific island that is, as the book's translator Donald Keene surmises, Peleliu thinly disguised. (Japanese troops fight from caves in a mountain range, they make no banzai charges, their commander launches a tank-led counterattack on the afternoon of D-day.) Keene translates the Japanese title, *Gyokusai*, as *The Breaking Jewel*. One important theme is the racial discrimination that a Korean volunteer suffers from his Japanese fellow soldiers. Oda uses the racist underpinnings and brutality of Japan's expansion in Asia to develop a powerful critique of the war. He portrays the brainwashing of the soldiers, constantly exhorted to play their role as the heroic bulwark defending the homeland. But he also invokes American conduct in this battle, noting U.S. forces' reliance on overwhelming material superiority, their "barbarous" tactics, the havoc they wreak on the island with flame, and how they "killed Japanese soldiers inhumanly, not recognizing them as human beings."[32]

In a sad mirror image of history, Oda has his Japanese defenders realize the futility of their sacrifice precisely as E. B. Sledge describes this recognition dawning among the marines: if the Japanese garrison's mission was to prevent the American armada from advancing on the Philippines through Peleliu, then the landings at Leyte, in the middle of the ten weeks of slaughter on Peleliu, meant that "the main theater of the war had leaped over the heads of the Japanese and American forces even while they continued their life-and-death battle on this little island." Peleliu "no longer had the significance of a bulwark of any kind." The glorious death of a gyokusai, a crushed jewel, promised the men by their officers stands revealed as a meaningless waste, a dog's death. Oda ends his melancholy novel with a hallucinatory description of a woman fighting alongside the dying hero. Then decades later an elderly Japanese visitor to the island finds his native guide repeating this story and asking if it was true that she killed many Americans.[33]

In the early 1990s two American books appeared in which the authors employed a combination of documentary sources and interviews with marine veterans to produce the first narratives of the battle in which the experiences and opinions of infantrymen figured prominently. Bill D. Ross and James H. Hallas both provide a sense of immediacy and detail missing from previous accounts. Their books buttress the views of those historians who argue the value of oral histories to flesh out the documentary record.

Unfortunately, Ross's *Peleliu: Tragic Triumph* is marred by glaring errors any time he steps beyond the confines of the military history. But he was the first to focus attention on one crucial piece of the Peleliu story: the quality of the leadership of the marines, as revealed by the postinvasion fate of their commanding-officer, General William Rupertus. The failure to act on the intelligence concerning the existence of mountains, the prodigal expenditure of men's lives in a battering ram advance against those mountains, capped by his superior officer having to order him to accept reinforcements from the Army's 81st Division—all these errors were not lost on the head of the Marine Corps. In late October 1944 Commandant Alexander Vandegrift summoned Rupertus to Washington, D.C., and relieved him of command of the First Marine Division. Ross quotes an aide of Vandegrift as saying he was displeased with the campaign and its heavy losses and had no choice but to relieve Rupertus. It took nearly 50 years before a journalist uncovered what every official campaign history studiously ignores. No succeeding account has admitted and discussed the implications of the most salient fact concerning U.S. leadership at Peleliu: the commanding general was fired.[34]

Dick Camp's *Last Man Standing* uses marine archives and oral histories to provide a tightly focused account of the First Regiment's destruction as a fighting unit during the first week of battle across the beaches and against the southern ridges.[35] His account can be considered quasiofficial given his position with the National Museum of the Marine Corps. Despite its useful detail, this yard-by-yard narrative uses its narrow perspective to avoid addressing the two most pressing historical issues for the United States—whether Peleliu was worth the high cost, and whether much of that cost resulted from incompetent leadership.

Camp is particularly frustrating on the second question since his organizing theme provides an important addition to the literature on Peleliu. In every army a chasm exists between the officers and the enlisted men they lead. Official histories, written from reports made by officers, tend to airbrush out both this tension and the errors of officers. Camp, though, depicts well this caste-based conflict between the brave, disciplined marine infantrymen who suffered desperately under the slow-witted, inflexible command of two of their officers, Colonel Chesty Puller and General Rupertus. Camp describes how these two squandered their men's lives in futile assaults up the deadly slopes of the Omleblochel. Both men refused reinforcements from the army and tried to adhere to the unrealistic three- to four-day timetable Rupertus had declared to the press. As a result, Puller, the commanding officer of the First Marine Regiment, destroyed his unit, while Rupertus destroyed his, the First Marine Division.

For 300 pages Camp includes many harsh comments about Rupertus as a person and leader made by those who served under him, and makes plain his failures as commander at Peleliu. (The *NBC Dateline* episode also shows enlisted men angrily recalling that Rupertus ordered them to keep attacking without regard to their losses.) Yet concerning the dismissal of Rupertus, Camp simply repeats Vandegrift's mollifying remarks, as reported by Ross, carefully worded to protect Rupertus's reputation: "I had no choice but to relieve Rupertus of his command.... I knew the Peleliu campaign must nearly have exhausted him." Camp shrinks from making explicit the conclusion contained in his own argument. Certainly Rupertus and Puller were exhausted, but both men deserved to be relieved of command because of their performance at Peleliu. (Puller retained his.) American histories share an unflattering similarity here with their official Japanese counterparts—the refusal to take wartime commanders to task for their most blatant failures, which cost men's lives.[36]

Wartime Japan apotheosized its soldiers and sailors for their fighting spirit. No one among the Peleliu garrison deserves such admiration more than its commanding officer, Col. Nakagawa Kunio. Even the earliest American histories treat him with respect as a tough, creative, and skilled foe who fully utilized the terrain of Peleliu and his limited resources to force the invaders into a bloody drawn-out siege that none of them had anticipated. Max Hastings observes that the battles for the Micronesian islands were concentrated in space, so they were decided by the endeavors of foot soldiers with their immediate support, like tanks and light artillery.[37] This meant the island battles were fought largely on Japanese terms, where the overwhelming American advantages in fleets, manpower, materiel, and firepower could be diminished though not fully neutralized. Nakagawa added the keystone, the idea of placing his army underground to protect it and prolong its ability to fight. He did this so successfully that the Japanese commanders at the two final island campaigns, Iwo Jima and Okinawa, followed his example to horrifying effect. Nakagawa's brilliance as a commander and his troops' steely discipline thwarted his opponents' expectation of a quick sharp fight that would allow Peleliu to support the return to the Philippines. Even though Nakagawa and his men were given the assignment to expend themselves as yet another gyokusai garrison and duly suffered annihilation, those in Japan knowledgeable about the battle draw comfort from remembering that their brave fighting men were led by such a competent commander. Neither side has yet added the conclusion that Nakagawa's success in defeat demolished the career of the nominal victor, the Colonel's less imaginative, less able American adversary.

Three other books devoted to Peleliu add incrementally to our knowledge. That by Moran and Rottman is derivative, but Derrick Wright's *To the Far Side of Hell* is thorough in its brevity and judges the historical controversies fairly; it is the best study of the campaign for the general reader among the works now in print. It contains a good choice of photos and reproductions of the memorable paintings Tom Lea made of the battle for *Life* magazine. Bill Sloan's *Brotherhood of Heroes* fits among the Greatest Generation—Band of Brothers publications of the late 1990s. Its title makes clear its perspective. Like Ross and Hallas, Sloan uses oral histories of aging vets to add immediacy to the story he tells. But the minute, small-unit detail comes at the price of a self-referential view of history, where ground that was covered in previous books is crunched underfoot once again to add a bit of personal testimony, and the reader is given no guidance concerning the larger historic and strategic matters surrounding the island clash.[38]

The Army's 81st Wildcat Division irked many marines by raising three monuments to itself before departing Peleliu, while the marines left none. American books and films about the battle, however, devote a disproportionate share of attention to the First Marine Division. The Wildcats' seizure of Angaur and their nine weeks on Peleliu receive only slight notice. A recent study improves this imbalance with its careful accounts of the Wildcats' actions on Angaur, their quick capture of Ulithi (an atoll east of Yap, which, as a fleet anchorage, proved the most valuable American acquisition in the western Carolines), and their determined fighting for Peleliu. Palauans are mentioned once: "Finally, in addition to the Japanese troops on Angaur, there was a civilian population, both Japanese and natives."[39]

Wil Hylton's *Vanished*, which received an unusual amount of attention for a book dealing with Palau's wartime past, relates the extraordinary efforts private organizations and families have made in conjunction with U.S. government agencies to locate and recover the remains of 30 or so American airmen whose B-24 bombers were shot down in the Palau lagoon in 1944. The planes that Hylton focuses on were bombing Palau just prior to the invasions of Peleliu and Angaur. The material and technological advantages of the American searchers and their resilience in the hostile tropics echo the fundamental American narrative of the Pacific war: the book's dust jacket tells how "a maverick team of scientists and scuba divers . . . trolled the water with side-scan sonar, conducted grid searches on the seafloor, crawled through thickets of mangrove and poison trees, and flew over the islands in small planes to shoot infrared photography."

Hylton's depiction of the families and interested parties who make up the American POW/MIA community (prisoners of war/missing in action) reveals how much they have in common with the war-bereaved families of Japan, the Nihon Izokukai. Both are well-organized and influential pressure groups, single-minded, intent on recovering the remains of lost men. Their deep emotional investments keep their vision narrowly focused and locked firmly on the past. As with the Izokukai on Peleliu, tensions erupt over methods and leadership between the U.S. government agencies devoted to locating POW/MIA remains and the private parties.[40]

Yet, in a book devoted to the hunt for war remains in the archipelago, Hylton never mentions the Izokukai and their half century of efforts to gather 12,500 men lost in battle or the additional 10,000 dead of starvation in the siege of Babeldaob. Nor is there mention of how the people of Palau lived in terror and lost loved ones, homes, villages, infrastructure, and an ordered society from 18 months of incessant American bombing. Seventy years after the war, on Palau the gulf between the two former enemies remains unbridged. Each side appears unaware that the other exists. Neither of them is prepared to respond to the plea of the Angaur survivor Kurata Yoji: to let the past go and look instead to the future to find ways to aid the Palauan people.

The final Japanese book I will discuss, Sawachi Hisae's *Berau no sei to shi* (*Life and Death in Palau*) remains untranslated into English, like most other Japanese accounts of Peleliu. A respected journalist with liberal leanings, Sawachi focuses on Japanese, especially Okinawan, civilians and their experiences as migrants to Palau and as conscripts and laborers when trapped on Babeldaob under the Japanese Army's authority during 1944–45.[41] No American account of the war in Palau considers the fate of the 30,000 Japanese troops, 15,000 Japanese and Asian civilians, and 5,000 islanders besieged by the United States on Babeldaob for over a year (see chapter 5). It was Sawachi who published the Japanese Army data, which, when later analyzed, revealed that 5,000 of these civilians had likely starved to death along with a similar number of soldiers.[42]

For all their gritty depictions of battle, however, none of these accounts truly renders the dehumanization of war's violence, forces the reader to abandon comforting notions of "terrible but necessary," or confronts the truth about organized mass murder. It was left for a marine from the Fifth Regiment at Peleliu to write the memoir that once and for all stripped away the glory of combat and unforgettably captured the hatred, ferocity, stink, and mayhem of the Pacific War. Paul Fussell describes the disappearance by the 1970s of the concept of "prohibitive obscenity," the reluctance to reveal to the public the full degradation and inhumanity of war, which had acted as a censor on earlier memories of warfare. E. B. Sledge's *With the Old Breed at Peleliu and Okinawa*, first published in 1981, is the outstanding example of how this new freedom allowed a PFC assigned to a mortar unit at Peleliu to reveal, as never before, the obscenity of war.[43] John Keegan, preeminent among historians of warfare in our time, called it "one of the most arresting documents in war literature." John Gregory Dunne wrote, "Of all the books about the ground war in the Pacific, it is the closest to a masterpiece." Today, no serious study of the Pacific War fails to include it for its chilling insights into the heart of what has been called "the most American of our great wars."[44]

Sledge does not give us battle displaying honor, nobility, and respect for the foe. Rather, it is battle of grim determination and brutality, merciless in execution. No reader can forget Sledge's description of a U.S. marine slashing the cheeks of a still-living but paralyzed Japanese in order to pry out his gold teeth for souvenirs. Sledge's experiences and his words appear prominently in the episodes on

Peleliu and Okinawa in Ken Burns's documentary *The War*, and he is one of three marines whose battle experiences were re-created in the HBO miniseries *The Pacific*. Three of the ten episodes in *The Pacific* concern Peleliu. The miniseries also features Robert Leckie, who was wounded on Peleliu, and whose memoir *Helmet for My Pillow* was a best seller. Sloan's brotherhood of heroes are in fact survivors from Sledge's unit on Peleliu, which allows Sloan to refer to and quote liberally from the mortar man, who died in 2001.[45]

A second memoir about Peleliu, Captain George P. Hunt's *Coral Comes High*, has become neglected despite its gripping portrayal of the two days of fighting for the Point at White (Ngebedangel) Beach.[46] Both Hunt and Sledge push themselves beyond the heroic bromides of battle and confront the darkness in the human psyche released by organized violence. Sledge in particular agonizes at watching decent young men seduced by the evil of war. It may well be these two vivid personal accounts of warfare that will secure for Peleliu permanent lodgment in American memory.

Japan remembers its two crushing defeats in Palau in much the same way the Americans prefer to recall their victories, as examples of the spirit and heroism of the nation's fighting sons. Celebrating bravery at this microcosmic level allows nations to duck the harder questions surrounding war: Could it have been avoided? Did it have to be so wasteful of lives? Did it accomplish what the nation declared as its purpose? Why did Japan lose? Japanese and American official histories of Peleliu share the same faults of accumulating detail while avoiding critical judgment, especially of their high commands. The United States, however, has gradually produced other works that faced inconvenient truths and provided long-overdue analysis and interpretation. In the historiography of war, narrow definitions of what is relevant to conflict continue to encourage writing about it from a confined military perspective. For the Pacific War, most studies exist in an ecological and social vacuum as well. Still overlooked by both sides is what the conflagration of war and its aftermath did to the natural environment of Peleliu and to the human society that made its home there. The people who know this best receive scant attention. Above the din of what the combatants bruit about themselves in their histories, memoirs, novels, films, and memorials, the voices of the chad ra Beliliou have difficulty reaching the ears of others.

Quiet Voices: The chad ra Beliliou

When Palauans remember their own intervillage wars from the past, they speak of them in personal, family terms. Even as late as the mid-19th century Palauan villages fought each other in a type of warfare recognizable within the *Iliad*, warriors closing on each other in hand-to-hand combat. (And, as Keate's description of Koror's invasion of Peleliu makes clear, many of the battles involved amphibious assaults from fleets of canoes.) Palauan speakers of today will recall, for example, a fighter from their family who bested one from a rival village or a chief from their lineage who led a successful raid. Chronologies are imprecise. There would be no public commemoration of the event, a battle without a name, but possibly an olangch that survives to trigger the memories of descendants.

Compared to the two belligerents, the resources available to the Palauans from which to forge their memories of World War II are meager—no books, films, plays, musicals, journals, newspapers, or national holidays, only individual memory and family oral history, supplemented by song, chants, dance, and graves. It is history at the level of households and small communities, mostly private, without the mass media to both celebrate and mold public remembrance.

"We're invisible in the U.S. books," Chief Obak Isao Singeo observed in an early interview. But he attributed this to the fact that the residents had been evacuated before the invasion, so the Americans believed themselves fighting "on a Japanese island." The older generation, however, knew the experience of war. "They were in the war though they did not fight." Since many visitors read the available books before their trips, the invisibility of the natives in these accounts dampens travelers' curiosity about their lives and about their memories of the war. The remainder of this chapter provides a review of how the Palauan people have been portrayed in foreign-produced books devoted to the battle. Then follows a discussion of how the islanders themselves view the Japanese and American Ireidan who return to the battlefield today, and what the islanders say about the foreign types of olangch they leave behind.

Funasaka Hiroshi explains in *Sakura, Sakura* (1967) that he felt a deep obligation to return to Palau to collect the remains of his fallen comrades. He condemns his national government's pusillanimous abandonment of the soldiers who died in World War II, chastising its failure to recover remains of the men who sacrificed themselves to protect the homeland. His books, which were widely read, played an important role in prodding the Japanese government into a response that has led to 50 years of official attempts to return the fallen from Peleliu. It was this necessity among those in Japan who lived through the war that brought the war back to Peleliu, a necessity that has pressed Ireidan into frequent, insistent, sometimes intimate, sometimes contentious contact with the chad ra Beliliou. It is also within these difficult relationships that the best opportunities for sharing losses and understandings have occurred.

Yet Funasaka devotes little space to the inhabitants of Peleliu in his book. He calls them "tōmin," which, as previously discussed, is a not-necessarily pejorative term for "islander." He describes the people of the 1960s as living peacefully, with fishing as the main industry. He correctly records that they were reluctant to go into the caves in the mountains because of their fear of the spirits of the dead. In *Falling Blossoms* he repeats this and adds that he has hosted many of the natives—translated as "Kanaka"—in his home. (When my Peace Corps colleague Fred Davis and I visited Funasaka at his Tokyo home in 1968, two guests of his at the time, from Angaur, translated our Palauan into Japanese.) Like his former enemies, Funasaka goes on to lament, "The world's memory has also relegated this particular chapter to its own little retirement bin; we can see that everyone is eager to forget the miseries of the war."[47]

Bill D. Ross's 1991 book, *Peleliu, Tragic Triumph* (subtitled *The Untold Story of the Pacific War's Forgotten Battle*) found a wide audience with its weaving of oral history and the documentary record into a compelling narrative. Unfortunately, this means his ignorance of the Pacific Islands and his open contempt for Palau's natives also reached far. A journalist, he visited Palau and Peleliu in 1990, at a dark time in the islands' postwar efforts to establish a new political status with the United States. His discussion of Palau is the most extensive to appear in any of the works on the Peleliu battle. But clearly he interviewed no one from Peleliu. The island "appears unchanged from the way it looked before the pre-invasion bombardment blasted and burned away the dense primeval foliage." It is once again "what it was before World War II—a reef-fringed backwater atoll [*sic*] with little value or use to anyone except its some 500 inhabitants," whose houses are "shacks" and whose village "has no public school system." (It has had an eight-grade public school, which dominates the center of Kloulklubed, since 1954.) Pentagon planners consider the island "without an iota of military value," while Palauan officials "largely ignore the island as useless for anything except the illegal growth . . . of marijuana."[48]

Ross garbles the terms of the compact offered Palau and the structures of the four political entities that emerged from the TT through democratic plebiscites. He never pauses to consider the extent to which the invasion he celebrates and the rudderless decades that followed under American administration were implicated in the poverty that obviously gripped Peleliu at the time of his visit. He sneers at the money Palau received from the United States, ignoring that these sums were designed to bind Palau to America for the role it could play in projecting American power in Asia. He misspells the names of both the Palauan presidents he mentions. Another writer, James Hallas, works three errors into his one-sentence description of the chad ra Beliliou: "The island is home to a handful of natives who survive by fishing and know little of the events that took place there 45 years ago."[49]

One American writer, however, did arrive in Palau without preconceived notions of what was worth observing there. Alerted by local hosts, Larry Woodard traveled to Peleliu to meet and learn from four men who had participated in the war era as conscripted laborers for the Japanese authorities. (One was later of enormous help to me, Spesungel Ichiro Dingilius of Ngesias.) While his book is devoted to the experiences of a marine amphibian tractor battalion, Woodard includes a sympathetic description of the losses of the islanders and their year of hardship on Babeldaob.[50]

Some Japanese visitors to Peleliu are eager to assert that Japan is well-regarded by the local people. A Right-wing website carries photos of Palauans worshiping at the first Shinto shrine on the island, and some Japanese remark on the similarities between their national flag and that created for independent Palau (a yellow circle, the full moon, against a blue background, the sea). A returned Imperial Army veteran tells the film crew of *Tears of Peleliu* that in the 1940s Palau "was Japanese territory. We were often invited into their homes and were able to communicate. There were Japanese schools. The people were friendly to us." The skeptical American filmmakers juxtapose this with Palauan elders complaining of being forced to labor for the Japanese military. "They had the guns; they would beat us." Another Imperial Japanese Army veteran points out that his commander on Peleliu removed the people to Babeldaob, which the film follows with an elder from Peleliu saying, "We didn't know where we were going."[51]

Certainly, the people of Peleliu and Palau tell some imaginative stories concerning the fighting in 1944. In *Sakura, Sakura* Funasaka repeats two of the local tales we Peace Corps volunteers regularly heard in the 1960s. One insists that the Americans tried to land on the northwestern beaches of Ngerchol three times but were repulsed. This probably traces to inaccurate messages that Colonel Nakagawa sent to General Inoue saying that the first landings had been thrown back.[52] The second tale explains that when the marines did land they suffered so many casualties that the water turned orange with their blood; hence the name the beach carries to this day, Orange Beach. In 2002 a young boy repeated for me a story unchanged from 35 years earlier, one that Oda Makoto repeats at the end of his fictional treatment of the battle: the tale of the mysterious Japanese female sharpshooter who, the boy believed, had single-handedly killed 1,000 marines. It was probably fanciful legends like these that spurred marine vets to be sure the Peleliu tour guides learned "the truth" about the battle.

In considering the attitudes of the chad ra Beliliou toward their visitors from Japan and the United States, one should keep several things in mind. First is their reluctance to complain about the war and its impacts on them. Palauans do not wrap themselves in the cloak of victimhood. But when they agree to discuss the war's terrible hardships, most of them articulate a keen sense of the *injustice* done them by both of the colonizers who caused such destruction and trauma, yet accepted so little responsibility for them. Second is the islanders' ambivalence, and the disparity of opinions among them, toward both the foreign powers, coupled with the requirement not to offend Palau's two largest aid donors. Closely related is the way they dampen criticisms of whichever nation their interlocutor comes from. Next is their sense that history is largely personal and familial and is therefore a private matter that ought to be respected by others—so that they owe the foreign visitors privacy and the chance to tell their stories as they see fit. In return, the islanders' personal stories may be shared with outsiders who show an interest in learning something of a family's past. Finally, tourists of any sort—Ireidan, divers, fishermen, or military buffs—still represent, for most people, the most promising source of economic development for the island as it struggles to hold its young people and rebuild what can be salvaged from the old way of life. Tourists, that is, must be treated with discretion and consideration. This fits how Palauans view their role as hosts, while also recognizing the foreigners' vital economic contributions.

"Peleliu treats foreigners well, we like them," Chief Obak Isao Singeo told me. Then he said something whose significance I did not appreciate at first: "We don't speak with them telling how we were hurt, or our disappointments at many things in the past. We know it all and keep it in our mind." This forbearance, combined with the limited curiosity of most tourists, means the natives' stories get told infrequently.

Another major hurdle to communication arises from the way tourism operates on the island. The wave of Ireidan—who came multiple times, often stayed for several days, and interacted, at least a bit, with the Japanese-speaking elders—has long since receded. They have been replaced by smaller numbers of visitors who come only for day tours. This change was mentioned obliquely when I asked Chief Obaklechol Ichiro Blesam about tourists' ignorance of the islanders' wartime experiences. He replied, "They are only here for a short time."

The comments of these two chiefs are rooted in Palauans' different conceptions of history and its transmission. They were saying this: "To be understood, our histories depend on the prior creation of personal relations because the stories are private, about our families and our lives. They can only be shared with and become meaningful to those who have learned who we are and have grown to care about us." A visitor would need time, curiosity, sympathy, and patience to acquire such personal relationships, to gather a sense of Palauans' cultural values and what their lives were like before the war, and thus to begin to see the war's effects from their point of view. The role of respectful hosts deters the Palauans even further from volunteering their stories. These are formidable barriers to mutual understanding. Against the ceaseless outpouring of histories and dramas broadcast by the combatants, the islanders offer stories that are private, told as kelulau, whispers, not meant for public consumption. Olangch are the opposite of books, films, documentaries, or inscriptions in stone. They are silent until decoded by the qualified elder, who shares the story selectively. His audience often has just one opportunity to lend attentive ears—ears, the elder hopes, tugged by Apollo.

Some of the elders remain unabashedly angry at Japan. The two sisters, Ungil Besul and Mesiou Matareklai, blame Japan for bringing the war to the island and credit the United States for providing extensive free education during the TT years. Mesiou, expressing her dislike of Japanese visitors, said, "I'd prefer they not come at all." In 2003, when Japanese officials were scouting possible sites for Emperor Akihito to visit, she dismissed the event: "He's not coming here to thank us for taking care of the Japanese when they were here. He'll just come to pray for the souls of those who died and thank them for fighting in the war." I suggested that a visit might boost tourism from Japan. The sisters argued that it would have the opposite effect, since the already-declining Ireidan would stop coming at all. The chief of Teliu, Renguul Donald Haruo, though better disposed toward the guests from Japan, made the same point, perhaps inadvertently. He told me that if the emperor comes to Palau he will definitely go to Peleliu "to give respect to the dead soldiers. As long as the bones are here the war isn't over until the emperor comes."

In April 2015, Emperor Akihito and Empress Michiko did finally make a two-day visit to Palau in order to pay their respects to the fallen at Peleliu and Angaur. The royal couple laid bouquets of chrysanthemums at the Peace Park Memorial at the south end of Peleliu and then bowed toward Angaur, visible across the strait. They then laid a wreath at the nearby stone memorials to the United States Army's 81st division, at the site of the former American cemetery on Orange Beach. But if the visit represents the closing of a chapter in the history of commemoration on Peleliu, new chapters continue to be written: both the Republic of Palau and the Peleliu State government are cooperating with Japan to open sealed caves and bunkers. The first of these was opened at the shoreline in Ngerkeyukl just days before the emperor's arrival; the remains of six men were found. Palau now seems prepared to allow unlimited openings in the future.[53]

Smau Amalei Ngirngesang's opinions of the Japanese colonizers had softened by the time of the 50th anniversary celebrations. "But in the wartime I felt very angry at the Japanese. I blame them for the hard times and hunger and bad food on Babeldaob. When I look back I'm mad at the Japanese, but glad they forced us out of Peleliu [to Babeldaob] or else there would be none of us left." Former minister Temmy Shmull sees a marked difference in Japanese behavior as compared to the past. "My father [Chief Uchelsias Etibek Shmull] and others on Peleliu remember the Japanese as *really mean*, very hard disciplinarians, especially during the war. Japan seems much changed from the horror stories I heard about them as a child on Peleliu." Former governor Yuki Shmull expressed a common opinion: "It was a war of Japan and the U.S., but they came to our island instead of fighting

Figure 16. Peleliu historian Smau Amalei Ngirngesang, of Ngerdelolk and Ngerchol, 2007

it elsewhere. Since Japan was here, the U.S. had to come. We were in the middle although it was not our war. I personally have no ill feelings toward Japan, though they fortified the island contrary to the League Mandate." Gene Tkel, of the Peleliu land office, considered the war to be Japan's fault. "We didn't ask them to come to Palau," he said, recalling the magistrate Saburo Ngirablai in his confrontation with the Diet official 30 years earlier.

Some elders, like Susong Smau of Ngerchol, were unhappy with both sides. "I'm somewhat angry at the Ireidan and U.S. They are the ones who destroyed our homeland. But I'm willing to forget it and let them come in." When asked if he felt ignored by the two nations, he replied, "I'm not sure; they destroyed our land but it seems they don't care. If we ask for help they'll answer us, but otherwise they just don't care about the people who live here and have to get on. . . . When they finally collect all the bones and take the ashes, they'll forget about Peleliu."

Many who spoke about attitudes toward foreigners drew distinctions according to age, since different generations grew up under different colonial regimes. Renguul Kelbasang Soalablai of Ngerdelolk, too young to recall the war itself, said, "Parents told their kids the U.S. and Japan had their war here, and we fell in the middle, got caught in it although it had nothing to do with us. The younger people feel a bit of animosity toward both. They are generally more favorable to the U.S., who fed them, and know stories of mistreatment by the Japanese at the time of construction of the airfield and so forth. They tend to look warmly toward the U.S. vets who come." He said of the younger generation, "They're pleased to be Westernized, but I worry about the loss of traditional ways. Democracy is acceptable to the youth generally, but it has caused the fading of some traditions. We need to preserve our Palauan way of life, keep our heritage intact."

"Palauans would have been pushed out as a people if the Japanese had stayed and not been expelled by the U.S.," insisted Koichi Wong, an engineer trained in the American era. "The Japanese gave Palauans only the most basic education. Although people suffered in the war, they benefited from the way the U.S. came in and improved things, and foremost was what the U.S. did with education. We're fortunate the Americans won the war, and they treated the locals better; so we're thankful for the war in that sense. Otherwise, there would be no land left for Palauans."

Robat Olikong, born after the war, recalled, "Our parents talked a lot about the war and said we were lucky the U.S. won since the Japanese treated people really badly. We wouldn't be here now otherwise." When asked what benefits Peleliu received under American rule, Robat and Gene Tkel replied that the educational opportunities had been key. After a bit of nudging by my colleague, Fuanny Blunt, they added another, democratic government.

Robat agreed with many on the island when he distinguished between the past and the present. "We like the Americans, and the Japanese nowadays; we're one family, they can support Palau and Peleliu [with tourism]." Haruo Esang, from Teliu, and Chairman of Peleliu's Economic Development Authority, similarly believed that young Palauans were not resentful over World War II, though they did not like that the war occurred there. Chief Renguul Donald Haruo of Teliu credited the Palauan people with a nuanced appreciation of the actions of the two colonial powers. "My grandparents and their generation appreciated the Japanese for giving them education, technical skills, and technical advances. Palauans trained by the Japanese became the country's leaders after the war. Palauans are sympathetic to the Japanese when they return here. They are also grateful to the U.S., which gave them opportunities and freedoms and knowledge. There are no bad feelings."

What do the chad ra Beliliou and other people of Palau make of the many monuments that foreigners have erected to bear witness to their time in the islands and tell their versions of history? Several men and women recognized as knowledgeable in Palauan affairs and history provided their views of these artifacts. Jonathan Emul, of Koror, was unusually blunt on the topic, and, fully aware of my profession, offered a bracing assessment of anthropology's contributions to Palauan discourse. "We don't depend on the Japanese or American stories about our land, unless we use one of the Palauan textbooks in school. We don't care much what American anthropologists say about something. You ridicule yourself if you quote a Japanese or American source. People will say you don't know your own clan or ancestry. You must know the people of your past in order to be believed. People might use an outside book, but if they can tell the story themselves without referring to anything else, they will do it. Many times kids have asked for my story of the war; you tell your own experience of war, your involvement."

Speaking of the foreign memorials throughout Palau, Emul said, "Palauans don't read or pay much attention to them. The attitude is, they are their monuments, like decoration, scenery. Palauans may enjoy them; it's good to have them for the historical record. But we don't take pride in them; they belong to the Japanese and Americans. It's good for them to have their versions of history, but we don't necessarily like or agree with the monuments. The foreigners built them for themselves. The Palauans see them as Japanese and American olangch, to tell their stories."

When asked what people in Palau know of the combatants' versions of the conflict on Peleliu, Kathy Kesolei replied, "Those never get to us. It doesn't get told to us, maybe in scattered bits and pieces, but the average person wouldn't have the knack to piece together credible documentation for the war." As for the foreigners' appreciation of the war's impacts on Palau, "I doubt that either of these two powers understands the Palauan experience during the war, doubt they can even follow it."

"We understand that they have to memorialize the dead," she continued. "Put up a plaque, a grave, a marker, because we have it in our legacy. We point to a hill or river where someone died, or battle took place. Olangch we understand, and we have to have them, they remind us and help us understand our history." But while Palauan olangch have a "sacred" feel to them, "we don't have the same feeling for this [foreign] monument, don't revere it as we would something Palauan. . . . It's not the same as for my relatives' graves."

Antonio Tewid of Ngerkeyukl expressed the same distance from the messages the foreigners leave on Peleliu. "They are their monuments, not ours. They are not Palauan, so we're not interested in them. Only the Japanese are interested. I don't care what they write, they and the Americans are writing for themselves, not us." Haruo Esang believed that "people realize that the visitors put up monuments because many of their citizens died. And it's good for Palau to learn more about World War II. The Japanese and U.S. lost many people, and the residents are willing to encourage them to honor their dead. Plus it's good promotion [for the economy], so it's not resented." Yet the memorials "are theirs not ours." Kent Giramur said of Peleliu's monuments, "They don't have much influence on locals. People know what happened, the hardship they [Palauan families] went through, without the monuments. It's passed on orally to the younger generation. Children know the war brought destruction and death."

Most Palauan natives, then, regard the memorials, the Japanese and American olangch, with tolerance and indifference. Part of this tolerance stems from Palauans' recognition that history always involves discordant versions of the past. With their lack of interest, the chad ra Beliliou also remind us that the memorials tell the foreigners' wartime stories, not their own. Outsiders often remark on the islanders' seeming ignorance of the details of the battle. Even the academic historian, Harry Gailey, wrote that the "friendly young men" of Peleliu "know little of the events that at one time made the name Peleliu a recognizable word" far beyond the confines of the island.[54] To some extent, the islanders return the indifference that most visitors and foreign histories accord them—except that the islanders are deeply aware of the painful losses suffered by nationals of both sides, which compel so many of them to make the expensive voyage to Peleliu. Beyond this sympathetic understanding, however, in the totality of its ecological ruination and its massacre of thousands, the war lies outside Palauan calculations of what is possible in their history. Their indifference, then, also declares that the people of Palau do not recognize the foreigners' events as legitimate—or anyway, *defining*—components of *Palauan* history. They cannot escape the battle's effects today, but they do not have to let it define either their past or present. Distancing themselves from the war is how the people of Peleliu reject the foreigners' conceptions of where their homeland's value lies.

Tourism development on the scale envisioned by JICA seems improbable for Peleliu at this time. Creation of a heritage area holds promise for protecting historical resources and bringing badly needed regulation to the activities of foreign tourists. But this new approach to preservation also challenges the chad ra Beliliou to think carefully about their own cultural heritage and to identify which of its elements are suitable for the kind of treatment anticipated for foreign resources. If Palauan artifacts, history, and ways of life are to be presented as the context in which the actions of the Japanese and Americans occurred, then the residents have to find effective ways to impress upon visitors the richness and the continuity of native life on Peleliu.

One necessary step will be to add displays at the Peleliu museum devoted to the local society, as it was in the past and as it functions today. Texts describing Palauan history, photographs and relics, models and replicas can all be effective here. To these could be added efforts to show foreigners the way of life that existed before the war swept it away and how that life continues today in a modified but recognizable form. Each village still has living elders who remember the site and appearance of the main bai, the council house of chiefs, and the layout of the village. The beluu could start by raising traditional style bai on rebuilt odesongel, as has been done in five Palauan states in recent years. Involving as they do the organizational and technical skills of an entire beluu, these reconstructed bai are physical, aesthetic, and cultural marvels. They attract tourists and allow locals to explain Palauan social and political organization and the legends painted on the gables and tie beams. Rebuilt bai with up-to-date paintings showing the war and its aftermath would tell the local story in the local medium, the most stunning of all olangch. Palau's adult generations now living have a responsibility to attempt these vital reconstructions. Time is of the essence; the elders who remember the old villages and ways of life will not be available much longer.

If the traditional bai were erected on Peleliu, the heart of each village would start to beat again and people would be encouraged to reestablish at least one family home as soon as practicable—the dream of almost every person on the island. More than any other symbol, these bai would represent the people's return to their land, to the places that define their identities as chad ra Beliliou. Even casual tourists would encounter authentic and unforgettable evidence that a native society on Peleliu thrived before the war and has carried on after it. The war and the years afterward changed much on the island but not everything. People still farm and fish, maintain their lands, recognize identity through lineage, clan, and village, retain the traditional titles of leadership, and honor their ancestors and their histories. Used again for meetings of the klobak and other functions, bai would be the visible manifestation of the evolving social order, and of people's reverence for their past, a reminder to the people of Palau and foreigners alike that not everything was consumed in the furnace of war.

Conclusion

The Roots of the Plant

For the chad ra Beliliou, the battle for Peleliu was an unmitigated social, cultural, and environmental disaster. This book tries to present it as they view it, as an event that obliterated the way of life that, in their minds, stretched back in time from the 1930s to its mythic beginnings. Their ancestors had established human society on the island before Homer chanted of Achilles dragging the body of Hector behind his chariot. The patterns of life underwent sudden alterations as the Europeans brought Palau into the global commercial and geostrategic network. Their lives since 1914 have, according to their many different personal opinions, been expanded and constrained, improved and diminished, by the imperial ambitions of Japan and the United States. When Japan imposed its strict rule on Palau, it seized vast tracts of land, sent 25,000 immigrants to occupy them, disrupted traditional patterns of life and rule, damaged the environment while exploiting resources solely for its benefit, and prepared the archipelago to support the Japanese empire's military expansion into Asia and the western Pacific. But nothing in Peleliu's previous experience compared to the devastation wrought on the island and its people by the implacable intruders who waged war there in 1944.

Therefore, in order to approach what the war means to the chad ra Beliliou, the listener has to give them the time to express, in their terms, the loss of their way of life, the demise of their long-established communities, the damage to their fragile island. The fundamental difference between their perceptions of the war and those of the combatants is that for the islanders Peleliu was their ancient home. Outsiders displaced them in order to fight their battle, but when it was over, the survivors sailed away, leaving behind their dead and debris. The people returned to their home to find it transformed and unrecognizable; their previous way of life had vanished. They had no choice but to start their lives anew.

To foreign veterans, their families, tourists, and the history minded, the island is a time capsule, floating in a distant sea. It is a site they can visit or shun as they choose. Many of the war's participants and their countrymen expelled it from their memories. Those who come today out of need or curiosity will, with few exceptions, abandon it when they have achieved their purpose. The chad ra Beliliou, however, have to make a living there, from its soil, its seas, and its past. For them the war is an episode in their long and continuing history on the island, to which time has now added another 70 years. It is a memory that none can ignore; its effects are everywhere.

Elements of the human and natural landscape, particularly villages and clan and lineage lands, illuminate much of the people's lives and frame their reckoning of the war's legacy. The five villages lay at the center of their prewar life. Political arrangements, patterns of production, kinship, notions of personal and collective identity, and emotional attachments—all these were connected to the village. Beneath them all lay the lands belonging to the lineages: gardens, taro paddies, shores, beaches, reefs, and seas that were indispensable productive resources, but also the foundation of wealth, power, identity, and social structure within a complex hierarchical society. Just as the physical environment of small islands is especially vulnerable to disturbance, so too was the human culture, based on the island's environment, that clung to Peleliu.

The extensive damage to Peleliu's lands, the loss of much productive farmland to military facilities, and the disappearance of all they had ever built constituted the immediate obstacles the people faced upon their return from exile. Longer-term difficulties have included the slow relinquishment of lands seized by colonial governments, the threats posed by lethal unexploded ordnance that poisons large tracts of the island's surface to this day, and the still-unresolved disputes to title for most parcels on the island. During this wait, Palau has undergone unprecedented political and economic change. Yet chad ra Beliliou of all ages express the desire to rebuild the villages and maintain what they see as distinctive Palauan values, customs, and social organization.

Lacking a precise baseline of prewar natural resources and biological species, we cannot say for certain whether the war exterminated certain species or seriously altered the balance among those that survived. The chances are it did not: a study conducted on Guam after World War II found that no native bird species or other vertebrates were lost as a result of its invasion; and the Rock Islands provide short stepping stones for terrestrial species to come down from Babeldaob or Koror. The elders of Peleliu themselves do not agree whether the quality of soils and farming has returned to prewar levels. There is no question, however, that large tracts of farmland and immensely valuable taro paddies disappeared forever beneath the runways, aprons, roads, and encampments constructed by the two belligerents. This devastation implies that, especially for Ngesias, Ngerkeyukl, and Teliu, the fondly remembered prewar model of clustered village homes surrounded and sustained by fertile gardens is one that cannot be retrieved. Most elders also believe that the types of fish or their abundance in the western lagoons were altered to some degree. (The most thorough catalog of postwar species may be the survey in the NPS report.)[1]

The landscape had also performed the vital function of helping the people maintain their histories. History was conceived as events occurring in spatial and geographic frames and as human movement among places. Housing plots, gardens, taro paddies, boat landings, reefs, fishing grounds, channels, moorages all had names and stories tied to them. A lineage title itself repeated the name of the land on which sat the titleholder's home. The odesongel likewise carried histories of migrations, relations to other clans, and how titles, land, and influence had been acquired. Like other kin property, they contained the stories justifying membership and claims to access for the present and the future. All these and many other tangible objects and landmarks, like the council houses with their painted legends, functioned as olangch, the mnemonic devices that bear coded, private stories of the past and bring them into the living present.

Thus the destruction of the landscape of Peleliu, with its olangch, had the additional effect of cutting the people off from their past. When the islanders returned after the invasion, not only had the physical evidence of their society disappeared, their histories were gone as well, except what they carried in their memories. Recording these memories from before, during, and after the war was the primary purpose of my research. James Young is surely right that history is enriched by including commemorative forms, so it becomes the study of both what happened and how it is passed down to us. Palauan conceptions of history tell us that the natural landscape itself can contain the primary substance of history and be the principal means by which it is remembered.

While the islanders discussed their war experiences and losses with persistent reference to their lands and villages, these same physical features—including the seas, beaches, reefs, and caves—also reveal how differently the many foreigners who invite themselves to Peleliu regard the island. These features help structure the discussion for this book's second goal, the comparisons among the three parties involved in the war. All who have engaged with Peleliu—geostrategists from both Japan and the United States, Nan'yō authorities seeking resources and labor to exploit, wartime defenders and amphibious attackers, veterans and the families of those who fought and died there, war historians, tourists attracted to Palau's underwater beauty, planners of tourism development, creators of historic parks—all these have viewed Peleliu Island in their own particular and limited ways.

Given the numbers of their casualties—there were 11,000 dead Japanese defenders, 1,600 dead American soldiers and marines, and 6,800 wounded Americans—it is understandable that both adversaries would consider Peleliu consecrated by the events of 1944. Both the victors and the defeated have struggled to find appropriate ways to remember the cataclysm. Each nation has concentrated on its own experiences and needs, to the exclusion of the foe and the inhabitants of Peleliu. Both combatants have relied on selective remembering and forgetting, obscuring painful or awkward issues. In this process they arrived at the same solutions found by nations in previous wars. Historians Kurt Piehler and David Blight describe how, to promote reconciliation after the Civil War, Americans emphasized the need to honor those who had fought in it. In particular, by focusing on battlefields, Piehler writes, "they hoped to gloss over the causes of the conflict. . . . Except by a few novelists, the dissension, brutality, alienation, and anger of the war was forgotten or ignored by creators of memorials. Instead . . . monuments and ceremonies portrayed the [war] as one in which the qualities of loyalty, valor, duty, and comradeship reigned supreme." Blight describes how public memory of the war "came increasingly to exalt the soldier and his sacrifice, disembodied from the causes and consequences of the war."[2]

In the contest of memory for the Second World War, the advantages have lain with the United States. Rich and triumphant, it had the postwar resources to create a military-historical complex, whose portrayal of the great crusade in film, literature, historical studies, and art overwhelms awareness of the war's losers and innocent victims and inhibits careful consideration of all the means used to achieve victory. The struggle in the Pacific allows storytellers to combine the timeless allure of tropical islands with the theatricality and prurient fascination of war. American memory views the battle for Peleliu as one chapter in this tale, which is most often told with an unambiguous moral thread running from the treachery at Pearl Harbor to the proper and inevitable conclusion in Tokyo Bay.

Concentrating on this proximate cause of war avoids America's exertions of power throughout the Pacific dating from Commodore Perry's forced "opening" of Japan in the 1850s and the fit of imperialist expansion in 1898 that ended with the United States possessing the Hawaiian Islands, Midway, Wake, Guam, and the Philippines. America suddenly spanned the Pacific just as Meiji Japan surged out of its isolation, acquiring Taiwan, Asian mainland possessions, and Korea by 1910. From this time the two nations planned for war with each other, a prophecy fulfilled in 1941. Yet the American memorials on Peleliu and every documentary and written account devoted to the battle place it within the restricted context of the United States responding with might and righteousness to an unprovoked attack.

The United States crushed an empire that had brutally subjugated Asian and island populations and had behaved atrociously toward combatants and civilians alike. Yet scrutiny of the war by scholars has identified troubling moral complexities in the way it was fought on *all* sides. To this day, many Americans remain loath to recognize that we killed hundreds of thousands of women and children with the firebombing of Japanese cities, while our soldiers shot prisoners and mutilated corpses for souvenirs. In the Pacific both antagonists fought with wanton disregard for the effects their combat had on local populations and on their ability to sustain themselves after the conflict ended. I have tried to document what this meant for the people of Peleliu.

The American victory at Peleliu remains shadowed by nagging questions that are only fitfully engaged. These include the necessity of the battle, the quality of the preinvasion intelligence, and the competence of the leadership of the marines. Peleliu proved to be a prize of little value, purchased at a higher cost than necessary, and one that should not have been paid at all. In mid-1944 General Inoue had formidable ground forces in Palau but no means of interfering with U.S. operations in the western Pacific. He had no air force, no ships; he could not project his power beyond Palau's reefs. His own government had abandoned his command of 30,000 soldiers and sailors, and the 14,000 Japanese and other Asian civilians marooned in Palau. His situation has been likened to that of a badger in its burrow: he could only hurt his American enemies if they thrust their hands down the hole. The United States did not oblige the badger to the degree he had hoped by invading Babeldaob. But America expended men against Inoue's forces to an extent that haunts the national memory still. If the U.S. siege of Babeldaob killed an additional 10,000 military men and civilians, most by starvation, then the war's victors have another set of difficult questions to consider as well.[3]

America's veterans are pained by the deaths of their comrades, a waste even by the profligate calculus of world war. They complain of the historical obscurity to which Peleliu has been consigned. But the passage of time and the emotions created by a visit to the island can soften the grief and anger. At the 50th anniversary ceremonies on Peleliu, marine Tom Quinn said to former IJA Lieutenant Yamaguchi, "Today is a victory for both of us. I'm glad we're both alive." Comparing the muted American commemoration on the island to the more intense Japanese efforts, marine veteran Richard Gettell, who returned to the island in his eighties, said to me, "Well after all, they lost more sons here than we did."

The postwar treatment of its island wards while trustee for the United Nations is another memory that America tends to avoid. Decades of stingy and torpid administration isolated and frustrated people who were eager for lives connected to the wider world. Trust Territory personnel would loudly deny it, but like that of the Nan'yō, U.S. rule in Micronesia was colonial; in Anthony Lane's words, it "controlled and corrupted even in its efforts to assist." American rule was based on compulsion and on confiscation—of property, of personal rights, of the dignity of independence, and of life chances for two generations of its unwilling subjects. With its massive power in world affairs after the war, the United States had difficulty recognizing how its professions of benevolence could mask self-interest.

"Power always thinks it has a great soul, and vast views beyond the comprehension of the weak," warned one of America's founding fathers, John Adams.[4]

Yet in contrast to Japan's Nan'yō regime, the U.S. Trust Territory lacked the overt and institutionalized racism of the former, prohibited immigration like that promoted by Japan, which, but for the war, would have eventually engulfed the native societies of Micronesia, and prevented the massive extraction of natural resources and exploitation of labor that Japan had pursued as fundamental policy. Most important, the United States steadfastly expanded public education in the islands, even during the most penurious of the early budgets. While Japan had restricted Micronesian youngsters to three years of schooling, the United States provided 12 years of free education for all boys and girls by the early 1960s, and scholarships that funded college educations for rapidly growing numbers of Micronesian high school graduates.

Once exposed to America's ideals of self-determination and the freedoms due all mankind, the people of Micronesia inevitably asked, "Why not us?" New leaders forced political change onto their trustee earlier than the United States expected and in forms it did not anticipate, like compacts of free association. Yet, through coercion and massive subventions the United States retained its grip on all its strategic interests in Micronesia. Again in contrast, Mark Peattie reminds us that Japan had no intentions, ever, of granting its island colony political freedom and offered absolutely no preparations for this to its indigenous peoples.

Japan also views Peleliu as a site of hallowed and sorrowful national history. Eleven thousand of the nation's men were sacrificed there to buy time for the Japanese leadership; but like their adversaries, their sacrifices achieved honor yet had no significant effect on the course of the war. In the following year Japan's government achieved no diplomatic or military breakthroughs and only dragged the people of Asia and of Japan itself further into the abyss. In the postwar era, absent consistent leadership from the central government, contentious civic groups have led Japanese war memory on Peleliu. They have pursued their debates on the island through conflicting interpretations of Japan's imperial ambitions, of the attempt to defend the island from American assault, and in disagreements over collection of the remains of Japanese dead. Opposing judgments of Peleliu's historical meaning reflect the continuing discord within Japan over the larger issues surrounding its role in the wars in Asia and the Pacific from 1931 to 1945.

Peleliu, then, is a much more politicized site for Japan than for the United States. Its distance from Japan and the tolerance that the island's residents have shown toward the Japanese visitors have given greater freedom to the voices of commemoration than what they enjoy back in Japan. Associations from the Left and Center have built memorials lamenting war and praising peace. The Japanese government memorialized the conflict on Peleliu more readily than it remembered the wars back in the home islands. This same government maintains a studied silence regarding the obligations it incurred toward Palau and Micronesia as colonizer and wartime aggressor. But its generous financial aid is recognized, if not universally accepted, as an expression of remorse. The Japanese Right has been the most active and visible faction on Peleliu. Its memorials honor the fallen soldiers as heroic defenders of the homeland. In the extreme, Rightist organizations promote a return to the imperial era through Shinto ceremonies and a celebration of Japanese expansion into Micronesia. Although Japanese Ireidan have been the mainstay of battlefield tourism to Peleliu, their numbers have declined as those familiar with the war have passed on.

This distant foreign site lends little support to the notion that war commemoration is eagerly hijacked by the nation-state to forge national identity and distract attention from the crushing costs of war. Rather, private groups and individuals from both sides have promoted a wide array of viewpoints regarding the significance of the battle for Peleliu. Among these competing statements in stone and ritual, grief is displayed by victor and vanquished alike. Politics and mourning are particularly entwined in the Japanese commemoration.[5]

As involving and revealing as war monuments can be, their messages are inherently limited, both in space and intent, which is always more commemorative than pedagogic. But the combatants' books and films about Peleliu have largely failed to provide the missing analysis and interpretation that all three of the participants need in order to comprehend the battle's place in their national histories. Four decades elapsed before Professor Gailey's study probed the American conduct of the invasion. One filmmaker focused on the plight of the chad ra Beliliou at the 1994 ceremonies, while NBC marred an otherwise fine presentation with false drama and careless inaccuracies. E. B. Sledge left a searing personal testimony of what the infantrymen suffered on Peleliu, while Funasaka Hiroshi's memoir of Angaur helps us appreciate what the battle was like for the doomed Japanese defenders.

In keeping with Palauan notions of history, Palauan memory of the war resides primarily at the level of families, lineages, clans, and villages. The klechedaol provide occasions for Ngaraard and Peleliu to exchange memories and renew and revise the public stories that they share—precisely the opportunities that have eluded the wartime adversaries. The new national government of Palau does not use the wartime experience to bolster its legitimacy. It does use it effectively, however, to secure aid and financial benefits from both the belligerents. Palauans' memories of the two powers during their respective eras of dominance are mixed and nuanced, influenced by one's generation, family heritage, personal or family experiences, and education. Nationals of Japan and the United States, meanwhile, come to Peleliu "for their own reasons," as a resident observes. Their attitude toward the island's inhabitants recalls Nick Carraway's description of the crowds who flocked to Jay Gatsby's lavish parties—people who came without invitation, but "accepted Gatsby's hospitality and paid him the subtle tribute of knowing nothing whatever about him."[6]

The obsequies due the human dead and the disposition of their remains created anguish and conflicts that trouble Peleliu to this day. The combatants lost comrades in arms. The chad ra Beliliou lost relatives, friends, and fellow villagers during the 17 months of hostilities. The proper resting place for their dead should have been their homeland, Peleliu. In her remarks to the 50th anniversary conference, Tokie Morei of Ngesias told how her mother became ill while the family hid in Ngiwal on Babeldaob. After a frantic search they found a Japanese doctor, who advised she needed better nutrition. "But what food can we find while hiding in the forest?" asked Mrs. Morei. Her mother died and was buried in Ngiwal. "The hardest part, the saddest thing for us, is that our mother was never able to return home"—to see Peleliu again or to be buried there. Palauan memories of the war return constantly to the ties forged when relatives were buried in the lands of others. These connections extended to the U.S. servicemen who had been buried in Palau. Residents of both Peleliu and Angaur were deeply distressed to have the remains of the Americans who had been buried on their islands removed after the war.[7]

The West, too, has its long traditions of giving proper burials to the dead. Priam, the king of Troy, entreats Achilles to return the body of his son; the warrior relents, and the *Iliad* ends with Hector's funeral. Antigone risks death rather than leave her brother unburied. American troops on Peleliu went to extraordinary lengths to recover the bodies of comrades, even if it took repeated assaults up mountainsides over several days.

When finally allowed to search the battlegrounds, the Ireidan and Izokukai feverishly scoured Peleliu's caves and fortifications, spurred by emotions that had been pent up for 20 years. The NPS prized Peleliu as a "pristine battlefield" to display combat. But for the Ireidan and Izokukai, Peleliu's landscape was priceless as a source of undisturbed remains of their loved ones. They argued passionately with the chad ra Beliliou when the islanders forbade further collection of bones. The searches continue today, with opposition coming sometimes from the younger generation of Palauans who have less sympathy with the former overlords, sometimes from Palauan preservationists, and sometimes from other thoughtful people from Japan who argue it is time to let the war go.

The Battle over Peleliu has much to say about the physical aftermath of the war on Peleliu, about the obliteration of the human and natural landscape. David Blight writes in his *Race and Reunion* how, following the vast destruction of the Civil War, Americans became a people "with so much tragic, bloody history that their modern society would forever be burdened by its historical memory. America's 'historic landscapes' became more *interesting* because of the Civil War."[8] For the chad ra Beliliou the war had no such redeeming qualities. Peleliu's landscape may now be more "interesting" to some who visit from outside, to some historians and tourists. But it is not more interesting to the island's inhabitants, who yearn for the vanished prewar landscape and way of life that was so deeply shaped by that landscape.

Kent Giramur offered this insight: "The war in Peleliu is a small thing as far as we're concerned; it's tiny compared to what Peleliu has to offer. It's a big thing for the U.S. and the Japanese. I want people to know Peleliu as a happy place, not come to Peleliu and be reminded of bad things that happened. I want people to come to enjoy themselves, to see Peleliu as Peleliu, not be reminded of the ugliness national governments get into. I want them to remember Peleliu as paradise, not a place of massacres, of wars that didn't have to happen."

Giramur's fervent wish for how visitors will perceive his island touches on another aspect of the war's immaterial aftermath. The two warring nations left Peleliu a charnel house, clotted with dead. With this the two armies succeeded in changing the people's perceptions of their island. In the islanders' minds, the slaughter defiled Peleliu, scarred it in ways that the regeneration of the forests and gardens cannot conceal. The destruction of the villages, especially of the odesongel and graveyards, desecrated the past and the memories of the people's ancestors. In Palauan folk beliefs the spirits of those who died violently or were not properly buried are said to haunt the locales of their deaths. The whole island, then, was polluted spiritually as well as physically by the war. This conception of the battle as a stain on the island caused by foreigners runs as a countercurrent against the people's desire to turn the battlefield to economic advantage.

In using islander ways of telling the past, I have relied not only on oral histories but also on olangch, the physical prompts of remembrance in Palau. They are important to all three people involved in the story of Palau and World War II. The fate of olangch from Peleliu abounds with ironies. One of the most sorrowful memories of the chad ra Beliliou is the very loss of these aids to memory. The battle demolished all of theirs, with the single exception of the odesongel in Ngerdelolk. They have reconstructed only a few, like the shrine for the chelid (god) at Ngerdelolk and the repairs on Ngebungel, the village pier of Ngesias. The two warring nations, by contrast, eventually returned to the island to raise numerous stones and memorials to themselves and their fighters. They tell revealing, abbreviated, sometimes contentious versions of events, while urging the world to remember a battle that the chad ra Beliliou prefer to forget.

One feature of the island was rebuilt 10,000 miles away. The U.S. Marine Corps constructed an exact replica of the coral Point, from the beach of Ngerkeyukl, at Quantico, Virginia, to use for military training. Thus the one portion of the western villages to be "reconstructed" was a model used for yet more warfare. For a decade after World War II, marines skirmished over this rocky outcrop, learning incidentally from this olangch the story of the First Marine Division at Peleliu.

At the end of the war the chad ra Beliliou themselves raised only one olangch to the war. The Odesangel Bad in Ngaraard singles out their paramount memory of the era. It symbolizes their gratitude toward the people of Ngaraard and the other beluu who risked their own chances of survival in order to shelter and feed the exiles from Peleliu. In this it is quintessentially Palauan—commemorating not conquest or bloodshed but human compassion and decency as a quieter form of heroism. The stone and five coconut palms brought from Ngaraard in 2006 symbolize the renewal of this bond for the three generations born since the conflict.

But if the most enduring Palauan olangch are stones worked by man, then the largest, the most monumental, of them all is the island of Peleliu itself. From this platform of raised coral limestone Japanese enterprises dug out minerals, carved roads, and built an airfield. Japanese military engineers, using thousands of conscript laborers, expanded the many natural caves and excavated new ones. The American invaders rained explosives on the island, cratered its surface, destroyed cliff faces in order to annihilate their enemy. Afterward they filled in lowlands, leveled terrain, and dredged coral from the reefs for construction of their base. With willfulness and inexhaustible sources of power the strangers shaped the very rock of Peleliu to their ends. However much its residents would like the island remembered for other reasons, Peleliu is fated forever to tell the story of war to those willing to decode it.

The caves of Peleliu tell the observer much about the disparate people who have sought out the island. The islanders stored food in the coolness of caves. One cave is an olangch in which the mythical monster of Ngesias lived. Residents took shelter in them during the air attacks and lived in them after losing homes to Japanese troops. The Japanese military used them for storage, hospitals, gun emplacements, and as near-impregnable defenses against invasion. American tales of the Peleliu campaign are dominated by descriptions of the awful fighting to destroy the enemy inside the caves. The Ireidan and Izokukai returned to Peleliu to recover the bones that lay in caves decades after the end of the fighting. It is the caves, many still littered with remains and military equipment, that lend Peleliu its unique potential as a historic battle site.

Not until 50 years after the war did scientists discover another legacy of the combat on Peleliu. Researchers have learned from the fossil record that the arrival of the first indigenous settlers on islands coincided with dramatic declines in the populations of vertebrates, mostly native sea and land birds. These settlers sheltered in caves, and the debris they left in them makes caves the best source of fossil evidence for the fauna that existed when humans first arrived. When two leading researchers, Gregory Pregill and David Steadman, examined Palau and Peleliu in the mid-1990s they were concerned at what they found. They discovered that "Palau's paleontological potential had been seriously diminished by events of World War II. The best and most likely caves with potentially fossiliferous sediment were used by the Japanese military." The losses in Palau are so extensive that "no vertebrate bone record exists in either a cultural or noncultural context. . . . .In fact, the scarcity of rich, fossiliferous sediment in Palau is thus far unequalled for tropical Pacific islands." On Peleliu Steadman and Pregill looked for fossil sites that might have been spared the invasion's disturbances; they found none. "Beliliou is by far the most cave-rich island in Palau and, if not for wartime activities, almost certainly would have yielded an important record of prehistoric vertebrates."[9] Thus the war severed the islanders not only from their remembered past but possibly from their prehistoric past as well.

Yet the picture may not be as gloomy as Pregill and Steadman paint it. The archaeologist Nancy Farrell believes that the deeper middens of previously opened caves may not have been fatally disturbed and that further research may find less disturbed sites, especially among the remaining sealed natural caves. Professor Mike Jochim of the University of California at Santa Barbara fully agrees, noting that in Europe caves had been poorly excavated in the past, yet significant remains were found when these caves were explored again using more modern, meticulous methods.[10] Research on Tinian found significant precolonial remains in natural caves that had been used by Japanese troops.[11] The recent careful excavations of caves in Peleliu by Price and Knecht yielded cheering results of prehistoric remains, justifying the confidence of Farrell and Jochim.[12] Standards need to be set, however, and maintained vigilantly. Japanese bone-collecting expeditions badly damaged a rare prehistoric Chamorro site on Tinian, and most of the bones gathered were actually remains of native Chamorros. The team had illegally used a bulldozer and, with heedless ignorance, looted ancient Chamorro graves.[13] As Professor Jochim observes, these serious blunders argue the more for strictly controlling excavations on Peleliu. They should be done only by experienced archaeologists. The caves contain not only Japanese history but a priceless Palauan history that can be lost forever through a single act of carelessness. A handful of caves may hold the last opportunity for discovering what the island was like when the ancestors of the chad ra Beliliou first crossed its beach and held their breath as the fresh, green breast of this new world flowered before them.

Peleliu's future, on the other hand, almost certainly will involve tourism, Palau's dominant industry. JICA proposed massive infrastructure development on Peleliu to serve marine-oriented tourism. The National Park Service favored an even larger amount of land, beaches, and waters devoted to remembering World War II. A more modest ecotourism model that emphasizes the natural world of the tropics, which is what attracts the vast majority of travelers to Palau, warrants consideration. Ecotourism can grant the war era a niche within the range of experiences offered to visitors but denies it primacy, in keeping with the residents' preferences. Coupled with the protection of historic resources and continued production of lands and waters offered by a heritage area, ecotourism could develop into a sensible and sustainable source of income for the islanders in this century.

Ultimately, in their multitude and complexity, the memories of the three peoples who have lived the story of war and Peleliu appear commensurable only in that the battle for this island was a tragedy for each of them. Yet the three have much else in common. All carry a burden of regret and painful loss, and all struggle to keep their particular memories alive as time wears them away. If they were aware of it, most residents of the island would agree with the pacifist view expressed by the Hiroshima monument, agree reluctantly that their island and their experiences teach us that, of all the ways to pursue national interest or settle disagreements, resorting to war is the worst. But however useful Peleliu may seem as an object lesson in man's capacity for gallantry, folly, or hate during warfare, none of its inhabitants wants it remembered this way.

If those for whom Peleliu is sacred ground abandoned their self-absorption and mutual alienation and instead sought out each other and the Palauans who live there, the rewards seem certain. The foreigners would enjoy the advantage of tapping into the powerful Palauan sense of obligation toward those whose relatives died away from home and within a Palauan setting. The three far-flung people living with the story of Peleliu and war are actually a single community, bound together by that story. Each, as a partial owner, has the responsibility to remember and share his portion, however divergent, with the others. For the American and Japanese visitors this would require overcoming Palauans' reticence by demonstrating sincere concern for their wartime experiences. Doing so would require the foreigners to face unpleasant truths about their nations' roles in causing the war, their conduct of it, and the harm they inflicted on innocents. It would also create the best chance of bridging the gap between the foreigners' conviction that the Peleliu battlefield now exists to present memories that honor and justify their sacrifices—memories that are public yet exclusive—and the conviction of the native people that histories are instead kelulau, whispers that are private and various, yet, in the right circumstances, are conversational and open to exchange and revision. In either case, whether concealed or shared, the islanders consider them ill-suited for proclamations in brass or stone.

Consolation would be the first goal. Next would be for the three peoples to achieve not a consensus on meanings, not a definitive "true" version of Peleliu's history, but rather the comprehensiveness and sympathetic awareness of differing viewpoints that are the aim of Palauan history telling. Such listening and learning would remove each story from the personal and national, and place it finally in its greater whole. Requiring as it does time and respectful attention, this storytelling would also provide the chance to forge new personal relationships, living connections that could replace the tormented and ever more marginal searches for lifeless artifacts and remains.

For their part, the Palauans have gathered oral histories from Peleliu under the auspices of the Republic's Historic Preservation Office, opened a museum on the island dedicated to the battle and its era, established a structure for creating heritage areas, and cooperated with the National Park Service in its cultural and archaeological surveys and preservation efforts. With patience and tact Peleliu's residents continue to accept the steady stream of foreign visitors for whom the trip may be an emotional pilgrimage or just a casual tour of an island curiosity. Through the klechedaol ceremonies, gatherings that are by design public and inclusive, the citizens of Peleliu and Ngaraard have salvaged from the horror and wreckage of the war benefits of deep value: shared memories, expanded understandings, comfort in loss, gratitude for help rendered, and unexpected yet significant friendships, which flow beyond individual lifetimes.

When the difficult exchanges of memories and opinions do occur, what will distinguish even the most heartfelt stories told by Japanese and American families touched by the war from those told by the chad ra Beliliou will be the islanders' tenacious attachment to place, to their home. Underlying any conversation with them about Peleliu, their lives, and the impacts of imperialism and war lies an unspoken conviction, which, as with so much of their history, they are too polite to insist on to an outsider. If they gave voice to the conviction, to this important kelulau, they would likely say: *We are talking to you about* our *island. We named these beaches, gardens, hills, and waters, gave the island a history, and sustained its capacity for human life for 150 generations. We are the ones forever bound to this place, to its lands and seas, its past and future.*

The fighting men in World War II were youngsters, many still in their teens. It is common to compare them with flowers when speaking of their youth and their sacrifices. The Japanese are most explicit in likening warriors to the sakura, the lovely but fleeting cherry blossom. Shortly before the 1944 invasion of France, Winston Churchill confided his fear to General Dwight Eisenhower that the beaches of Normandy would be "choked with the flowers of American and British youth."[14]

One man of the island told how his grandmother employed this same metaphor when discussing Peleliu and the foreigners who changed it so thoroughly. She said to him, "We of Peleliu come from here and we are taking care of it for the world. We are the roots of the plant. They—the Americans and Japanese—are flowers: they are beautiful, but they wither eventually. We take care of the roots for the whole world."

Notes

Introduction

1. Seraphim 2006; Yamazaki 2006.

Chapter 1

1. Hanlon 2003; Hau'ofa 1993; 2000; Borofsky 2000; Linnekin 1997.
2. Nero 1987:44–46.
3. Petersen 2009:112.
4. Stewart and Strathern 2003.
5. In Palauan orthography "ch" represents a glottal stop, the catch of air that occurs in the first syllable of the exclamation "uh-oh." I will frequently use two Palauan terms that have this glottal stop spelled with ch: olangch and that for the residents of Peleliu, chad ra Beliliou. The reader should avoid scanning these as having the "ch" sound of "beach." It is better to ignore the glottal stop and mentally pronounce them as shown in the glossary: ō-lang' and ath-ra-Be-lee-lee-ō', ath as in "father."
6. Parmentier 1987.
7. Useful writers are Ashplant et al. (2000a); Winter and Sivan (1999); Winter (1995); Hutton (1993); Connerton (1989); and Young (2003).
8. Nearly everyone who discusses war and memory, from historians to politicians to veterans, assumes that wars and the men who fought them are exceptionally worthy of public commemoration and inclusion in the texts of national history. Dissenters exist. George Orwell, writing during the Battle of Britain (2005 [1940]:18), insisted that "in England all the boasting and flag-wagging, the 'Rule Britannia' stuff, is done by small minorities." The common people "do not retain among their historical memories the name of a single military victory." English of all classes loathe "the swaggering officer type, the jingle of spurs and the crash of boots." Michel de Montaigne was even harsher on the glories that armies deserve postbellum: "So many names, so many victories, so many conquests buried in oblivion, render ridiculous our hope of eternalizing our own names by the capture of ten insignificant troopers or of a hen-roost, known only by the fact of its fall" (1958:64).

9. Young 2003:277–78, 283.

10. Connerton 1989:18.

11. I have not adhered to any particular theory of memory in this book, whether psychological, sociological, or neurological. Connerton (1989) is useful for considerations of collective memory, Lowenthal (1985) for discussions of memory and history, and Hutton (1993) has an excellent analysis of various theories of memory. Indigenous ways of using objects and landscapes as aids to remembering find counterparts in the Western methods that also attach a memory to a place or object, that preserve it by making it visual or spatial. One of the most effective involves building an imaginary "memory palace" of rooms or spaces into which the creator lodges images that prompt memories. See Yates (1966), Spence (1984), and Foer (2011).

12. U.S. Army 1956:26.

13. Paulay 1994; Quammen 1996.

14. Kirch 2000:53–54; Wiles et al. 2003; Grimmett et al. 2000:15–16; see also Quammen (1996:321–24).

15. Fosberg 1963:5.

16. Quoted in Kirch 2000:58.

17. Kirch 1997:13; 2000:313–14, 59–62; see also Quammen (1996:312–21) on Hawaii.

18. Callaghan and Fitzpatrick 2008; Clark 2004; Kirch 2000:167–73, 187–91, 234–35; Fitzpatrick 2003; Rainbird 2004:79.

19. Johannes 1981.

20. D'Arcy 2001.

21. For contacts with Palau in the 19th century see Palau Community Action Agency (1977) and Hezel (1983). Parmentier (1987:79–98) and Liston and Tuggle (2006) discuss indigenous warfare in Palau. On the expedition to Peleliu see Palau Community Action Agency (1976), Nero and Thomas (2002:176–79), and Krämer (1917–29, vol.2:267 n. 1). Palauan money (*udoud*) consists of small pieces of ceramic and beads from foreign sources; it circulates today only as valuables used for discharging debts from customary obligations.

22. Gorenflo 1996:47; Useem 1946:64; Hezel 1983:271.

23. Dening 1980:31–32; 1992:175–87.

24. Faulkner 1974:13–16; Rottman 2002:8–10; Mueller-Dombois and Fosberg 1998: 11–19.

25. Kirch 2000:48–50. The Hawaiian Islands are good examples of high islands. For an atoll, picture a string of small beads laid out in an oval on a kitchen counter, which represents the sea: the ocean lies outside the beads, the lagoon inside them, and the beads themselves are the small sandy islets, connected by reefs. Usually there are one or more passages through the reefs into the lagoon. For a makatea island, place a cutting board on the counter and imagine a fringing reef shelf attached to it. With Peleliu, the cutting board platform also has a ridge of mountains.

26. U.S. Department of Agriculture 2001; National Park Service 2003:45–51.

27. Johannes 1981:63–67; on tenure of sea and land in Palau see also McCutcheon (1981).

Chapter 2

1. Germany's holdings in the central Pacific—the Marshall, Caroline, and Mariana Islands, except for Guam—fixed the *political* boundaries of what came to be called Micronesia in common usage. This same grouping of islands became the Japanese Mandate (Nan'yō) and then the United States Trust Territory of the Pacific Islands after World War II.

2. On the Spanish and German eras see especially Hezel (1995). Harder to find but helpful too is Palau Community Action Agency (1977).

3. McCutcheon 1981:49–54, 177–80.

4. Peattie 1988b:14–15. This study of the Nan'yō is indispensable for understanding Japan's era in Micronesia.

5. Peattie 1988b:2, 7, 36–38; Yamashita 2000; Peattie 1996; Akimichi 1997.

6. Myers and Peattie 1984:8; Hezel 1995, ch.4; Peattie 1988b, ch.2.

7. Peattie 1988b:47–51.

8. Peattie 1988b:53–57; Hezel 1995:153–56.

9. Peattie 1988a:238.

10. Peattie 1988b, ch.5; Hezel 1995, chs. 4 and 5.

11. Dower 1986:203–33, 262–90; 1993.

12. Peattie 1988a:238–44; 1988b:85–86, 103–11, 114; 1984a:7; Duus 1996:xxi.

13. Peattie 1988b:157–61, 335; Sawachi 1990:38; Tomiyama 2002.

14. Mita 2009:258 n. 10; Palau Community Action Agency 1978:322–53; Poyer, et al. 2001, chs.1 and 2; Peattie 1988b:170–76 and ch.5; Hezel 1995, chs. 4 and 5.

15. This discussion draws primarily on McKnight (1960, ch. 2); Smith (1983); Palau Community Action Agency (1976); Palau Society of Historians (1997); and Parmentier (1987, ch. 2).

16. Krämer 1917–29, vol.2:1; see also Klee 1976.

17. Krämer 1917–29.

18. Alkire 1977:87–88, 22.

19. Smith 1991:155 and n.7.

20. On Palauan social structure and its relationship to lands see Smith (1983); McCutcheon (1981); and McKnight (1960).

21. Petersen 2009:76–77.

22. For more on these structures, see Nero (1987:104–14); Telmetang and Rehuher (1993); Robinson (1983).

23. Palau Community Action Agency 1978; Peattie 1988b, ch.3.

24. Palau Community Action Agency 1976:55.

25. Smau Amalei Ngirngesang explained to me that although this odesongel was damaged in the war, villagers were able to repair it after their return to Peleliu.

26. Nero 1989:138; see also Parmentier (1987:32, 56).

27. Sources are personal interviews with Muchucheu Augusto Sengebau, Smau Amalei Ngirngesang, and Renguul Kelbasang Soalablai, all of Ngerdelolk.

28. Hijikata 1973:79.

29. Parmentier 1987:33.

30. Nero and Thomas 2002:176–79; Krämer 1917–29, vol.2:267 n.1; Price, et al. 2013.

31. D'Arcy 2001.

32. Sources are my interviews with Chief Uchelsias Etibek Shmull, Spesungel Ichiro Dingilius, Tokie Morei, and Edelboi Ruul, all of Ngesias.

33. Chapter 4 explains how a much-corrupted form of the name for these ridges above Ngesias would enter the annals of Pacific war history as the "Umurbrogol" Mountains.

34. Krämer 1917–29, vol.2:279.

35. Today this ceremony is widespread throughout Palau, although it originally was confined to the wealthy.

36. Semper 1982 [1873]:231–33.

37. Sources, all from Ngerchol, not otherwise identified: Diltpak Merkii, Dirribukel Ngirametuker, Ungil Besul and Mesiou Matareklai, and anonymous mechas.

38. Liston and Tuggle 2006.

39. The word for a rocky promontory is *chelbacheb*, which is also the Palauan term for the hundreds of Rock Islands that lie between Koror and Peleliu.

40. Ngerkeyukl is a fascinating archaeological site. Matichau showed me the remains of this *odesongel*—scattered shaped stones lying along the eastern flank of Cheuatel ridge, just to the south of the cut across the ridge for the path to Ngesias. Other mostly intact *odesongel* from village homes lie east of the ridge as well. Their condition is surprising considering the heavy fighting that occurred here; they may have been rebuilt after the war.

41. Krämer 1917–29, vol.2:275–77; Hijikata 1973:81.

42. Krämer (1917–29, vol.2:278) gives a different version of this founding story, in which the Angaur village of Ngabeanged was destroyed. The ibedul of Koror was then married to a woman of Bkulabeluu, so he brought the refugees to Peleliu, settled them in Bkulabeluu, and told the uchelsias of Ngesias to protect them.

43. Krämer 1917–29, vol.2:278.

44. Palau Community Action Agency 1978:381–85; Hezel 1995:163–66; Peattie 1988b:78; Aoyagi 2002.

Chapter 3

1. Sources are interviews with Chief Obaklechol Ichiro Blesam, Ngerchol; Obechad Tabelong Olkeriil, Teliu; Spesungel Ichiro Dingilus and Edelboi Ruul, Ngesias; Smau Amalei Ngirngesang, Ngerdelolk and Ngerchol; Matichau Ilemelong, Ngerkeyukl.

2. Sources are interviews with Antonio Tewid, Ngerkeyukl; also Diltpak Merkii Napoleon and Ungil Besul Matareklai, Ngerchol; Obechad Tabelong, Teliu. Home construction: Dilchuuch Ermang, Ngerchol.

3. McCutcheon 1985.

4. Semper 1982 [1873]:229.

5. Tapioca, also called cassava or manioc (*Manihot esculenta*) was introduced to Palau probably in the late 19th or early 20th century (Mary McCutcheon, pers. comm.). Elders also said that a variety of brak, giant swamp taro called *belulechab* or *yap*, was introduced from the island of Yap at about the same time. Sources for this discussion: Tokie Morei,

Ngesias; Sammy Ocheraol, Ngerdelolk; Matichau Ilemelong; Chief Obaklechol Ichiro; anonymous mechas; Dirribukel Ngirametuker, Ngerchol.

6. Besides those previously identified, sources are interviews with Chobechad ra Eliou Song of Ngerkeyukl and Mesiou Matareklai of Ngerchol.

7. Peattie 1988b:219 and Poyer, et al. 2001:31.

8. Overviews of the period appear in Peattie (1984b; 1988b); Poyer et al. (2001); Hezel (1995).

9. Palau Community Action Agency 1978:367–68; Nero 2005:303; Hezel 1995:161–62; Ballendorf et al. 1986:124, 147.

10. Shuster 1979; Peattie 1988b:90–96, 104–5, 114; Poyer et al. 2001:28–29; Palau Community Action Agency 1978:373–81.

11. See also Peattie (1988b:111–12).

12. Ballendorf et al. 1986:182; Higuchi 1987:31; see also Peattie 1988b:111–16.

13. This plant appears in Vincent 1973:126 and in Palau Community Action Agency 1978:323. The Peleliu war museum has a badly damaged snapshot of the mining rails and carts in operation in the mountains.

14. Hezel 1983:199.

15. Sources are Tokie Morei and Spesungel Ichiro Dingilius of Ngesias and Dilchuuch Ermang and Susong Smau of Ngerchol.

16. Iitaka 2011.

17. Discussions of economic development within the Nan'yō are found in Peattie 1988b:100–103 and ch. 5, Hezel 1995, chs. 4 and 5, and Poyer et al. 2001, ch.2.

18. Peattie 1988b:96–100; Palau Community Action Agency 1978:324.

19. Peattie 1988b:230–56.

20. Peattie 1988b:251–52; Frank 1992:612.

21. Higuchi 2006:145.

22. I thank Wakako Higuchi for providing me with the data from appendix 2 of her dissertation. The two crossed runways were 1200 meters and 1700 meters long; see U.S. Army 1956, maps of air facilities, attachments to text.

23. Ballendorf et al. 1986.

24. Peattie 1988b:251–52.

25. Ballendorf et al. 1986:291, 342–44.

Chapter 4

1. Morison 1948:162–63; Peattie 1988b:257.

2. Kennedy 1999:500–515, 533–35; Spector 1985:54–57; Miller 1991.

3. Dower 1986:293; Miller 1995:195; Kennedy 1999:534; Spector 1985:184–219; van der Vat 1991:170–250.

4. Morison 2001 [1951]:69–70; Shaw et al. 1966:11–13; Miller 1995:328–29, 366–67, 402; Spector 1985:252–56; Taaffe 1998, chs.1 and 2.

5. Isely and Crowl 1951:17–21.

6. Alexander 1997:5.

7. Morison 2001 [1951]:109–10. Paul Kennedy (2013, ch.5) summarizes well the problems of distance in the Pacific and how the United States overcame them. Still the best single volume on the war in Asia and the Pacific is that by Ronald Spector (1985). Willmott's fine overview (2004 [1999]) should not be missed. I discuss the American published histories of the battle for Peleliu in chapter 9.

8. Alexander 1997:vi.

9. Morison 2001 [1951]:109–10.

10. Spector 1985:260–67; Morison 2001 [1951]:127.

11. Dower 1986.

12. Cameron 1994:17.

13. Bix 2000:281; Ienaga 1978:48–50.

14. Gailey 1983:49.

15. Alexander 1997:4.

16. Spector 1985:257–58; Morison 2001 [1951]:85–92; Alexander 1997:86–103.

17. Butow 1969 [1961]:425.

18. Bailey 1991; Morison 2001 [1953]:27–34; 2001 [1951]:315–32.

19. Garand and Strobridge 1971:67–68.

20. van der Vat 1991:330–31.

21. Ballendorf et al. 1986:148, 232, 363, 284.

22. The Japanese command in Palau had learned in advance about the approach of the American fleet. Morison (2001 [1953]:31) describes the escape of Japanese warships, including the super battleship *Musashi* on March 29. Spesungel Ichiro remembered seeing the *Musashi* at anchor in the western lagoon during the month it moored in Palau after its escape from Truk. See also Ugaki (1991:342–44, 349) and Bailey (1991:44, 105). No general warning was given the populace.

23. The most detailed account of the carrier raids against Palau appears in Bailey (1991); see also Morison (2001 [1953]:13, 27–34).

24. Another Palauan boat operator who survived this sinking was Ngiratkel Etpison, a future president of the republic. See Bailey (1991:215–18). On the Palauan men taken to the Sailors Training Center in Makassar, see Ballendorf et al. (1986:75–79).

25. Ngercheu is called Ngergoi on British Admiralty chart 977 and Garakayo, the name the Japanese used, in the official Marine Corps monograph of the battle (Hough 1990 [1950]:5). It is actually a group of one large and several small islands; the large island is the site of today's popular Carp Resort. For a fascinating narrative of a young Palauan woman growing up on this island in a traditional Palauan subsistence manner during the postwar, see Callaghan 2012.

26. Ballendorf et al. 1986:293, 297.

27. Peattie 1988b:279, 299–300.

28. Peattie 1988b:170–74.

29. Gailey 1983:36–40; Gayle 1996:8–11.

30. Hough 1990 [1950]:10–13, 190–91; Garand and Strobridge 1971:51–69; Isely and Crowl 1951:392–94.

31. Morison 1966 [1958]:12–18.

32. Morison 1966 [1958]:47; Miller 1995:456. Although given extensive support by the navy, Morison, a professor of history at Harvard, wrote his 15 volumes of the history of U.S. naval operations free of any editorial control by the navy. He was not an "official" historian but was not fully independent either.

33. Alexander 1997:87; Bix 2000:462–96; Garand and Strobridge 1971:71.

34. Hough 1990 [1950]:192–93; Isely and Crowl 1951:401.

35. Gailey 1983:35–51; Garand and Strobridge 1971:72–73; Gayle 1996:9–10.

36. Leckie 1962:396.

37. The marines applied the vivid label "Bloody Nose Ridge" to peaks in the southern end of the mountains that were also called the "Five Sisters" (Hough 1990 [1950]:83 n. 47). At Guadalcanal in 1942, these same marines had repulsed Japanese attacks on a height that Americans dubbed "Bloody Ridge" or also "Edson's Ridge" (Kennedy 1999:556; Spector 1985:198–99). The Peleliu term may hearken to this earlier sanguinary formation.

38. Gailey 1983:43–45; Hough 1990 [1950]:194–97.

39. Gailey 1983:62–63; Hough 1990 [1950]:17–19; Richard 1957a:152; Garand and Strobridge 1971:58.

40. McMillan 1949:280.

41. Quoted in Garand and Strobridge 1971:104.

42. Sledge 1990 [1981]:56; Hunt 1946:35, 39.

43. National Broadcasting Co. 1995.

44. Gailey 1983:170; Hough 1990 [1950]:203.

45. Hough (1990 [1950]:57) gives 1,111 casualties on D-day, including 210 killed. In U.S. military parlance, the term "casualties" includes dead, wounded, and missing. Although the best known "D-day" is that of the Normandy invasion of June 6, 1944, American planners normally labeled the first day of any amphibious landing as D-day. In the Pacific this was true for Tarawa, the Marianas, Peleliu, and Iwo Jima, among many others.

46. Hunt 1946:139.

47. Alexander 1997:n. 118–19.

48. Garand and Strobridge 1971:147; Gailey 1983:121.

49. Hough 1990 [1950]:94.

50. Gayle 1996:34.

51. Blair and DeCioccio 2011.

52. Garand and Strobridge 1971:279, 283; Gailey 1983:154–55; Isely and Crowl 1951: 421; McMillan 1949:342–43.

53. Schrijvers 2002:101–35; Bergerud 1997:55–118.

54. Gayle 1996:38–39.

55. Regarding fire, see esp. Schrijvers 2002:244–52; Hough 1990 [1950]:158; and Alexander 1997:99–101.

56. Hough 1990 [1950]:139.

57. Gayle 1996:42.

58. Hunt 1946:136–37.

59. Gailey 1983:175–76; Gayle 1996:42.

60. Dower 2012a:75.

61. Gayle (1996:48) says 202 men were taken prisoner; Hallas (1994:280) says 302 were captured but agrees that only 19 were regular troops; he says 73 were Japanese laborers and most of the rest Korean laborers.

62. The American figures come from Garand and Strobridge 1971:Appendix H and pp.284–85; Smith 1984 [1953]:530, 573; and Gayle 1996:48; the Japanese from Bōeichō Bōei Kenshūjō Senshishitsu 1968:235; Sawachi 1990:65; and Peattie 1988b:297. Cameron notes the marines claimed 10,695 Japanese fighters killed and the 81st Infantry another 3,249, but he cautions how such estimates are "rife" with errors (1994:137 n. 14). American estimates for Japanese defenders sealed within caves obviously contain uncertainties.

63. Vandegrift 1966 [1964]:274; Garand and Strobridge 1971:285–86; Hough 1990 [1950]:181.

64. Gailey 1983:152–55; Denfeld 1988:45–48.

65. Gailey 1983:191.

Chapter 5

1. Richard 1957a:613; Useem 1946:70.

2. Ngaraard had a population of about 775 at the time (Useem 1946:69–70). Almost all of Peleliu's 825 inhabitants initially accepted refuge there, along with the 160 from Angaur, but many refugees sought out relatives in other beluu on Babeldaob in the following 12 months.

3. Walter 1993.

4. Murray 2013.

5. Written accounts of Palauan experiences in the war years appear in Hezel 1995; Peattie 1988b; Nero 1989; Poyer et al. 2001; Walter 1993; Murray 2013, 2006, 2005, 1971; Palau Community Action Agency 1978; Higuchi 1991; Ballendorf et al. 1986; Rechebei and McPhetres 1997; and Tellei 1991. Falgout et al. (2008) also offers valuable comparative material on how other Micronesian communities remember the war.

6. The search to recover remains of crews from B-24s is recounted in *Vanished* (Hylton 2013).

7. Walter 1993:119, 136–37, 177–79.

8. Francisco Morei testimony in Ballendorf et al. 1986:130; for Palauan history text see Rechebei and McPhetres (1997:189).

9. Collingham 2012:284–300; Morison 2001 [1951]:308.

10. Nero 1989:130.

11. A bureaucrat from the Nan'yō era recalled, "We did not regard [the natives] with contempt. The only thing that I disliked was the skin smell of coconut, which was very strong and smelled from one meter distance. Surprisingly, I did not smell any of the [odor] when I visited Palau in recent years" (Higuchi 1987:190).

12. Peattie 1988b:347–48 n. 85; 300–307; Poyer et al. 2001:233–34.

13. Higuchi 1991.

14. Murray 2013.

15. Walter 1993:119.

16. Ballendorf et al. 1986:294.

17. See also Nero 1989:120, 124; Walter 1993:Appendix A; Peattie 1988b:301; and Ballendorf et al. 1986:68–79.

18. Drea 2009; Straus 2003.

19. These figures come primarily from volume 13 of the official Japanese history of the Pacific war, the Senshi Sōsho, Bōeichō Bōei Kenshūjō Senshishitsu 1968:234–36. They are augmented by data from Sawachi Hisae's book (1990:79–115). I am indebted to Professor Iitaka Shingo for reviewing these Japanese sources with me. Three English language sources contain numbers of survivors on Babeldaob as of the surrender in September 1945, but they lack information on deaths incurred by either military or civilians on the island: Walter 1993:113, 195–96, Richard 1957b:18, and the postwar report by Admiral Nimitz's command (CinCPac-CinCPOA 1946:175–76). Of the 120,400 Japanese military personnel trapped on the 15 bypassed garrisons in the Nan'yō, including Babeldaob, 24,600 died, 77 percent from famine and illness. Not one of the 15 Japanese commanders released a single soldier or civilian until the final surrenders in September 1945. I discuss the Palauan and Micronesian data in detail in Murray 2013; see especially its note 3.

20. Richard Parmentier (1987:98 n. 26) says this klechedaol occurred in 1948 and that the anthropologist H. G. Barnett witnessed it. In his "Palauan Journal" (1970:19–20) Barnett defines a *kledaol* as "a display of native dances and a feast." He then describes a klechedaol that occurred in Ulimang, Ngaraard about January 24–26, 1948. It honored American officials "along with members of Peleliu village, which is a kind of brother community to Ulimang." But, as in his famous study, *Being a Palauan* (1960:78), he mentions only dancing and skits. If Barnett had translated the words to the dancers' songs, he would have learned why Peleliu was visiting. He might then have learned of and attended the central event, the olangch ceremony, and left us a written account of it.

21. Nero 1989:137–38.

22. Nero 1989:138.; Parmentier 1987:98.

Chapter 6

1. Richard 1957a:18. American forces were unconscionably slow to provide food to the starving populations under their control. Walter writes (1993:197–207) that not until October 2, 1945, did the United States bring 70 tons of food to Renrak in southern Babeldaob and that the occupation of the whole of Palau did not begin until October 29. Marines did not begin "the patrolling and occupation of Babeldaob Island" until the end of December.

2. Walter (1993:215 n. 182) cites navy documents stating they were sent in June and September.

3. Bergerud 1997:55–118.

4. The most accessible set of photos showing the extent of the devastation caused by the battle and the base construction, as well as the state of the battlefield today, appears in the report of the battlefield survey performed by Knecht, Price, and Lindsay, (Knecht, et al. 2012).

5. Camp 2008:162.

6. Garran 2010.

7. U.S. Army 1956:12.

8. Walter 1993:220–21; A&E Home Video 1985.

9. Hough 1990 [1950]:96–98.

10. A recent survey found massive amounts of unexploded ordnance still on the island (Price and Knecht 2012). See the carpet of rusting but still lethal munitions shown in Knecht et al. 2012:81–82. Ordnance specialists calculate that 31 percent of the homes on Peleliu contain unexploded munitions on their property.

11. U.S. Department of Agriculture 2001:4.

12. Additional discussions of the war's effects on Pacific island landscapes may be found in Poyer et al. 2001, ch. 9, and in Bennett 2009, ch.10.

13. Nero 1989:132; Hezel 1995:244–45.

14. Useem 1946:65.

15. See, for example, McKnight (1960).

16. Hallas 1994:283–84.

17. Richard (1957c:147–48) describes the sale of the scrap and writes that the garrison force remained until May 1948. She also says that the United States began removing the remains of its interred military personnel from Micronesia in April 1947 (1957b:25). Hugh Ambrose writes (2010:362) that there were 1,058 U.S. dead buried at Orange Beach.

18. McDougall 1993:662; Kiste 1994:227.

19. The constituent islands of the TT were the former islands of the Nan'yō, which is the Micronesia of post-1898: the Marshall Islands, Kosrae (Kusaie), Pohnpei (Ponape), Chuuk (Truk), Yap, and Palau of the Caroline Islands, and the northern Mariana Islands of Saipan, Tinian, and Rota. Each of these six groupings was called a "district." Guam remained a U.S. unincorporated territory, governed separately.

20. Gale 1979:47–69; Kiste 1994; Hezel 1995, ch.6.

21. Gale 1979; Hezel 1995, ch.6; Kiste 1994; Richard 1957b.

22. Kiste 1994:229–30.

23. Hezel 1995:359; Poyer et al. 2004.

24. For the stories of other Micronesian citizens who faced similar postwar hardships, see Poyer et al. 2001; 2004; Falgout et al. 2008, and Hezel 1995, ch.7.

25. In general usage *Kloulklubed* refers to several small, distinct communities clustered at the island's north end since the war.

26. Sources for this information were Postol Remeliik, Koichi Wong, and Balkuu Kumangai. Cortés (2013) offers a good discussion of Palauan land and the influences of the American legal system.

27. Tia Belau newspaper 2003.

28. Higuchi 1995; Lee and Goodman 1981.

29. Australia and New Zealand made prompt and generous payments in the southwest and central Pacific; see Bennett 2009, ch.8.

30. Gale 1979; Leibowitz 1996; Roff 1991; Aldridge and Myers 1990.

31. Pers. comm. J. Victor Hobson, Freely Associated States Federal Programs coordi-

nator for the Department of Interior, 2003, whom I thank for providing these official figures. Palau's compact was priced at $589.5 million, to which were added $12 million for services like weather forecasts and the post office. The perimeter road around Babeldaob at $149 million is included in this $602 million. The figures for fiscal years 1987–2001 for the RMI were $945 million, for the FMS $1.347 billion. Additional "federal services" of $139 million brought their grand total to $2.431 billion. In 2010 the United States agreed to provide Palau with $265 million in aid between 2011 and 2024 (Shuster 2012:163), But as of mid-2015, the U.S. Congress had still not given its final approval. On Palau's tortuous path to sovereignty see Hezel 1995, ch.7); Kiste 1994; Leibowitz 1996; Wilson 1995; Murray 1996; U.S. Congress 1986.

32. U.S. Department of Agriculture 2001.

33. McHenry 1975:15–25. It was an open secret that the crash program of the Peace Corps to emplace the first four groups of volunteers in Micronesia between November 1966 and early February 1967 drew its urgency from the American need to have them laboring visibly and happily prior to the arrival of the 1967 visiting mission, which toured in February.

34. *Ireidan* actually means association for repose or consoling of souls. Their hosts in Palau apply the term to any Japanese persons who return to commemorate their war dead; they refer to them in English as "the *Ireidan*."

35. Tourist arrivals in Palau grew from about 4,000 in 1980 to 45,000 in 2000; they fluctuate, but reached almost 120,000 in 2012 (Palau Visitors Authority 2013). Japan and ROC Taiwan each usually accounts for 25–35 percent of total arrivals. Korea provides nearly 20 percent, and the U.S. mainland 6 percent. With a rapidly growing influx of tourists from China as well, these market shares remind us how close to the east Asian mainland Palau lies.

36. Pers. comm. Kyosuke Takaoka, Palau Resident Representative of JICA, 2003; the Peleliu wharf figure appears in the Tia Belau newspaper of December 23–30, 2005. The Koror-Airai road project is in Shuster (2009).

37. Higuchi 1995, esp. pp.96–98.

38. The 2005 census counted 19,907 people residing in Palau, of whom 14,000 were citizens and 5,900 noncitizens. Of these latter, 4,300 came from Asia, 3,000 of these from the Philippines (Republic of Palau 2005). Another 5,000–6,000 Palauan nationals lived outside of Palau and are not included in the 19,907 figure (Kyonori Tellames, pers. comm.).

39. Republic of Palau 2001:25, table 3.1; Republic of Palau 2000:13–14, 31, table 14; Republic of Palau 2005.

Chapter 7

1. Young 2003:283.

2. Gallicchio 2007; Buruma 1994; Seraphim 2006; Henshall 2001.

3. For comparisons of the very different ways Germany and Japan have dealt with their war memory, see Buruma 1994; Hein and Selden 2000; and Seraphim 2006:263–70, 318–22. In early 2015 German Chancellor Angela Merkel visited Japan. She pointedly discussed

Germany's reconciliation efforts after World War II, and clearly implied a contrast with Japan's efforts. She said Germany had "faced its past squarely," helping it move forward. She noted that Germany's acceptance into the international community following World War II was possible because Germany had dealt with its past. "There was the acceptance in Germany to call things by their name," Merkel said. What also helped were "generous gestures by our neighbors" like France in reaccepting Germany (BBC News Asia, March 9, 2015).

4. The literature on both Japan's struggles with war guilt and responsibility and the impatient and angry reactions from its regional neighbors is large. Recommended are Cook and Cook 1992; Buruma 1994; Duus 1996; Asada 1998; Dower 1999; 2012b; Orr 2001; Seraphim 2006; Hastings 2007; Seaton 2007; Hasegawa and Toga 2008.

5. Dower 2002:226.

6. Yamazaki 2006.

7. Seraphim 2006:5.

8. Dower 1999:643; Seraphim 2006, chs. 2 and 8.

9. Szymkowiak and Steinhoff 1995; Kaplan 2003.

10. Funasaka 1986:3.

11. Dower 1999:486.

12. Peattie 1988b:314–15.

13. For a discussion of bone collecting and war memorialization on Guam and Saipan see Camacho 2005, 2011. Interestingly, Camacho found that U.S. authorities allowed a Japanese bone-gathering expedition to gather remains on Guam, U.S. territory, as early as 1953 (2005:168 n. 69). This was 12 years before Japanese veterans or Ireidan were allowed into Palau.

14. Seraphim 2006:182–83.

15. Both U.S. and Japanese sources placed 2,460 Korean residents in Palau as of June 1943 (U.S. Army 1956:14; Senshi Sōsho 1968:45–46.) More would have come with the 14th Division as forced labor. Hundreds worked on the Peleliu airfield and on the island's defenses and were trapped during the invasion. A Korean memorial at the Palauan capitol in Melekeok states that Korean nationals had been forcibly brought to Palau for their labor before the war, and that as many as 6,000 were "literally enslaved" as laborers during the war, including 500 "comfort women" for the Japanese Army. It estimates 2,000 Korean citizens died in Palau.

16. Saipan Tribune 2005.

17. Linenthal 1993.

18. On memorials and commemoration see also Pye 1996; Piehler 1995; Young 2002; Ashplant et al. 2000a.

19. Levinson 1998:10.

20. Buruma 1994:234–38.

21. Ma 2007:172; on peace museums see Smith 2002.

22. Ma 2007; Smith 2002; Seraphim 2007.

23. Linenthal and Engelhardt 1996; Heinrichs 2007.

24. Camacho 2011.

25. Initially I understood that the stone dated to 1978, and provided this date to

Franziska Seraphim (2006:341). I thank Jeff Boal, who, as a Peace Corps volunteer on Peleliu, attended the dedication of these first two memorials and gave me a photo of the ceremony and the 1967 date.

26. Dower 1999:489–90.

27. Seraphim 2001:252; Bix 2000:658.

28. In 1980 Japan erected an identical set of trilingual plaques at Rabaul, Papua New Guinea. The only difference is that they refer to the "South Pacific," and the indigenous language is pidgin. E. M. Gardiner, who informed me of this memorial, refers to such trilingual texts as "Rosetta stones."

29. Ryan 2007:14; Dower 1999:643.

30. Ma 2007:156–59; Bix 2000:680–81.

31. Dower 1996a:123.

32. Bix 2000:30–32, 560–61; Dower 1993.

33. Tia Belau newspaper 2002.

34. Szymkowiak and Steinhoff 1995:283.

35. Breen (2008:156–57) observes that Yasukuni Shrine calls the military dead the "cornerstone" of today's peace and prosperity. He cites Emperor Akihito's statement before his visit to Saipan in June 2005: "It is vital that we all bear constantly in mind that the Japan of today is, indeed, built on the cornerstone [*ishizue*] of the sacrifice made by the fallen." This provocative remark came just weeks after the massive demonstrations against Japan that occurred in China in April 2005.

36. Shuster 1982.

37. *Heisei* is the name given to the reign of the current emperor, Akihito. It began in 1989.

38. Peattie 1988b:301.

39. Dower 1993:272–75.

Chapter 8

1. Dower 1986, 1996b; Kennedy 1999:855–56; Zinn 1990, ch. 16; Ferguson 2005.

2. Beidler 1998:3–4, 45, 91–92.

3. Ashplant et al. 2000b:46, 51–52; Fox 1997.

4. Manchester 1979:372.

5. Fussell 1989:285–97.

6. Frank 1999:330.

7. "K-3-1" means Company K, Third Battalion, First Marine Regiment of the First Marine Division. "Semper Fidelis," "Forever Faithful," is the motto of the Marine Corps.

8. Ross 1991:168.

9. National Park Service 2003:13.

10. Their remarks have been transcribed into Palauan but have not been translated into English. The transcripts are kept at the Belau National Museum in Koror.

11. Tia Belau newspaper 2004:19

12. Hongo, *The Japan Times*, 2013.

13. Hoshi 2008.

14. National Park Service 2003. The NPS wrote a preliminary draft of the Bliliou Peleliu Historical Park Study in January 1991. This was updated as *Special Resources Study: Peleliu Battlefield National Historic Landmark*, dated January 2003 and released in January 2004. This latter report adds 38 pages of text to the front of the 1991 draft without changing the pagination of the draft. The 2003 document thus has two separate sets of pages numbered 1–38. I refer to the first set of page numbers as SRS, for example, "SRS:12" and the second set as 1991 Draft, for example, "1991 Draft:26". Pages 39 and higher refer to the 1991 Draft; these will be noted parenthetically in the text.

15. Japan International Cooperation Agency 2000.

16. From the 1991 Draft: 55–56. The 4.78 square miles of land surface surveyed by the U.S. Army (U.S. Army 1956) equates to 3,059 acres. This excludes mangroves and reefs.

17. From conversations with staff of NPS in Honolulu.

18. Price and Knecht 2012; Price et al. 2013.

19. Japan International Cooperation Agency 2000; references will be noted parenthetically in the text.

Chapter 9

1. McMillan 1949; Falk 1974.

2. Garand and Strobridge 1971:288.

3. Dower 1999:486; Grayling 2006:264–65.

4. Bōeichō Bōei Kenshūjō Senshishitsu 1968.

5. Peattie 1998:57; Peattie and Evans 1994:219.

6. Peattie 1998:56.

7. Hoshi 2008.

8. Kennedy 1999, ch.18.

9. Mawdsley 2007:242; Alexander 1997:150; Morison 2001 [1960]:90; Spector 1985: 532; Schwarz 2007; Frank 1992:615; Dower 2002; Willmott 2004 [1999]:34,128; Wood 2007:111. Total Americans killed in action in World War II were 291,600, with another 114,000 killed by accidents or disease (Kennedy 1999: 668, 716).

10. Funasaka 1986; out of print.

11. Funasaka 1966.

12. Funasaka 1967.

13. Funasaka 1968.

14. Peattie 1988b:273–74.

15. Funasaka 1986:23.

16. Dower 1999:492–96.

17. Funasaka 1986:9, 12–13, 28–29, 40, 54.

18. Willmott 2004 [1999]:34; Keegan 1989:167.

19. Cook and Cook 1992:261–66; Drea 2009:212–13, 231, 253–62.

20. Richard Overy (1996) shows that the Allied triumph involved far more than the sheer weight of material force, colossal as it was. Victory required complex economic organization, technological innovation, production of high-quality armaments, training sol-

diers to use them effectively, leadership and strategic judgment, close coordination among sometimes fractious allies, and powerful support from the home front. Japan lagged seriously in all these categories, except civilian morale.

21. Yet one of America's most hallowed battlegrounds is the Alamo, where the defenders chose annihilation over surrender. FreeHart Productions 1999.

22. John Dower (2012a:75) explains that this exhortation "became the morbidly romantic catch-phrase that men prepared to die for the nation were supposed to utter upon taking leave of one another." Funasaka 1986:22, 48.

23. Hough 1990 [1950]:179; Smith 1984 [1953]:575; Morison 1966 [1958]:47; Garand and Strobridge 1971:52.

24. Gailey 1983:x–xi.

25. Gailey 1983:189–91. As if to underscore the small contribution Peleliu made in the American campaigns against Japan, even as compared with other Micronesian islands, the day Colonel Nakagawa burned his regiment's colors, November 24, 1944, was the day that the first raid of B-29s flew against Japan from the new airfields on Saipan. There is some danger, however, that Peleliu is becoming known as *the* needless invasion of the Pacific War. Ken Burns's PBS documentary series *The War* (2007) consigns Peleliu to an episode devoted to bungled and wasteful operations. It is inaccurate to single out Peleliu this way. The Allies engaged in 78 landings in the Pacific War (Wood 2007:107). Dozens of these proved of limited value. Van der Vat (1991:301–2) stoutly argues the entire Micronesian campaign wasted men and resources that would have been better employed on the axis through New Guinea and the Philippines. The one Micronesian archipelago the United States needed to capture in support, he writes, was . . . Palau. Paul Kennedy (2013) and H. P. Willmott (2004 [1999]), however, are convinced that the Micronesian campaign proved to be the most efficient route of attack against Japan. Of the First Marine Division's four campaigns in the Pacific, Guadalcanal and Okinawa were of unquestionable military necessity; Cape Gloucester and Peleliu were costly mistakes.

26. Gailey 1983: 187–88; National Broadcasting Co. 1995.

27. Gailey 1983: 19–21; Morison 1966 [1958]; Hough 1990 [1950].

28. Gailey 1983:190; Gayle 1996:25–26, 35, 45.

29. National Broadcasting Co. 1995.

30. A&E Home Video 1985; *Peleliu 1944*: Kenwood Productions 1991; FreeHart Productions 1999.

31. National Broadcasting Co. 1995. See Sledge 1990 [1981]:163–64.

32. Oda 2003:99–100.

33. Oda 2003: 95, 112–16. When General Inoue learned of Leyte, he realized the United States would never bother invading Babeldaob. He and his 30,000 troops and 20,000 civilians would be bypassed by the American forces and abandoned by Tokyo and left to starve (Murray 2013).

34. Ross 1991:346. The issue receives no mention in the official and semiofficial histories of the battle. See Hough 1990 [1950], Morison 1966 [1958], Smith 1984 [1953], Garand and Strobridge 1971, or Gayle 1996. Vandegrift did not go on record with a detailed explanation of his action (1966 [1964]:278–79).

35. Camp 2008.

36. In his 1983 study Gailey observes that the leadership of Rupertus "must have been seriously questioned by his superiors" and notes that he was replaced as commander of the Division (171). He does not quite sheet the sail home and confront the firing as having been forced by field command errors, which only compounded Nimitz's mistake of proceeding with the invasion in the first place. Hugh Ambrose (2010:365) says that Rupertus was fired for his failures but does not elaborate. Before Rupertus, at least six American general officers had been relieved of divisional command in the Pacific for unsatisfactory performance (Spector 1985:314).

37. Hastings 2007:119,182.

38. Moran and Rottman 2002; Wright 2005; Sloan 2005.

39. Blair and DeCioccio 2011:20.

40. Hylton 2013. See transcripts of the National Public Radio broadcasts from March 6 and 7, 2014: http://apps.npr.org/grave-science/, accessed November 12, 2014.

41. Sawachi 1990.

42. Murray 2013.

43. Fussell 1975:334; Sledge 1990 [1981]. Sledge's book remains in print today.

44. Keegan 1990:598; Dunne 2001.

45. Sledge 1990 [1981]:120); Burns 2007; Franklin and Patten 2010; Leckie 2001 [1957].

46. Hunt 1946.

47. Funasaka 1986:277.

48. Ross 1991:350–55. Peleliu is a makatea island, not (as Ross claims) an atoll.

49. Hallas 1994:x–xi.

50. Woodard 1994:77–82.

51. The website is http://www2s.biglobe.ne.jp/~nippon/nagoshi/palau.htm, accessed March 21, 2015. FreeHart Productions 1999.

52. See, for example, Camp 2008:180.

53. The event was heavily covered by the Japanese press. See http://the-japan-news.com/news/article/0002069464. The opening of the first sealed bunker (not a cave) is described in Tia Belau newspaper 2015.

54. Gailey 1983:x.

Conclusion

1. Rodda et al. 1997; National Park Service 2003.

2. Piehler 1995:177; Blight 2001:31.

3. Murray 2013.

4. Lane 2013: 93; Burleigh 2010 [1969]: xi.

5. Ashplant et al. 2000a; Seraphim 2006.

6. Fitzgerald 1995:65.

7. Wahl 2000:229–32.

8. Blight 2001:33.

9. Pregill and Steadman 2000:141, 138, 148.

10. Personal communications.

11. Allen et al. 2002.

12. Price and Knecht 2012; Knecht, et al. 2012; Price et al. 2013; for a description of disturbances to the material remains of Peleliu's battlefield and the effects of souvenir hunting see Price, et al. 2015.

13. Ward and Pickering 1985.

14. Perry 2007:283

Glossary

The Palauan language is generally considered to be an independent branch of the Malayo-Polynesian languages, within the family of Austronesian languages. In Palauan orthography "ch" indicates the glottal stop, but for phonetic spellings I drop it. The "r" is trilled, as in Spanish. The "ng" sound frequently appears in initial position. Singular and plural forms of nouns are identical, so rubak *can mean an elder man or elder men. For pronunciations, the syllable before a stress mark is the one that receives the emphasis.*

Babeldaob (bab'l-dowb). "Upper Seas." Name of largest island in Palau; also name of northern moiety, led by the high chief reklai of Melekeok. *See also* **Eouldaob; ibedul.**

bai (bī). Large wooden community structure, the most important of which was the council house of each village in which the council of chiefs, klobak, met. This bai is also sometimes called the *rubak bai* since it seats the male elders.

Bai ra Ibesachel (ee-be-sa'l). The Its main rubak bai in Ngerchol.

Belau (bay-low' as in "plow"). Native name for the archipelago. *See also* **Palau.**

Beliliou (Be-lee-lee-ō'). "The Land Downwind"; native name for Peleliu island. Its five traditional villages in rank order are Ngerdelolk, Ngesias, Ngerchol, Ngerkeyukl, and Teliu. Home to a people of fortitude.

beluu (be-loo'). Village; community; place; country.

Bibuiich el bad (bee-byoo '-ye-el-bath). A clear, glasslike olangch from before the war,.

Bkulabeluu (be-kool-a-be-loo'). Alternate name for village of Teliu, q.v. *See also* **Chelechol ra Bkulabeluu.**

blai (blī). House or home, also a constituent unit of a telungalek, lineage.

chad ra Beliliou (ath-ra-Be-lee-lee-ō'). The inhabitants of Peleliu.

chedil (e deel). Mother; as exclamation expresses surprise or woe.

cheldecheduch (el-the-e-doo). A settlement of money and land at the time of the death of a spouse.

Chelechol ra Bkulabeluu (el-e-ol-ra-Be-kool-a-be-loo'). "The beach of Bkulabeluu," alternative name for the village of Teliu. The southwestern beach that the United States code-named Orange Beaches 1–3 for the 1944 invasion.

Chelechol ra Ngebedangel (nge-be-thang'l). Beach of the Peleliu village of Ngerkeyukl on the southwest coast; code-named White Beaches 1 and 2 by the United States during 1944 invasion.

chesols (e-sols'). Chants performed by men and women of advanced age and rank.

chutem (oo-tem). Land parcel.

dui (doo-ey). Chiefly titles that denote leadership, high rank, and the power to direct the disposition of lands.

eirei (ay-ray). "Spirits of the glorious/honorable/heroic war dead." A highly contentious term in Japan and a key word in the idiom of the ultranationalist Right. Newspapers avoid it in favor of the more neutral *senbotsusha* (those who died in war).

Eouldaob (yol'-dowb). "Lower Seas." Name of southern moiety of Palau, led by the high chief ibedul of Koror. Peleliu is part of Eouldaob. Cf. Babeldaob.

ewaul saus (ay-wal-souse). The four corner post chiefs of a village ruling council; these four are the most powerful in the full council of chiefs, the klobak.

ibedul (ī'-be-dool). Title of the high chief of Koror; leader of the southern moiety of Palau, Eouldaob, "Lower Seas." Written "Abba Thulle" in early texts.

Inoue (ee-no-oo-ay) **Sadae**. Commander of Palau's defending forces.

Ireidan (ee'-ray-don). (Japanese) "Association for consoling souls." Used by Palauans as a term for Japanese who visit for war commemoration.

Izokukai (ee-zo-koo'-kī). Full name Nihon Izokukai, the Japan Association of War-bereaved Families; powerful Rightist pressure group active on Peleliu gathering remains.

kebliil (ke-bleel'). Term commonly glossed as clan. Made up of constituent lineages, telungalek, which are in turn made up of several blai, houses. Typically each Palauan village has ten clans. *See also* **klobak.**

kelulau (ke-loo-lau', as in "plow"). Literally whispers, applied to knowledge guarded from those not qualified to know it.

klechedaol (kle-e-dowl'). Large, multiday commemorative feast between two villages.

klobak (klō'-bak). The full ruling council of chiefs of a village, usually ten in number, made up of the male chief of each of the ten clans (kebliil) of the village. *See also* **ewaul saus.**

Kloulklubed (klōl-klu'-beth). "Great boat landing." The name of the new community that Peleliu residents were settled into by the U.S. Navy upon their return to the island in 1946. Primary settlement on the island today.

Koror (ko-roar'). Name for both the island and its town, main urban center in Palau today; the capital town of the Japanese Nan'yō; "Oreor" in Palauan.

kukau (goo-gow'). Taro, *Colocasia esculenta*. The preferred variety throughout Palau, grown in deep, heavily mulched paddies called mesei.

mechas (me-oss'). Respectful term for, or of address to, female elder; in past, reserved for female title holder. *See also* **rubak.**

mengkar (meng-kar'). Trustee or guardian, as of family land.

mesei (me-say'). Taro patch, esp. the deep and heavily mulched pits used to grow kukau. Highly valuable plots of land in Palau traditionally because of their high productivity and the heavy labor that goes into their creation and maintenance.

Modekngei (mō-thek-ngay'). Native religion and revitalization movement from Nan'yō time; extant today.

Nan'yō (nan'-yō). Japanese for "south seas." It was applied broadly to the Japanese Mandate of Micronesia.

Nan'yō-chō (nan'-yō-chō). The Japanese colonial government or bureau that administered the Nan'yō Mandate.

Nan'yō Jinja Shrine. Kampei Taisha Nan'yō Jinja, the great Japanese Shinto shrine dedicated in Koror in 1940.

Ngaraard (nga-rard'). Large village in northern Babeldaob Island that gave refuge to residents of Peleliu during invasion of their island, 1944–45.

Ngchereu (nger-ay'-oo). Small Rock Island to the north of Peleliu to which most people fled after the air raid of March 1944.

Ngebedangel. *See* **Chelechol ra Ngebedangel.**

Ngerchol (nger-ōl'). One of the five traditional villages of Peleliu. Ranked third among them. *See also* **Beliliou** for list of villages.

Ngerdelolk (nger-the-lolk'). One of the five traditional villages of Peleliu. Ranked first among them. *See also* **Beliliou** for list of villages.

Ngerkeyukl (nger-kyu'-kle). One of the five traditional villages of Peleliu. Ranked fourth among them. *See also* **Beliliou** for list of villages; **Chelechol ra Ngebedangel.**

Ngermeskang (Nger-mes-kang'). Hamlet in Ngaremlengui where Japanese dropped the refugees of Peleliu, who then walked to Ngaraard. Also called Asahimura for Japanese farm of 1930s.

Ngesias (nge-shas'). One of the five traditional villages of Peleliu. Ranked second among them. *See also* **Beliliou** for list of villages.

Nihon Izokukai (nee-hōn-ee-zo-koo'-kī). *See* **Izokukai.**

Odesangel (ō-the-sang'l). Traditional and ceremonial name for Peleliu. Not to be confused with odesongel. Odesangel Bad (stone, pron. "bath" as in "bother"; see figure 11) is the olangch commemorating the aid given the exiles of Peleliu by Ngaraard villagers.

odesongel (ō-the-sōng'l). House or burial platform made of stone in which significant ancestors, who watch over affairs of the living, are buried; see figure 3. Not to be confused with Odesangel.

odoim (ō-thoy'-em). Foods higher in protein, obtained by men. A proper Palauan meal must contain both this and the higher-energy carbohydrate foods (**ongraol**) produced by women.

olangch (ō-lang'). Objects that contain histories and information; mnemonic markers for stories of the past; external signs or distinguishing marks.

Omleblochel (ōm-le-blō'-el). The name of the portion of mountains immediately north of the village of Ngesias in central Peleliu. In corrupted form it became the "Umurbrogol" mountains in accounts of the 1944 battle.

ongraol (ōng-rowl') Foods higher in carbohydrates, produced by women. A proper Palauan meal must contain both this and the foods higher in protein (**odoim**) obtained by men.

Palau (pa-low', as if "plow" were spoken in two syllables). Adopted as the official name of the Republic of Palau. People of Peleliu often use it to refer to the northern portion of the archipelago, Koror and Babeldaob. *See also* **Belau.**

Peleliu (pel'-le-lew). Western version of native name Beliliou. Southernmost of the islands within the main system of reefs in the Palau archipelago, one of 16 states of the Republic of Palau. Site of World War II battle, September–November 1944.

rael (rī-l). Road.

ream (ray-am'). A type of weed

ringko (ring-kō). (Japanese) Phosphates, mined for fertilizer.

Rock Islands, Chelbacheb (el-ba'-eb). The numerous small and now uninhabited islands that lie in the lagoon between Koror and Peleliu. Refuges for people of Peleliu during air attacks; popular with foreign tourists today.

rois (royce). mountains.

rubak (rū'-bak). Respectful term for, or of address to, male elder; in past, reserved for male title holder. *See also* **mechas.**

sers (rhymes with "bear us"). Dry land garden used to grow crops like tapioca, sweet potato, vegetables, and greens. *See also* **mesei.**

Teliu (te-lew'). One of the five traditional villages of Peleliu, ranked fifth among them. Also called Bkulabeluu. *See also* **Beliliou** for list of villages.

telungalek (te-lew-ngal'-ek). A lineage, made up of several blai, houses; several telungalek make up a kebliil, clan.

tochi daicho (to-chee-dī-cho). (Japanese) The land surveying and registration program carried out during the Japanese era.

tōmin (tō-min). (Japanese) Islander, viewed by many Palauans as a pejorative term for themselves.

TT. The U.S. Trust Territory of the Pacific Islands, 1947–94: the Marshall Islands, Kosrae (Kusaie), Pohnpei (Ponape), Chuuk (Truk), Yap, Palau, and the Mariana Islands other than Guam.

Bibliography

A&E Home Video

1985 World War II: The War Chronicles, vol. 6: The Bloody Ridges of Peleliu (video documentary). New York: New Video Group.

Akimichi, Tomoya

1997 Japanese Views on Oceania: Modernist Images of Paradise. *In* Images of Other Cultures. K. Yoshida and J. Mack, eds. Pp. 244–49. Osaka: NHK Service Center.

Aldridge, Bob, and Ched Myers

1990 Resisting the Serpent: Palau's Struggle for Self-Determination. Baltimore, MD: Fortkamp Publishing Company.

Alexander, Joseph H.

1997 Storm Landings: Epic Amphibian Battles in the Central Pacific. Annapolis, MD: Naval Institute Press.

Alkire, William H.

1977 An Introduction to the Peoples and Cultures of Micronesia. Menlo Park, CA: Cummings Publishing.

Allen, Jane, Dennis Gosser, Richard Nees, and Boyd Dixon

2002 Final Report Cultural Resources Survey of the Military Leaseback Area, Tinian, Commonwealth of the Northern Mariana Islands, vol. 5: Synthesis and Interpretations. Prepared for the Department of the Navy, Pacific Division, Naval Facilities Engineering Command, Pearl Harbor. Honolulu: Ogden Environmental and Energy Services Company, Inc.

Ambrose, Hugh

2010 The Pacific: The Official Companion to the HBO Miniseries. New York: New American Library.

Aoyagi, Machiko

2002 Modekngei: A New Religion in Belau, Micronesia. Tokyo: Shinsensha Press.

Asada, Sadao

1998 The Mushroom Cloud and National Psyches: Japanese and American Perceptions of the A-Bomb Decision, 1945–1995. *In* History of Contemporary Japan, 1945–1998.

E. R. Beauchamp, ed. Pp. 133–54. Dimensions of Contemporary Japan: A Collection of Essays. Honolulu: University of Hawai'i.

Ashplant, T. G., Graham Dawson, and Michael Roper, eds.

2000a The Politics of War Memory and Commemoration. London: Routledge.

2000b The Politics of War Memory and Commemoration: Contexts, Structures and Dynamics. *In* The Politics of War Memory and Commemoration. T. G. Ashplant, G. Dawson, and M. Roper, eds. Pp. 3–85. London: Routledge.

Bailey, Dan E.

1991 World War II Wrecks of Palau: The Japanese Occupation, Operation Desecrate One, Operation Snapshot, Operation Stalemate II Preliminaries. Redding, CA: North Valley Diver Publications.

Ballendorf, Dirk A., Donald R. Shuster, and Wakako Higuchi

1986 An Oral Historiography of the Japanese Administration in Palau. Final Report Submitted to the Japan Foundation International Project Support Program. Mangilao, Guam: University of Guam, Micronesian Area Research Center.

Barnett, H. G.

1960 Being a Palauan. New York: Holt, Rinehart, and Winston.

1970 Palauan Journal. *In* Being an Anthropologist: Fieldwork in Eleven Countries. G. D. Spindler, ed. Pp. 1–31. New York: Holt, Rinehart and Winston.

Batty, David

2004 Japan at War in Color. London: Carlton Books

BBC News Asia

2015 Germany's Merkel addresses WW2 reconciliation in Japan, March 9. http://www.bbc.com/news/world-asia-31792313, accessed March 12, 2015.

Beidler, Philip D.

1998 The Good War's Greatest Hits: World War II and American Remembering. Athens: University of Georgia.

Bennett, Judith A.

2009 Natives and Exotics: World War II and Environment in the Southern Pacific. Honolulu: University of Hawai'i Press.

Bergerud, Eric M.

1997 Touched with Fire: The Land War in the South Pacific. New York: Penguin.

Bix, Herbert P.

2000 Hirohito and the Making of Modern Japan. New York: Harper Collins.

Blair, Bobby C., and John P. DeCioccio

2011 Victory at Peleliu: The 81st Infantry Division's Pacific Campaign. Norman, OK: University of Oklahoma Press.

Blight, David W.

2001 Race and Reunion: The Civil War in American Memory. Cambridge, MA: Belknap Press of Harvard University.

Bōeichō Bōei Kenshūjō Senshishitsu (BBKS), Self-Defense Agency, Self-Defense Research Institute, War History Office

1968 Senshi Sōsho [War history series], vol. 13: Chūbu Taiheiyō rikugun sakusen, part 2:

Periryū, Angaru, Iōtō [Army operations in the Central Pacific, part 2: Peleliu, Angaur, and Iwo Jima]. Tokyo: Asagumo Shimbun Sha.
Borofsky, Robert
2000 An Invitation. *In* Remembrance of Pacific Pasts: An Invitation to Remake History. R. Borofsky, ed. Pp. 1–30. Honolulu: University of Hawai'i Press.
Breen, John
2008 Yasukuni and the Loss of Memory. *In* Yasukuni, the War Dead, and the Struggle for Japan's Past. J. Breen, ed. Pp. 143–62. New York: Columbia University Press.
Burleigh, Anne Husted
2010 [1969] John Adams. Rutgers, NJ: Transaction Publishers.
Burns, Ken
2007 The War. Hollywood, CA: Public Broadcasting System.
Buruma, Ian
1994 The Wages of Guilt: Memories of War in Germany and Japan. New York: Farrar, Straus and Giroux.
Butow, Robert J. C.
1969 [1961] Tojo and the Coming of the War. Stanford: Stanford University Press.
Callaghan, Paul
2012 Flight of the Dudek: A Story of One Person's Journey. Available on Amazon.com. ISBN 978-1475109498.
Callaghan, Richard T., and Scott M. Fitzpatrick
2008 Examining Prehistoric Migration Patterns in the Palauan Archipelago: A Computer Simulated Analysis of Drift Voyaging. Asian Perspectives 47(1):28–44.
Camacho, Keith L.
2005 Cultures of Commemoration: The Politics of War, Memory, and History in the Mariana Islands. Ph.D. dissertation, Department of History, University of Hawai'i.
2011 Cultures of Commemoration: The Politics of War, Memory, and History in the Mariana Islands. Honolulu: University of Hawai'i Press.
Cameron, Craig M.
1994 American Samurai: Myth, Imagination, and the Conduct of Battle in the First Marine Division, 1941–51. Cambridge: Cambridge University Press.
Camp, Dick
2008 Last Man Standing: The 1st Marine Regiment on Peleliu, September 15–21, 1944. Minneapolis, MN: Zenith Press.
CinCPac-CinCPOA
1946 Report of Surrender and Occupation of Japan: Washington, D.C., Chief of Naval Operations. (Commander in Chief Pacific Fleet and Pacific Ocean Areas). http://www.dtic.mil/dtic/tr/fulltext/u2/a438971.pdf, accessed March 21, 2015.
Clark, Geoffrey
2004 Radiocarbon Dates from the Ulong site in Palau and Implications for Western Micronesian Prehistory. Archaeology in Oceania 39(1):26–34.
Collingham, Lizzie
2012 The Taste of War: World War Two and the Battle for Food. London: Penguin Books.

Connerton, Paul

1989 How Societies Remember. Cambridge: Cambridge University Press.

Cook, Haruko Taya, and Theodore Failor Cook

1992 Japan at War: An Oral History. New York: New Press, distributed by Norton.

Cortés, A. L.

2013 Land in Trust: The Invasion of Palau's Land Tenure Customs by American Law. Asian Pacific Law and Policy Journal 14(3):167–240. http://blog.hawaii.edu/aplpj/files/2013/05/APLPJ_14-3_Cortes_FINAL.pdf, accessed April 17, 2015.

D'Arcy, Paul

2001 Connected by the Sea: Towards a Regional History of the Western Caroline Islands. Journal of Pacific History 36(2):163–82.

Denfeld, D. Colt

1984 Korean Laborers in Micronesia during World War II. Korea Observer 15(1):3–14.

1988 Peleliu Revisited: An Historical and Archaeological Survey of World War II Sites on Peleliu Island. Micronesian Archaeological Survey Report # 24. Saipan: Micronesian Archaeological Survey.

Dening, Greg

1980 Islands and Beaches. Discourse on a Silent Land: Marquesas 1774–1880. Honolulu: University of Hawai'i Press.

1992 Mr. Bligh's Bad Language: Passion, Power, and Theater on the Bounty. Cambridge: Cambridge University Press.

Dower, John W.

1986 War without Mercy: Race and Power in the Pacific War. New York: Pantheon Books.

1993 Race, Language, and War in Two Cultures. *In* Japan in War and Peace: Selected Essays. Pp. 257–85. New York: New Press.

1996a The Bombed: Hiroshimas and Nagasakis in Japanese Memory. *In* Hiroshima in History and Memory. M. J. Hogan, ed. Pp. 116–42. Cambridge: Cambridge University Press.

1996b Three Narratives of Our Humanity. *In* History Wars: The Enola Gay and Other Battles for the American Past. E. T. Linenthal and T. Engelhardt, eds. Pp. 63–96. New York: Metropolitan Books, Henry Holt.

1999 Embracing Defeat: Japan in the Wake of World War II. New York: W. W. Norton/New Press.

2002 "An Aptitude for Being Unloved": War and Memory in Japan. *In* Crimes of War: Guilt and Denial in the Twentieth Century. O. Bartov, A. Grossmann, and M. Nolan, eds. Pp. 217–41. New York: New Press, distributed by W. W. Norton.

2012a Japan's Beautiful Modern War. *In* Ways of Forgetting, Ways of Remembering: Japan in the Modern World. Pp. 65–104. New York: New Press.

2012b Ways of Forgetting, Ways of Remembering: Japan in the Modern World. New York: New Press.

Drea, Edward J.

2009 Japan's Imperial Army: Its Rise and Fall, 1853–1945. Lawrence: University Press of Kansas.

Dunne, John Gregory
2001 The Hardest War. New York Review of Books, December 20: 50–53, 56.
Duus, Peter
1996 Introduction. Japan's Wartime Empire: Problems and Issues. *In* The Japanese Wartime Empire, 1931–1945. P. Duus, R. H. Myers, and M. R. Peattie, eds. Pp xi–xlvii. Princeton, NJ: Princeton University Press.
Duus, Peter, Ramon H. Myers, and Mark R. Peattie, eds.
1996 The Japanese Wartime Empire, 1931–1945. Princeton, NJ: Princeton University Press.
Falgout, Suzanne, Lin Poyer, and Laurence M. Carucci
1995 "The Greatest Hardship": Micronesian Memories of World War II. Isla: A Journal of Micronesian Studies 3(2):203–22. http://www.uog.edu/schools-and-colleges/college-of-liberal-arts-and-social-sciences/publications/isla-journal-of, accessed May 23, 2015. Click on issue and volume number; search for the title of the article.
2008 Memories of War: Micronesians in the Pacific War. Honolulu: University of Hawai'i Press.
Falk, Stanley L.
1974 Bloodiest Victory: Palaus. New York: Ballantine.
Faulkner, Douglas
1974 This Living Reef. New York: Quadrangle/New York Times Books.
Ferguson, Niall
2005 V-E Day—a Soiled Victory. *In* Los Angeles Times, May 8: .M5.
Fitzgerald, F. Scott
1995 The Great Gatsby. New York: Simon Schuster, Scribner Paperback Fiction.
Fitzpatrick, Scott. M.
2003 Early Human Burials in the Western Pacific: Evidence for a c. 3000 Year-old Occupation on Palau. Antiquity 77(298):719–31.
Foer, Joshua
2011 Moonwalking with Enstein: The Art and Science of Remembering Everything. Eastbourne, East Sussex, UK: Gardners Books.
Fosberg, F. Raymond
1963 The Island Ecosystem. *In* Man's Place in the Island Ecosystem: A Symposium. F. R. Fosberg, ed. Pp. 1–7. Honolulu: Bishop Museum Press.
Fox, Fred K.
1997 My Ten Foot Circle of Space. Old Breed News 47(4):18–20, 22–25, 30–32.
Frank, Richard B.
1992 Guadalcanal: The Definitive Account of a Landmark Battle. New York: Penguin.
1999 Downfall: The End of the Imperial Japanese Empire. New York: Penguin Books.
Franklin, Carl, and Timothy Van Patten
2010 The Pacific. New York: HBO.
FreeHart Productions
1999 Tears of Peleliu (video documentary). New York: Cinema Guild.

Funasaka, Hiroshi

1966 Eirei no Zekkyō: gyokusaitō Angauru [Scream of the Eirei: Angaur, an island of crushed jewels; Transl. to English as "Falling Blossoms"]. Tokyo: Bungeishunjyu.

1967 Sakura Sakura: Periryū tō dōkutsu sen [The Battle for the Caves of Peleliu Island]. Tokyo: Mainichi News Press.

1968 Gyokusai: Angō denbun de tsuzuru Parao no shitō [Crushed Jewels: Deadly Battle for Palau Written in Coded Radio Transmissions]. Tokyo: Yomiuri News Press.

1986 Falling Blossoms. H. Funasaka and J. D. Rubin, transl. Singapore: Times Books International.

Fussell, Paul

1975 The Great War and Modern Memory. New York: Oxford University Press.

1989 Wartime: Understanding and Behavior in the Second World War. New York: Oxford University Press.

Gailey, Harry A.

1983 Peleliu, 1944. Annapolis, MD: Nautical and Aviation.

Gale, Roger W.

1979 The Americanization of Micronesia. Washington, D.C.: University Press of America.

Gallicchio, Marc

2007 Introduction. *In* The Unpredictability of the Past: Memories of the Asia-Pacific War in U.S.-East Asian Relations. M. Gallicchio, ed. Pp. 1–12. Durham, NC: Duke University Press.

Garand, George W., and Truman R. Strobridge

1971 History of U.S. Marine Corps Operations in World War II, vol. 4: Western Pacific Operations. Washington, D.C.: Historical Division, Headquarters, U.S. Marine Corps, and U.S. Government Printing Office.

Garran, Daniella Defilippo

2010 Beyond Plymouth Rock. Tufts Magazine, Winter 2010: 10–11.

Gayle, Gordon D.

1996 Bloody Beaches: The Marines at Peleliu. Washington, D.C.: History and Museums Division Headquarters, U.S. Marine Corps, and U.S. Government Printing Office.

Gorenflo, L. J.

1996 Demographic Change in the Republic of Palau. Pacific Studies 19(3):37–106.

Grayling, A. C.

2006 Among the Dead Cities: The History and Moral Legacy of the WWII Bombing of Civilians in Germany and Japan. New York: Walker.

Grimmett, Richard, Carol Inskipp, and Tim Inskipp

2000 Birds of Nepal. New Delhi: Prakash Books.

Hallas, James H.

1994 The Devil's Anvil: The Assault on Peleliu. Westport, CT: Praeger.

Hanlon, David L.

2003 Beyond "the English Method of Tattoing": Decentering the Practice of History in Oceania. The Contemporary Pacific 15(1):19–40.

Hasegawa, Tsuyoshi, and Kazuhiko Toga, eds.
2008 East Asia's Haunted Present: Historical Memories and the Resurgence of Nationalism. Westport, CT: Praeger.
Hastings, Max
2007 Retribution: The Battle for Japan, 1944–45. New York: Alfred A. Knopf.
Hau'ofa, Epeli
1993 Our Sea of Islands. *In* A New Oceania: Rediscovering Our Sea of Islands. E. Waddell, V. Naidu, and E. Hau'ofa, eds. Pp. 2–16. Suva, Fiji: University of the South Pacific.
2000 Epilogue: Pasts to Remember. *In* Remembrance of Pacific Pasts: An Invitation to Remake History. R. Borofsky, ed. Pp. 453–71. Honolulu: University of Hawai'i Press.
Hein, Laura Elizabeth, and Mark Selden, eds.
2000 Censoring History: Citizenship and Memory in Japan, Germany, and the United States. Armonk, NY: M. E. Sharpe.
Heinrichs, Waldo
2007 The Enola Gay and Contested Public Memory. *In* The Unpredictability of the Past: Memories of the Asia-Pacific War in U.S.-East Asian Relations. M. Gallicchio, ed. Pp. 201–33. Durham, NC: Duke University Press.
Henshall, Kenneth G.
2001 A History of Japan: From Stone Age to Superpower. New York: St. Martin's Press.
Hezel, Francis X. S. J.
1983 The First Taint of Civilization: A History of the Caroline and Marshall Islands in Pre-Colonial Days, 1521–1885. Honolulu: University of Hawai'i Press.
1995 Strangers in Their Own Land: A Century of Colonial Rule in the Caroline and Marshall Islands. Honolulu: University of Hawai'i Press.
Higuchi, Wakako
1986 Micronesians and the Pacific War: The Palauans. An Oral Historiography of the Japanese Administration. Guam: University of Guam, Micronesian Area Research Center.
1987 Micronesia under Japanese Administration: Interviews with Former South Sea Bureau and Military Officials. Mangilao, Guam: University of Guam, Micronesian Area Research Center. Sponsor: L. J. Skaggs and Mary C. Skaggs Foundation.
1991 War in Palau: Morikawa and the Palauans. *In* Remembering the Pacific War. G. M. White, ed. Pp. 145–56. Honolulu: University of Hawai'i, Center for Pacific Islands Studies, Occasional Paper 36. http://www.hawaii.edu/cpis/publications_6.html, accessed March 17, 2015.
1995 Japan and War Reparations in Micronesia. Journal of Pacific History 30(1):87–98.
2006 A U.S. Territory of Japan's South Seas Islands: Japanese Navy Administration of Guam. Ph.D. dissertation, Pacific and Asian Studies Department, Australian National University.
2012 The Japanese Administration of Guam, 1941–1944: A Study of Occupation and Integration Policies, with Japanese Oral Histories. Jefferson, NC: McFarland.
Hijikata, Hisakatso
1973 Stone Images of Palau. Guam: Micronesian Area Research Center (MARC).

Hongo, Jun

2013 Tojo's granddaughter, Yuko, dies at 73. Japan Times, February 16. http://www.japantimes.co.jp/news/2013/02/16/national/tojos-granddaughter-yuko-dies-at-73/#.VV5lWEZ5_iB, accessed May 21, 2015.

Hoshi, Ryoichi

2008 Angauru Periryū: senki gyokusai o ikinobite [Angaur, Peleliu: A record of the war survived through Gyokusai]. Tokyo: Kawade Shobo Shinsha.

Hough, Frank O.

1990 [1950] The Assault on Peleliu. Nashville, TN: Battery Press.

Hunt, George P.

1946 Coral Comes High. New York: Harper and Brothers. Reprinted 1957 by Signet Books.

Hutton, Patrick H.

1993 History as an Art of Memory. Hanover, NH: University Press of New England.

Hylton, Wil S.

2013 Vanished: The 60-Year Search for the Missing Men of World War II. New York: Riverhead Books.

Ienaga, Saburō

1978 The Pacific War: World War II and the Japanese, 1931–1945. New York: Pantheon Books.

Iitaka, Shingo

2011 Conflicting Discourses on Colonial Assimilation: A Palauan Cultural Tour in Japan, 1915. Pacific Asia Inquiry 2(1):85–102. http://www.uog.edu/schools-and-colleges/college-of-liberal-arts-and-social-sciences/publications/pacific-asia-inquiry-4, accessed May 26, 2015. Search for title of article.

Isely, Jeter A., and Philip A. Crowl

1951 The U.S. Marines and Amphibious War: Its Theory, and Its Practice in the Pacific. Princeton, NJ: Princeton University Press.

Japan International Cooperation Agency

2000 The Study for Promotion of Economic Development in the Republic of Palau. Typescript in library of Palau Community College.

Japan News, by Yomiuri Shimbun

2015 70 years after WWII / Emperor, Empress honor Peleliu dead. April 9. http://the-japan-news.com/news/article/0002069464, accessed April 12, 2015.

Johannes, Robert E.

1981 Words of the Lagoon: Fishing and Marine Lore in the Palau District of Micronesia. Berkeley: University of California Press, 1992.

Kaplan, David E.

2003 Yakuza: Japan's Criminal Underworld. Expanded edition. Berkeley: University of California Press.

Keegan, John

1989 The Price of Admiralty: The Evolution of Naval Warfare. New York: Viking.

1990 The Second World War. New York: Penguin Books.

Kennedy, David M.

1999 Freedom from Fear: The American People in Depression and War, 1929–1945. New York: Oxford University Press.

Kennedy, Paul

2013 Engineers of Victory: The Problem Solvers Who Turned the Tide in the Second World War. New York: Random House.

Kenwood Productions, Inc.

1991 Peleliu 1944: Horror in the Pacific (video documentary). St. Paul, MN.

Kirch, Patrick V.

1997 Introduction: The Environmental History of Oceanic Islands. *In* Historical Ecology in the Pacific Islands: Prehistoric Environmental and Landscape Change. P. V. Kirch and T. L. Hunt, eds. Pp. 1–21. New Haven, CT: Yale University Press.

2000 On the Road of the Winds: An Archaeological History of the Pacific Islands before European Conquest. Berkeley: University of California Press.

Kiste, Robert C.

1994 Towards Decolonisation: United States. *In* Tides Of History: The Pacific Islands in the Twentieth Century. K. R. Howe, R. C. Kiste, and B. V. Lal, eds. Pp. 227–57. Honolulu: University of Hawai'i Press.

Klee, Gary A.

1976 Traditional Time Reckoning and Resource Utilization. Micronesica 12(2):211–46.

Knecht, Rick, Neil Price, and Gavin Lindsay

2012 WW II Survey of Peleliu Island, Peleliu State, Republic of Palau, Final Report. Washington, D.C.: U.S. National Park Service, American Battlefield Protection Program. www.peleliuhistorical.org/Peleliu_REPORT.pdf, accessed Feb 7, 2015.

Krämer, Augustin

1917–29 Palau, II.B.3 (5 vols.). *In* Ergebnisse der Sudsee-Expedition, 1908–1910. G. Thilenius, ed. Hamburg: L. Friederichsen.

Lane, Anthony

2013 *Review of* Our Children. New Yorker (August 12 and 19): 92–93.

Leckie, Robert

2001 [1957] Helmet for My Pillow. New York: ibooks.

1962 Strong Men Armed: The United States Marines against Japan. New York: Ballantine Books.

Lee, Chae-jin, and Grant K Goodman

1981 Japanese Policies and Perspectives in Micronesia and Papua New Guinea. *In* The United States and Japan in the Western Pacific: Micronesia and Papua New Guinea. G. K. Goodman and F. Moos, eds. Pp. 243–89. Boulder, CO: Westview Press.

Leibowitz, Arnold H.

1996 Embattled Island: Palau's Struggle for Independence. Westport, CT: Praeger.

Levinson, Sanford

1998 Written in Stone: Public Monuments in Changing Societies. Durham, NC: Duke University Press.

Linenthal, Edward T.
1993 Sacred Ground: Americans and Their Battlefields. Urbana: University of Illinois Press.
Linenthal, Edward T., and Tom Engelhardt, eds.
1996 History Wars: The Enola Gay and Other Battles for the American Past. New York: Metropolitan Books/Henry Holt.
Linnekin, Jocelyn
1997 Contending Approaches. *In* The Cambridge History of the Pacific Islanders. D. Denoon, S. Firth, J. Linnekin, M. Meleisea, and K. Nero, eds. Pp. 3–36. Cambridge: Cambridge University Press.
Liston, Jolie, and H. David Tuggle
2006 Prehistoric Warfare in Palau. *In* The Archaeology of Warfare: Prehistories of Raiding and Conquest. E. N. Arkush and M. W. Allen, eds. Pp. 148–83. Gainesville: University Press of Florida.
Lowenthal, David
1985 The Past Is a Foreign Country. Cambridge: Cambridge University Press.
Ma, Xiaohua
2007 Constructing a National Memory of War: War Museums in China, Japan, and the United States. *In* The Unpredictability of the Past: Memories of the Asia-Pacific War in U.S.–East Asian Relations. M. Gallicchio, ed. Pp. 155–200. Durham, NC: Duke University Press.
Manchester, William
1979 Goodbye Darkness: A Memoir of the Pacific War. New York: Dell Publishing, 1982.
Mawdsley, Evan
2007 Thunder in the East: The Nazi-Soviet War, 1941–1945. London: Hodder Arnold.
McCutcheon, Mary S.
1981 Resource Exploitation and the Tenure of Land and Sea in Palau. Ph.D. dissertation, Department of Anthropology, University of Arizona.
1985 Reading the Taro Cards: Explaining Agricultural Change in Palau. *In* Food Energy in Tropical Ecosystems. D. Cattle and C. Schwerin, eds. Pp.167–88. New York: Gordon and Breach.
McDougall, Walter A.
1993 Let the Sea Make a Noise: Four Hundred Years of Cataclysm, Conquest, War and Folly in the North Pacific. New York: Avon Books.
McHenry, Donald
1975 Micronesia: Trust Betrayed. New York: Carnegie Endowment for International Peace.
McKnight, Robert K.
1960 Competition in Palau. Ph.D. dissertation, Department of Anthropology, Ohio State University.
McMillan, George
1949 The Old Breed: A History of the First Marine Division in World War II. Washington, D.C.: Infantry Journal Press.

Miller, Edward S.

1991 War Plan Orange: The U.S. Strategy to Defeat Japan. Annapolis: Naval Institute Press.

Miller, Nathan

1995 War at Sea: A Naval History of World War II. New York: Scribner.

Mita, Maki

2009 Palauan Children under Japanese Rule: Their Oral Histories. Osaka, Japan: National Museum of Ethnology.

Montaigne, Michel de

1958 On the Education of Children. *In* Essays: Pp.49–85. New York: Penguin Books.

Moran, Jim, and Gordon L. Rottman

2002 Peleliu 1944: The Forgotten Corner of Hell. Wellingborough, Northants, UK: Osprey Publishing.

Morison, Samuel Eliot

1948 History of United States Naval Operations in World War II, vol. 3: The Rising Sun in the Pacific. Boston: Little, Brown.

1966 [1958] History of United States Naval Operations in World War II, vol. 12: Leyte, June 1944–January 1945. Boston: Little, Brown.

2001 [1951] History of United States Naval Operations in World War II, vol. 7: Aleutians, Gilberts, and Marshalls June 1942–April 1944. Edison, NJ: Castle Books.

2001 [1953] History of United States Naval Operations in World War II, vol. 8: New Guinea and the Marianas March 1944–August 1944. Edison, NJ: Castle Books.

2001 [1960] History of United States Naval Operations in World War II, vol. 14: Victory in the Pacific, 1945. Edison, NJ: Castle Books.

Mueller-Dombois, Dieter, and Raymond Fosberg

1998 Vegetation of the Tropical Pacific Islands. New York: Springer.

Murray, Fermina Brel

1996 *Review of* Lynn B. Wilson, Speaking to Power: Gender and Politics in the Western Pacific. Isla: A Journal of Micronesian Studies 4(1):211–18. http://www.uog.edu/schools-and-colleges/college-of-liberal-arts-and-social-sciences/publications/isla-journal-of, accessed May 23, 2015. Click on issue and volume number; search for the title of the article.

Murray, Stephen C.

1971 The Americanization of Micronesia: Paradise Lost. Ramparts 9(7):35–37, 45–47.

1975 The Marianas: New Outpost of Empire. The Nation 220(15): 459–61.

2005 Catastrophe on Peleliu: Islanders' Memories of the Pacific War. International Institute for Asian Studies Newsletter, Autumn, Special Issue, The Asia-Pacific War: History and Memory (38):17. http://www.iias.nl/nl/38/IIAS_NL38_17.pdf, accessed December 18, 2014.

2006 War and Remembrance on Peleliu: Islander, Japanese, and American Memories of a Battle in the Pacific War. Ph.D. dissertation, Department of Anthropology, University of California at Santa Barbara. ProQuest catalog #3245927.

2013 The Palauan *Kirikomi-tai* Suicide Bombers of World War II and the Siege of Babeldaob: A Reconsideration. Pacific Asia Inquiry 4(1):30–57. http://www.uog.edu/schools-and-colleges/college-of-liberal-arts-and-social-sciences/publications/pacific-asia-inquiry-4, accessed May 26, 2015. Search for title of article.

Myers, Ramon H., and Mark R. Peattie, eds.

1984 The Japanese Colonial Empire, 1895–1945. Princeton, NJ: Princeton University Press.

National Broadcasting Co.

1995 Hell in the Pacific: Remembering Peleliu. NBC Dateline, August 4. New York: National Broadcasting Co.

National Park Service, U.S. Dept. of the Interior

2003 Special Resource Study: Peleliu Battlefield National Historic Landmark, Peleliu State, Republic of Palau. Honolulu: NPS Pacific Islands Support Office.

Nero, Karen L.

1987 A Cherechar a Lokelii: Beads of History of Koror Palau, 1783–1983. Ph.D. dissertation, Department of Anthropology, University of California at Berkeley.

1989 Time of Famine, Time of Transformation: Hell in the Pacific, Palau. *In* The Pacific Theater: Island Representations of World War II. G. M. White and L. Lindstrom, eds. Pp. 117–48. Honolulu: University of Hawai'i Press.

2005 Structuring a Peaceful Society: Reflections on Palau. *In* Securing a Peaceful Pacific. J. Henderson and G. Watson, eds. Pp. 298–309. Christchurch, NZ: Canterbury University Press.

Nero, Karen L., and Nicholas Thomas, eds.

2002 An Account of the Pelew Islands by George Keate. London: Leicester University Press.

Oda, Makoto

2003 Gyokusai [The Breaking Jewel]. D. Keene, transl. New York: Columbia University Press.

Orr, James Joseph

2001 The Victim as Hero: Ideologies of Peace and National Identity in Postwar Japan. Honolulu: University of Hawai'i Press.

Orwell, George

2005 [1940] The Lion and the Unicorn: Socialism and the English Genius. *In* Why I Write. Pp.11–94. New York: Penguin Books.

Overy, Richard

1996 Why the Allies Won. New York: W. W. Norton.

Palau Community Action Agency

1976 A History of Palau, vol. 1: Traditional Palau, the First Europeans. Koror, Palau: Palau Community Action Agency.

1977 A History of Palau, vol. 2: Traders and Whalers, Spanish Administration, German Administration. Koror, Palau: Palau Community Action Agency.

1978 A History of Palau, vol. 3: Japanese Administration, U.S. Naval Military Government. Koror, Palau: Palau Community Action Agency.

Palau Society of Historians

1997 Rechuodel: Traditional Culture and Lifeways Long Ago in Palau. D. R. Smith, transl. San Francisco: U.S. National Park Service.

Palau Visitors Authority

2013 Visitor Arrival Statistics. www.visit-palau.com/publication, accessed February 10, 2015.

Parmentier, Richard J.

1987 The Sacred Remains: Myth, History and Polity in Palau. Chicago: University of Chicago Press.

Paulay, Gustav

1994 Biodiversity on Oceanic Islands: Its Origin and Extinction. American Zoologist 34:134–44.

Peattie, Mark R.

1984a Introduction. *In* The Japanese Colonial Empire, 1895–1945. R. H. Myers and M. R. Peattie, eds. Pp. 3–58. Princeton, NJ: Princeton University Press.

1984b The Nan'yō: Japan in the South Pacific, 1885–1945. *In* The Japanese Colonial Empire, 1895–1945. R. H. Myers and M. R. Peattie, eds. Pp. 172–210. Princeton, NJ: Princeton University Press.

1988a The Japanese Colonial Empire, 1895–1945. *In* The Cambridge History of Japan, vol. 6: The Twentieth Century. P. Duus, ed. Pp. 217–70. Cambridge: Cambridge University Press.

1988b Nan'yō: The Rise and Fall of the Japanese in Micronesia, 1885–1945. Honolulu: University of Hawai'i Press.

1996 Nanshin: The "Southward Advance," 1931–1941, as a Prelude to the Japanese Occupation of Southeast Asia. *In* The Japanese Wartime Empire, 1931–1945. P. Duus, R. H. Myers, and M. R. Peattie, eds. Pp. 189–242. Princeton, NJ: Princeton University Press.

1998 Japanese Strategy and Campaigns of the Pacific War, 1941–1945. *In* World War II in Asia and the Pacific and the War's Aftermath, with General Themes: A Handbook of Literature and Research. L. E. Lee, ed. Pp. 56–71. Westport, CT: Greenwood Press.

Peattie, Mark R., and David C. Evans

1994 Japan. *In* Ubi Sumus? The State of Maritime and Naval History. J. B. Hattendorf, ed. Pp. 213–21. Newport, RI: Naval War College.

Perry, Mark

2007 Partners in Command: George Marshall and Dwight Eisenhower in War and Peace. New York: Penguin Press.

Petersen, Glenn

2009 Traditional Micronesian Societies: Adaptation, Integration, and Political Organization in the Central Pacific. Honolulu: University of Hawai'i Press.

Piehler, G. Kurt

1995 Remembering War the American Way. Washington, D.C.: Smithsonian Institution Press.

Poyer, Lin

1992 Defining History across Cultures: Islander and Outsider Contrasts. Isla: A Journal of Micronesian Studies 1(1):73–89. http://www.uog.edu/schools-and-colleges/college-of-liberal-arts-and-social-sciences/publications/isla-journal-of, accessed May 23, 2015. Click on issue and volume number; search for the title of the article.

1995 Yapese Experiences of the Pacific War. Isla: A Journal of Micronesian Studies 3(2): 223–56. http://www.uog.edu/schools-and-colleges/college-of-liberal-arts-and-social-sciences/publications/isla-journal-of, accessed May 23, 2015. Click on issue and volume number; search for the title of the article.

Poyer, Lin, Suzanne Falgout, and Laurence M. Carucci

2001 The Typhoon of War: Micronesian Experiences of the Pacific War. Honolulu: University of Hawai'i Press.

2004 The Impact of the Pacific War on Modern Micronesian Identity. *In* Globalization and Culture Change in the Pacific Islands. V. S. Lockwood, ed. Pp. 307–23. Upper Saddle River, NJ: Pearson Prentice Hall.

Pregill, Gregory K., and David W. Steadman

2000 Fossil Vertebrates from Palau, Micronesia: A Resource Assessment. Micronesica 33(1/2):137–52.

Price, Neil, and Rick Knecht

2012 Peleliu 1944: The Archaeology of a South Pacific D-Day. Journal of Conflict Archaeology 7(1):5–48. http://www.maneyonline.com/doi/full/10.1179/157407812X13245464933786, accessed February 14, 2015.

Price, Neil, Rick Knecht, and Gavin Lindsay

2015 The Sacred and the Profane: Souvenir and Collecting Behaviours on the WWII Battlefields of Peleliu Island, Palau, Micronesia. In Heritage and Memory of War: Responses from Small Islands. G. Carr and K. Reeves, eds. 219–33. New York and Abingdon, Oxon, UK: Routledge.

Price, Neil, Rick Knecht, Steve Ballinger, Steve Cypra, Calvin Emesiochel, Tangie Hesus, Errolflynn Kloulechad, Gavin Lindsay, David McQuillen, Sunny Ochob Ngirmang

2013 After the Typhoon: Multicultural Archaeologies of World War II on Peleliu, Palau, Micronesia. Journal of Conflict Archaeology 8(3):193–248. http://www.maneyonline.com/doi/abs/10.1179/1574077313Z.00000000026, accessed November 2, 2015.

Price, Willard

1944 Japan's Islands of Mystery. New York: John Day.

Pye, Lucian W.

1996 Memory, Imagination, and National Myths. *In* Remembering and Forgetting : The Legacy of War and Peace in East Asia. Significant issues series, vol. 18, no. 3. G. W. Gong, ed. Pp. xx, 123. Washington, D.C.: Center for Strategic International Studies.

Quammen, David

1996 The Song of the Dodo: Island Biogeography in an Age of Extinctions. New York: Scribner.

Rainbird, Paul

2004 The Archaeology of Micronesia. Cambridge: Cambridge University Press.

Rechebei, Elizabeth D., and Samuel F. McPhetres

1997 History of Palau: Heritage of an Emerging Nation. Koror, Palau: Ministry of Education.

Republic of Palau

2001 Republic of Palau 2000 Statistical Yearbook. Koror, Palau: Division of Planning and Statistics.

Republic of Palau, Office of Planning and Statistics

2000 2000 Census of Population and Housing of the Republic of Palau. Koror, Palau: Office of Planning and Statistics.

2005 2005 Census of Population and Housing of the Republic of Palau, vol. 1: Basic Tables. Koror, Palau: Office of Planning and Statistics. www.pacificweb.org/DOCS/rop/Palau%202005%20Census.pdf, accessed December 12, 2014.)

Richard, Dorothy E.

1957a United States Naval Administration of the Trust Territory of the Pacific Islands, vol. 1: The Wartime Military Government Period 1942–1945. Washington, D.C.: Office of the Chief of Naval Operations.

1957b United States Naval Administration of the Trust Territory of the Pacific Islands, vol. 2: The Postwar Military Government Era 1945–1947. Washington, D.C.: Office of the Chief of Naval Operations.

1957c United States Naval Administration of the Trust Territory of the Pacific Islands, vol. 3: The Trusteeship Period, 1947–1951. Washington, D.C.: Office of Chief of Naval Operations.

Robinson, David

1983 The Decorative Motifs of Palauan Clubhouses. *In* Art and Artists of Oceania. S. M. Mead and B. Kernot, eds. Pp. 162–78. Palmerston North, NZ: Dunmore Press.

Rodda, Gordon H., Thomas H. Fritts, and David Chiszar

1997 The Disappearance of Guam's Wildlife. BioScience 47(9):565–74.

Roff, Sue R.

1991 Overreaching in Paradise: United States Policy in Palau since 1945. Juneau, AK: Denali Press.

Ross, Bill D.

1991 Peleliu, Tragic Triumph: The Untold Story of the Pacific War's Forgotten Battle. New York: Random House.

Rottman, Gordon L.

2002 World War II Pacific Island Guide: A Geo-Military Study. Westport, CT: Greenwood Press.

Ryan, Chris, ed.

2007 Battlefield Tourism: History, Place and Interpretation. New York: Elsevier.

Saipan Tribune

2005 Imperial Saipan Visit Includes Korean Memorial. June 29. Saipan, CNMI.

Sawachi, Hisae

1990 Berau no sei to shi [Life and Death in Palau]. Tokyo: Kodansha.

Schrijvers, Peter

2002 The GI War against Japan: American Soldiers in Asia and the Pacific during World War II. New York: New York University Press.

Schwarz, Benjamin

2007 Stalin's Gift. *In* Atlantic, May: 103–6.

Seaton, Philip A.
2007 Japan's Contested War Memories: The 'Memory Rifts' in Historical Consciousness of World War II. London: Routledge.
Semper, Karl
1982 [1873] The Palau Islands in the Pacific Ocean. M. L. Berg, transl. Guam: University of Guam, Micronesian Area Research Center.
Senshi Sōsho [Japanese Government War History Series]
1968 See Bōeichō Bōei Kenshūjō Senshishitsu (BBKS), vol. 13. Chūbu Taiheiyō rikugun sakusen, part 2: Periryū, Angaru, Iōtō [Army operations in the Central Pacific, part 2: Peleliu, Angaur, and Iwo Jima]. Tokyo: Asagumo Shimbun Sha.
Seraphim, Franziska
2001 Negotiating the Post-War: Politics and Memory in Japan, 1945–1995. Ph.D. dissertation, Graduate School of Arts and Sciences, Columbia University.
2006 War Memory and Social Politics in Japan, 1945–2005. Cambridge, MA: Harvard University Asia Center.
2007 Relocating War Memory at Century's End: Postwar Responsibility and Global Public Culture. *In* Ruptured Histories: War, Memory, and the Post-Cold War in Asia. S. M. Jager and R. Mitter, eds. Pp. 15–46. Cambridge, MA: Harvard University Press.
Shaw, Henry I., Bernard C. Nalty, and Edwin T. Turnbladh
1994 [1966] History of U.S. Marine Corps Operations in World War II, vol. 3: Central Pacific Drive. Nashville, TN: Battery Press.
Shuster, Donald R.
1979 Schooling in Micronesia during Japanese Mandate Rule. Educational Perspectives 18(2):20–26.
1982 State Shinto in Micronesia during Japanese Rule, 1914–1945. Pacific Studies 5(2) (Spring):20–43.
2009 The Republic of Palau. Contemporary Pacific 21(1):136–43.
2012 The Republic of Palau. Contemporary Pacific 24(1):163.
Sledge, E. B.
1990 [1981] With the Old Breed at Peleliu and Okinawa. New York: Oxford University Press.
Sloan, Bill
2005 Brotherhood of Heroes: The Marines at Peleliu, 1944—the Bloodiest Battle of the Pacific War. New York: Simon and Schuster.
Smith, DeVerne Reed
1983 Palauan Social Structure. New Brunswick, NJ: Rutgers University Press.
1991 *Review of* Richard J. Parmentier, The Sacred Remains: Myth, History, and Polity in Belau. Pacific Studies 14(3):154–69.
Smith, Kerry
2002 The Shōwa Hall: Memorializing Japan's War at Home. Special Issue "Beyond National History: World War II Recollected," Public Historian 24(4):35–64.
Smith, Robert Ross
1984 [1953] The Approach to the Philippines. Washington, D.C.: Center of Military History, United States Army.

Spector, Ronald H.
1985 Eagle against the Sun: The American War with Japan. New York: Free Press.
Spence, Jonathan
1984 The Memory Palace of Matteo Ricci. New York: Viking Penguin.
Stewart, Pamela J., and Andrew Strathern, eds.
2003 Landscape, Memory and History: Anthropological Perspectives. London: Pluto Press.
Straus, Ulrich
2003 The Anguish of Surrender: Japanese POWs in World War II. Seattle: University of Washington Press.
Szymkowiak, Kenneth, and Patricia G. Steinhoff
1995 Wrapping Up in Something Long: Intimidation and Violence by Right-Wing Groups in Postwar Japan. Terrorism and Political Violence 7(1):265–98.
Taaffe, Stephen R.
1998 MacArthur's Jungle War: The 1944 New Guinea Campaign. Lawrence: University Press of Kansas.
Tanaka, Yuki
1996 Hidden Horrors: Japanese War Crimes in World War II. Boulder, CO: Westview Press.
Tellei, Ubal
1991 Palauans and the Japanese Military Experience. *In* Remembering the Pacific War. G. M. White, ed. Pp. 157–60. Occasional Paper 36. Honolulu: University of Hawai'i, Center for Pacific Islands Studies.
Telmetang, Marciana, and Faustina K. Rehuher
1993 Bai. Koror, Palau: Belau National Museum, 2000.
Temengil, JeRome
1995 A Collection of Palauan Legends, vols. 1 & 2. Koror, Palau: Island 21st Century Publications.
Tia Belau Newspaper (Koror, Palau)
2002 8th Independence Day Feted. October 5–11.
2003 Appeals Court Rules on Peleliu Land Dispute. March 14–21.
2004 Battle of Peleliu Remembered. September 17–24.
2005 Japan Approves $5.25M Grant. December 23–30.
2015 Peleliu WWII Cave Re-Opened After 70 Yrs. March 26.
Tomiyama, Ichiro
2002 The "Japanese" of Micronesia: Okinawans in the Nan'yō Islands. *In* Okinawan Diaspora. R. Y. Nakasone, ed. Pp.57–70. Honolulu: University of Hawai'i Press.
Turner, James West, and Suzanne Falgout
2002 Time Traces: Cultural Memory and World War II in Pohnpei. Contemporary Pacific 14(1):101–31.
Ugaki, Matome
1991 Fading Victory: The Diary of Admiral Matome Ugaki, 1941–1945. M. Chihaya, transl. Pittsburgh: University of Pittsburgh Press Reprint in English from Japanese edition, 1953.

U.S. Army

1956 Military Geology of Palau Islands, Caroline Islands. Washington, D.C. Copy in Micro-Pacific Collection, oversize cart, Palau Community College Library.

U.S. Congress

1986 Public Law 99–658, 99th Congress. Compact of Free Association, Approval. Congressional Record, vol. 132.

U.S. Department of Agriculture

2001 Peleliu and Angaur Soil Assessment: Natural Resources Conservation Service.

Useem, John

1946 Report on Yap and Palau. Economic Survey, October. Honolulu: U.S. Commercial.

Vandegrift, A. A.

1966 [1964] Once a Marine: The Memoirs of General A. A. Vandegrift, Commandant of the U.S. Marines in WW II. New York: Ballantine Books.

van der Vat, Dan

1991 The Pacific Campaign: World War II. The U.S.-Japanese Naval War, 1941–1945. New York: Simon and Schuster.

Vincent, James M., ed.

1973 Micronesia's Yesterday: Illustrations for an Understanding of Micronesia's History. Saipan, Mariana Islands: Trust Territory Press.

Wahl, Cecilia Hendricks

2000 Number One Pacific Island. Bloomington, IN: Woodcrest Publishing.

Walter, Karen R.

1993 Through the Looking Glass: Palauan Experiences of War and Reconstruction, 1944–1951. Ph.D. dissertation, Department of History, University of Adelaide.

Ward, Graeme, and Michael Pickering

1985 The Japanese Bone Collecting Expedition on Tinian, March 1985: Its Impact upon Historic Resources. A Report to the Historic Preservation Co-ordinator, Tinian, and the Historic Preservation Office, Commonwealth of the Northern Mariana Islands, Saipan. Canberra, Australia: Tinian Archaeological Survey.

Webster, Donovan

1996 Aftermath: The Remnants of War. New York: Pantheon Books.

Wiles, Gary J., Jonathan Bart Jr. Robert E. Beck, and Celestino F. Aguan

2003 Impacts of the Brown Tree Snake: Patterns of Decline and Species Persistence in Guam's Avifauna. Conservation Biology 17(5):1350–60.

Willmott, H. P.

2004 [1999] The Second World War in the Far East. Washington: Smithsonian Books.

Wilson, Lynn B.

1995 Speaking to Power: Gender and Politics in the Western Pacific. New York: Routledge.

Winter, Jay

1995 Sites of Memory, Sites of Mourning: The Great War in European Cultural History. New York: Cambridge University Press.

Winter, Jay, and Emmanuel Sivan, eds.

1999 War and Remembrance in the Twentieth Century. Cambridge: Cambridge University Press.

Wood, James B.
2007 Japanese Military Strategy in the Pacific War: Was Defeat Inevitable? Lanham, MD: Rowman and Littlefield.
Woodard, Larry L.
1994 Before the First Wave: The 3rd Armored Amphibian Tractor Battalion—Peleliu & Okinawa. Manhattan, KS: Sunflower University Press.
Wright, Derrick
2005 To the Far Side of Hell: The Battle for Peleliu, 1944. Tuscaloosa: University of Alabama Press.
Yamashita, Shinji
2000 The Japanese Encounter with the South: Japanese Tourists in Palau. Contemporary Pacific 12(2):437–63.
Yamazaki, Jane W.
2006 Japanese Apologies for World War II: A Rhetorical Study. London: Routledge.
Yates, Frances Amelia
1966 The Art of Memory. London: Routledge and K. Paul.
Young, James E.
2002 Germany's Holocaust Memorial Problem—and Mine. Special Issue, "Beyond National History: World War II Recollected," Public Historian 24(4):65–80.
2003 Between History and Memory: The Voice of the Eyewitness. *In* Witness & Memory: The Discourse of Trauma. A. Douglass and T. A. Vogler, eds. Pp. 275–83. New York: Routledge.
Zinn, Howard
1990 A People's History of the United States. New York: Harper Perennial.

Index

www.ingramcontent.com/pod-product-compliance
Lightning Source LLC
LaVergne TN
LVHW100817200826
845923LV00028B/231